Praise for *Getting to the Heart of the Matter*

"[Carl Levin is] the model of serious purpose, principle, and personal decency, whose example ought to inspire the service of new and returning senators."

—U.S. Senator John McCain in a speech honoring Senator Levin upon his retirement

"Carl and I served together for five terms—thirty years—and we developed a very strong bond of personal trust. Our word was our bond and the security of our nation was always foremost. Even though we are from different political parties, we share a love of country, a commitment to do what is right, and a deep mutual admiration and respect for each other. We never let our policy differences turn into personal differences. And we served in a Senate where bipartisanship was something to be sought after, where compromise was not a dirty word but an essential ingredient to make our government function better."

—Senator John Warner

"*Getting to the Heart of the Matter* reminds us there are patriots like Carl Levin who define 'honesty, integrity, and civility.' In a lifetime of dedicated service, he made government more accountable, the nation more secure, and fought for opportunity for all. He is an American hero."

—U.S. Senator Jack Reed

"The Dingell and Levin families have shared decades of friendship and public service. *Getting to the Heart of the Matter* is a heartfelt, thoughtful narrative of his career, which had a positive impact on so many people. Everyone interested in public service should read this."

—Congresswoman Debbie Dingell

"Carl Levin's life and work continue to be an inspiration to each of us who have had the privilege of knowing him. His commitment to public service and the leadership he exemplifies have made a remarkable and historic contribution to the country. His beautifully written autobiography makes me wish we had more like him now."

—U.S. Senator Tom Daschle

"Care about integrity? Read this book. Given up on finding truly selfless politicians? Read this book. Senator Carl Levin's riveting biography is food for our decency-starved souls and is a page-turning must-read for future public servants and all who love Michigan."

—Jennifer Granholm, 47th governor of Michigan

"Over fifty years of immersion in the Senate—writing about it, interacting with its members, and working inside it—I have seen very few of its members garner the universal admiration and respect of Carl Levin. *Getting to the Heart of the Matter* is a memoir, but it is much more than that. Writing about his six terms in the Senate, Levin gives us an intimate, inside portrait of thirty-six years of key policy decisions and political developments in the country—and his role, often a pivotal one, in many of them. Along the way, we get a sense of how the Senate worked during those decades. This book is a tribute to a remarkable, important career and is a must-read for all who care about the country, its values, and the workings of its institutions going forward."

—Norman Ornstein, resident scholar,
American Enterprise Institute

"Senator Carl Levin is the epitome of a dedicated statesman. His wise, effective, and collegial service to our nation is admirable. His memoir is a must-read for those who seek to understand how our government should work."

—Reginald Turner

"Carl Levin served as the de facto conscience of the United States Senate for thirty-six years. He never forgot the people he grew up with in Detroit where he started out driving a taxi and working in an automobile factory. As chairman of the Permanent Subcommittee on Investigations, Levin ferreted out wrongdoing, abuses of taxpayers, and failed policies, its reports all issued with bipartisan agreement, a remarkable feat of dignity, duty, and moral strength in our era."

—David Cay Johnston, Pulitzer Prize–winning
investigative reporter

Getting to the Heart of the Matter

Getting to the Heart of the Matter

My 36 Years in the Senate

Senator Carl Levin

WAYNE STATE UNIVERSITY PRESS
DETROIT

ISBN 978-0-8143-4839-0 (jacketed cloth); ISBN 978-0-8143-4840-6 (ebook)

Library of Congress Control Number: 2020947287

Wayne State University Press
Leonard N. Simons Building
4809 Woodward Avenue
Detroit, Michigan 48201-1309

Visit us online at wsupress.wayne.edu

On cover: Carl Levin questions a witness at one of the hearings he led on the 2008 financial crisis. (Photo courtesy of Carl M. Levin Papers, Bentley Historical Library, University of Michigan)

*I lovingly dedicate this book to my wife, Barbara;
our three daughters, Kate, Laura, and Erica;
and our six grandchildren, Beatrice, Ben,
Bess, Noa, Olivia, and Samantha.*

Contents

Foreword by Linda Gustitus   ix
Preface   xiii

1. Origins   1

2. Eight Years on the Detroit City Council   21

3. Campaigning for the U.S. Senate   40

4. Coming to the Senate   53

5. Early Efforts at Government Accountability   64

6. The Rise of Global Competition   74

7. The Armed Services Committee   87

8. Foreign Policy and America's Role in the World   112

9. Afghanistan and Iraq   141

10. Protecting the Great Lakes and the Environment   175

11. Earmarks and Private Bills   193

12. The Filibuster   207

13. Ethics and Impeachment   222

14. The Permanent Subcommittee on Investigations   240

15. Bipartisanship   277

16. The Role of an Elected Official and American Values   290

17. Why I Loved the Senate, Why I Left the Senate   304

18. Retirement   308

Acknowledgments   313
Levin Senate Staff, 1979–2015   317
Index   323

Foreword

I first came in contact with Carl Levin in 1974 as a twenty-six-year-old law student assigned to help Detroit's Central Business District Association (CBDA) develop legislation to create a tax increment financing district. Working at CBDA enabled me to come to know and appreciate the workings of a big, complicated city like Detroit and to follow Carl Levin's work on the City Council in some proximity. I liked what I saw—an honest, down-to-earth, compassionate, smart public official.

Four years later Carl won election to the U.S. Senate, and I pulled out all the stops to get my résumé in front of him and have a chance at a job as a legislative assistant. It worked, and for twenty-four years I never looked back. I had what I frequently termed the perfect professional marriage: working for a person who was whip-smart, hardworking, prescient, decent, funny, and thoughtful. His love of opera and stamp collecting were both enlightening and endearing. And, oh—he also smoked cigars at the time, but I could live with that.

He had a passion for fairness and facts, and that led to dozens of investigations and hearings into greedy schemes where people sought a shortcut to either power or money at the expense of anyone who was in the way. After two years I became Carl's staff director for various subcommittees on the Senate Governmental Affairs Committee that did oversight, ethics legislation, and investigations into everything from defense contracting to sweepstakes solicitations to money laundering by some of our biggest banks. I couldn't have asked for a more satisfying and enjoyable career.

So when Carl left the Senate, several of us worked on the establishment of the Levin Center at Wayne State University Law School to carry on his legacy of good government, civil discourse, and, most prominently, fact-based, bipartisan, in-depth legislative oversight. I also encouraged him to write an autobiography, which he resisted. (He is almost biologically unassuming.) But at the urging of family and friends, he finally saw the value of writing this memoir.

As you will see from reading this book, Carl is a man of impressive accomplishments, always working to make government better and wiser and the world fairer. What you may not see enough of from this book is his kindness, his humor, his empathy, his love of children and family, his courage, and the respect in which he was held by his colleagues.

When I decided I needed to cut back my hours to have more time with my children, Carl would often be the person reminding me to leave the office. "Didn't you want to be home by now?" he would say. "Go. We've got this here." And his thoughtfulness is best reflected in how he answers the phone almost every time: "How are you?" or "How's it going?" he'll say—and mean it. He wants to know.

And he could laugh, sometimes to the point of tears. One time he was telling the subcommittee staff a joke, and he couldn't finish it—he was laughing too hard at the punch line.

The accolades over his lifetime have been many. *Time* magazine listed him as one of America's ten best senators, noting the respect he had from both parties for his attention to detail and his "deep knowledge of policy." David Cay Johnston in the *American Prospect* asked, in looking back at Levin's career and his absence from the Senate, "Who will possess the personal integrity, never touched by the slightest hint of scandal, along with the backbone and brains to take on the most powerful institutions in America on behalf of not just the little guy, but of a healthier republic?" And in tributes on the Senate floor when he left the Senate, his colleagues from both sides of the aisle, conservative and liberal, effusively praised his accomplishments and his character: "a wonderful human being," "a level-headed mediator," "honest—totally honest—decent honorable man," "a model of firm purpose, firm principle, and personal decency," "calm, measured, patient, thoughtful," "a foot soldier for justice," "keeps his word," "pursued the powerful on behalf of the powerless."

Those of us who had the privilege to work for and with him remember it as the best time of our professional lives. This memoir will give you a sense of why that was so.

Linda Gustitus

Preface

Few moments in my long political career were as satisfying as that cool morning in October 1975 when, as president of the Detroit City Council, I pointed at a dilapidated, vacant bungalow on Detroit's Drexel Street and told the man operating a bulldozer to "knock it down." That house, an eyesore and haven for criminal activity for several years, was owned not by a slum landlord or a drug dealer. It was one of the ten thousand–plus Detroit single-family homes owned by the federal government's Department of Housing and Urban Development, better known simply by its acronym, HUD, or, as I once told Mike Wallace in a *60 Minutes* interview, "Hell Upon Detroit."

Abandoned, dilapidated HUD houses in Detroit were a huge problem in the 1970s. The homes in question had been purchased by low-income families with HUD-subsidized loans for as little as $200 down. Unable to afford the upkeep and monthly payments, they defaulted on the mortgages, and HUD ended up owning the properties after handsomely paying off banks and speculators. The 1968 law that established the program was well-intended, but HUD's refusal to either protect or repair the properties after default was preposterous. To my mind, HUD-owned properties were no different than the properties owned by the slumlords who took advantage of the government-subsidized poor, indifferent to the blight that was killing our neighborhoods.

Based on dozens of articles by Don Ball, a top reporter at the *Detroit News* who exposed the HUD housing fiasco, and with the backing of Detroit's mayor

Coleman A. Young, we at the City Council declared thousands of these houses to be public nuisances and ordered that they be torn down. HUD told us it was a federal crime to do that and if we did, we would be indicted. I told HUD, "Let me get this straight—You are going to indict us? Do you think a jury is going to convict us for tearing down buildings that are nuisances in their neighborhoods? Do you think even one out of twelve jurors would vote to convict? Forget twelve out of twelve. They are not going to convict us. They will convict the federal government! Go ahead and indict us because we are tearing down your houses."

The incompetence of HUD in Detroit in the 1970s convinced me that our elected members of Congress were not taking responsibility for overseeing the programs they had voted to establish. During my eight years on the City Council, I did everything I could think of to make Detroit's government work; protecting our neighborhoods from the blight of vacant houses became one of our top priorities. But the federal agencies that oversaw the distribution and impact of tens of millions of federal dollars flowing into Detroit were largely unresponsive, and HUD was the worst of the lot. When I tried engaging with our elected representatives in Washington to do something about HUD, I was politely told that it was a regulatory problem and I should take it up with the agency. That response was unacceptable to me. In light of HUD's gross mismanagement, which cost U.S. taxpayers hundreds of millions of dollars, I expected Congress to take action to make sure the agency did what Congress and the legislation it passed intended, but that didn't happen.

After two terms on the City Council, I decided to run for the U.S. Senate. I realized that as a senator, I would be in a unique position to make a difference in the programs that affected the people of Michigan. Through my running battle with HUD, I had an intimate understanding of how federal agencies can obstruct reform and avoid oversight. As a senator, I felt I could help get Congress to fulfill its duty through the power to oversee federal programs, in order to ensure that the programs it authorizes operate effectively and that taxpayer dollars are not wasted. This was particularly important to me as a Democrat, since most of the programs at stake were ones Democrats had created and supported. I thought that Democrats who believe in an active role for government to address real human problems have an obligation to care at least as much about how their programs are implemented as the Republicans who believe in a lesser role for government.

Once I decided to run for the Senate, that became the theme of my campaign—that we should go after wasteful programs, not only because it is the right thing to do and saves taxpayers money but because mismanagement jeopardizes important programs.

Holding government accountable and ensuring that legislatively authorized programs are run effectively and efficiently were major guideposts during my service on the Detroit City Council, during my first campaign, and throughout my Senate career. As a former local official, I understood the importance of responding to people in need, listening to even the smallest voice, and working hard on behalf of the people with honesty, integrity, and civility.

It was my honor to serve for thirty-six years as one of Michigan's senators. I hope this book will provide a new generation of leaders the benefit of lessons I learned and perhaps inspire those who want to dedicate their lives to public service and the noble ideal of making government work for the welfare of all Americans.

1

Origins

Family

It's no understatement to say that public service and politics are in my genes. My father, Saul, a lawyer and strong Democrat, served on the Michigan Corrections Commission. His brother, Theodore, my Uncle Ted, was a federal judge, and his son, Charles, was a state supreme court justice. My cousin, Avern Cohn, was a federal district judge for over forty years. My mother's brother, David Levinson, served for thirty-five years on the Oakland County Michigan Board of Supervisors. And, of course, my brother, Sandy, served in the U.S. House of Representatives for thirty-six years. Upon Sandy's retirement, his terrific son Andy followed in Sandy's footsteps and, at the time of this writing, represents the same congressional district.

Our family's love affair with America began when my four grandparents immigrated to the United States in the late 1800s from Lithuania, Poland, Russia, and Moldava, some of the places from which Jews fled to escape persecution. My mother's father, Morris Levinson, and my grandmother, Gittelle, found their way to Birmingham, Michigan, where they were the only Jews in the 1890s. Morris started as a peddler, going with a horse and buggy to farms in northern Oakland County to sell spools of thread, needles, and other small household items. They saved their pennies and bought property at the town's main intersection, Woodward Avenue and Maple Road, where they opened a little store that eventually grew into four storefronts.

My mother, Bess, was born at home in 1898. She was a strong woman, very independent, and ahead of her time in many ways. She graduated from the University of Michigan long before women attended in large numbers. And she volunteered in many organizations, including Hadassah, the American Jewish women's volunteer organization, which at the time advocated for a Jewish homeland and became famous for, among other things, the Hadassah Research Hospital in Jerusalem, which treats people of all religions and races and supports the education of poor children in Israel and around the world.

My father's parents, Joseph and Ida, had eight children. My uncle Ted was the oldest, and next oldest was my father, Saul, born in Chicago where Grandpa Joe worked in a cigar factory. When Joe was fired for trying to organize a union, he later landed a job as a foreman in a cigar factory in London, Ontario, part of the tobacco belt on Lake Erie's north shore. To help their family financially, Ted and Saul as teenagers worked the trains between London, Ontario, and Port Huron, Michigan, selling candy and gum to passengers. In 1913 the family moved to Detroit.

After high school, my father and Ted both attended the University of Detroit School of Law at a time when you didn't need a bachelor's degree to study law. They got their law degrees and opened an office in Detroit. They mainly represented immigrants, usually for free, but when the new arrivals later opened small businesses, they hired lawyers they trusted—like the Levin brothers—to handle their legal work. My father and Uncle Ted were recognized not only for their legal acumen but also for their ethics and passion for justice. In 1946, President Harry Truman nominated Uncle Ted to be a judge on the United States District Court for the Eastern District of Michigan where he served until his death in 1970, including as chief judge from 1959 to 1967.

My father was a strong liberal. He represented migrant farm workers *pro bono*. He picked up the Spanish language and taught it to U.S. Navy flyers during World War II. He frequently traveled to Mexico, including once, he told us, with the author John Steinbeck. Honduras named him its honorary Consul General in Detroit. He served for years on the Michigan Corrections Commission where he was considered an expert in penology, caring about prison conditions and corresponding with several inmates. He was widely known and respected for his gentle nature and was beloved by a host of nieces and nephews.

I was born in Detroit in 1934, three years behind my brother, Sandy, and six years behind our sister, Hannah. After 1940 we lived in a house on Boston Boulevard, part of the well-established Boston-Edison neighborhood, and the three of us attended Roosevelt Elementary, Durfee Intermediate, and Central High School, all excellent public schools. We had the benefits of loving parents; a warm, extended family; a middle-class lifestyle; and the freedom to explore and grow in a city we loved.

While our immediate neighborhood wasn't Jewish, our family were proud Jews. As a four-year-old Jewish kid, I remember the exhilaration of my family when Joe Louis knocked out Max Schmeling, who, though not a Nazi, was for many the symbol of Hitler's racist regime. As an eleven-year-old, I remember how, on a Sunday afternoon with my brother's and my ears glued to the radio, we shrieked and hollered when Hank Greenberg, the Jewish community's pride and joy, recently back from the war, hit the pennant-winning home run for the Detroit Tigers in the last game of the season. And as a teenager, as the full impact of the Holocaust and its horrors unfolded, I understood why the Jewish people, my people, needed a homeland, a place where the Jewish survivors in Europe could find safety and where Jews forever could find refuge when danger appeared.

I remember how my family celebrated when President Harry Truman recognized Israel. I also remember the gratitude that my parents instilled in my sister, my brother, and me for living in America as a haven for minorities and refugees. As children of immigrants, our parents taught us to appreciate the sacrifices that so many immigrants make and the risks they take to reach our shores. They told us to never complain about paying taxes—a small price to pay, they said, for living in America.

As a kid I had a group of friends we called "the gang," many of whom became lifelong friends, and despite our differences in age, Sandy included "my" group with "his" group in the games we played. The gang included Dick Bernstein, Norman Bolton, Mel Fishman, Eugene Gordon, Bob Marans, Merrill Miller,

Dennis Ormond, Fritzi Roth, Fred Shulak, Arthur Vander, Ben Wasserman, Joe Weiss, and Sheldon Wigod.

Sandy and I were extremely close buddies all our lives. Almost every summer we went to camp together. During the last two summers of World War II, in 1944 and 1945, we went to Camp Cobbossee in Maine, a great sports camp for boys. I was ten and Sandy was not quite thirteen. We played a lot of baseball at that camp, but we also picked beans two or three afternoons a week to assist in the war effort. With so many off to war or working in jobs those in the military left behind, even we campers needed to help. I'm sure our parents wondered why they spent their money sending us to camp to pick beans, but they also knew it made us feel part of something bigger than ourselves. That message drove a lot of what they taught us growing up, and it was a message we carried throughout our lives.

We helped with the war effort at home, too. We collected tinfoil from gum wrappers and cigarette packs dropped in the streets. I remember peeling the foil off the paper wrappers and wadding it into little balls to bring to school. All the homerooms did the same. We felt we were doing our bit to help win the war. We also collected tin cans. My job at home was to take off the ends of the cans, flatten them, and box them up to take to school. I often talk about the value of every-one pitching in during wartime as we did in World War II. That sense of common purpose, of people of every age and background doing what they can, sacrificing for the good of the country, is something we've sorely missed of late.

My family often discussed politics at dinner. My parents were strong sup-porters of Franklin Roosevelt, and my dad was involved in a number of politi-cal campaigns, including that of Congressman John Dingell Sr. Our family ate dinner together, and we always waited for my father to get home no matter how late he was. During dinner my parents asked for our opinions, making us feel an equal part of the discussion. They carried that spirit into family life in general, scrupulously playing no favorites among their kids or grandkids. No doubt that helped shape my own deeply held belief in the equality of all people.

Their willingness to listen to us was particularly meaningful when President Harry Truman was running for election in 1948. Dad supported Henry Wallace, FDR's third vice president who ran as the Progressive Party's candidate. Sandy and I argued that a vote for Wallace would help Republican Thomas Dewey. Despite our pleas, Dad left for work election day vowing to vote for Wallace. When he came home from work that evening and we asked him whom he voted for, his answer was a satisfying, "Aw, I voted for Truman!"

Once Sandy got his driver's license, we took a number of trips together. We drove to Lake of the Clouds in the Upper Peninsula to fish, but we didn't do much fishing. We liked to read so we'd tie our fishing rods to the boat and read books while we waited for some action, but we never got a bite. Later we took a road trip to Mexico with his buddy Bill Broder in Bill's mother's car. The car took a beating from fording streams and driving up mountains on dirt roads and came back significantly worse for the wear.

We also worked to make money for college and law school. I worked in three Detroit auto plants: DeSoto, Lyon Wheel Cover, and the Ford Tractor Plant in Highland Park. At DeSoto I worked in the "white body department," so called because the cars weren't painted yet. My job was to be inside the car's shell when strong guys would lift the left-side doors and hold them in place while I tightened the bolts. It was noisy—particularly if a door didn't fit quite right and the guys on the outside had to use their rubber mallets to pound it into place. Bam! Bam! Bam! I was also told to take care of just the specific bolts on the left-side door hinges—and nothing else. If I saw a problem with any other part, it wasn't my responsibility to report it or fix it even if that made good sense. That culture would haunt the auto industry when Detroit started to face global competition.

Sandy and I also drove cabs one summer and had a friendly competition as to who would make more money. Sandy always made more on the fares because he drove faster and thus got more trips. But I got more tips because I was younger and people probably felt they wanted to help this young guy.

Sandy got involved in politics early. In high school he was president of his class and an activist. At the University of Chicago, he was president of the student government and active in the National Student Association and Students for Democratic Action, the student component of the Americans for Democratic Action.

My first campaign came when I ran for treasurer of my high school class. I had posters with pictures of a piece of matzo (unleavened bread eaten during

Passover) that said, "This is what happens to bread without Levin." I won that election and never lost an election after that, although I came pretty close a few times.

Swarthmore

I didn't follow Sandy to the University of Chicago. I decided to go to Swarthmore College, a Quaker-founded college just outside of Philadelphia. I loved the beautiful campus, and it had a great academic reputation. It also had a geographical diversity program. I probably got in because I came from the Midwest instead of the East Coast. I started in the fall of 1952.

I had a fabulous four years there with so many fond memories. I was barely 5 feet, 10 inches tall, but I made the school's basketball team as a sophomore. In one particular game in November 1953, the *Swarthmore Phoenix* reported that we defeated Dickinson College 62–55 and that "Carl Levin, playing a smart and steady game, was the only player to go the full forty minutes." The box score shows that I sank a two-pointer and four free throws. That was the high point of my one-year varsity basketball career. I also played junior varsity baseball. Sandy's fungoes to me at shortstop as a kid paid off, because I developed a great pair of hands. Unfortunately I never practiced my throwing arm, and I swear people used to duck when I picked up a grounder and tried to throw somebody out at first base.

I majored in political science, got deeply into politics, ran for the Student Council, and won. One issue I wanted to address involved a fraternity whose alumni were pressuring the campus chapter to deny admittance to Jews, threatening to cut off financial support if they did. In January 1956, I proposed a resolution to the Student Council asking that it take jurisdiction over any fraternity activity that affected the rest of the student body. My resolution failed, but the members of the council came together to adopt a resolution to create a mechanism to study the issue and report back. It wasn't what I wanted substantively, but it was a healing, consensus-building way to address an otherwise contentious issue and taught me an early lesson about bringing people together after a divisive fight.

I chaired the Student Council's National and International Affairs (NIA) committee and got involved in a number of matters with respect to students abroad. I sponsored a letter to the University of Moscow seeking an exchange of information (this, despite our college president's concerns that dealing with a Soviet university might reflect poorly on our college); I proposed we use International Students Day as a fundraising opportunity to provide a scholarship to Swarthmore for a foreign student; we raised money to help the students of Utkal University near Bombay, India, which had been devastated by a flood; I helped lead a book drive to establish a library for the students of a Catholic university in Vietnam who had fled Hanoi's totalitarian regime for Saigon; and seeing people flee Hungary when Soviet tanks moved into Budapest in 1956 to crush a democratic uprising moved me to speak out in support of the Hungarian Revolution.

My most newsworthy effort at Swarthmore occurred in 1954 when the nation was riveted by live coverage of the famous Army-McCarthy hearings. For years Senator Joseph McCarthy had used the U.S. Senate's Permanent Subcommittee on Investigations (PSI), which he chaired, as a platform to malign and accuse hundreds of people in and out of government of being communists. He abused its broad subpoena power and berated witnesses who invoked their constitutional right under the Fifth Amendment and declined to testify.

McCarthy's hearings showcased claims that suspected communists had infiltrated the U.S. Army. In this set of hearings he claimed the army was abusing a draftee who was a PSI staffer and close friend of McCarthy's chief counsel, the lawyer Roy Cohn, in retaliation for the committee's investigation. The hearings exposed McCarthy for the dangerous demagogue he was and greatly contributed to his loss of public support. But would the U.S. Senate do anything about it?

A resolution to censure McCarthy was introduced in July 1954. In the weekend preceding the Senate debate on the resolution, news broke that citizens supporting McCarthy and opposing censure had gathered more than a million signatures. Using the slogan "Ten Million for Justice," they were planning on delivering the signatures in an armored truck to the Capitol where they would hand them over to Vice President Nixon, a McCarthy ally.

My buddy Mike Douty and I, with a few friends, decided the voices of Swarthmore students should also be heard. On Monday, just days before the vote, we set up a table outside the dining hall and collected 650 signatures, about two-thirds of the student body, on a statement urging the two Pennsylvania senators, James H. Duff and Edward Martin, both Republicans, to vote "yes" on censuring McCarthy.

Early in the morning on the first day of the Senate debate, having notified the press, we piled into an old Dodge and drove to Washington, D.C. We got to Senator Duff's office while his staff faced a scrum of reporters and photographers asking about the group from Swarthmore. We were told Senator Duff wasn't in but that he'd meet with us at noon. So, there we were, facing a host of journalists angling for the story. As the early birds we basically had the news media to ourselves. We took full advantage, answering all questions and posing with our scroll of signatures. We presented Senator Duff our petition when we met him in the reception room next to the Senate chamber later that day, and he graciously posed for photographers.

The pro-McCarthy people were also there, expecting to get all the media attention only to find some college kids had somehow upstaged them. The next day papers nationwide published two photographs side by side: one of a couple of armored truck guards with guns drawn—believe it or not—supposedly protecting a million signatures supporting McCarthy; the other, of five cherubic-looking students handing our petition to Senator Duff. It was great. (No one ever found out whether the McCarthy supporters had the signatures they claimed.)

The Senate would go on to vote to censure McCarthy, holding him to account and shaming him and McCarthyism forever. Senator Duff voted for censure. Senator Martin, with whom we were not able to meet, voted against.

In an irony of history, I would decades later become chairman of the PSI and wield the same gavel that Joe McCarthy had abused. As you will read, I tried to exercise the power of subpoena judiciously and not for partisan reasons. The McCarthy hearings left an impression on me, and I was particularly careful to respect a witness's Fifth Amendment right to refuse to testify.

During the summer of 1954, my friend Art Vander and I traveled through Europe on small motorcycles. My father did some import-export business with an English motorcycle maker, Excelsior, and we bought two motorbikes that we arranged to pick up at the plant in Birmingham, England. They were the smallest bikes Excelsior made, 98 ccs with only two gears and saddlebags to carry our meager possessions.

The whole thing turned out to be a comedy of errors. We discovered that our motorcycles' two gears would not carry us over the mountains, so in some cases we had to walk the bikes. We also lacked the proper licenses and insurance, and while we were able to talk our way through those problems and get into Belgium, Germany, and Switzerland, it took us three tries to get into Italy. South of Florence, while gawking at some vineyards, I crashed straight into a stone wall. My leg was badly hurt, and the bike was out of commission. Art helped me hobble to the nearest town where a doctor was summoned as a crowd gathered around us. Before I knew it, a group of villagers had retrieved my bike, carrying it into town. I ended up in a hospital in Rome where I was put in a full-length cast because of a broken kneecap. The Italians treated this bearded, bedraggled American student in the ward like a hero, because Americans had liberated their country just nine years earlier. Poor people even brought me English magazines and newspapers they couldn't afford. I've had a special fondness for Italy ever since.

The accident ended my varsity basketball career. In truth it was going nowhere fast anyway, and its demise helped me focus on my academics.

Before I graduated from Swarthmore in 1956, I learned a lesson that I pass on to students today: take the teacher, not the course. Two faculty members at Swarthmore were particularly memorable to me—an astronomy professor and a Russian teacher. The astronomy professor put his whole heart into his subject. He would take our class out at night and show us the stars with a childlike zeal. His love of the subject, love of teaching, and love of young people was powerful and contagious.

The Russian teacher was a woman named Olga Lamkert who had taught the czar's children before escaping the revolution by fleeing to China where she lived for many years, eventually making it to the United States. There were maybe eight students in our Russian class, and after our lesson she'd invite us to her house for tea. She made each of us feel that we had a personal relationship with her. When she retired a few years after I graduated, we former students felt strongly enough about her to supplement her small pension. About forty of us pledged and sent her a total of a couple thousand dollars a year. When Ms. Lamkert passed away, we sent the balance of almost ten thousand dollars to Swarthmore to set up a small endowment in her name for students taking Russian. To be frank, I'm not really sure why I even took Russian, but I'm glad I did. The right teacher can make you see things in a subject you never expected and show you new paths.

I made a number of close friends at Swarthmore, including Carolyn (Cotton) Cunningham, Christopher Lehmann-Haupt, Eric Osterweil, Norman Hilsenrad, Bob Adler, Michael Douty, Gretchen Handwerger, and Alex Shakow.

Harvard Law

From Swarthmore, I went to Harvard Law School. My first year was the best, because I roomed with Sandy, who was in his third year. We took up the great game of squash, which we played together into our eighties. (Over the course of sixty years we probably played over ten thousand games against each other.) We usually came back to our dorm room to have lunch together, invariably making Kraft macaroni and cheese with tuna fish, and then went right to the books. I found Harvard to be overly abstract and theoretical, but I do remember having a number of good professors, including one who took our class, which included my great buddy Larry Levy, to witness an autopsy. The person doing the autopsy said, as he picked up a large knife, "Let me tell you right now. This is just a piece of meat." Then he plunged the knife in the body. It made a lasting impression on us, to put it mildly. Larry, his wife, Stephanie, and their children became great friends with our family, and we visited them in Cleveland and Maine many times over the years before their too-early passing.

I stayed politically active at Harvard, volunteering in Adlai Stevenson's 1956 campaign for president against Dwight Eisenhower. I learned a lesson in retail politics one October afternoon. A group of us drove in a caravan down to Woonsocket, Rhode Island, where Stevenson was having a rally. It was a perfect afternoon, sun shining, leaves changing, in a gorgeous little town with a quaint town square. When Stevenson got to the microphone, he greeted the crowd in French! We found out that many French-speaking immigrants from Quebec had long ago migrated to Rhode Island. I took Stevenson's cue fifteen years later when I was campaigning in Hamtramck, a small town within the boundaries of Detroit that was the center of Detroit's Polish community, and started my remarks with a few sentences in Polish.

Home to Detroit

After graduating with my law degree in 1959, I returned to Detroit and joined Grossman, Hyman, and Grossman, a small downtown law firm. I also started a two-person law firm with Marvin Gerber, an old classmate from high school, in a vacant store near the corner of 12th Street and Clairmount, just a few doors away from where a police raid on an after-hours establishment would spark the devastating Detroit rebellion in July 1967. My work in private practice would later include working part time from 1971 to 1973 for the Schlussel, Lifton law firm in Detroit.

I did some trial work when I started out but didn't feel confident doing it. One of my mentors told me that if you're going to be a professional trial lawyer, you've got to be able to stand up, do your thing, and leave the courtroom behind when you go home at night. But I took the cases too personally. I couldn't handle the thought that my client could lose based on something I did or failed to do. At one misdemeanor trial I was so obviously worried about what would happen to my client, who had been arrested for missing a scheduled court date, that when he saw my concern he took off during a break and I never saw him again. Fortunately I was more comfortable arguing appeals, which would later become my specialty.

During my early years as a lawyer, I was minimally involved in politics but what I did see left a lasting impression. In 1960 I was a precinct delegate during John Kennedy's campaign. My job on election day was to drive Kennedy voters to the polls. The first voter I was assigned to pick up was a disabled veteran in the V.A. hospital in Allen Park, a Detroit suburb. I drove out there, loaded him and his wheelchair into my car, and drove him back to Detroit, where he was registered to vote. He voted after waiting in a long line, and I drove him back to the hospital. The whole process took me half the day. At the time I didn't think it was worth it. But when Kennedy won by just over one vote per precinct nationwide, I thought, "That vote was my veteran!" I still get tears in my eyes telling that story. That was my veteran, and his vote was worth the time. I tell this story often when I urge people to get out and vote. One vote can make all the difference!

Barbara

Around this time, I had a blind date that lasted the rest of my life. My cousin Joe, Uncle Ted's youngest son, was dating a fellow law student, Rena Katz, who was best friends with a young woman named Barbara Halpern and urged me to ask her out. I learned that she was born in Ypsilanti, Michigan, and moved with her family to Detroit when she was three. She attended Detroit public schools, including Central High School, the same school I attended, but was three years behind me. She earned a bachelor's degree at the University of Michigan, then moved to New York where she earned a master's in mathematics at Columbia University.

I had a record for embarrassing myself on first dates. On one memorable occasion I left my wallet at home. The record remained intact when I invited Barbara to my uncle's farm for a swim in the lake there. When I picked her up, Barbara came out of her parents' house wearing a bathing suit, and I knew I had done it again. I had forgotten my bathing suit. So when we arrived at the lake, I stripped to my underwear and jumped into the water, wondering how she would react. She didn't flinch, and I began to fall in love.

We dated for about a year. I was practicing law in Detroit while Barbara was in New York working at Bell Laboratories as a computer programmer on missile defense. Barbara provided my first exposure to military research when she told me about the effort to figure out how to protect against missiles carrying nuclear weapons. She explained that it was easy to track a missile trajectory and predict when and where it would land if you could see its trajectory for a short time. However, a problem had developed with the invention of decoys, that is, creating false trajectories surrounding the original one. Little did I know that twenty years later I would be opposing President Reagan's Strategic Defense Initiative, known as Star Wars, because it had not been adequately researched and seemed totally impractical.

After several visits and trips together, we knew we wanted to get married. Barbara moved back to Detroit and went to work as a computer programmer at the General Motors Research Center in Warren, Michigan. She earned more than I did as a new attorney and helped pay off my law school loans. We were married on August 31, 1961, in Beth Achim Synagogue in Detroit.

It was a great wedding, thanks in large measure to cousin Joe. We started out thinking we'd like a small wedding with only our closest family and friends. But when we realized that we couldn't leave out cousin Joe, I knew that we would also have to invite some of my other twenty-five Levin cousins and their spouses. We both realized it would be fun to include more of our families and friends, such as my old school gang and their spouses. Since Barbara's extended family was not nearly as large as mine, her parents, Ben and Esther Halpern, also invited a group of special friends, fellow immigrants from Eastern Europe who, like them, made it to America before World War II and the Holocaust. The wedding grew to over two hundred guests. In the end, cousin Joe didn't make it to the wedding, but we were always grateful that he gave us the reason to have such a big and joyous celebration.

We had a short but wonderful honeymoon in and around Quebec City, Canada, but it didn't quite satisfy our wanderlust. So, the following year, we decided to do some real traveling. Foreign travel was cheap then, and we both took a three-month leave from our jobs and went on a grand trip to Europe, Israel, and Turkey.

We had also decided to visit Bulgaria, a communist country midway between Turkey and Greece, which welcomed American visitors who paid in advance for a guided tour. The 1962 Cuban Missile Crisis erupted during our trip, and both the United States and Russia were arming for a potential military confrontation. We didn't know if we should go to Bulgaria. We passed a U.S. Air Force base in northern Turkey and went in to get their advice. It was clear and practical. We were told we would most likely not be harmed if we went there but that we might not be able to leave on time because Bulgaria was also getting ready for the possible conflict. It was my first encounter with military professionals. As I discovered many years later in the Senate, military leaders' advice was typically helpful and reliable. We decided not to go to Bulgaria. We've always shared a love of travel and have been fortunate throughout our lives to visit countries all over the world.

Our happiest memory of that trip occurred in Paris when we learned that Barbara was pregnant with our first child. We returned home looking forward to the beginning of family life, and over the following six years we had three daughters, Kate, Laura, and Erica. In those early years, Barbara, who was a skilled classical pianist, brought live music into our home, a gift that I enjoy to this day. She continued her musical training and even found time to build a harpsichord. We have always shared a love of classical music and going to hear it live has been one of our favorite pastimes.

Beginning of a New Family

When our three daughters were in school all day, Barbara enrolled in Wayne State University Law School and worked hard to complete her degree while juggling family life. Her legal and policy career would focus on environmental preservation, nuclear disarmament, and alternative energy. And until my last years in the Senate, she worked full time, helping to support our family while running our household and looking after the kids.

Throughout my career, Barbara (and at times our daughters) has been my thought partner on many issues and projects on which I've embarked, her keen intellect helping me think through the decisions and actions that I've taken. I have been very fortunate to have both a challenging and meaningful work life and a rich family life. This was due in great part to the support and understanding of Barbara and our daughters.

Barbara was immediately welcomed into my family, which remained very close even as Hannah and Sandy had families of their own. By the time we were married, Hannah and her husband, Bill, had two daughters, Debbie and Judi, in elementary school, and Sandy and his wife, Vicki, had two young children, Jenny and Andy. (Their daughter Madeleine was born shortly thereafter, and their son Matt the same year as our youngest daughter, Erica.) Although my dad had passed away just before Barb and I met, we maintained a tradition of all of us having Sunday night dinner with my mother, alternating between her apartment in downtown Detroit and our respective houses. Our daughters grew up in this tradition, seeing their grandmother, uncles, aunts, and cousins each week, as well as Barbara's parents on Friday night for Shabbos dinner. Sometimes the Sunday night dinners were preempted by political events, in which case we'd gather for brunch.

Politics was always the subject of family conversation, as it had been when I was growing up. In the years to come, as Sandy and I ran for office and Hannah, Bill, Vicki, and Barb also became involved in Democratic party politics, the political conversation could last a while and the kids would leave the table to play outdoors. Eventually, Sandy and I would follow and organize a game of pickle or basketball (leaving the dishes for others, I'm afraid). Another special experience that we shared over these years was going to a piece of property of about a hundred acres just north of Kensington Metropark, about an hour northwest of Detroit. It's an undeveloped area of steep hills and a beautiful valley where we built a small one-room cabin, fondly known as the Lion's Den. We would meet out there throughout the seasons for a few hours on the weekend, when our schedules permitted. To this day we still enjoy going out there.

Michigan Civil Rights Commission

In 1963, when I was still in private law practice, Michigan voters approved a new constitution that, among other things, created the Michigan Civil Rights Commission. The first cochairs of the commission were respected lawyers who would go on to serve on the federal bench: John Feikens and Damon Keith. They recommended me to Michigan's attorney general, Frank J. Kelley, a progressive hero of mine who used the law to help people, and in January 1964 I became the first General Counsel to the newly formed commission.

Racial discrimination by certain local government officials and in private housing was a major issue when I started representing the commission. In Arkansas there was an infamously racist governor named Orval Faubus who, in 1957 in response to a federal court order, sent his National Guard to block African American students from entering an all-white public school. We had our own "Orval" in Michigan, and not just figuratively. His name was Orville Hubbard, the long-time mayor of Dearborn, a suburb west of Detroit and the home of the Ford Motor Company. Hubbard was notorious for his very public stance that African Americans were not welcome in "his" city, either to live, work, or visit. The Michigan Civil Rights Commission decided its first major effort would be to take on Mayor Hubbard.

Anyone entering the public lobby of Dearborn City Hall in those days was confronted by a huge bulletin board filled with newspaper clippings featuring stories and photos from around the country about crimes committed by African Americans. Hubbard had personally ordered this grotesque display. It wasn't clear whether the Civil Rights Commission had jurisdiction over local government activities, but we aimed to find out.

We took a photograph of the bulletin board and re-created an exact replica to use as an exhibit at a public hearing. It was very dramatic, because Hubbard denounced the hearing, publicly contested our jurisdiction, and refused to attend. The commission, chaired by Feikens and Keith, ordered Hubbard to take down the board, which Hubbard refused to do. So, we sued to enforce the commission order in Wayne County Circuit Court, alleging that the racist, public bulletin board violated the equal protection clause of the Michigan constitution. Our main goal was not to simply get the bulletin board removed but to establish a precedent that would give the commission jurisdiction over discriminatory actions of local governments. Fortunately, before trial, Ralph Guy Jr., Dearborn's corporation counsel who would later become a federal judge, called me to say that Hubbard was taking down the bulletin board. Not only that, he said the City of Dearborn and Hubbard would concede that the Michigan Civil Rights Commission had jurisdiction to take appropriate action to stop discriminatory actions by local governments. The order resolving the case explicitly provided that the equal protection clause of the Michigan constitution gave the Michigan Civil Rights Commission jurisdiction to address discriminatory actions by local governments.

When I spoke at Rosa Parks's funeral in 2005, I referenced the Orville Hubbard incident. I was later criticized by some friends who lived in Dearborn and thought I should have mentioned the significant changes in their city that had occurred in the fifty years since Rosa Parks was arrested. They were right, because the changes were dramatic and provided a ray of hope that progress is achievable.

But the Hubbard decision did not address the commission's role with respect to private property. Could the commission prohibit the owners of private property from discriminating against potential buyers based on their race? At that time, there was widespread discrimination against African Americans who wanted to buy homes in white neighborhoods, particularly in the fast-growing suburbs of Detroit. Many African Americans, for example, faced "covenants" in deeds of real estate that forbade owners from selling to minorities.

An opportunity to challenge discrimination in housing came to the commission when an African American public school counselor, Freeman Moore, filed a complaint with the commission. It involved a suburban subdivision called Georgetown Green, which was planned to include 140 homes. The builder was William J. (Bill) Pulte, one of the biggest developers in metro Detroit and later in the country. Pulte's Beech Grove Investment Company was offering four-bedroom colonials for $29,000, and Moore expressed an interest in buying one. Moore was mailed a plot plan for a house he liked and sent a down payment check for $1,000 to Pulte. Pulte called Moore's school to ascertain his race. When he was rebuffed, someone working for Pulte set up a meeting for Moore in Pulte's office, the result being Pulte's refusal to sell to Moore. When we took Pulte's deposition, he freely admitted that he wouldn't sell Moore and his wife a home because "if I sold him a lot it wouldn't be advantageous to the subdivision from our business standpoint." Responding to this open challenge, the commission ordered Pulte to "cease and desist from any practice or policy" that discriminated against persons based on race or color.

I argued the case in the Michigan Supreme Court, which found in a 5–3 opinion that the discrimination against the Moores violated both their civil rights to acquire property and the Michigan Public Accommodations Act of 1931. It was a major victory for both the Moores and the commission because it gave the commission jurisdiction to go after discrimination in private housing.

Legal Aid

I left the Michigan Civil Rights Commission in 1967 to join a new division in Detroit's Legal Aid Office representing indigent citizens. Previously, Legal Aid assisted poor people in civil matters like divorces; now it would also represent indigent citizens charged with crimes. This additional authority was important, because indigent defendants in criminal cases had been given court-appointed lawyers who often were inadequate and who were assigned in some cases by judges based on friendship instead of competency. Moreover, these lawyers were paid just a small amount for each case they handled, which meant the more cases they could churn out and the more clients who pled guilty, the more money they would make. There was also no provision for investigators to help the defense, so these attorneys were often working without all the pertinent information, including records, documents, and witness testimony. Legal Aid, on the other hand, paid salaries to its attorneys and budgeted for several investigators. I ran its appellate division.

The importance of having investigators available to the defense was demonstrated to me in the case of an African American man who spent twenty-five years in prison after a jury found him guilty of killing a white store owner during a robbery, a first-degree felony murder. The injustice in this case was so blatant that two governors offered to commute the man's sentence, but he turned them down, saying he'd either leave prison as an innocent man or die in prison because he felt that accepting commutation implied he was guilty.

One of our detectives, Bob Gartner, went looking for the only witness to the crime, the daughter of the victim. After twenty-five years, it required a lot of shoe leather to find her, but Bob did. She forthrightly told Bob that she had never seen the killer's face. She said she had identified the defendant only because the police detective on the case had told her that he was the killer. She readily affirmed these facts in an affidavit that led to a hearing, and the conviction was vacated. Such miscarriages of justice are why I oppose the death penalty in all cases.

Another case I handled involved a woman named Geraldine Shamblin, who had been convicted of second-degree murder for killing her boyfriend. She had two young children and had already been in prison a few years when I handled the appeal. She acknowledged that she went after her boyfriend with a pen knife, apparently aiming for his private parts because he was sexually assaulting her. She hit an artery in his thigh and he bled to death. She was convicted of second-degree murder, an intentional crime, and sentenced to a minimum of ten and a maximum of twenty years in prison.

At the sentencing, the judge, Thomas Poindexter, said, in reference to the ten-year minimum, that given he had sentenced people convicted of manslaughter to ten years in prison, he couldn't impose a lesser minimum sentence for second-degree murder. The statute, however, said he could sentence her to any term of years. The case went to the Michigan Court of Appeals. My very technical argument was that the judge had said he *couldn't* sentence her to less than ten years but the law said he could, so the judge was wrong. The appeals court panel looked at me like I was a bit naive. They said something to the effect of, "If we reverse and send it back for resentencing, won't the judge just re-sentence her to the same ten years?" "Maybe he will; maybe he won't," I said. "All we know is that he said on the record that he couldn't give her less than ten years, and that was wrong."

I won the appeal, and it went back to Judge Poindexter for re-sentencing. I watched in the courtroom as our trial division attorney, George Lee, argued to Judge Poindexter that he had been wrong on the law. He reminded the judge that the woman had two young children, no previous record, and unintention-ally killed a man who was abusing her.

"For heaven's sake, Judge!" Lee said. "What's the point of keeping her in prison?"

The judge listened, then said, "I'm sentencing her to time served." The courtroom exploded in cheers. Her family cried tears of joy, and I added a few of my own. Those cases had an effect on me; they still do.

I worked in that appellate division until the year after the devastating 1967 Detroit rebellion, when I decided to run for public office.

2

Eight Years on the Detroit City Council

The events that took place in Detroit in July 1967 have been called the Uprising, the Detroit Rebellion, the Riots, and a civil disturbance. Whatever name is used, the event itself was a disaster for many individuals and for the city. For five days Detroit burned, looters took to the streets, and police and the National Guard at times used excessive force. U.S. Army troops were needed to help restore order.

It all began just a few doors from my old law office, and by the time it was over forty-three people had died and hundreds of homes and businesses had been looted, burned, or destroyed. The city spent millions in overtime for police officers, firefighters, and other city employees. Dozens of conventions booked for downtown were canceled. The extent of the damage was calculated to be over $130 million. Detroit was on its knees.

On a more personal level, I was heartbroken. Detroit is my hometown. It had been home to three generations of my family. I love Detroit. I revere its past, and I've always had faith in its future. It's a large part of who I am. Indeed, when Barbara and I finished our thirty-six years in Washington, all we wanted was to be full time in Detroit.

After the riots or days of rage, all over the city people were searching for answers and direction and hope. As chief appellate attorney at the Legal Aid and Defender Association of Detroit, I was pressed into service at bail hearings to help represent over 7,000 defendants, including 700 juveniles, accused of looting or curfew violations. Our office wasn't very successful in that effort, given the chaos going on in Detroit's streets and the fear of returning into the fray anyone suspected of being a participant.

In the aftermath of the riots not only in Detroit but also in Chicago, Los Angeles, and Newark, President Johnson established the Kerner Commission to investigate the causes of the urban violence. The commission reported in April 1968 that the United States was "moving toward two societies, one black, one white—separate and unequal," and that white racism was largely to blame, citing a history of racial prejudice in housing, education, employment, and social service programs. In Detroit, for example, which had an African American population at the time of over 30 percent, only one member of the City Council was black, and 93 percent of officers in the Detroit Police Department were white. Moreover, many police officers, the report found, harbored racist attitudes toward black residents, who were well on their way to becoming the majority a few years later.

My First Campaign

I agreed with the Kerner Commission's conclusions but wondered what a young, white lawyer could do to help improve those conditions. A number of friends and some long-standing political gurus urged me to run for what was then called the Common Council (later called City Council), Detroit's legislative body. They believed I could draw significant support from the African American community because of my work as first General Counsel of the Michigan Civil Rights Commission and my involvement in the creation of the Legal Aid and Defender Association in 1966.

What moved me to run was my deep feeling that Detroit needed healing and that if I could draw support from both the white and African American communities, I might be able to help start the process of rebuilding and improving my shattered hometown. So in 1968, with encouragement from family and friends, I announced my candidacy for Detroit Common Council.

I received valuable encouragement from many friends but none quite as persuasive as that of Eugene and Elaine Driker. The Drikers, with their two children, Elissa and Stephen, who were close in age to our girls, remain our dear friends, and they lived a few doors away until I was elected to the Senate in 1978. Like us, they were stalwart Detroiters, committed to our city through "thick or thin" and to its people, neighborhoods, and institutions like Wayne State University, the Tigers, the art museum, the library, and the symphony.

I campaigned that year with a strong network of volunteers who knocked on doors, handed out leaflets, and contributed to my campaign in countless other ways. The Detroit neighborhood we lived in, Green Acres, was a vibrant community, proud of its diversity and cohesion. It was a middle-class neighborhood where people knew everybody on the block and looked out for each other, taking in a neighbor's newspapers if they were out of town. Kids played together—our yard being one of the favorite places, because we had a basketball hoop, and we flooded the yard during freezing spells in winter so kids could do a little ice skating. We even knew each other's pets—and if a dog or cat went missing, a note taped to a light pole alerting the neighborhood that a search was on usually produced results. We made great friends on the block, and we were fortunate to live directly across the street from Art Johnson, a close friend of ours with whom I worked during my time with the Michigan Civil Rights Commission.

Our closely knit neighborhood gave us an idea for my political campaign. In an effort to help build and demonstrate support in diverse racial, ethnic, and economic neighborhoods, we circulated "neighborhood letters" all over town. The text of the letters was the same from neighborhood to neighborhood, but we customized them with endorsements from local supporters, so people could see that their neighbors, people they knew, knew me and were behind me. Organizing a hundred or so letters, getting the names and addresses right, and then getting them distributed in the right neighborhood takes a significant amount of work. But it is a great way to organize a campaign, to localize a candidate, and to make use of volunteers. A lot of people worked hard for me in that campaign, and I owe them a huge debt.

Another key to my campaign was my family name, Levin. A number of Levins had been involved for decades in Detroit's African American community. My cousin, Dr. Mort Levin, for example, was a general practitioner on the east side of Detroit in a very poor neighborhood. He must have had ten thousand patients for whom he delivered babies and made house calls. He was beloved. It happened all the time, and it still happens: people from that neighborhood walk up to me and say, "Senator Levin, is your brother a doctor?" And, I say, "You mean Mort Levin? He's my cousin." They'll say "he delivered me" or something about Mort coming to treat their mother when she was sick and she couldn't afford to pay, and Mort said that was okay and to pay him "when you're on your feet." He sent out thousands of postcards for me when I ran for City Council.

Perhaps most importantly, Sandy ran for the Michigan Senate in 1964 and had served for five years when I made my first bid for the Council. While Sandy's district wasn't in the city, he guided me through that first election, serving as a mentor and friend, as he has done throughout my life. My sister, Hannah, and her husband, Bill, who was the Democratic Party chairman in their congressional district, also provided critical support with political savvy and connections where they lived in northwest Detroit. Our kids grew familiar with meetings being held in our living room and learned how to pitch in, stuffing envelopes for campaign mailings.

All seats on City Council at that time were at-large, meaning members were elected citywide, an approach I always favored as a way to keep a city as united as possible. Out of the eighteen finalists running for nine seats in November 1969, I came in third, behind the incumbent Council president, Mel Ravitz, and the long-serving African American Council president pro tem, Reverend Nicholas Hood. Notably, two additional African Americans were also elected that year.

First Term

Elections in Detroit are nonpartisan, and City Council members consequently can have a wide variety of political views. It was a real challenge to get nine people with diverse views and backgrounds on the City Council to work together, and over the course of my time there I gained a lot of respect for the legislative process. You need to work together, compromise, and respect the fact that different people can have very sincere but very different views about the best ways to solve problems you both care about. It's a lesson I took to the Senate, where you need a majority of 51 or at times a supermajority of 60 to get things done.

At the City Council I also learned patience. One member, Jack Kelley, who was a wonderful blue-collar guy, had a drinking problem and blew his stack from time to time. One time in a debate he yelled at me, "You're a whore, Levin! All you lawyers are whores!" All I could do was shake my head and say, "Aw, come on, Jack!" The next day's paper laid it all out: "Kelley calls Levin a whore; Levin says, 'Aw, come on, Jack.'" It was a good lesson: the importance of keeping my cool in challenging situations and the way cool could defeat hot in the media. Equally important, because I hadn't yelled back or insulted Jack, we were able to put the "fight" behind us and work together on many issues. By keeping lines of communication open, by not contributing to tense interpersonal situations, you could leave the door open and get things done. Finally, working with Jack and my other colleagues taught me how important it was to understand where they were coming from, what political or personal forces led them to take the positions they did. In this case, I really didn't think Jack believed I was whore. It wasn't a personal attack on me; it was just a guy letting off some steam. Recognizing that helped me keep my cool and helped diffuse the situation both rhetorically and personally.

My legal training prepared me to listen closely to witnesses who appeared before the City Council, many of whom were agency heads. And, if the words in an answer were not responsive to a question, I learned to bore in—repeating the question until I got a responsive answer. It also helped that as a lawyer I knew how to use documents and exhibits to get to the facts. I learned how important it is to be prepared by digging into previous statements of a witness and relevant documents. Only "by getting into the weeds" can you know whether or not a witness is being evasive. The lessons I learned as a legislator in local government were, as they say, priceless. My reputation in the Senate for tenacity in asking questions goes back to those Council days.

In 1971, *Detroit Free Press* reporter Peter Benjaminson described my style this way:

> Levin calls officials to the Council table with all the friendliness and good nature of a party host on New Year's Eve. But once the official has settled himself . . . he is often confronted with a suddenly implacable Levin. . . . Levin, 36, a lawyer by training and a modern populist by inclination is the recalcitrant official's most formidable foe. Nothing seems to please Levin as much as confronting a quavering official with a contradictory statement from a letter that official had previously written . . . [Levin] fairly overflows on occasion with righteous indignation for the poor and mistreated. . . . Levin masterfully rolls his baleful eyes from his papers to the face of his victim in one easy, guilt-inducing motion, before remarking that it "intrigues" him that, say, $500,000 has mysteriously disappeared between letter and lip. He is the only councilman with the inclination or expertise to push defensive officials all the way into the bullpen of contradictions they themselves have constructed.

On the Council, I focused my attention on trying to improve the state of the city after the riot. I'd like to think of myself as an idealist, but I don't want to be naive, and I am basically a practical person. I knew then and I know now that no one, certainly no politician, can wave a magic wand and displace the hate and fear that people carry in their hearts. Nor can any politician make people love or respect or even tolerate each other. But I do believe that a politician has an obligation to identify injustice and try to eliminate or at least minimize it. And I do believe that politicians can write laws that will improve the lives of the people they seek to serve.

And that is what I tried to do.

HUD

As I mentioned in the preface, one of the biggest problems Detroit faced while I was on the City Council was the impact of the housing programs of the Department of Housing and Urban Development (HUD). The lack of safe and suitable housing in Detroit was one factor in the rioting of 1967, but the response of the federal government—making FHA (Federal Housing Administration) mortgages with inflated value available to people who often did not have the ability to pay—was a total failure. It produced a glut of abandoned houses, devastating our neighborhoods. Action was required by the city and the Council to take on HUD.

A Council member's staff was limited to a secretary, but fortunately I enjoyed the assistance of a bright young man named Tom Clark, a graduate student who worked for me with a small salary paid through a work-study program at Eastern Michigan University. With Clark's help I rolled up my sleeves—literally, because I am more comfortable working that way—and got to work on the HUD issue.

Through Don Ball, a *Detroit News* reporter, we learned troubling things about HUD's failings and the impact they were having on the quality of life in Detroit. In May 1972, Ball reported that HUD was selling houses it had repossessed to the public without a city inspection for building code violations, which was in violation of Detroit ordinances designed to keep unsafe homes off the market. HUD promised to change that policy, but nothing happened. Ball also reported that unscrupulous inspectors hired by HUD had approved homes for sale that were in bad shape and could not pass a city inspection. According to Ball, and later to federal prosecutors, the inspectors were taking kickbacks so mortgages could be approved on run-down homes that were not up to code. The houses were then purchased by unsuspecting people who could not afford the repairs. Since they couldn't even get loans to make repairs, houses deteriorated to the point where many people simply walked away. Defaults soared, but the banks didn't care because the mortgages had been backed by the federal government, so the banks got paid anyway.

Clearly we needed help from Congress, and I introduced a resolution in City Council asking Congress to investigate HUD's abuses, including selling homes to the public without a city inspection for building code violations. The resolution passed unanimously. I publicly declared that HUD—and therefore the federal government—was "giving up on the city."

I thought that Detroit would have had a leg up in dealing with HUD because it was then headed by our former governor, George Romney, who had been appointed by President Richard Nixon as HUD secretary in 1969. We met with Secretary Romney during a visit to Detroit, and he promised to look into it. Months later there was no sign that an investigation had begun. Our frustration with HUD grew. We were angry. We produced a 150-page report that included photocopies of Don Ball's articles and documented HUD's dismal record of failure in the city. We mailed the report to President Nixon on July 25, 1972, with a cover letter asking the president to fire Secretary Romney.*

At the center of our battle with HUD was our ordinance allowing the city to tear down thousands of buildings owned by HUD that were a danger because they were open to trespass. HUD's response was an offer to sell to the city some 3,000 abandoned houses for $1 apiece, which would have the effect of putting responsibility for the maintenance costs of about $500 a year per house onto the city of Detroit. I suggested that HUD instead sell the houses for $1 to adjacent owners, who would have a vested interest in making sure the property next door was kept secure. HUD rejected that idea but then began selling houses in "as is" condition with the buyer assuming responsibility for rehabilitation. Their advertising for this plan was misleading and prompted speculators, instead of families, to try to "flip" houses to make a quick profit while doing little to nothing to bring the houses up to code. It seemed that every time we identified a problem with HUD's programs the "feds" created a

---

* To be fair, Secretary Romney was progressive on many issues. He had tried to dismantle racial segregation exemplified by what he called a "high-income white noose" formed by the white suburbs surrounding increasingly black cities. Under his Open Communities initiative, Romney instructed HUD bureaucrats to reject applications for sewer and highway projects from cities and states with segregationist policies. But then, in a move that became public only after the Watergate scandal broke, President Nixon ordered his domestic policy chief, John Ehrlichman, to shut down the project, an act that may have been the cause of Secretary Romney's resignation.

"fix" that actually made matters worse. Indeed, HUD's inventory of dilapidated, unusable homes would soon be 10,500. It was time for drastic action.

Armed with a legal opinion from the City Corporation Counsel's office that outlined the city's right to order demolition of HUD houses the same way we did for private owners, I said that we would no longer rely on false promises from HUD. We would rely on our city's ordinances to deal with this disaster. We had the legal basis to fulfill our duty of protecting citizens by tearing down HUD-owned houses not securely boarded up and open to trespass or worse, and so we ordered that it be done. With the destruction of that first house, I felt we were clawing our way out of the blight and into the fight.

Other Issues

Another fight for Detroit's neighborhoods involved the proliferation of "adult" businesses—porn shops, strip clubs, and the like. Some of the neighborhood theaters that used to show family films were now showing X-rated movies. "Adult" bookstores were springing up in residential areas. I felt the City Council had an obligation to try to do something about it, but the United States Supreme Court had previously ruled that sexually explicit material had some First Amendment protection.

So I hit upon a new way of tackling the issue—one that was ultimately upheld by the Supreme Court. We wrote an amendment to our "Anti–Skid Row" zoning ordinance to regulate the location of these businesses, including prohibiting them from operating closer than 1,000 feet to a similar business and prohibiting them from operating within 500 feet of residential zoned neighborhoods. In other words, we were creatively using our zoning law to restrict objectionable uses instead of trying to ban them. The owners of two adult movie theaters sued the city, alleging violation of their First Amendment rights. We won in U.S. District Court but lost in the Circuit Court of Appeals. Then, in *Young v. American Mini-Theaters, Inc.*, the U.S. Supreme Court in 1976 overturned the appeals court. Writing for the majority, Justice John Paul Stevens said that zoning was an instance where the right to free speech could be balanced against the right of a municipality to protect its neighborhoods from blight and crime. It was extremely gratifying to see a law I'd written get upheld by the nation's highest court. And while that law didn't deal broadly with the many problems Detroit faced, it did at least allow us to make some progress in that area.

That first term I also got deeply involved in the effort to ban phosphates from detergents. The 1970s marked a key turning point in our country's consciousness about environmental problems. Wisconsin senator Gaylord Nelson had established the first Earth Day on April 22, 1970, to bring environmental issues to national attention. During this time, I became aware of scientific studies about the harmful effects of phosphates on the environment, particularly on Great Lakes waters. Detroit was the single largest polluter of Lake Erie, a lake so heavily polluted at the time that it was considered "dead." Laundry detergent, often containing 40 percent phosphorus by weight, was one of the worst culprits. I proposed an ordinance banning the sale of laundry detergent in Detroit containing over 8.7 percent phosphates after July 1, 1971, with a goal of zero phosphates by July 1, 1972. The 8.7 percent level was the limit set by Canada. Despite protests from companies like Procter & Gamble and market owners who said people would simply do their shopping for detergents in the suburbs, the City Council unanimously passed the ordinance in January 1971.

As part of a public relations campaign, manufacturers voluntarily agreed later that year to meet the 8.7 percent standard. The following year, the Michigan legislature used our ordinance as a model to impose the same limit statewide. However, apparently bowing to industry pressure, the legislature declared that no Michigan municipality could impose an outright ban on phosphates, effectively nullifying our effort to completely eliminate phosphates in 1972.

Environmental activists would not let the issue die. In 1976, the Michigan legislature passed a law setting the phosphate limit at 5 percent by weight. The law took effect in 1977, and that year a bill on reducing phosphate use in laundry detergent nationwide was introduced in Congress. As then-president of the Detroit City Council, I was asked to testify about Detroit's efforts to limit phosphates before the newly renamed Senate Environment and Public Works Committee chaired by West Virginia Democratic senator Jennings Randolph. Of course, I spoke in support of a national ban on phosphates in laundry detergent. People had mocked our ordinance as ineffective because of its geographical limits, but it was proof that the slogan "think globally, act locally" can sometimes lead to a global response.*

I also created a big stir in 1971 when I proposed a ban on the sale of coats and other clothing made out of the furs or skins of endangered species of animals such as cheetahs. Although such items of clothing were rare and extremely expensive, Detroit furriers raised a howl, complaining that customers would take their business to the suburbs. The City Council passed the ordinance, but Mayor Gribbs vetoed it in July 1971 only to change his position a year later, allowing us to enact it. That ordinance, too, became the model for a later state law that banned the sale of pelts from endangered species.

Another ordinance I proposed in 1971 created an ombudsman with powers to champion the cause of citizens with complaints against city government. Given my belief that government, at all levels, has to be responsive to the legitimate concerns of citizens, and given the number of citizen complaints and how aggrieved many Detroiters felt about city services, I thought an ombudsman was a good approach. That proposal was adopted by the Detroit Charter Revision Commission and approved by voters in 1973. Giving people more power to make government listen to them is a way to ensure that government will serve them. And, equally important, that process gives people greater faith that the government can operate efficiently.

---

* Unfortunately, Michigan and Congress had left a big loophole—phosphates in automatic dishwasher detergents. Granted, at the time few people owned automatic dishwashers, but within a decade, they were ubiquitous. As before, manufacturers claimed limiting phosphates would make their products less effective while environmentalists and, eventually, the public clamored for more action. In 2009 Senator George Voinovich, Republican of Ohio, and I introduced a bill in Congress to impose the same phosphate limits on automatic dishwasher detergents. That bill died in committee, but the Michigan legislature passed a law that took effect in 2010 to set the same 0.5 percent phosphate limit on dishwasher detergents, as have seventeen other states.

A key part of the effort to improve conditions for Detroit citizens was to improve the educational opportunities available to them. Detroit schools in the 1970s were underperforming and underresourced and, because most neighborhoods were de facto segregated, they were not racially diverse. There was little the Council or the mayor could do about it because under state law elected school boards controlled public schools, and the money needed to provide a quality education for our children was tied to property taxes. Unfortunately, in Detroit the revenue from this source was decreasing.

In 1970, the NAACP filed a federal lawsuit alleging that the state was providing unequal (discriminatory) educational opportunities in Detroit. The plaintiffs, who had cited the landmark 1954 *Brown v. Board of Education* case, prevailed at trial. U.S. District Court Judge Stephen J. Roth in Detroit ordered the state to begin cross-district busing of students among fifty-three school districts. That would mean many Detroit students would be enrolled in suburban schools and vice versa. But Roth stayed his ruling when the state said it would appeal.

Most suburbanites opposed cross-district busing, but many Detroiters did as well, believing that Detroit needed to be capable of educating its own children without busing them long distances and that Detroit could do that well if funding and other resources were equalized. Mayor Coleman Young and I filed an amicus brief against cross-district busing in the case when it got to the U.S. Supreme Court. In the *Milliken v. Bradley* decision in 1974, the Supreme Court partially overturned Roth's remedy. There would be no cross-district busing, but the Detroit school system was ordered to begin intradistrict busing. That meant that within Detroit, African American students would be sent to predominantly white schools and white kids to mostly African American schools. That did not have a positive outcome either, as racial divisions intensified and contributed to the mainly, at that time, white exodus from the city to the suburbs.

In the 1960s and the 1970s, our three daughters went to integrated public and private schools in the City of Detroit. Barb and I believed in the value of diversity as an important part of one's education. Our kids benefited from it and were able to get a good education in Detroit. As our daughters grew older and had children of their own, they appreciated more and more their own positive experiences with diversity.

In 1977, Barbara and I and a number of our Jewish friends came together to help maintain Jewish religious services in Detroit. Only one synagogue, the downtown synagogue, remained in the city, but they didn't hold Jewish holiday services. Using St. Mary's Church School in Detroit's Greektown neighborhood to hold services, we formed the congregation T'chiyah with ten other families. We preserved some artifacts from old Detroit synagogues, including pews, chandeliers, and a magnificent stained glass window. Eventually we needed to find other space and have been able to remain a small Reconstructionist congregation using different downtown locations over the years.

Second Term

The political environment had changed in Detroit by the time I ran for reelection in 1973. The race for mayor that year was between Police Commissioner John Nichols and Coleman A. Young, a Tuskegee Airman and a state senator. Young became a hero for African Americans and progressives when, during a 1952 field hearing in Detroit, he defied the House Un-American Activities Committee by repeatedly refusing to answer whether he was a member of the Communist Party. When one congressman remarked that Young seemed reluctant to fight communism, Young said: "I am here to aid in any fight against un-American activities. I consider un-American activities those of the Klan [and] the denial of the right to vote of Negroes all over the south." On the other hand, Nichols, who'd been appointed police commissioner by Mayor Gribbs, had created a controversial crime-fighting unit called STRESS (Stop the Robberies, Enjoy Safe Streets). It used undercover cops posing as easy victims as bait for potential muggers. The idea came close to entrapment, and the implementation was deeply flawed: the STRESS cops shot to death twenty civilians—seventeen of whom were African American. STRESS divided the city and the City Council, where I voted against continuing it.

Young campaigned effectively against maintaining an overwhelmingly white police department, while Nichols opposed the creation of a civilian board to oversee the Detroit Police Department. Young won and shortly thereafter dismantled STRESS.

The makeup of the City Council also changed in that election; it was now comprised of five whites and four African Americans, seven men and two women. And, as the top vote-getter, I became its president. Reverend Nick Hood came in second and continued to be president pro tem. Nick Hood was a blessing for me—he was wise and sensitive. He was a true partner and friend. I still think of him often and how lucky I was to serve together with him.

Now that we would have Detroit's first black mayor and a white City Council president, it was particularly important that we work well together. Our city was divided in many ways, including by tensions over court-ordered integration of Detroit's public schools and the school busing that had been mandated to achieve it. Crime was rising, businesses were moving out, and white flight was accelerating. A national economic crisis prompted by the first oil embargo imposed by OPEC on the United States in 1973 had weakened the national economy. We were suffering from self-inflicted wounds like the 1967 riot but also from things we could not control such as a severe downturn in the national economy, particularly in the auto industry.

The discriminatory practices of insurance companies contributed significantly to the decline of our neighborhoods. In August 1976 we issued a report documenting rampant "redlining" in Detroit—the refusal to provide insurance to people based on the zip code in which they lived. Using that report, we petitioned the state insurance commissioner to ban all redlining and to treat all customers in Michigan in accordance with the same standards. The Insurance Bureau held investigative proceedings, but nothing changed. I testified before the state legislature on the redlining problems, and in January 1977, U.S. senator Howard Metzenbaum, Democrat of Ohio, invited me to present the report to the Judiciary Committee's Subcommittee on Citizens and Shareholders Rights and Remedies, but it would take many years for the courts to clarify its illegality.

That June I exposed a new form of redlining—credit card redlining. That secret practice involved using zip codes to determine whether an applicant would get a credit card. Banning this form of discrimination was the subject of the first bill I introduced as a U.S. senator, and the practice was finally stopped by the industry.

For the most part, I worked well with Mayor Young. I liked and respected him. He had put his life on the line in World War II as part of an extraordinary group of black aviators for a country that discriminated against them. But we had differences of opinion about specific policies. For example, I believed that regional cooperation was essential. His rhetoric wasn't just pro-Detroit; it was perceived to be anti-suburb, which I thought was shortsighted and counterproductive. The truth of the matter is that if you want to have a healthy city, you need people, wherever they live in the metropolitan area, to work together.

The mayor's perceived "we don't need the suburbs" approach affected a number of issues. For instance, Young told criminals to "hit Eight Mile Road," meaning "get out of town." But many suburbanites took that to mean he was encouraging criminals to victimize the mainly white suburbs.

Another issue that divided the mayor and me was the construction of the Detroit People Mover, which was built with federal funds committed by President Jimmy Carter. I had thought the huge amount of federal funds should be used to begin construction of a transit system radiating from downtown Detroit—west toward the airport, north toward Pontiac, and east toward Mt. Clemens. Mayor Young opted for a light rail system that operated on an elevated single-track loop around Detroit's downtown area. Critics called it "the train to nowhere." In building it, an opportunity to start connecting Detroit to other centers in the region and to the airport was lost, and a lot of federal money was left on the table.

During my second term as City Council president, I had the benefit of four years of experience and a strong reelection vote. I decided that one of my priorities would be to try to make the legislative branch of city government more open to the public. We wanted our citizens and the news media to observe what we were doing and understand how it impacted their lives. We set aside time at meetings to allow citizens to bring issues to our attention. I also believed in a strong legislative branch as valuable insurance against a secretive executive branch. I told the *Detroit Free Press* in November 1977 that since the executive branch, by its very nature, doesn't deliberate in the open, the legislative branch was the one place "where we can debate and discuss policies and issues" in a public forum.

During my first year as Council president in 1974, I held the first open Council session on budget matters. Handling financial matters at public sessions is a safeguard against the misappropriation of funds or even the appearance of such misappropriation. We passed an ordinance to give City Council veto power over all city contracts exceeding $5,000. Though Mayor Young vetoed that ordinance, the Council overrode his veto unanimously. We refused to approve a painting contract, let by the Public Lighting Commission, that was $110,000 higher than the lowest bid. We also voted to deny a $900,000 contract for billing services because competitive bids had not been received. That saved the Water Department tens of thousands of dollars.

In April 1975, Mayor Young took the position that under a new City Charter passed in 1974, the Council had no power to change or add programs to his lump-sum program budget. The core of the issue was which branch of city government would control spending. I argued that Mayor Young's interpretation made the Council a mere rubber stamp for the administration and was a serious challenge to the legislative body's fundamental duty. The Council sued the mayor and lost, but we didn't give up. We proposed a charter amendment to ensure that the Council had authority over the city budget. The voters agreed with us. They adopted our amendment in 1976, a big step toward ensuring legislative oversight of city finances.

It was necessary on a number of other occasions to defend the power of the Council with respect to financial matters. For instance, the Council was required to approve a large number of settlements agreed to by the City Law Department in lawsuits against the city. The near automatic approval of small settlements was an incentive for filing dubious claims against the city, and we faced an avalanche of such claims. We thus instituted semi-annual comprehensive reports to City Council on the status of all litigation against the city and stopped the rubber-stamping of settlements.

Over those eight years on the City Council, I developed an understanding of and a deep appreciation for the role of the Council in Detroit's governance and the value an effective legislature could provide in our tripartite system of government. It is an essential check on the efforts of strong chief executives who seek to assume powers that are not theirs and was an effective tool to go after bureaucratic waste, abuse, and neglect. My experience in local government as a legislator overseeing the activities of the executive branch would prove to be a valuable training ground for later tussles—and sometimes battles—with presidents and federal agencies when I became a member of the U.S. Senate.

Time for a Change

It was a good eight years on Council, but I decided not to run for a third term. It was time for a change. I was gratified by the response to my decision. Even the conservative editorial page of the *Detroit News*, which disagreed with me on many policy issues, said I had served as Council president with "serene yet firm leadership that had helped remove the dirty connotation from the word 'politician.' " One of their columnists, Jake Highton, wrote that "checking Levin's public record, it is difficult to find something bad to say about him."

But what to do now? I tried to be appointed U.S. Attorney for the Eastern District of Michigan. Its office is in Detroit where the U.S. District Court is located, and there was a vacancy in the position for which Senator Don Riegle would recommend someone to President Carter. I met with Senator Riegle to make the case that I should be that "someone," but Senator Riegle selected Jim Robinson, a fine person and a highly qualified lawyer.

Plan B didn't pan out any better when I didn't make the cut for a Fulbright scholarship, either. Two disappointments and, as it turned out, two lucky breaks, because if I had succeeded at getting either the U.S. Attorney appointment or the Fulbright, I would not have been able to seek election to the U.S.

Senate when a Senate seat opened up shortly thereafter. It was a great lesson about the role of chance in one's life and how disappointment can turn out to be a lucky break.

I have frequently shared that bit of my personal history with high school students I have talked to over the years. I tell them one may hope, for example, to go to a particular college and be crushed if you are turned down and you end up going to your second or third choice. But, after you've swallowed your disappointment, it may turn out that you fall in love and marry someone you never would have met, or you take a course with a teacher who inspires a new career choice. So there are many reasons not to be too disheartened when what appears to be an unlucky break comes along. Most people who have been around a while have learned this.

In January 1978 I joined what was then a small law firm led by my friend Ira Jaffe. Later that year, two political commentators, TV's Lou Gordon and the *Free Press*'s Judd Arnett, suggested that I run for the Senate. Most importantly, my wife, Barbara, woke me from a sound sleep one morning at 4 a.m. and said, "You know, you really ought to consider running for the U.S. Senate." As I remember it, I urged her to go back to sleep. But I began more and more to think back to the day when as president of the Detroit City Council I ordered the demolition of the house that presented a clear danger to the community—despite the threats of prosecution—and I realized that I might be in a unique position as a senator to make a difference by overseeing federal programs that affected the people of Michigan. I had engaged in a running battle with a key federal agency for several years and had an intimate understanding of how these agencies with important missions can obstruct reform and avoid oversight.

The Senate seat we were thinking about was held by a powerful incumbent and former Republican whip, Robert Griffin, who had been appointed to the Senate by Governor George Romney in May 1966 to fill a vacancy. He defeated former governor Soapy Williams that same year, then won reelection in 1972 by besting Attorney General Frank Kelley. But in early 1977, Griffin said he would not seek reelection in 1978. Several big-name Republicans like L. Brooks Patterson and Clark Durant were said to be in the race to succeed him.

I was still mulling it over while visiting friends in the village of L'Anse in the Upper Peninsula and snoozing on the couch when we heard on the news that Griffin had changed his mind and would run for reelection. Griffin was now vulnerable. When he said earlier that he wouldn't run, he also said that he was tired and proceeded to miss a lot of votes. Many Republicans resented that he had reversed course. I told my friends: "That's it! I'm going to go home and announce." I headed back to Detroit and talked it over with Barbara and our daughters, Kate (age 14), Laura (age 12), and Erica (age 9), and the rest of the family, including Sandy, of course, and our sister, Hannah, who had great political instincts. They supported my decision.

3

Campaigning for the
U.S. Senate

The first high hurdle after deciding to run for the Senate in 1978 was to win the primary. There were five other solid Democrats who had also decided to run. During the campaign one of them ran a radio ad claiming that I was running on my brother Sandy's name, even though by that time I had served on the Detroit City Council for eight years and had been Council president for four of those years. I am proud to be a member of the Levin family and was proud of the two positive and impressive campaigns for governor that my brother ran despite the fact that they were unsuccessful. I was also proud of my cousin Charles Levin's successful campaigns for the Michigan Court of Appeals and Supreme Court. The candidate who ran that ad miscalculated, because I've found the electorate admires families in public life that are close and supportive of each other, provided the person running is qualified to run on his or her own merits and experience. Laughably, when Sandy ran for Congress four years later, he was accused of running on *my* name despite the fact that he had served in the Michigan Senate for six years and had been involved in two competitive races for governor.

Another of my primary opponents dramatically outspent me, but we were able to prevail, and I immediately became the underdog challenger to the formidable Senator Griffin. Fortunately, all my primary opponents joined in helping me in the general election.

Challenging Senator Griffin

I anticipated that the attack on me would be that I was a Detroit liberal (an unpopular label in the rest of the state). Senator Griffin had previously defeated Frank Kelley, the long-serving and beloved Democratic Michigan attorney general, primarily based on the claim that Kelley had supported cross-district busing, which was so unpopular in the Detroit suburbs. Senator Griffin made that same attack against me, but it failed to have any traction because not only was it untrue but Coleman Young and I had filed that amicus brief opposing cross-district busing.

My radio ad against Senator Griffin was powerful because we used his own words against him, namely that he was "tired of the job." And, we landed a haymaker punch by adding that after Griffin first announced he wasn't going to run, he missed more votes than any other senator "except for one senator who died in office." The ad went "viral," so to speak, well before someone coined that phrase in reference to the Internet. Senator Griffin was livid about that ad, even though it was factually accurate and his words were not taken out of context.

In addition to Griffin's poor attendance record, one of my campaign issues was something that most voters had never heard of: I supported the principle of a "legislative veto" that would allow either house of Congress to overrule or suspend a regulation issued by a federal agency. Legislation to allow that had been introduced by Congressman Elliott Levitas, a Democrat from Georgia. Given my experience on City Council with HUD and the many times members of Congress had told us they were unable to affect the decisions of regulatory agencies, I thought Levitas's bill was a good approach. It was at the core of my Senate campaign. My main piece of campaign literature read: "For eight years Carl Levin battled waste and bureaucratic bungling. Because he knows the cost, he'll fight against them—full time—as a U.S. Senator. The Congress must have the power to veto rules made by unelected bureaucrats. Making existing programs work isn't as glamorous as dreaming up new ones, but it's a big part of what we pay our Senators to do."

When I spoke about this issue across the state, I heard example after example of how federal agencies were not effectively addressing the issues that were within their area of responsibility. That was one problem. The other was that when they drafted and implemented regulations, they failed to recognize that in many situations one size doesn't fit all because of the differences between different places.

So while campaigning, I talked about my HUD experience in Detroit, but I focused on the broader issue of whether or not Congress has the responsibility to oversee the regulations and activities of agencies. The idea that citizens should be able to go directly to their representatives in Congress to ask them to accept some responsibility to oversee the agencies involved in the environment, water, housing, immigration, veterans' rights, and a host of other issues appealed to Michigan voters, especially those who felt federal agencies in Washington were ignoring their needs.

As I campaigned across the state, Barb often appeared and spoke for me. She was a big hit, and wherever she spoke they wanted her to come back. I had a small staff, including my sister, Hannah, who planned out each stop. The very creative Bob Seltzer, my campaign manager, was new to politics; Rick Weiner, already wise in the ways of politics, ran my field operation; Linda Grossman was an all-around force; and Ruth Broder was a superb fundraiser.

At the first debate I had with Griffin, I saw that he was miffed about that ad about his missing votes. Sometime later we were at the Detroit Economic Club for another debate where he went first. In his opening statement he came out swinging, trying to stereotype me as a "big-city liberal." The "high cost of Levin" was one of his lines, in the effort to label me as a big spender. When it was my turn, I thanked the moderator for his very kind introduction, and then I turned to Griffin and said, "And I thank you, Senator, for your kind words." The crowd burst out laughing. It was a spontaneous quip, a highlight of my first campaign, and made use of the "keeping cool" lesson I had learned on City Council. I then answered Griffin's attacks, well aware that the audience was made up mainly of businesspeople: "On what does Senator Griffin base a claim that I am a big spender? It beats me, because in all eight years I was on

City Council in Detroit we had a balanced budget, a lot better than Griffin's Senate record on deficits."

One of the many memorable events during that campaign was triggered by President Carter's request to come to Michigan to campaign for me. I believed, given the president's great unpopularity, that his visit would not be helpful, and I let the White House know that I would prefer he not come. When that somehow leaked, I explained to the press that I wanted to run an independent campaign. The president decided to come anyway, because he sensed that I might win, and he wanted to be connected to some positive election outcomes in what appeared to be a bad year for Democrats. Senator Griffin tried to capitalize on the situation and, perhaps in an effort to overcome his partisan reputation, announced that while I was "insulting" the president, he would welcome the president to Michigan.

That left the White House and me with some strategizing to do, since I obviously was willing to appear with President Carter if he came to Michigan. So when Air Force One landed, it immediately pulled into a side area where I was taken to meet privately with the president. After talking about Michigan issues (and sharing a few stories) for half an hour, Air Force One taxied to where the large press turnout was waiting. I led the way down the steps where Senator Griffin was standing at the front of the receiving line. I very warmly "introduced" the president to Senator Griffin (saying something like, "Of course you know Senator Griffin, Mr. President"). The president would later tell the press that he and I had an in-depth discussion about a number of Michigan issues in our time together on Air Force One.

I learned a lot of lessons in my first campaign. Perhaps the most important one was the role of luck and chance. I also learned the importance of maintaining and using a sense of humor. My father-in-law, Ben Halpern, supplied me with a number of humorous stories. For instance, when some observers wondered whether or not a Jew could be elected to statewide office in Michigan (I would be the first one if I succeeded), Ben told me to break the ice when I arrived late to a meeting by telling the audience that I hoped they were on "Jewish time." Then I added an example for those who might not know what Jewish time was. "When I was adjusting my watch upon my arrival in Jerusalem," I said, "I called to find out the time on the phone. The voice at the other end said, 'At the tone the time will be 8 p.m. . . . . 8:30 at the latest!'" The joke worked time after time, particularly with ethnic groups because most poke fun at themselves for running late.

Another of my father-in-law's jokes was based on a phone call that he received from a young man raising money for my campaign. The fellow didn't know he was talking to my father-in-law, so Ben decided to have some fun. After telling my father-in-law why he should vote for me and asking him to contribute $25 to my campaign, Ben said, "I wouldn't give that bum 25 cents. He got my daughter pregnant three times!" My father-in-law told that story when he introduced me at the Michigan Democratic Convention. Word spread and it was quoted on national radio. People remembered it, and over the years I was asked to tell that story again and again, and I would often use it when introducing my wife at events. She laughed with the audience, even after she had heard it for the hundredth time.

Senator Griffin outspent me 3 to 1, and it was a hard-hitting, contentious campaign. Election night was a cliff-hanger, and Senator Griffin did not concede until late the next day. When the dust settled, I won with 52 percent of the vote. It turned out that while a number of new Democratic senators were elected that year, I was the only one who defeated an incumbent Republican. My family and I would soon be heading to Washington, D.C. Little did I know that I would spend the next thirty-six years of my life in the U.S. Senate and successfully run for reelection five times.

Reelection Campaigns

My second campaign was also very close. My opponent was Jack Lousma, a retired astronaut. He was a political novice and a nice guy. His military background was probably the reason why his campaign biography started with his physical characteristics. As I remember, it said something like "Jack is 6'3" tall, 195 pounds, and has blond hair and blue eyes." Some of my staff thought the "blond hair and blue eyes" reference was intended to be a contrast to my Jewish religion. I was sure that it wasn't and decided to have some fun with it. In my speeches I would pull out a piece of paper from my pocket and quote my opponent's literature and say that we were going to reprint my biography so that it would start with my physical characteristics: "5′9″ tall, plump, balding, and disheveled." I would then add "our pollsters tell us that it's a winner because there are more of us than there are of them." It produced a laugh every time. Jack actually sent me a letter of apology which, while unnecessary, was a thoughtful thing to do. But it took away a great opener from me.

Lousma made a serious mistake before he was a candidate that turned out to be a real break for me in the campaign. He had given a speech in Japan at Toyota Hall and said how proud he was that his son had a Toyota automobile in his garage. We had a tape of the speech, and we put it to good use in our television ad, contrasting what he had said in a paid speech in Japan with what I had said at almost the same time in testimony before a Senate committee in Washington, D.C., describing Japan's unfair trade advantages: that we allowed them to sell their products freely in the United States while they were restricting our products from being sold in Japan. There was one problem with the tape and that was the presence of a Japanese flag with its rising sun on the wall behind Lousma as he spoke. Feelings were so high against Japan at that time that an autoworker had killed an Asian man who he mistakenly thought was Japanese. At a focus group testing our ads, a woman said she was troubled by the prominence of the flag. Sandy, Barbara, and I immediately saw why and decided to letter-over the flag with the location and date of the speech. The ad, even without that unnecessary inflammatory element, turned out to be particularly effective.

The 1990 campaign against Bill Schuette was less memorable but for one incident during a televised debate. In violation of the agreed-upon rules, Schuette walked across the stage and presented me with a no-tax-increase pledge card, which he challenged me to sign. My response was that most people don't buy political gimmicks or posturing. Also memorable in that campaign was the excellent leadership of my Washington chief of staff, Gordon Kerr, who took leave to come to Michigan to manage the campaign.

The next three campaigns were somewhat easier for me, but the amount of time I had to spend on fundraising always troubled me, and over the years I favored many different types of reform to reduce the role of money in campaigns. I spent about $800,000 on my campaign against Senator Griffin, and I had a surplus of $25,000. By the time of my last campaign, I raised and spent over $8 million. Inflation accounted for only a small part of the increase.

I always enjoyed campaigning and particularly relished campaigning with Democratic candidates for president, governor, or state legislative offices in Michigan. Bill Clinton's 1996 campaign train with its whistle-stops for speeches was truly memorable. It may have been on that trip, when returning on Air Force One, that President Clinton invited me to be the fourth in a game of Hearts, a card game he loved to play. I told him I was rusty, but he insisted that I play. On the first hand I "shot the moon," which in baseball is like hitting a grand slam. He said, "You shithead—and you said you were rusty." He laughingly signed the scorecard.

But the campaign most etched in my memory was Barack Obama's in 2008, which was also a reelection year for me. It evoked more passion and more enthusiasm, particularly among young people, than any campaign in which I was involved since John Kennedy's run for the president in 1960. As I campaigned around the state, the momentum toward an Obama victory was palpable.

One of my warmest campaign memories occurred in 1996 when I was running against Ronna Romney. One of my truly good friends in the Senate was Virginia Republican John Warner. It was his job to raise money to elect Republican senators. He told me that he was going to come to Michigan to raise money for my opponent but that he would be positive about her and say nothing negative about me. I told him I understood, of course. One of the attacks against me by my opponent in that election was that I had done a lot of traveling, which she characterized as "junkets." When Warner was being interviewed by the press during his visit, he was asked whether he had traveled with me, and when he said he had, he was questioned about the characterization of those trips as junkets. He responded by saying, "Are you kidding? Traveling with

Levin is like being in a seminar," or words to that effect. Warner then recounted a trip across Paris when we were on our way to meet with a French minister and I was so busy reading my briefing books that I didn't even pick up my head to look at the Eiffel Tower. The story in the press the next day recounted that Warner story and blew the junket accusation out of the water.

John Warner's response to my opponent's attack on me was an example of the true friendships spawned by working in the Senate. It was also evidence of the importance of being factually accurate if you are using paid media to go after an opponent. My first two campaigns involved the use of negative ads, but we were extremely careful to make sure they were totally accurate. Much of the public says that they hate negative television commercials, but history shows they are effective at times. History also shows that they can backfire.

The Presidential Primaries

Another type of campaign that I waged was not for my own election or reelection but to end the stranglehold that New Hampshire and Iowa have had for decades over the process of nominating candidates for the most powerful position in the world, the president of the United States. They are two of the least diverse states, but their huge advantage in the Democratic and Republican primaries allows them to get their issues before the next president and unfairly boosts their ability to attract national support. Despite the obvious violation of democratic principles inherent in this situation, it remains unchecked and, for the moment, unchallenged, which is surprising because of its importance and the ease with which it can be remedied. It is a self-inflicted wound that the political parties can easily fix by themselves.

Early in my career, I felt strongly that I should do what I could to end that stranglehold. The privileged position of being the first two primaries should be rotated, that is, shared by the states, probably on a regional basis, as provided for in a bill introduced by my brother, Sandy. It was clear to me as a lawyer that there was no legal basis for challenging the privilege and that only a direct challenge within the party could strip the privilege that the two states had held onto so fiercely for so long. That was the beginning of my one-man crusade, which became a two-person crusade when Michigan representative Debbie Dingell became my partner.

At the beginning of the 1988 election year, I spoke out against New Hampshire and Iowa having a disproportionate effect on the candidate selection process. At a news conference in Lansing I said then that "some state that uses a caucus needs to stand up and say we're going to have our caucus the same day as Iowa, and we're willing to take a risk in order to break that monopoly." I said that I was "worried about the people who had little or no say in other states because Iowa and New Hampshire insist on always going first." I said that "we've got to find a way to end this distortion, so that every state gets a turn at going first." Little did I know the lengths that New Hampshire and Iowa would go to maintain their stranglehold and the power they held over candidates to get them to comply with what amounted to political extortion. Their domination enables them to have a greater impact on the issues they care about and gives their economies a huge boost when the flood of volunteers and media hordes move into their motels and patronize their restaurants for a year every four years.

I testified before the Democratic Party's Rules Committee in November 1999 that the party's rules guaranteeing a preferred position for those two states needed to be changed and that no two states should have this kind of impact. New Hampshire's secretary of state responded that letting any other state have an earlier primary than the date the rules set for New Hampshire's primary would be "like say you're going to let 'M' be the first letter of the alphabet." How's that for an extreme, absurd defense of the status quo?

But it was more than tradition on which New Hampshire and Iowa relied. It was bare-knuckled political power. Candidates are asked right off the bat by the leaders in those two states when beginning their campaigns whether they will pledge to maintain their preferred positions into the future. Candidates know that if they hedge in answering, they can kiss goodbye their chances of doing well. So, they all give their pledges not only to maintain the current system but also to not campaign in any state that would set a date competing with Iowa's early caucus or New Hampshire's early primary.

Vermont governor Howard Dean, in his run for the presidency, said, "I'm going to live in Iowa and New Hampshire for the next two years" and also that his wife and family "have taken an apartment in Manchester, New Hampshire." Candidate Joe Lieberman said, "I will pledge to the death to protect the New Hampshire primary."

Candidates try to prove their commitment to Iowa by visiting all of its 99 counties. We in Michigan, with a far greater population than Iowa, rarely see candidates in more than 3 of our 83 counties. And, of course, candidates strive to be responsive to issues of concern when seeking votes, be it protecting the ethanol industry in Iowa or making a no-tax-increase pledge in New Hampshire's Republican primary.

In advance of the 2000 presidential election, my chief of staff and political guru at the time, Chuck Wilbur, and I urged the Michigan Democratic Party to take on the National Democratic Party. To do that, it was obvious to me that we would have to set Michigan's primary the same day as New Hampshire's. We would then have to fight against the penalty that the DNC would try to impose, refusing to seat our delegates to the Democratic Convention. I knew with certainty that we would win that fight when we appealed the penalty to the Convention, because the candidate it nominated wouldn't jeopardize winning Michigan in the upcoming election by enforcing that penalty. Even former New Hampshire senator John Durkin once said: "Let's face it, if it ever gets to the floor of the (Democratic) convention, New Hampshire loses." But the Michigan Democrats didn't want to chance it in 2000, and my effort went nowhere that year.

But I was picking up support for the 2004 cycle. Our Democratic committeewoman Debbie Dingell, wife of "dean of the U.S. Congress" John Dingell, and a powerful force in her own right, joined the effort. The two of us met in my office in April 2003 with Democratic National Chairman Terry McAuliffe to discuss what we were planning to recommend to the Michigan Democratic Party for the 2004 nominating process. Nationally, public opinion overwhelmingly supported getting rid of the Iowa-New Hampshire preference by an 80–20 percent margin in one poll. We threatened a head-on confrontation but accepted a compromise suggested by Chairman McAuliffe. He promised to establish a Commission on Presidential Nomination Scheduling and Timing and to get it approved at the July 2004 National Convention. The commission would report to McAuliffe's successor, former Vermont governor and presidential candidate Howard Dean. It was approved, and Debbie Dingell and I were appointed as members.

The first real skirmish in what the *Detroit News* political columnist George Weeks called "Levin's Twelve-Year War" took place in Chicago in May 2005 at the commission's first meeting. Debbie and I railed against the status quo. I said the Democratic Party is supposed to be the "party of the people, not the party of the privileged." I told the commission members how much I would love for our presidential candidates to spend as much time in Michigan as they spend in Iowa or New Hampshire, so they could hear about our loss of manufacturing jobs or the need to preserve the Great Lakes. I argued that any state would appreciate a similar opportunity, and more states should have it, and that the lesson my mother taught me about people applies to the fifty states as well: each state is just as good as every other state but no better.

Perhaps the most common argument I heard from those defending Iowa and New Hampshire's privileged position was that they practice "retail politics" and the voters there give candidates a thorough evaluation. I countered that all states would like to partake in retail politics because it is indeed the best way to hear from candidates and present one's views.

After a year of study and public hearings, the commission's December 2005 report expressed support for our argument. It concluded that there are "serious concerns that Iowa and New Hampshire are not fully reflective of the Democratic electorate or the national electorate generally—and therefore do not place Democratic candidates before a representative range of voters in the critical early weeks of the process."

In August 2006 the DNC adopted a rule providing that four states—Iowa, Nevada, New Hampshire, and South Carolina, in that specific order—could hold their primary or caucus in January 2008 before the opening of the window for all other states. New Hampshire was the only state to vote "no." While Debbie and I expressed our disappointment that Michigan wasn't chosen as one of the four January states, we said it did represent some progress in ending the domination of two states, and we were satisfied that our effort had borne some fruit.

Our Michigan Democratic Party chairman, Mark Brewer, announced that Michigan would comply with the rule and that its primary would be held on February 9, 2008, *provided* all other states abided by the new rule. To drive home the point, he said if any other state moved its primary or caucus in violation of the rule, Michigan would not comply either. The DNC rule had moved the Nevada caucus to that number two position, after the Iowa caucus, so there would be two caucuses first and then two primaries, before the window would open for all other states.

New Hampshire would have none of it because it wouldn't give up coming right after Iowa. It announced on August 9, 2007, that it would hold its primary on a date before the January 19 date set for the Nevada Caucus—period. While it asked for a waiver from the new rule from the DNC, it didn't wait for an answer. Michigan followed suit and asked for a waiver so it could go before February 8, 2008. In a complete cave to New Hampshire, on December 3, 2007, the DNC granted New Hampshire its waiver request but denied Michigan's waiver request. The power of New Hampshire to dominate was never clearer. It not only preserved its privileged position; it did so by pressuring a national party to adopt a double standard. Even our partial victory and their own hard-fought-for rule was reversed by a weak-kneed DNC.

Michigan did what it had threatened to do and scheduled its primary for January 15, 2008, to compete with New Hampshire. The major Democratic candidates did not campaign personally in Michigan because of their pledge to New Hampshire. Barack Obama also decided to take his name off the primary ballot, while Hillary Clinton left her name on the ballot. Michigan party leaders had to deal with the understandable hard feelings that resulted. They urged Obama voters to vote for "uncommitted." Six hundred thousand Michigan Democrats voted in the January 15, 2008, primary. When the votes were counted, Clinton got 55 percent of the votes and 40 percent voted for uncommitted, with 5 percent voting for other names on the ballot.

After some intense negotiations, Michigan party leaders decided to divide its delegates, with 69 going to Clinton and 59 to Obama. The leaders concluded that both candidates had legitimate arguments and, after broad consultations, that such a division would unify our party. On May 12, 2008, the Michigan Democratic Party notified the National Party of the delegate split and formally asked it to reverse its decision to disqualify the entire Michigan delegation.

I had always been confident that whoever our candidate was would support our delegation being seated with full voting rights, and if that decision wasn't made before the National Convention, that it would be overwhelmingly supported at the convention itself. Both major candidates did indeed agree to our full delegation being seated at the convention without a penalty, and, in fact, we all were.

The battle we waged remains front and center, given the visibility of the issue in the 2020 primaries. I'm hopeful that some future candidates will skip the primaries and caucuses of the few privileged states and appeal to the people in other states. Or, perhaps more likely, Michigan, or some other populous state that never has the chance to go early with retail politics, will schedule its primary or caucus early to challenge the dominance of New Hampshire and Iowa. The state making the challenge will hopefully be reassured by our experience in Michigan in 2008.

We demonstrated that the only way to change the status quo, in order to produce greater balance, fairness, and diversity in the process, is with a direct, upfront challenge and that it can be pursued without fear of a penalty being imposed for doing so, that is, that the penalty threat is a hollow one. What we demonstrated, in other words, was that our effort, with all its uncertainty and angst, was worth it.

The battle will bubble to the surface again for the reasons a *New York Times* editorial gave just days before the 2008 primary season kicked off: "We believe the time has long passed for parties to break the Iowa-New Hampshire habit." As the paper put it, "The honor of going first should rotate among regions. That would give a far broader range of American voters a say in this vitally important choice."

4

Coming to the Senate

I made my first trip to Washington as a senator-elect about three weeks after my election, with the Democrats in control of the Senate. I met with Senate Majority Leader Robert Byrd and a number of other Democratic senators. The advice they gave me was remarkably consistent: make a quick decision about the committees on which I would seek to serve and leave decisions about staff for later.

Choosing Committees

I was actually being recruited for two committees by two distinguished senators—Ted Kennedy of Massachusetts, chairman of the Judiciary Committee, and Abraham Ribicoff of Connecticut, chairman of the Governmental Affairs Committee. Kennedy knew about my uncle Theodore Levin, the federal judge in Detroit, as well as my legal background. Judiciary is an important committee that handles criminal law, oversight of the Justice Department, and the president's appointments to the federal bench, including the Supreme Court. Membership on the Judiciary Committee is one of the most important and high-profile posts in Congress. The downside was that I wouldn't get my own committee staff; all staffers would be selected by and work for Senator Kennedy.

Senator Ribicoff, on the other hand, had apparently heard about my interest in government oversight and offered to create a subcommittee for me and give me a few staff of my own. While the Governmental Affairs Committee was usually not as active as the Judiciary Committee, the opportunity for a subcommittee chairmanship and staff was compelling.

There was also an opening on the Senate Armed Services Committee (SASC) and some competition for it. I decided to try for a seat on that committee, not because I knew about the armed services but because I didn't. My old knee injury from the 1954 motorcycle accident in Italy caused me to be classified 4-F for the draft, so I had never served, and I wanted to learn, to fill the gap in my experience so I could knowledgeably address the military issues that came before the Senate. Also, I hoped my oversight experience in local government and my determination to focus on oversight of federal agencies would help me contribute to not only a strong military but also a smart and efficient one.

My decision to seek membership on the SASC surprised my family and friends who said the SASC members are generally "hawks," and they didn't think of me in that way. (Of course, I've come to learn that categorizations like that, though easy to throw around, are usually not accurate or all that helpful.) I didn't have any ideological ax to grind by joining the Armed Services Committee, other than the belief that nuclear weapons were highly redundant and needed to be reduced. I thought their only function was to deter an aggressor, and it didn't take that many to deter. Given their destructive capacity, it takes only a couple dozen nuclear weapons to destroy any enemy along with much of the world, but there were thousands of them. I thought the excess was a mistake financially and was the wrong way to move toward a more peaceful and stable world as well. Other than my belief about nuclear weapons, I didn't come to the Senate thinking that the military was too big or too small or with any other preconceptions.

The third committee I sought to join was the Small Business Committee. During my campaigns and years of public service I had been struck by the special problems facing the small business community in Michigan. Many of those problems came from the demands made on small businesses by federal regulations that were often designed to apply to large companies. If I could take a seat on Governmental Affairs along with a seat on Small Business, I'd be in a position to ease some of their challenges.

Wanting certain committee assignments and getting them, however, are not the same thing. Committee assignments for Democrats are made by members of the Senate Democratic Steering Committee, a group of senators who are selected by the Democratic leader. The leader is interested in satisfying the interests of as many senators as possible, and that often puts the leader in the middle of competing interests and ambitions. I talked with as many members of the Steering Committee as I could, and I thought I was in reasonably good shape. While a few freshman senators expressed an interest in the committees I wanted, particularly Armed Services, most of them indicated that there were other assignments they wanted even more.

With that thought in mind, I sat down to write the required formal letter to Majority Leader Byrd indicating my choices in order of preference. It was likely the Steering Committee could not give me all my top choices while having to deny some other new members theirs. I knew, for example, that at least four of my fellow freshmen were indicating that the Finance Committee was their first choice—but there were only two open seats there. It would be difficult for the leader to give me all three of my choices if two fellow freshmen were denied their first choices. So I decided to try another approach with my preferences: I listed a committee I wanted less than the three I actually wanted, knowing that my apparent first choice was in high demand and the likelihood of being assigned that committee was minimal. I played a little poker—guessing that doing it that way might make it easier for the members of the Steering Committee to give me what I really wanted. Soon after I submitted the letter based on my Byzantine strategy, I was informed that while the Steering Committee regretted that it could not honor all my requests, they hoped I would be pleased with my assignment to Armed Services, Governmental Affairs, and Small Business, and indeed I was. I had achieved my goal. And with my membership on Governmental Affairs secured, the Subcommittee on Oversight of Government

Management (OGM) was born, giving me the opportunity to do what I primarily came to the Senate to do, namely, to make federal government agencies responsive to people at the grassroots.

The First Few Months

My swearing-in was a blur of activity and family. My brother, Sandy, who had been in Washington with the Agency for International Development (AID) for more than a year, and his wife, Vicki, hosted a party the night before the ceremony for family and friends who had come to Washington to witness the event. Everyone wanted to know what it was really like to be a United States senator. I wanted to know how I was going to get more than the five tickets I was allotted so that all the people who meant so much to me could get to see the swearing-in. And my family wanted to know where we were going to live in Washington. In the two months since the election, we had seen what seemed like every real estate agent in the city, and we still hadn't been shown a house yet in the Capitol Hill neighborhood we liked that was under $200,000. It was beginning to look like a long winter.

We wanted, and finally found, a house we liked and could afford eleven blocks from the Capitol. The more upsetting part of the move was uprooting the children from our Detroit home and finding a new home in Michigan for our great but hyper dog, Freddie, who would not have done well in our D.C. house with its tiny yard.

My first months in the Senate were slow. There was little legislation being considered since Majority Leader Byrd had decided that committees, many with new members, needed time to organize and consider new proposals. My mind was on mundane tasks like juggling meetings of three committees and a half dozen or so subcommittees, as well as figuring out the light and buzzer system used to announce session openings, quorum calls, and votes. After spending four months making a campaign issue of my predecessor's poor attendance record, I certainly wasn't going to miss any votes. On February 22, 1979, I cast my first vote as United States senator in favor of a motion to table an amendment that would have changed the 100-hour limit on debate following cloture to an aggregate of 100 one-hour time periods. Try explaining that to your kids.

Shortly after coming to the Senate, I introduced my first bill—S.15, designed to end the practice of credit card redlining that was an issue I identified and worked on when I was on the Detroit City Council. A colleague agreed to hold hearings on my bill in the subcommittee he chaired, and I asked my staff to get to work and make sure those hearings established a solid record. They worked so hard that the Federal Trade Commission (FTC) became active in the area and ultimately settled one case that had been in litigation for over three years against a company that habitually redlined. When the FTC's decision against the firm was announced, the subcommittee decided that my bill was no longer needed since the commission had already decided to end the practice on a case-by-case basis. I didn't agree, but it wasn't my committee and there wasn't much I could do. So, while the bill died, I put out a press release saying that at least we had won an administrative victory. I had learned a little more about the way Washington worked.

Panama Canal Treaty Implementation

While I was promoting my credit card redlining bill, I started to get some pressure on another issue: the Panama Canal Treaties. Before I came to the Senate, President Carter had signed treaties with Panama to return the canal back to that country, and the treaties had been ratified by the Senate. I soon learned that implementing legislation would be needed to actually put the treaties into effect. That legislation would have to go through the Senate Armed Services Committee. Chairman John Stennis approached me about the possibility of my managing the legislation—that is, accepting the responsibility of moving it through the Senate. At first, I was flattered. Then I realized that the only people on the committee who had voted for the original treaties were up for reelection in 1980 and didn't want to add to their problems by being the "point person" or floor manager of the unpopular legislation that "gave away our canal." A process of elimination rather than talent had made me the logical choice.

Initially I was reluctant to do it, although I had favored the treaties. I hadn't followed the ratification debate, I didn't know the issues all that well, and I was too new to the Senate to feel comfortable with the responsibility of managing a major bill. But my staff urged me to take it on. They thought that managing the bill would give me an opportunity to learn more about the nuts and bolts of the legislative process and to make a real contribution. I agreed and told Chairman Stennis I would accept the assignment.

Not long after I agreed to manage the bill I was on a military jet flying to Panama for a round of meetings with our ambassador, some of the leaders of the American community, and high-ranking Panamanian officials including its president. I came back from that trip with a keen appreciation of the problems associated with the political and legislative situation and an awareness that my work was cut out for me.

I was deeply involved in the process of preparing to hold hearings on the Panama Canal legislation that was being supported by the Carter Administration. Since I would chair those hearings, I spent weeks poring over the debate on the treaties in an effort to anticipate the issues that might be raised. I also spent days negotiating changes in the administration's bill with representatives of the State Department in an effort to improve the legislation. It was a grueling process, but at the end I felt we had a better bill, and I knew I was in a better position to manage it.

After the hearings, it was time to get ready for the debate on the Senate floor. It was a long debate, beginning in the morning and ending in the late afternoon. One after another, opponents of the treaties rose with amendments to the implementing legislation which, if adopted, would violate those treaties. They were labeled "killer" amendments. And time after time, I rose to make essentially the same speech: "I wasn't here when the treaties were signed; I don't know if I agree with everything in them, but I do know that they represent a commitment. I do know that this country has an obligation to honor its commitments. Now is not the time to debate again what we decided a year ago.

Now is the time to keep faith with what we did a year ago." No amendments were adopted in the Senate that violated the spirit of the treaties, although one came close.

On the House side, however, things did not work out as well. Political pressure over there resulted in the adoption of a bill that did violate the treaties. It also resulted in a very difficult conference—a meeting between representatives of the House and Senate designed to resolve their legislative differences. The issue was emotional, and arguments in the conference were sometimes heated. Finally, though, we had an agreement that I thought was consistent with the commitments our country had made. I took it back to the Senate and got its approval, but the House rejected it. That meant another conference, another set of compromises, another round of concessions, another series of conflicts. But, finally, again, an agreement was reached. Again, the Senate accepted it. And this time the House did too. The legislation was approved and, most significantly, the treaty commitments that had been made were honored. President Carter called to thank me for my efforts and congratulate me on the successful outcome, and I remember the way he closed that call. He said: "You did a great job, and I know from personal experience how hard that is for a freshman around here."

I often thought about my involvement with that bill. It's such a great example of how things work in Washington. I got the assignment by chance, really, and because I handled it well, I think I grew a little bit in the eyes of my colleagues. My colleagues saw me move a difficult bill through the Senate and then preserve the essential elements of that legislation even in the face of sustained opposition in the House. And I saw myself dealing with the complex procedures and personalities that constitute legislative life. I grew more confident in my ability and a little more certain of my place in the United States Senate.

Frances Perkins Bill

I also had the thrill of introducing a bill on a lighter note that year. My bill renamed the Labor Department headquarters in Washington as the Frances

Perkins Department of Labor Building. It passed the Senate, it was enacted into law, and President Carter spoke at the building's dedication ceremony in the spring of 1980.

Frances Perkins was the nation's first female cabinet member when she was appointed by President Franklin Roosevelt as secretary of labor. When Roosevelt was governor of New York, he had appointed her as the state's industrial commissioner, so she had plenty of experience when taking on some of the most important initiatives of the New Deal, including the Civilian Conservation Corps, the Works Progress Administration (which provided temporary employment for the millions of workers who were unemployed in the Great Depression), and apprenticeship training programs designed to provide more permanent employment. Her leadership led to the adoption of child labor laws and the minimum wage, the setting of a ceiling on hours worked, and the protection of workers' rights to organize and bargain collectively. When I drive by the Perkins Building, which is at a prominent spot on Pennsylvania Avenue between the Capitol and the White House, the name on the building reminds me, as it does millions of other passersby each year on our nation's Main Street, of Miss Perkins's singular achievement, not just in smashing a glass ceiling but of the Labor Department's mission to ensure that American workers are treated with dignity and fairness.

ADA Speech: "Keepers of the Dream"

About halfway through my first year, the Americans for Democratic Action (ADA), recognizing me as the only Democrat to beat an incumbent Republican senator in the previous election, asked me to give the keynote address at their annual conference in Washington in June. The ADA was organized by Eleanor Roosevelt and others after the death of Franklin Roosevelt to "keep the New Deal alive." The speaking invitation was an opportunity for me to share the message I brought to Washington and to articulate my ideas on how liberals—by then a label used with contempt by Republicans—must change their focus in order to remain relevant. The speech, which got some attention, was drafted by my chief of staff, Bob Seltzer, who had a great flair for public speaking. It was excerpted by the *New York Times* and published as an op-ed six weeks later with the headline "Keepers of the Dream." It's still relevant today. Here's some of what I said:

As you know, "liberal" is not a term widely used anymore. Members of Congress—and liberals increasingly are *former* members of Congress—hide their prior use of that label as protectively as news reporters hide their sources. The polls tell us that "liberals" are an endangered species and that one of the first tasks of any member of this vanishing clan ought to be to adopt the protective coloring of a new label. . . . While changing labels probably isn't the answer, we do need to change a few things if we are to remain a viable and creative voice in American political thought.

It seems to me that liberalism was born of idealism and optimism. It was conceived in the belief that human beings faced a perfectible future. It was nursed by the faith that our destiny remained under our control. It matured in a world which seemed to confirm these beliefs and which moved, admittedly at a slow pace, toward an improving social order. . . .

[But] we confront a time in which the conservative community is laying claim to the political imagination of the country. In the Senate, they often have the initiative and frequently control the movement of issues on the floor. Every other day we are confronted with amendments which seek to eliminate Federal court jurisdiction over school prayer cases, or mandate a balanced budget, or reduce spending on needed social programs. The list is as long as the fertile imagination of the new conservative coalition. The liberal-minded are too often relegated to the role of rear-guard actors—desperately trying to prevent the dismantlement of the good in what we had accomplished, but not having the mandate or the momentum to strike out and move for the adoption of our own programs. . . .

In our zeal to safeguard our achievement and to solidify our accomplishments, we institutionalized them. In the almost 50 years since the first

Roosevelt Administration, we have seen the policies we produced spawn a new administrative branch of government which is in some ways more powerful than the Congress, the Courts and the President combined. That power comes, in part, from the administrative control these agencies have over the entire range of issues which pervade public life. But in larger part it comes from their structural independence—their exclusion from the delicate mathematics of our system of checks and balances. The result of that independence is a branch of government which is not directly accountable to the political process and not directly subject to effective public evaluation.

Creating and tolerating this situation was a mistake. . . .

People haven't rejected the goals of our programs but they have begun to reject the *claim* that our programs have anything to do with our goals. . . .

. . . And I can tell you the result—a good liberal boy like me has matured into a man with *fear* in his gut and a *fire* in his eyes. The *fear* is that the programs I so strongly supported are going to be doomed—doomed not by a flaw in intent but rather by a flaw in implementation. The people and the local elected officials have become so tired—so exhausted—by the battle to save what is good, that the fight may no longer seem win-able. And then when enough people reach that conclusion, then the "new right" will have been proven right—they will have reached the point at which they can do more than dismantle our programs, they can gut our goals.

The *fire* is a burning desire to prevent that. The way to do that, I submit, is to regain control of the way the government runs, to re-establish our mastery of detail, to reaffirm our commitment to serving society and helping people. The mechanisms exist to do that. We can "sunset" programs and thereby require the Congress to rethink the mission of those programs on a regular basis. We can give Congress a "legislative veto" which would return some accountability over regulations to the elected officials of the people. To those who say that these and similar mechanisms will make it difficult to sustain our programs and continue our policies—I say that the alternative is to continue as we are and watch silently as our opponents sustain their attack and continue to build public support for abandoning the liberal dream.

The liberal philosophy I was reared on held that the political process was the place to make public policy. It held that if people were given sufficient information and were involved early enough in the decision-making process, they could be trusted to reach wise decisions. If we really do not think that we can mobilize a constituency for social programs, then we ought to fade away into our tents. And if we do not believe that we can mobilize a constituency for our social goals, then we do not even deserve tents. . . . [I]f we return to the task of relating our programs to people, then we can mobilize massive public and political support for our vision.

And we *must do that* because there is much that we still need to do. If we are to achieve the vision of Franklin Roosevelt and provide decent housing for all, then our implementation of housing programs must be carried out as carefully as the forces which shaped his conception.

If we are to achieve the vision of Adlai Stevenson and provide a decent education for all, then the execution of our education programs must be as fine as Stevenson's dream.

If we are to achieve the vision of John Kennedy and provide decent medical care for all, then we must administer health care programs with the same idealism that conceived them. . . .

If we are to achieve these visions, and more, then we must administer our programs with the common sense that conceived them. That is our heritage—and that is our task.

As I read these words four decades later, there is much that is relevant today. All in all, it was quite a first year for me in the U.S. Senate—getting the committees I wanted, managing a major bill, and speaking with conviction to the ADA. I also turned to the issues on which I had campaigned: legislative veto, sunset, accountability, and congressional oversight.

5

Early Efforts at Government Accountability

Probably the most controversial bill on government accountability that I cosponsored my first year in the Senate was S. 2, the Sunset Act, a bill that required Congress to review existing programs to determine if they were worth continuing. It was Senator Ed Muskie's bill, but few Democrats supported it because it was strongly opposed by the unions, environmental groups, and the organizations that had fought so hard to get the various programs established in the first place. The bill would have required a review by Congress every ten years to determine if those programs continued to make sense. I continued my support despite its unpopularity with groups that were normally my allies. In retrospect, I'm glad it didn't pass. It's an example of a bill that sounds good in principle but would be a nightmare in practice unless it was very selective in terms of the programs to which it was applied. With the thousands of federal programs requiring a complete review every ten years, the amount of member and staff time devoted to that work would have been overwhelming.

Legislative Veto

Most importantly, I cosponsored legislation to put into effect that obscure issue I ran on: legislative veto. I introduced the bill, S. 1945, in October 1979 with

Democratic senator Dave Boren, a good friend from Oklahoma. It would give Congress thirty days to review major rules issued by federal agencies before they could take effect. If during that period a committee of either house passed a joint resolution disapproving the rule, that rule could not take effect for sixty days while both houses could consider a disapproval resolution. I sponsored a similar provision as an amendment to the Federal Trade Commission bill that year and later, with Senator Harrison Schmitt, a Republican from New Mexico, to an omnibus regulatory reform bill.

There were actually hundreds of program-specific legislative vetoes in various forms enacted into law by that time but nothing comprehensive. Some provided for just one house of Congress to stop a rule from taking effect, some required both houses to agree to stop a rule, and some, like my bill, required the full legislative process—a joint resolution requiring not only both houses of Congress to disapprove a rule but also presentment to the president for his possible veto, which in turn could be overridden by a two-thirds vote of both houses of Congress. All three approaches provided an expedited procedure with a set period of time for congressional consideration before a regulation took effect.

The constitutionality of the one-house and two-house legislative veto was questionable, and an important case on the subject was winding its way through the courts at that time. In June 1983 the Supreme Court issued its decision in the *Chadha* case and ruled that anything less than a joint resolution of disapproval was unconstitutional. It wasn't until 1996 that an across-the-board legislative review like the one I proposed in my 1979 bill became law. I always told my Democratic opponents of legislative veto that it was a two-edged sword. Yes, as they feared, it could be used to stop good regulations, and it could also be used to stop bad regulations (usually because they are weaker than the statute), and over time that proved to be true. Both parties have used the process to stop rules with which they disagree, but that's what I've always supported—giving elected officials a bigger say over the decisions of unelected agency officials and providing constituents an opportunity to support or fight the rules through their elected members of Congress.

Legislative veto was just part of the omnibus regulatory reform effort undertaken by the Governmental Affairs Committee in the 96th Congress. Chairman Abraham Ribicoff released a multivolume study on the regulatory process and developed an omnibus regulatory reform bill that addressed the need to rein in the bureaucracy in part by controlling the scope of regulations and requiring an analysis of the costs and benefits of regulations. These were the issues near and dear to my heart, and I jumped into the fray with both feet. And fray it was. Business was pressing for major reform, and while many Democrats were willing to make modest reforms, major changes in the regulatory process were strongly opposed by the unions, environmental organizations, and a host of NGOs (nongovernmental organizations). I supported most of the major changes and found myself, again, often on the opposite side of groups with whom I was usually aligned. The best I could offer them was an honest explanation of why I supported the reforms that I did—legislative veto and cost-benefit analyses—because I wanted more political accountability in the regulatory process.

Regulatory Reform

One recurring issue was the use of cost-benefit analyses before major regulations were adopted. Business interests wanted agencies to assess the costs and benefits of regulations to ensure that the benefits outweighed the costs. That sounds like a good idea, but the groups that supported strong regulations in the environmental, health, and safety fields were concerned that the figures could be manipulated and that it was impossible to fairly quantify the value of a life, for example. I said that insurance companies do that all the time and that the opponents of regulations will gain support if government can't show that the benefits of a regulation justify the costs. We fought over that issue at some length in the Governmental Affairs Committee and in the Senate. In the meantime, President Reagan issued an unprecedented executive order requiring all agencies to send their proposed rules to the White House's Office of Management and Budget (OMB) before they were published for public comment so the OMB could review them to make sure the benefits exceeded the costs. That was like a lightning strike in the regulatory community. It came fast, something of a surprise, and shook things up. There were numerous hearings in Congress on whether the president had the authority to do that (he did), just what standards were being applied, and whether it injected politics into what was supposed to be an unpolitical process aimed at objectively and fairly carrying out congressional intent. The decision-making process in the OMB was also not transparent; there was no provision for public documentation as to why the OMB would be telling an agency to modify a rule in a particular way.

As a supporter of cost-benefit analysis I wasn't an opponent of the OMB reviewing rules as were many of my Democratic colleagues, but I did think it would be better and more appropriate for Congress to determine the standards for applying a cost-benefit analysis and to make the process open to the public. So I continued to work on getting our committee's major regulatory reform bill, with a requirement for cost-benefit analysis, enacted into law. The president's authority to issue executive orders governing the conduct of the executive branch is valid only as long as Congress has not legislated in that same area. So enacting a law to address cost-benefit analysis in agency rulemaking would supersede the president's executive order.

We were finally able to pass a fairly comprehensive regulatory reform bill in the Senate unanimously, but it didn't make it through the House, which was heavily Democratic and saw regulatory reform as a way to roll back the programmatic gains Democrats had fought for over the years. Obviously, I disagreed. I saw regulatory reform as a way to ensure that the programs for which Democrats fought so hard would continue to have public support. Unfortunately, despite the efforts of many and having a large number of Senate cosponsors (80 at one point), we were never able to enact an omnibus regulatory reform bill.

The OGM Subcommittee

As chairman of the Subcommittee on Oversight of Government Management (OGM), I was in a great place to oversee—and hopefully improve—the management of government programs. By chairing this new subcommittee, I was also given a pot of money to hire subcommittee staff in addition to my personal office staff—an uncommon opportunity for a freshman. It was a small staff, varying between five and eight people at any one time, but with a staff director as extraordinary as Linda Gustitus and with the right people and the power of the Senate behind you, even a small staff can do big things. It was also very helpful to have a hardworking and fair-minded Republican, Bill Cohen from Maine, who, like me, was elected to the Senate in 1978, as my first ranking member. We worked well together, because we both believed in the importance of an efficient, effective, and ethical government, and we were both committed to finding the facts. For years, as the Senate shifted its majority between Republican and Democratic, Bill Cohen and I switched back and forth between chair and ranking member on the OGM subcommittee without missing a beat on the oversight work we were doing.

In the early years of the 1980s we spent a great deal of our time looking into wasteful defense spending and practices. I started with an investigation into debarment and suspension of bad federal contractors because we learned that while a bad contractor may be debarred from getting a government contract at one agency, that contractor could go to a different agency and still get government work. That didn't make sense, so we did the research, held a hearing, and introduced legislation to require government-wide debarment and suspension of bad contractors, which eventually passed.

We then tackled the problem of the lack of competition in defense contracting. Too many contracts were being awarded on a sole source basis, denying the Department of Defense (and in effect, the taxpayer) the advantages of competition. The examples of ridiculous prices being paid by the Department of Defense (DOD)—like a $640 toilet seat—were fodder for the evening news and helped pass the Competition in Contracting Act that Bill Cohen and I introduced following our investigation and hearings. It was estimated that the federal government saved several billion dollars during just the first few years it was operational.

We also looked at the amount of inventory in the DOD supply chain and found it to be disorganized and wasteful. Our staff went out and visited various military depots, and the amount of "stuff" in storage—trucks, parts, tents, and a host of other items—was staggering. If they were being well-organized for future use, that would have been one thing, but so much of it was just sitting there and costing us millions of dollars to store and keep secure. We had a hearing on it and got *60 Minutes* to do a segment on the problem.

The Defense Department was ripe for oversight in the 1980s. It was a behemoth that hadn't figured out how to manage all it had and all it would need. It has improved somewhat over time, but given the size of its budget, constant bipartisan congressional oversight is an absolute must.

Leading the OGM subcommittee also enabled me to respond to concerns being expressed by Michigan residents in a way that an individual member cannot. As chairman, I could have the subcommittee actively investigate allegations of mismanagement and wrongdoing by federal agencies and not just write a letter to that agency on behalf of my constituents.

Social Security Disability Oversight

One good example of this in those early years was when we reformed the Social Security Disability Insurance (SSDI) program. In the early 1980s, my Senate office caseworkers in Michigan were receiving a high volume of complaints about the way the Social Security Disability program was operating. Truly disabled people who had been receiving SSDI were being thrown off the program and new applicants faced serious financial hardship and bankruptcy because they were not able to get a reasonably prompt hearing on their claims. There were reports of some six or seven suicides of disabled people in Michigan who simply gave up—they couldn't face the delays, the denials, and the labyrinth of the application and review process. It was a perfect issue for the OGM subcommittee, and the staff went to work to find out what was happening and how it could be fixed. Bill Cohen was hearing similar stories in Maine, so we took on this issue with the urgency and intensity it deserved.

We held hearings both in Washington and in our respective states. By this time Bill and I had such confidence in each other that as chair, I approved a hearing for Bill in Maine without me being present and let him chair it. When he became chair, he did the same thing for me.

Through our investigation and hearings we learned that the major culprit of the backups and distress was a law passed by Congress in 1980 requiring reviews of persons already on SSDI every three years unless the individual's disability was considered permanent. The agency's rather mindless application of the review requirement made matters worse. Before 1980, these reviews had been conducted only where there was an expectation that the person was going to improve or the person had returned to work. The new law required everyone to be reviewed regardless of the extent of their disability—and the anxiety and backlogs were disastrous. People who had been on SSDI for years and who were clearly disabled were being required to prove their disability claim de novo, as if there were no presumption that they were disabled; there was no requirement for a showing of medical improvement before a person was denied future benefits; and the requirements to prove mental impairment were exceedingly strict. It was a national mess.

As a result, Cohen and I sponsored a major reform bill that was finally enacted on October 9, 1984—but not without some dramatic moments. When the bill was finally brought to the floor, Senator Russell Long, a senior Democrat from Louisiana with jurisdiction over the bill, required—as a delaying tactic—that the bill be read in its entirety. He wasn't too pleased that we had done so much work on a program that fell into his wheelhouse as ranking member of the Finance Committee. I'll not forget that moment when I was sitting in the Senate chamber, multiple files on hand to begin the debate on and help shepherd to passage this major piece of legislation—and instead of going forward, Senator Long stood up, called for a point of order, and required the clerk to read the entire bill. It could take days to do so. My staff director, Linda Gustitus, and I looked at each other, and neither of us knew quite what to do.

In the end Senator Long backed off, since we had the votes and were able to fix a problem that had been devastating to thousands of disabled people nationwide, not, I might add, because government was heartless but because prior efforts by Congress to legitimately reduce costs were enacted without realizing the full impact of the reforms on the program recipients. Legislation is an art, not a science, and despite best efforts to have all the necessary information when passing a bill, there are simply too many variables to guarantee perfection. You can fix one aspect of a program today, but that fix has the potential to create a new problem that needs fixing tomorrow. It's why there is a need for continuous legislative oversight to track closely how well programs are functioning.

The IRS

Another important investigation by our oversight subcommittee in those early years was the IRS seizure policy. We were getting reports in Michigan that the IRS was seizing the assets of small businesses in payment for back taxes even though the small business had entered into a payment plan with the IRS and even though the assets were crucial to allowing the small business to make money to pay the taxes. Our subcommittee investigated the claims and found that the IRS had an informal quota for seizures that IRS agents were expected to meet, whether or not they made sense either to the IRS or to the taxpayer. As a result of the hearings, I introduced the Taxpayer Bill of Rights in 1980, which I worked on diligently to get passed but to no avail. When Senator David Pryor, a friend and Democratic colleague from Arkansas who served on the Finance Committee with jurisdiction over the IRS, asked if he could give it a try, I was happy to join in his effort—which succeeded years later.

Wedtech and Ed Meese

The OGM oversight investigation I led that probably had the most press interest began in 1986 and involved Attorney General Ed Meese. We were looking into allegations that Meese had improperly helped a small company in the South Bronx called Wedtech get significant government contracts when Meese was an assistant to President Reagan in the White House. The investigation, staffed in large part by Peter Levine, who later became my extremely effective General Counsel on the Senate Armed Services Committee, took eighteen months and included a battle over access to White House documents. It took time and some serious discussions, one of which occurred in the White House Situation Room for lack of other available space, but we were able to negotiate an outcome to the satisfaction of both the White House and the subcommittee. We held two hearings that revealed numerous irregularities, including the fact that the army would not have awarded a $32 million contract to Wedtech to manufacture small engines and the Small Business Administration would not have issued the grants and loans that it did to Wedtech had there not been pressure from the White House.

Wedtech's legal counsel for the hearing, who had come in after the fact to clean up the situation and in doing so discovered numerous illegalities, testified to a "looted treasury" at the company and evidence of "the bribery of city, state, and federal officials." He disclosed that senior Wedtech officers took over $30 million out of the company despite its financial problems and that consultants with political connections were paid millions of dollars.

One central figure was Robert Wallach, a Wedtech consultant who was a long-time friend of Attorney General Meese. The subcommittee's investigation revealed that Meese had been the beneficiary of unusually profitable stock trades made for him by another Wedtech consultant and director, Franklyn Chinn. Meese had entered into an investment partnership with Chinn that he failed to disclose to the public as required by law, in which Chinn assigned only the stock trades that realized gains to Meese's account and didn't assign losses. In less than two years Meese's undisclosed $54,000 investment had an 80 percent return.

I called Attorney General Meese to a hearing to explain these trades and his relationship with Wedtech. He said his failure to disclose the "Meese Partners" investment fund on his federal financial disclosure form was inadvertent, that there was no conflict of interest, and that he did not know that Chinn had given him preferential financial treatment. I didn't believe him. Working with Bill Cohen and the other members of the subcommittee, we issued a hard-hitting bipartisan report without any dissent, concluding that Meese had violated a White House policy against contacting procurement officials about a specific contract and had improperly favored Wedtech. In a *Washington Post* opinion piece, I also called for Meese's resignation.

The Wedtech scandal led to the appointment of an independent counsel, who found that Meese had likely filed a false income tax return and violated federal conflict-of-interest law in connection with Wedtech. The independent counsel did not charge him with a crime, and Meese claimed vindication, but he soon resigned from office.

The Meese investigation is a good example of the difference in the roles between Congress and the executive branch on official misconduct. Congress can investigate and conduct oversight, but it cannot prosecute. However, where appropriate, it can make referrals for possible prosecution to the executive branch. The decision of whether or not to prosecute is in the hands of the Department of Justice or, in this case, an independent counsel. In this way, Congress's investigative and oversight function is often the principal way people in public office are held accountable for their misdeeds.

6

The Rise of Global Competition

By the time I got to the Senate in 1979, trade issues involving the auto industry were a primary economic concern. Unfair trade practices had led to an alarming rise in Japanese car imports in the United States, and that put our own auto industry on the ropes. Workers with good, union-protected jobs were being laid off by the tens of thousands. Those working for small companies without unions fared even worse, often left high and dry when their shops lost contracts to foreign competition. Our trading relationships were a fiasco. No other country did what we did—that is, open our doors to products from every other country no matter how much or in what way they discriminated against American goods. That's how the Japanese captured 35 percent of our nation's automobile market. Both blue- and white-collar auto workers in the United States were losing their livelihoods while foreign competitors, subsidized by their government in many ways, enjoyed virtually unlimited access to the American market.

I didn't mince words when I testified in October 1980 before the U.S. International Trade Commission (ITC) about how unfair competition from Japan was creating "a tragedy of a degree unmatched since the Depression of fifty years ago." Many proud men and women laid off from the auto assembly line had been forced to accept welfare or take minimum-wage jobs. Many lives were destroyed by forces beyond their control, and too few in power were willing to do something about it. Unemployment in Michigan back then was 12 percent, the worst in the nation, and I told the ITC that those statistics were more than just numbers. The ripple effect of the layoffs and unemployment was crippling Detroit, which had to lay off 750 police officers in 1979 due to dwindling property and income tax revenue. At the same time our auto jobs were being decimated, Japan was freely selling VCRs, cameras, automobiles, you name it, in the United States. No matter where you lived in this country, you saw people losing jobs because of unfair trade barriers against American products. My colleagues on this issue and I were not looking for protectionism; we were looking for fairness. What we were insisting on was no more and no less than a level playing field.

Chrysler Loan Guarantee

For Chrysler and its workers, the consequences of our trade practices was a life-and-death issue in 1979. Chrysler needed substantial help, a government bailout in common parlance, in order to survive, and that help was not a foregone conclusion. Congress and the president essentially had to decide whether the United States was going to have an auto industry. With Michigan's senior senator, Don Riegle, leading the effort, we did everything we could to make sure the answer to that question was "yes."

We both knew that if Chrysler came to Congress for help, Don's membership on the Banking Committee, which would handle the Chrysler loan guarantee bill, would put him in a critically important position in the Senate just as Michigan congressman Jim Blanchard's membership on the comparable committee in the House made him the key leader there.

Over the course of several months, the Michigan delegation worked together to save Chrysler. It was a cooperative, bipartisan effort to move the legislation through a Congress full of skeptics, and it was tough going. Chrysler needed $1.5 billion in loan guarantees, which meant that if the company went bankrupt the federal treasury would have to pay back the lenders. Part of the deal was that Chrysler was required to raise another $2 billion in unsecured loans from private sources.

Many Republicans didn't like the idea of enacting legislation to help a single company. Even some Democrats were against the idea. Senator Paul Tsongas of Massachusetts didn't believe Chrysler's workforce was sacrificing enough. (He was wrong. United Auto Workers members agreed to accept $446 million in wage concessions, meaning Chrysler workers would earn $4,500 less in annual compensation than their counterparts at Ford and GM.) Illinois senator Adlai Stevenson III suspected that Chrysler would just keep producing large automobiles instead of the fuel-efficient small cars that he claimed people wanted (or should want) because of rising gas prices. The chairman of the Senate Banking Committee, William Proxmire of Wisconsin, also derided Chrysler board chairman Lee Iacocca as someone enamored with making large, gas-guzzling vehicles.

The stakes for Michigan and the entire country couldn't have been higher. Thousands of workers in more than a dozen states were at risk of losing their jobs, which would have created a ripple effect in other sectors of the U.S. economy. True, many decisions made by the Big Three automakers in the 1970s were regrettable, based on short-term profits (the larger cars were more profitable). And with sharply rising fuel costs, many consumers were beginning to buy smaller cars, a category dominated by foreign carmakers. Detroit automakers were also late to develop more fuel-efficient large cars.

During our successful fight for Chrysler, the lobbyist network was very helpful. Most Americans think of lobbyists as people who influence congressional votes with drinks, dinner, and political contributions. In fact, the vast majority of lobbyists responsibly and factually represent the interests of organizations, companies, and individuals. They perform a valuable service by providing information to decision makers about the necessity for and consequences of various options.

The lobbyists representing the range of interests in the Chrysler bailout took two important actions. First, they energized a communication system that ensured that members of Congress heard directly from Chrysler dealers, suppliers, contractors, and workers in their home districts and states. Second, the lobbyists supplied Congress with factual information. Information is power in Washington. Almost everyone wants to make good decisions, and if you can provide persuasive facts to a decision maker, you have a better chance of achieving a decision favorable to your cause.

With strong leadership from the Michigan delegation, President Carter signed the Chrysler Loan Guarantee Act of 1979 on January 7, 1980. There's no question it saved one of our major auto manufacturers and thousands of jobs, and in that regard it was a major step forward. But in terms of government and industry collaboration to address the consequences of globalization, it was just the beginning of a road down which our country and its workers needed to travel.

Industrial Policy

One reason Chrysler was brought to the brink of bankruptcy was that Japan was using tax and trade policies to protect its markets from foreign competition in order to grow its auto industry while the United States had relatively open markets. Our government was not only foolishly and naively allowing a "one-way street" in trade with Japan, but it also refused to collaborate and partner with our industry even on joint research projects. Collaborative efforts between government and industry were anathema to most Republicans and some Democrats as well. If the label "industrial policy" was applied to a proposal, it was almost certain to kill it. But Japan's approach—with the government being a full partner with industry—gave their companies capital to expand exports and protected their home market, leaving American carmakers at a severe disadvantage. Our auto industry was competing not with Toyota and Honda but with the Japanese government, which we called "Japan Inc." And our Congress and successive administrations (Republican and Democratic) were not standing up for the most important domestic industry in the United States: autos and auto parts.

The basic argument against industrial policy in Washington was that government should not pick winners and losers and that doing so would inevitably be skewed by politics. Those of us who believed that there should be a close working relationship, indeed partnership, between government and industry, including support mechanisms for industry, argued that peer review and transparency of government decision-making would protect the public against political favoritism. The risk of abuse had to be taken if our industries were to be competitive with those in other countries.

The resistance to partnership and collaboration went to extremes. For example, in the 1980s I proposed an amendment in the Governmental Affairs Committee to create an office in the Department of Commerce that would be available to help industry, labor, academia, and government come together to discuss how an industrial sector, like steel, could become more globally competitive. We were losing our steel industry to foreign, government-supported steelmakers. I believed then as I do now that the only way to save a domestic industry that is losing out to overseas competitors supported by their governments is to find a way for the stakeholders in our industry to work together with government support and the participation of academia to jointly utilize the benefits of research to reduce costs and to become more efficient and more cost-effective. This would at times require modifications of our anti-trust laws, or tax incentives, or shared sacrifice on the part of the stakeholders.

The amendment I offered provided that participation in such discussions would be totally voluntary; government could not order the components of any particular sector to meet. But the chairman of the Governmental Affairs Committee, Delaware Republican William Roth, called my amendment "industrial policy," and that label was its death warrant. The amendment was defeated.

As I looked for different ways to advance the cause of government-industry partnerships, I saw a real opportunity in the Senate Armed Services Committee (SASC). I used my position on that committee to bring together the commercial vehicle world and the military vehicle world. Together, they could work on innovations like lighter, more durable materials; fuel-efficient engines; robotics; and dozens of other technical advances that were under research and development by the military, commercial, and academic sectors. A good example of who might benefit from such an arrangement was staring us in the face. The General Motors Tech Center and TARDEC (U.S. Army Tank Automotive Research,

Development and Engineering Center) at TACOM (Tank-Automotive and Armaments Command) were near neighbors in the Detroit suburb of Warren. TACOM develops military vehicles, including tanks, which were getting very little gas mileage—as low as three miles per gallon. At the same time, Detroit's auto companies were working to improve miles-per-gallon ratings for their cars. Here we had engineers working separately on energy-efficient technologies at two facilities a stone's throw from each other. Shouldn't they be able to work together, sharing what they learned and collaborating on solutions?

But until we acted, if the army and an auto company wanted to conduct joint research and develop solutions together, they had to get lawyers to draft a legal agreement that resolved patents, royalties, and dozens of other issues. Extensive negotiations were required to produce a Cooperative Research and Development Agreement (CRADA) for each project—not a great way to facilitate the idea of working together on potentially hundreds of projects.

So, I proposed a uniform CRADA, making it easier for engineers from the public and private sectors to share information and work on joint solutions. We held the signing ceremony with the Defense Department in the SASC hearing room. The uniform CRADA did what I had hoped—it promoted government-industry collaboration, which consequently increased the effectiveness and reduced the costs of our products. That format has been used hundreds of times now with positive results.

Later on, as I gained seniority on the SASC, I promoted the TACOM facilities as an ideal place for joint innovation, research, and development. Toward the end of my Senate career, I was able to provide funding to create a joint energy lab there. TACOM now has a battery development program in a laboratory where engineers from private manufacturers and the Defense Department work together testing new energy storage technologies. Collaboration between industry and the Pentagon had already spurred TARDEC and the National Automotive Center (NAC) at TACOM to work on joint projects with industry. The industrial challenges from Japan—and now from China—had finally forced the United States to accept reality and openly use industrial policy to advance our technology and save American jobs.

CAFE

Another challenge the auto industry faced in the 1980s and 1990s was the fight over Corporate Average Fuel Economy (CAFE) standards. I had many battles in the Senate on this one. Of course, I supported energy efficiency, but the CAFE standards were highly discriminatory against American-made vehicles. CAFE used a miles-per-gallon number for a company's entire fleet (that is, the total sales of a company in the United States), relying on an average for all the cars, regardless of size, produced by a particular company. But given that the Japanese were focused on manufacturing cars that were smaller than ours, they had no trouble meeting the overall fleet average. The large vehicles built by the Japanese were no more efficient than our comparable large vehicles. But because we produced more large vehicles than they did, U.S. automakers were put at an unfair disadvantage. Japanese automakers were free to sell all the big vehicles they could though, again, they were no more fuel efficient than ours, while our companies were severely restricted in their sales of those vehicles. That state of affairs did nothing for the environment but cost us a large number of jobs. I argued for years that the fuel economy requirement should apply to the size of the vehicle, be it Japanese or American, not to a company's entire fleet.

I was making that point at a public hearing in the Senate where Senator Dianne Feinstein of California and I were testifying. California was taking the lead on imposing higher CAFE standards on cars, and Dianne is a fierce advocate for the environment. But when I testified and said we needed to address the discriminatory aspects of the CAFE standards that put American carmakers at an unfair disadvantage, with no benefit to the environment, Dianne turned to me and said she would work with me to correct that. It was a good day for U.S. vehicles and a major turning point for the CAFE battle. That year we changed the law, requiring the Department of Transportation to set the fuel efficiency standard by car size and not by fleet average.

NAFTA

During my entire Senate career I argued that common sense dictates that if another country won't let us sell our goods in their country, we should treat them no better than they treat us. President Clinton expressed the same sentiment in 1993 when he said that "we can no longer afford to wait for ten years while someone does something to us that we do not respond to." Unfortunately he came up with the North American Free Trade Agreement (NAFTA), which embodies the opposite approach.

Democrats had initially opposed NAFTA, the unbalanced trade agreements with Mexico and Canada that had been supported by both the Reagan and George H. W. Bush administrations. However, in 1993 when President Clinton proposed NAFTA, it was approved by Congress.

We had lost 2.6 million manufacturing jobs between 1979 and 1991. Backers of NAFTA claimed that it would create jobs for the United States, but that was based on half a balance sheet. While the Department of Commerce counted increased exports as job producers, they refused to offset that with the job loss caused by increased imports, which was far greater in manufacturing than any gains from exports. Senator Byron Dorgan of North Dakota and I wrote President Clinton that "most Americans understand [NAFTA] on balance threatens American jobs and ships them to Mexico. That is why $25 million was spent by the Mexican government to lobby the U.S. Congress." We called for NAFTA to be rejected.

Given the significance of NAFTA to jobs in Michigan, I studied the language of the proposed agreement intensely. I realized that many of the so-called exports to Mexico in NAFTA, as defined by the U.S. Department of Commerce, were car parts and components sent by U.S. manufacturers with plants in Mexico, where they would be assembled into automobiles after a period of just a few weeks and then shipped right back to the United States as assembled vehicles. Our Department of Commerce ignored this shell game. That meant that if an auto company closed an assembly plant in Ohio with 1,000 workers losing their jobs and opened an assembly plant in Mexico, as long as some of the assembled parts in Mexico were from U.S. suppliers, the Department of Commerce would count the arrangement a "job creator," because those U.S. parts were "exported," albeit, for a brief period, to a Mexican assembly plant. Taken to the extreme, that meant that if every assembly plant in America picked up and moved to Mexico and still used some U.S. parts suppliers, the way the Commerce Department figured things our exports and job growth would show a jump—despite the catastrophic loss of U.S. assembly plant jobs.

Another discriminatory provision allowed Mexico to continue to prohibit the sale of U.S. used cars in Mexico for twenty-five years. Another allowed—after three years—cars produced in Mexico to be counted as "American domestic" for purposes of meeting our fuel efficiency (CAFE) standards. Until we corrected the CAFE discriminatory division a decade later, this provided U.S. automakers another incentive to shift small-car production to Mexico since Mexican-built small cars would still help the company meet U.S. fuel economy standards for their fleet. And NAFTA's reduction of the U.S. tariff on Mexican-built light trucks provided a strong incentive for light truck production to be relocated to Mexico.

Our auto industry was struggling to modernize operations and regain profitability while Mexico's was rapidly expanding. And under NAFTA the rules were severely tilted in Mexico's favor. I never understood why we made such discriminatory concessions to Mexico, helping them build an auto industry when they already had the economic "advantage" of very cheap labor.

The Senate passed NAFTA with the support of 27 Democrats. While I knew at the time that NAFTA was wrong for U.S. workers, I surely didn't foresee that it would help give rise to the populist anger of recent years. With NAFTA, too many Americans were let down and forgotten by their own government, setting the stage for a demagogue, Donald Trump, to exploit blue-collar and working-class dissatisfaction in 2016 to win the presidency.

Japan and Autos

The battle over Japanese auto imports had been waged over many years by the time I got to the Senate. The one-way street—Japan exporting large numbers of autos to the United States while severely restricting the import of our autos and auto parts—had produced a bitter battle that gradually led to the building of "transplants" in the United States by Japanese auto manufacturers. Even then, high-value components of the transplants, such as engines, would often continue to be made overseas and simply shipped here for assembly.

Another major part of our job loss resulted from Japan's refusal to allow the import of American-made replacement auto parts for the so-called aftermarket. I decided to obtain firsthand evidence of discriminatory Japanese practices and show how our parts, if allowed in Japan, would be very competitively priced. So, when the flight I took from Detroit to Tokyo in January 1998 touched down, I had some unusual things to declare at Japanese customs—two brake pads, two spark plugs, and two oil filters. I'm not sure what the Japanese customs agent thought, but I brought the auto parts to make a point about unfair trade practices directly to the Japanese people.

After resting a few hours, I began my visit to Japan by going shopping for car parts in Chiba, a suburb of Tokyo, with the Japanese media in tow, and comparing the cost of the Japanese-made parts with the parts I had brought from the United States. I didn't know exactly what I would find, but I had a pretty good idea that proved to be true. Yes, Americans were being hurt by Japan's unfair trade policies, but so were Japanese consumers. Believe it or not, Japanese consumers paid more for Japanese-made parts than we were paying in the United States for the same parts shipped from Japan, and they were paying far, far more than they would pay for U.S.-made replacement parts if we were allowed to sell them in Japan.

Carrying those auto parts from Detroit to Japan in 1998 was not a stunt but a demonstration of unfair trade practices that I hoped policymakers in Washington would recognize. And I hoped Japanese consumers would see how restrictions on the sale of U.S. parts hurt their pocketbooks and, as a consequence, would put pressure on their government to open their market. The restrictions imposed by Japan on our exports of replacement auto parts continue, as part of a host of unfair trade practices with Japan that are tolerated in the name of "free trade."

China

China took unfair trade practices to a new level. I've seen up close and personal how China has made a shambles of the concept of "free trade." While trade agreements are reached with China, its total authoritarian control over the country and its people and its willingness to use tactics that no other country in the world uses to promote its economy have made the negotiation of agreements with China and the implementation of agreements already signed with China highly dubious enterprises. China's workers do not have rights to organize and choose representatives to negotiate for their wages and other working conditions. China also engages in massive counterfeiting operations (as detailed in chapter 8), that is, it makes and sells products overseas and the sources of which are not what China claims they are.

China's theft of intellectual property is also extensive and is used by them to make and sell a broad range of products, from communication equipment to handbags.

The advantages of genuine free trade are many. It is based on the theory that different countries have different efficiencies and that the "comparative advantage" that one country has in some products can be traded with other countries that have different efficiencies, and therefore have different "comparative advantages" in other products. This would be to the mutual advantage of the countries involved. And when trading between countries becomes a major part of the economies of many countries, a "global economy" is the result.

But the terms "comparative advantage" and "global economy" aren't accurate when applied to the situation in which the United States finds itself. The result of trade with China and its totalitarian regime, where the government owns the major means of production, is a massive loss of good-paying American jobs to China, whose workers make a tiny fraction of what our workers make and should make. The hollowing out of American workers and of our manufacturing jobs should not be tolerated or covered up with the terms "comparative advantage" and "free trade" or accepted as a natural product of "globalization." China's activities are not part of a natural order where free people trade.

The one use of the term "free" that China could accurately claim is a market free from moral or ethical restraints. Its human rights violations are massive, including its use of prison labor and child labor. It is a market that has run wild, where anything goes and where everything is sold, from human body parts for transplantation to exotic animal parts for their alleged aphrodisiac benefits. China should be treated as an economic outlier, whose workers aren't free and whose trade practices are abhorrent.

China has a self-described "communist" economy, but the label I would apply is "predatory economy." The failure to stop normal relations and trade discussions with China and its predatory practices will lead to ever-increasing trade imbalances and greater economic loss for us and much of the rest of the world and, potentially, to military conflict.

Small Business

As a member of the Small Business Committee during all the years I served in the Senate, I became involved in a host of efforts to foster the growth of our country's number one job producer: small business. Harnessing the creative energies of small businesses in the areas of innovation and technology was critical to meeting the demands of global competition.

In 1982 I introduced and got passed the law creating the Small Business Innovation Research (SBIR) program. It provided for the allocation to small business of a minimum 3.2 percent of federal agencies' research and development budgets that exceed $100 million. Eleven federal agencies are now covered and over $2 billion is granted to small businesses through the SBIR program in a typical year. The Defense Department awards the largest amount of funds (about $1 billion annually), with over half of those grants going to companies with fewer than twenty-five people and a significant percentage to businesses owned by minorities or women. The original legislation contained a sunset provision, requiring it to be reauthorized every five years or less. This has proven valuable by ensuring that taxpayer funds are efficiently and fairly spent and that the program is achieving its goal of utilizing the extraordinary creative energies of our people to advance new technologies.

In 1982, Sandy was elected to the House of Representatives. His presence there was a big boost to my legislative efforts in the area of U.S. competitiveness and was a major event for me personally. It began thirty-two years of working together, from fighting for our auto industry and manufacturing sector to multiple trade issues, to trying to force open Chinese markets closed to American exports, to our opposition to NAFTA. Sandy led a decades-long effort to persuade administration after administration to include provisions in trade agreements that would require other countries to protect the rights of their workers to organize and bargain collectively, which was not only right morally but also would, if put into practice, reduce some of the disparity between the labor costs of manufacturing in the United States and those in other countries.

Sandy's arrival was also the beginning of thirty-two years of confusion when people wrote to our offices or saw us on the street because we look so much alike. We had hundreds of examples of where people addressed letters to "Congressman Carl Levin" or "Senator Sander Levin." There were so many examples that we each built up a "confusion file" that we had fun reviewing. For instance, one of Sandy's House colleagues sent a letter to "Senator Sander Levin" congratulating him on his reelection to the Senate, a double confusion because I had not even run for reelection that year! One of my favorite examples was what happened when, as was often the case, someone greeted me on the street with "Hi, Sandy." Usually I would just say "Hi" and move on, but this time I decided to have a little fun. I asked the fellow whether or not he knew my brother, Carl, to which he responded: "I do, but not as well as I know you, Sandy."

Both of us have retired now but Sandy and I established a record for siblings serving in the House and the Senate that will be tough to beat. We served a combined total of seventy-two years (thirty-six years each), and sixty-four of those years we served together. A distant second is the Kennedy brothers, who served a combined total of fifty years together. There were many highlights to my career but none beat serving in Congress with my big brother and life-long mentor, Sandy.

7

The Armed Services Committee

I asked to be appointed to the Armed Services Committee because I wanted to learn about the military, but I also wanted to make a contribution to our nation's security. I believed that the destiny of my children and grandchildren, my country, and yes, even the world, might depend upon the military preparedness and capability that Congress funds, and I wanted to have a role in that process. I had a steep learning curve to climb, but climb it I did, with the help of a knowledgeable and highly competent SASC staff that operated largely in a nonpartisan manner and with the willingness of experienced colleagues and friends, like Sam Nunn and John Warner, to be helpful.

I started with the belief that well-trained, conventional forces equipped with effective ships, planes, and tanks were the key to a strong national defense. In the beginning of my second year in the Senate, the committee undertook a comprehensive investigation of our force structure and readiness, and I participated enthusiastically. Some members of the committee concluded that the quality of the U.S. Armed Forces was declining as measured by the smaller number of high school graduates entering the service. In response, the committee's majority, led by Chairman John Tower, adopted a reduction of 25,000 in the army's authorized strength. Those who advocated this approach thought that it would "send a message" to the army and convince them that they needed to tighten their recruitment standards and "improve the quality" of our soldiers. Despite my junior position, I spoke in opposition to the idea as unwise in terms of both our military needs and the erroneous signal it would send about the "quality" of our fighting men and women. I was convinced that any decline that had taken place was primarily statistical and didn't reflect a decline in the army's ability to fulfill its mission. I was also troubled by automatically equating the "quality" of a recruit with whether he or she had graduated from high school.

Although I lost the first round of the fight in committee, I decided to oppose the committee position on the floor and try to have the authorized strength restored by the full Senate. The SASC staff and I spent days poring over documents that helped establish the fact that a reduction would be the wrong policy at the wrong time.

But having the facts is not the same thing as having the votes. So, I set out to see if I could build a coalition that would be able to defeat the committee position. Although I think of myself as a "moderate" on defense issues, I was often perceived as a "liberal" and "soft" on defense. I wanted to buttress my position by garnering the support of some senators who were perceived as "hawks." We found several with whom we were able to build a coalition of perceived "liberals" and "conservatives" who would fight to maintain the authorized strength of the army.

Some amendments to bills being considered on the floor of the Senate can be resolved through staff negotiations. This was clearly not one of them. I offered the amendment to maintain the army's end strength, and it was debated for a day and a half. Neither side was sure who had the votes, and there was a reluctance to bring the debate to an end until every argument had been presented. Finally, someone called for a test vote—a motion to table my amendment—and the tabling amendment was defeated by a large majority, making it clear that we had enough votes to pass my amendment. But my opponents felt as strongly about the merits of their case as I did about mine. They indicated that they would offer a series of twelve amendments in an effort to reverse or modify my amendment. In parliamentary terms, they had the power to tie up the Senate for days on the issue, unless there was some way to reach a compromise.

So, five of us retreated to a small room, and with staff and representatives of the Department of Defense we began to work out an agreement. I found that process to be fascinating—an early opportunity to fully discuss an issue with colleagues. I also found that process to be typical (at least back then), with senators willing to find a way to accommodate each other even when they might have had the votes to prevail, applying a lesson Mississippi senator John Stennis had taught me early on: "Even if you have the votes, give the other guy ground to stand on. You don't have to kill a guy to win. Take 80 percent, even if you can win 100 percent." I took this advice to heart and found it to be an effective way to function in the Senate because even if you have the votes today, you are not guaranteed to have the votes tomorrow. You need to compromise. If you don't come to Congress willing to compromise, then you don't come to Congress to govern.

And that is what we did, reaching an agreement that reflected the will of the Senate but giving a nod to attempting to increase the number of army recruits with a high school diploma. We agreed to maintain the army's end strength without a reduction but set a non-binding goal of 68 percent of recruits having a high school diploma. It was a good example of how compromise can be achieved.

Military Strength: Conventional Weapons versus Nuclear Weapons

It has always been clear that the United States has more than enough nuclear weapons many times over to respond to a nuclear attack and that nuclear weapons can deter, but if nuclear war occurs there will be no winners. So commonsense wisdom, to me, means focusing on our conventional strength because it can actually be used to win a conflict, if conflict is necessary. I also believed during the Cold War that the conventional military capability of the United States and NATO as a whole was superior to, or at least an equal match to, that of the then–Soviet Union and the Warsaw Pact.

I had to fight hard for those positions throughout my time in the Senate. For example, President Reagan repeatedly used one-sided and misleading charts that understated American strengths and overstated those of the Soviets. Reagan often claimed that the 1970s were a decade of neglect and that we fell behind the Soviet Union in military capability. He wanted to go on a weapons-buying binge to make up the alleged difference. In 1983 our research into the so-called decade of neglect found that, for instance, during the 1970s the United States acquired nearly twice as many major ships as the Soviet Union. In some categories of weapons, particularly when you added our NATO allies' inventories, we had the quantitative edge. For example, we had more amphibious boats, more aircraft carriers, and more ground attack aircraft than the Soviets. I argued that we needed to selectively and carefully focus on where there were shortfalls, with an emphasis on capability, not just quantity. I didn't think we needed to recklessly spend on weapons to close a numerical gap between us and the Soviets where we were behind quantitatively, ignoring the superior capability and quality of most of our weapons.

My 1988 report "Beyond the Bean Count" reflected my approach to the discussion about the relative strength of our forces compared to those of the Soviet Union. The sixty-seven-page report, principally researched by staff aide Greg Weaver, was timed to coincide with a Senate debate on the ratification of the U.S.-Soviet treaty limiting Intermediate-Range Nuclear Forces (INF). Reagan had reached agreement with Mikhail Gorbachev on the INF despite opposition from several leading conservatives who argued that limiting our nuclear capability would leave NATO allies vulnerable to an attack by Warsaw Pact conventional military forces. Contrary to their position, my report showed that NATO had significant advantages in terms of conventional military capability over the Warsaw Pact. One example was tanks. While the Warsaw Pact nations had 52,200 tanks to NATO's 22,200, nearly 57 percent of their tanks had been designed before 1965 while under 20 percent of NATO tanks were that old, and our newer tanks were far superior to both their older and newer ones. Yes, NATO needed better communications systems and more ammunition stockpiles, but solutions to those kinds of problems were far cheaper and much more effective than building more nuclear or unneeded conventional weapons.

The divide between those who wanted to build more nuclear weapons and those who wanted to focus on troop readiness and weapons capability was a constant factor in the 1980s and 1990s. Generally speaking, Democrats tended to focus on conventional defenses whether on land, sea, or air, and Republicans were more inclined to support space-based and additional nuclear weapons. President Reagan, most of all, had a "Hollywood view" of missile defense. The prime example was his Star Wars idea. Reagan wanted to locate missile launchers in space, an incredibly complex, expensive, and dubious proposition. The more cautious, but still highly technological, approach was to defend against missiles with ground-based defenses.

SASC hearings were informative, but to really understand the issues I needed a broader perspective. So I visited the Strategic Air Command Headquarters in Omaha and questioned operational commanders there. I also visited the ICBM launch control center in North Dakota and a bomber base in Michigan's Upper Peninsula. I went to Europe to meet with the key defense people of several allied nations. And I went to Russia to speak with their leaders about the Strategic Arms Limitation Treaties.

I became more and more convinced that every billion dollars we spend on redundant nuclear weapons is a drain on our conventional capability, making us weaker militarily, and that nuclear arms limitations and a strong national defense are not only compatible but essential to each other.

My position relative to nuclear weapons and focusing instead on the preparedness of our troops and conventional capability was criticized by many conservatives and by one of my hometown newspapers, the *Detroit News*. In April 1982 the editorial page proclaimed that while I am an "honorable man in many ways," I "owe[d] it to [my] country to resign from the Senate Armed Services Committee—not only because [my] antagonism toward new strategic weapons ill-serves the nation, but because that antagonism has soured the Pentagon on letting the defense contracts in Michigan."

I rejected that advice and that conclusion. What the *News* claimed, of course, was a very serious charge—that my opposition to a number of new nuclear weapon programs had caused the Defense Department to stop contracting with Michigan companies. That was not an accusation against me but against the Pentagon. If the *News* had information that such a thing was happening, it should inform the House and Senate Armed Services Committees. More importantly, it wasn't true. I know from my experience representing Michigan's interests to the Department of Defense that while there are always those noteworthy exceptions, most decision makers at the Pentagon look at contracts on their merits.

As I said in response to the *News* editorial, I fully supported additional defense spending to restore our conventional military strength, but I also believed that our best hope for being able to do that and remain strong militarily comes from verifiable ways to safeguard and reduce the nuclear arsenals that both sides possess.

Chairmen and Ranking Members

The Reagan landslide of 1980 made John Tower, a Texas Republican, SASC chair. Tower was highly partisan and authoritarian in his approach to running the committee. At one point, he proposed reducing the size of the committee (for better efficiency, he claimed), which would have knocked me, the junior member on the minority side, out of committee membership. He didn't succeed in implementing that proposal.

Tower retired from the Senate in 1985 and was succeeded as SASC chair for two years by another Republican, Senator Barry Goldwater of Arizona. Goldwater was very tolerant of differing opinions and was a wonderful human being. He took a courageous stance in 1986, his last year as a senator, by sponsoring a bill to reorganize the four branches of the military. The need for Pentagon reform had been demonstrated during the 1983 U.S. invasion of the Caribbean island of Grenada following a military coup. According to President Reagan, protecting the 600 American medical students on the island required military intervention, although most of their parents thought otherwise. The brief war on a small island with a population of 91,000 exposed weaknesses in communications and a lack of coordination among our country's armed services. It made clear we needed greater unity among the services in peacetime so that they could fight efficiently in wartime.

Chairman Goldwater named five Republican SASC members and ranking member Sam Nunn appointed four Democrats, including me, to a "task force" to review the way our four military branches work together. It was an impressive bipartisan effort, and, in the end, we recommended having one commander over the members of all services during a military mission or in each region where our forces were located in peacetime. We also recommended that the Chairman of the Joint Chiefs of Staff be the principal advisor to the president and the secretary of defense. There was significant bureaucratic infighting and opposition to these recommendations. Not surprisingly, the services wanted to keep their own power and authority. Defense Secretary Caspar Weinberger opposed the recommendations. The navy opposed them. John McCain, who was then in the House, opposed them. The opposition was reflective of the situation inside the services. But our recommendations were in the nation's best interest, and the bill implementing them, to be called the Goldwater-Nichols Act, passed the Senate 95–0. It was the most sweeping reorganization of the Pentagon since World War II, and I was proud to play a significant role in its evolution.

I had an unusual conversation on an altogether unrelated subject one day on the Senate floor with Goldwater, who had a wry sense of humor. I suggested to him that he take the whole committee to visit the Soviet Union. I told him I know we don't trust them, and we don't like what they stand for, but they are there and maybe there are some things that can be done in terms of arms reduction. Barry's startling answer was, "Carl, if you and I got into the Soviet Union, they wouldn't let us 'Jew boys' out!" A couple of non-Jewish senators standing next to us didn't have the vaguest idea of what the hell he was talking about. I knew that although Goldwater was raised Episcopalian, his father was Jewish. I admired him for his straight talk and independent spirit.

Other SASC chairmen I worked with included Sam Nunn (1987 to 1995) and Strom Thurmond (1995 to 1999). Thurmond was a character, at least in his last years, often lecturing us about our unhealthy eating habits. I sat next to him as ranking Democrat, and I can't tell you how many times he told me how close he came to being elected president as a third party Democrat in 1948. I can still hear him saying in his Southern drawl, "If I just had gotten fifteen-hundred more votes in one state it would have gone to the electoral college, and I could have won there." He was a person who had plenty of illusions and foibles but was very dependent upon his staff, which helped make him easy to work with.

Thurmond was succeeded by one of my best friends in the Senate, John Warner, with whom I traded roles as chairman and ranking member for some fifteen years. Nunn and Warner were masterful at being chairman. They were both ideal for the job—fair, thoughtful, strategic, open to ideas and debate, thorough at weighing pros and cons.

John McCain was my ranking member my last years as chairman, from 2007 to January 2015. He was an extraordinary man—courageous to the extreme in wartime and politically gutsy.

Each year the SASC has the responsibility to develop and pass the annual Department of Defense reauthorization bill, an extensive piece of legislation, typically a thousand pages in length. The chairman, with his staff, drafts the initial bill for committee consideration. SASC majority and minority staff then work closely together on the bill, fostering a bipartisan approach to the committee's work.

Being an effective committee chairman requires the establishment of trust with the ranking member in particular but also with all members of the committee, and it requires getting to know the other committee members' views and goals. An effective chairman needs to understand his colleagues' positions in order to either work something out or be able to argue effectively against them. I found that, with effort and patience, you can resolve most differences, and that was something that I was determined to do as chairman of the SASC.

During my tenure, I developed a knack for getting colleagues to find common ground in the hundred or so amendments that were typically offered in our mark-ups on the annual authorization bills. That's partly because having been in the legislative branch since my Detroit City Council days, I understood the importance of compromise and the need to understand the details on which different points of view are based if compromise is to be achieved. It also may be because I came from a close family where you learn to work things out instead of walking away angry. Whatever the reason, I found that capability to be invaluable to me as chairman.

There are many ways to build a relationship with a ranking member. For instance, generally as chairman I would make the opening statement at a hearing. That was usually the only realistic way news reporters and the public could follow the complex details. In the few cases when the ranking member had initiated the hearing, I might make a short opening statement and show deference to the leadership of the ranking member by turning to him to make the more extensive opening. I also would routinely support the issuance of a subpoena for a witness if requested by the ranking member, whether or not I thought it would be productive. I found this approach aided comity and bipartisanship and helped get the committee's vital work accomplished.

Close relationships also resulted from the extensive amount of time SASC members worked together in hearings, in mark-ups of bills, and in traveling together. One of the most memorable trips I took with a colleague was when John Warner and I traveled to Somalia in 1993, where our troops were providing security for U.N. humanitarian aid workers helping to stave off mass starvation. Two months earlier anti-government insurgents had used rocket-propelled grenades to bring down two U.S. Black Hawk helicopters. When some 90 U.S. and U.N. soldiers began a rescue mission, they found themselves surrounded and in a heavy gun battle in the densely populated city of Mogadishu. Eighteen of our soldiers died that day, October 3, and another of our soldiers was killed in the same area three days later. More than a thousand insurgent fighters and civilians also were killed. Chairman Nunn wanted us to write a report on the tragic incident to help him prepare for hearings about our policy in Somalia. The matter was extremely sensitive politically. President Clinton's defense secretary, Les Aspin, was under fire in the wake of the tragedy for having denied an early request for more armored vehicles from the U.S. Commander in Mogadishu.

We were a two-man CODEL (shorthand for a congressional delegation) on a fact-finding mission. To learn as much as we could, we talked to the president of Somalia, several generals and commanders, and our Pakistani and Malaysian allies on the scene. We also met with a couple of warlords one night on the outskirts of dusty, hot, and humid Mogadishu, feeling secure, despite the setting, given the fact that we had an Army Ranger covering our backs. We followed each other up a narrow flight of stairs to a barely lit room for a discussion with armed Somali leaders who were not part of the government.

Our highly professional staff directors, Rick DeBobes and Les Brownlee, worked closely together on drafting the trip report. Together they had interviewed witnesses to, and participants in, the Somalia operation and labored through over twenty drafts before John and I sat down and went through their product line by line. The only major issue we could not resolve was whether or not tanks and Bradley Fighting Vehicles should have been deployed with U.S. forces as they moved into the capital. Warner believed they could have made a difference. I believed that they were not used properly in the first operation and that it was impossible to determine if any lives would have been saved if the armor had been used in the rescue effort after our troops got into trouble. We otherwise agreed on the fifty-one-page report and inserted our own commentaries where we had disagreement.

It was a good example of how John Warner and I worked so well together even when we had some differences. It evoked in me the image in my favorite poet Robert Frost's best-known poems about two men who had different jobs working in a field of grass. One man cut the grass and the second man then came later after it dried to gather it. The poem was written from the perspective of the second man, who, at first, thought that after the cutter "had gone his way, the grass all mown, and I must be as he had been—alone." But then the grass gatherer's eyes follow the path of a butterfly from a tuft of wildflowers that the first man had left untouched because of their beauty. The poet mused that the second man spoke silently to the first as a kindred spirit: "'Men work together,' I told him from the heart, 'Whether they work together or apart.'"

Those words have always deeply moved me about how people with different views should work when pursuing a common cause.

The report was not ready until the following year. I hoped the Pentagon learned lessons from it and the tragic experience in Somalia about urban warfare, lessons that would be helpful in the conflicts that lay ahead.

Working on the Armed Services Committee issues with John Warner was a joy, a highlight of my years in the Senate. Our many travels brought us ever closer together, and our wives, Barbara and Jeanne, became good friends as well.

I had many other great relationships with colleagues. One of the closest in my later years was with Jack Reed, a Democratic senator from Rhode Island, who bent over backward to support me as chairman of the SASC. His military background was invaluable to the Senate and to me personally. His integrity and thoughtfulness were omnipresent, as was his sense of personal loyalty.

John McCain, who succeeded me as chairman and with whom I also served on the Permanent Subcommittee on Investigations (PSI), was another colleague with whom I had a solid relationship. We had total trust in each other, whether we agreed or disagreed on an issue. John was often alone among Republicans in his views. I deeply valued his support of our report describing how defense contractors trained CIA personnel in the use of torture, including waterboarding detainees. John's support came despite stiff opposition from the Bush administration and strong resistance from all but one of his Republican colleagues on the SASC.

John's strong objections to the Bush administration's illegal, unconscionable torture was based not just on his being tortured for years in captivity during the Vietnam War; it was also based on his conviction that approving the torture of the people we captured would jeopardize our own troops when captured in future conflicts. John had also concluded and eloquently argued that information obtained through torture is unreliable and leads to false leads and wild-goose chases. And like so many of us, he also felt deeply that America was dishonoring itself by using torture.

John had as keen a sense of honor as any person I have ever known, and he displayed great political courage in numerous ways. He was unafraid and uncowed by powerful interests, as he also demonstrated through his work on our investigations at PSI. Together we took on Apple, one of the world's most profitable companies, for engaging in dubious tax-avoidance schemes, and he didn't flinch. Our staffs worked together as a team when identifying issues, interviewing witnesses, and issuing subpoenas, reflecting our mutual determination to do bipartisan fact-finding. While we didn't always agree on the remedies to problems we uncovered, we always agreed on a bipartisan process, a tradition that his successor as PSI ranking member, Tom Coburn, maintained. Tom was another example of a senator who was willing to gore some sacred cows without fear or favor, and we also became very close.

One of the most meaningful moments for me in my years in the Senate came when John, commenting on the Senate floor about my retirement, said:

> Carl might never have served in the military, but he has surely served the military well, and he has served the national interests our Armed Forces protect in an exemplary manner that the rest of us would be wise to emulate. . . . Of course, the greatest compliment one Senator can pay another is to credit him or her as a person who keeps his or her word. That has become too rare in Washington but not so in my experiences with Carl Levin. He has never broken his word to me. He has never backed out of a deal, even when doing so would have been personally and politically advantageous. . . . When SASC Members disagree in committee—often heatedly—it is because we feel passionately about whatever issue is in dispute. Even then we try to behave civilly and respectfully to each other and we do not let our disagreements prevent us from completing the committee's business. Carl won't let us. That we have managed to keep that reputation in these contentious times is a tribute to Carl Levin. He has kept the committee focused on its duties and not on the next election or the latest rush-to-the-barricades partisan quarrel. He does so in a calm, measured, patient, and thoughtful manner. He seems, in fact, to be calmer and more patient the more heated

our disagreements are. As members' emotions and temperatures rise, Carl's unperturbed composure and focus bring our attention back to the business at hand.

I was as touched by John's comments as any I have ever received.

Waste

With knowledgeable and dedicated staff at both the Governmental Affairs subcommittee and the SASC, I was able to lead many efforts over the years to improve the Pentagon's contracting practices. In 1983, for instance, I used my Governmental Affairs Subcommittee on Oversight of Government Management (OGM) to hold hearings into why the Defense Department promulgated pointless rules and specifications for goods that were commercially available at a much lower cost. A lengthy list included military officials buying a five-cent plastic part for $2 because of packaging requirements and 15 pages of specifications for bakers to make cookies for our troops.

In the 1984 defense authorization bill, I made sure to include a procurement-reform law meant to force the Defense Department to promulgate regulations setting out how defense contractors might properly allocate overhead expenses in their billings for products supplied to the Pentagon. We also wanted military procurement officers to stop reimbursing contractors for outrageous expenses such as pricey hotel rooms, entertainment, vacations, and even the boarding of a company official's dog. And we tried to close the "revolving door" whereby procurement officers at the Pentagon would retire from the military and take lucrative jobs with the very defense contractors to whom they'd been awarding contracts. For example, General Dynamics, a major defense contractor, hired over a hundred former Pentagon procurement officers in 1985. Despite having the authority to end such practices, the Pentagon dragged its feet on writing the necessary regulations, which I considered a violation of the law for which someone should be held accountable. Instead, the military brass disciplined three navy officers in connection with the purchase of $659 ashtrays.

As I said at the time, this was small potatoes compared to the huge wasteful contracts we were uncovering.

I went after conflicts of interest in defense contracting in other ways. In 1988 my Governmental Affairs subcommittee identified a Defense Department consultant who played a major role in recommending that the department fund a particular research project. He did not disclose that he was being paid by the contractor that submitted an unsolicited proposal and received the contract to provide the suggested research. This was happening too often. I was astonished to learn that there was nothing in Defense Department regulations to require consultants to disclose such conflicts of interest. My colleague on the Governmental Affairs Committee, Senator David Pryor, and I wrote an amendment to require defense contractors to disclose such conflicts of interest.

My efforts were not without opposition, often embodied by Caspar Weinberger, President Reagan's secretary of defense from 1981 to 1987, who appeared before the SASC on numerous occasions. Any cuts to Reagan's defense budget, he argued, would jeopardize national security. I often felt that Weinberger wasn't being straight with us—and the American people—about defense spending. At one hearing I got him to admit that he had not consulted with the Joint Chiefs of Staff before concluding that the U.S. Armed Forces were inferior to the Soviet military. And he sometimes contradicted himself, as when he said our navy was better than it had been a few years earlier, but then turned around and claimed it was "deteriorating" to justify a budget increase. In 1981 we cut $8 billion from the president's defense request, in 1982 we cut $18 billion, in 1983 $16 billion, and in 1984 $20 billion—all while defense budgets were growing sharply anyway. Yet despite those reductions from the amounts requested, the very same cuts Weinberger said would jeopardize national security, Reagan claimed in 1984 that "remarkable progress has been made . . . to strengthen America's defenses"—tacitly admitting that there were billions of dollars in military spending baked into his defense budget requests that could be cut without jeopardizing our national security.

Reagan's budget director, fellow Michigander David Stockman, openly acknowledged the waste in defense spending that several of us on the SASC were trying to address. While presenting the defense budget request in the early 1980s, Stockman shockingly said we had to keep spending large amounts of money at the Pentagon because fighting the inefficiency would take too long. Of course we ignored that position, and our effort to go after waste continued because to accept it meant borrowing from our grandchildren and diverting dollars away from domestic programs that provided for the health, safety, and welfare of our citizens.

The B-1 bomber was an example of the Reagan administration's exaggerations in the area of defense. The argument for building the B-1 was based on the fallacy that it was needed to replace the aging B-52. But the period of replacement was expected to be only as long as it took to develop the "Stealth" B-2 bomber. Each B-1 bomber was supposed to cost more than $100 million. The fleet of B-52s was still functioning well as a key element of our nuclear deterrence. I argued that we should not spend that amount of money on the B-1 when it would have such limited use. But Reagan and Weinberger argued that the B-1 was needed to fill a "bomber gap." We ended up building 100 of them. Yet those B-52s are still flying and protecting our nation; the B-1s are scheduled for retirement, and the B-2s are now giving us the stealth and capability we were promised.

Hate Crimes and Prejudice

One of the hardest battles we fought in a defense authorization bill involved the efforts of a great senator and a good friend, Senator Ted Kennedy of Massachusetts, and myself to attach a provision to increase penalties for people who commit hate crimes against minorities; to add gender, sexual orientation, and disability to the existing categories of hate crimes; and to give the federal government more authority to prosecute hate crimes. Efforts to pass hate crimes legislation in the Senate had failed despite the fact that it was endorsed by law enforcement groups, had 44 cosponsors in the Senate, and had the support of over 70 percent of the American public. Our effort to attach it to the annual defense bill faced stiff opposition from Republicans who said that such an amendment was not relevant to the defense bill, arguing that addressing domestic crime had nothing to do with our armed forces. Their argument had validity, but the only way to address this needed hate crimes legislation, I thought, was to attach it to the "must-pass" defense authorization bill, which was enacted every year because it was so essential to the support of our troops and the defense of our country. We argued that the values the men and women in our armed forces were fighting to defend included our nation's diversity and equality and that the military historically had led the way in such matters, including racial desegregation. However, even though we got it added to the defense bill in 2007 by both houses, President George W. Bush threatened to veto the bill if it were included, so it was stripped in conference that year. It was finally passed and signed into law in 2009 by President Obama. Unfortunately, that was a few months after Kennedy had died.

The following year a similar issue came to the forefront—the seventeen-year-old Clinton-era Defense Department policy of "Don't Ask, Don't Tell" (DADT). When the policy was adopted it was actually seen as progress because it ended the prohibition on homosexuals serving in the military if the men and women who were gay kept their sexual orientation a secret. In essence, the policy meant that many of our dedicated patriots had to live a lie while serving their country.

Repealing DADT was a highly contentious issue. It came to the forefront with the inauguration of Barack Obama in 2009. Any repeal would have to be run through the Armed Services Committee. Our former committee chairman, Barry Goldwater, believed that gay people had served their country heroically. "You don't have to be straight to shoot straight," he often said. But Goldwater was gone, and John McCain took his place on the committee. McCain was against dropping the "Don't Ask, Don't Tell" policy, saying it would break down the camaraderie needed among troops, especially those in war zones.

In SASC hearings, several leaders from three of the four military services testified in favor of repealing DADT, notably Chairman of the Joint Chiefs Admiral Mike Mullen. But there was resistance among Republicans and the commandant of the Marine Corps, my friend Jim Amos. He was against repeal and asked us to carve out an exception for the Marines. The committee heard him out when he testified against the provision, but I told him that making such an exception would be a bad precedent. He also was a true professional and said if you order the Marines to do it, they will of course do it and do their best to make it work.

In late 2010 a repeal of DADT was proposed to be included in our committee's defense authorization bill despite strong opposition from Republicans like Jeff Sessions of Alabama. McCain threatened to filibuster the bill if it contained the repeal. Obviously, as chairman, I didn't want our bill to be filibustered. McCain felt he had been "jammed" by the inclusion of our hate crimes amendment in a recent year's bill. I told John that this was different, that the DADT repeal clearly belonged in the annual defense bill, because it was a defense policy that was at issue. So I made a deal with McCain. I told him I would remove DADT from the defense bill if he would help me get a vote on a separate, freestanding repeal bill to DADT, that is, help me defeat a filibuster attempt in the Senate. He agreed to do so, and, as always, he kept his word. He was clear he would vote against the repeal, but that was not a problem. What was critical was that he let the separate bill come to a vote. And that's how we got DADT repealed—by a majority vote, instead of the 60 votes we would have needed if there had been a filibuster.

Repeal of DADT was an important victory for equality in America. Three days before Christmas that year, President Obama had a signing ceremony for it. I wasn't able to attend because I had to shepherd our defense authorization bill through the Senate before the end of the year, and debate on the bill was going on at the same time as the signing ceremony. I stole a moment from the Senate floor, however, to watch the bill signing on the television in the Senate cloakroom and heard the president's moving words: "As Admiral Mike Mullen has said, our people sacrifice a lot for their country, including their lives. None of them should have to sacrifice their integrity as well." Obama thoughtfully acknowledged my role in the legislation and sent me a signed copy of the law, which is proudly displayed in my office.

Another ceremony of which I have a picture on my wall occurred in 1982 with President Reagan, who was signing a bill I cosponsored to allow thousands of so-called Amerasian children, fathered by unknown American GIs who had served in Korea and Vietnam, to immigrate to the United States and later become American citizens. I was looking over Reagan's shoulder and saw that the word "pause" was typed into the remarks he was reading so the president would know when to do that. He faithfully followed the script. I saw firsthand how his acting experience helped make him a good communicator.

Shortly after the repeal of DADT another explosive issue came to the fore. Sexual assault in the American military became a major issue when more women enlisted and more allegations of assault arose. Such cases were handled, like other military discipline matters, by commanding officers. In 2014 Senator Kirsten Gillibrand, Democrat of New York, and a number of other female members of Congress in both houses pushed their colleagues to do something about it.

As a member and then chairman of the SASC, I wanted to help, but I had a fundamental disagreement with Senator Gillibrand. She introduced a bill that would take the handling of sexual assault allegations out of the chain of command entirely. She felt that the decision of whether to prosecute a member of the military for sexual assault should be removed from the commander, arguing that commanders were being too soft on members of their units against whom sexual assault claims were made. To an extent I agreed with her. We also had good reason to believe that victims of sexual assault or harassment were reluctant to report it because they didn't believe that commanders would punish perpetrators. But the majority of my committee members, both male and female in both parties, and I also agreed with the Pentagon's position that part of maintaining the good order and discipline in military units requires that such decisions be left to commanders. It is the commanders who must be responsible for, and held accountable for, ending the conditions that lead to such incidents and to set the overall climate in their units. Under Gillibrand's bill, commanders would be let off the hook because they would lose the ability to prosecute such cases. If they wouldn't have the responsibility to address the issue, they'd be less likely to take the steps needed to improve the climate and behavior in their units.

Although her bill was defeated, we did adopt several reforms in that year's defense authorization bill: commanders would no longer be able to overrule sexual assault convictions by courts-martial, victims of sexual assault would get lawyers, and the statute of limitations on prosecutions was eliminated. Following our reforms, the number of reports of sexual assault increased, and while that sounds like a bad outcome, it probably reflected the fact that more victims were willing to come forward. There were also actions taken by the military against commanders who weren't changing the climate of abuse in their units. It was long overdue.

Around the same time, the committee addressed another contentious issue, Guantanamo. I agreed with President Obama that the Guantanamo military prison erected at the U.S. naval base in Cuba in 2002 for suspected terrorists detained on the battlefield should be shut down and prisoners tried in U.S. courts. Some of the suspected terrorists being held in Guantanamo had been tortured, and the statements they made as a result of the torture would be inadmissible in a military or civilian court. The so-called enhanced interrogation—torture—tactics were illegal and immoral. The torture program was carried out by the CIA. In fact, the military and the FBI specifically refused to participate. But the military was not completely innocent of illegal treatment of prisoners. There were disgraceful things done to detainees at a military prison in Iraq called Abu Ghraib that fell short of torture, such as the flaunted humiliation and debasement exhibited in the pictures that military members took themselves and that went viral internationally.

It was April 28, 2004, when CBS's *60 Minutes II* broadcast pictures of American service members abusing detainees at Abu Ghraib, a facility notorious for the torture of prisoners held under Saddam Hussein's regime. The photos, taken between September and December 2003, showed U.S. soldiers engaged in what U.S. Army Major General Antonio Taguba would later call "sadistic, blatant, and wanton criminal abuses" of detainees. The pictures shocked the American public and damaged our efforts to win hearts and minds both in Iraq and around the world in the wake of the Bush administration's ill-considered invasion.

Appearing at an Armed Services Committee hearing the following week, Secretary of Defense Donald Rumsfeld laid out his "bad apples" argument, blaming the abuse depicted in the photos on "a small number" of military personnel at Abu Ghraib. I found Rumsfeld's statement incredible. I was struck by the fact that the photographs included large numbers of soldiers, some of whom were engaged in abusive behavior but others who were simply going about their business. It was obvious to me that the abuse captured in the photos was not an aberration or the product of a few bad apples but an accepted part of the process to extract information.

I was ranking member at the time and, along with John McCain, urged the committee to hold hearings on the abuses. Under John Warner's chairmanship, we held well over a dozen. The outcome was what is commonly referred to as the McCain Amendment, or the Detainee Treatment Act; it was passed in 2005 as an amendment to the DOD authorization and appropriations bills. (The same language was inserted in both bills.) The Detainee Treatment Act required all Defense Department personnel to use the guidelines in the Army Field Manual, which followed the Geneva Conventions in prohibiting torture when interrogating detainees, and it explicitly prohibited the "cruel, inhuman and degrading treatment or punishment" of anyone in the custody of the United States. In signing the bill, President George W. Bush issued a statement that the legislation would not take away what he saw as his constitutional authority to protect the country, implying that if he deemed it necessary, he would ignore the restriction. In 2009 President Barack Obama issued an executive order his first week in office requiring all agencies of the federal government, including the CIA, to comply with the Army Field Manual with respect to interrogations.

When I assumed the chairmanship of the committee in 2007, I created a small investigations team, headed by the very able Joe Bryan, to get the facts on the abuse of detainees in military custody at Abu Ghraib and elsewhere and to determine the role of Pentagon leadership in that misconduct. It was unacceptable that despite numerous military and executive branch investigations, higher-ups in the military and political leadership had avoided accountability.

Over the next eighteen months that staff poured over 200,000 pages of documents. With the help of subpoenas to compel testimony, they interviewed more than 70 people and sent written questions to more than 200 others. The two hearings and report that resulted from the committee's investigation helped set the record straight, tracking the abuses at Abu Ghraib back through Afghanistan and Guantanamo Bay and placed responsibility where it belonged—with political leaders like Secretary Rumsfeld, who had explicitly authorized U.S. interrogators to humiliate, demean, and physically abuse detainees. The investigation proved that officials at the highest levels of government had set the stage for the abuse at Abu Ghraib. Dick Cheney's "dark side" had become a reality. In the process we put our own soldiers, if captured, at grave risk of abuse and fractured U.S. relationships and our interests around the world.

The report of the committee's investigation, which was unanimously adopted in November 2008, started with General David Petraeus's observation that "what sets us apart from our enemies in this fight . . . is how we behave. In everything we do, we must observe the standards and values that dictate that we treat noncombatants and detainees with dignity and respect. While we are warriors, we are also all human beings." The report's overall conclusion was "that senior officials in the United States government solicited information on how to use aggressive techniques, redefined the law to create the appearance of their legality, and authorized their use against detainees. Those efforts damaged our ability to collect accurate intelligence that could save lives, strengthened the hand of our enemies, and compromised our moral authority."

In addition to establishing a connection from decisions made by Secretary Rumsfeld and others to abuses depicted in the photos released by *60 Minutes II*, the committee's report traced how "Survival, Evasion, Resistance, and Escape" (SERE) techniques used by American military trainers to teach U.S. soldiers how to resist abusive interrogations by our enemies had been adopted for use against detainees in our own custody.

After reviewing more than six million pages of documents, the Senate Select Committee on Intelligence (SSCI), chaired by Senator Dianne Feinstein and of which I was a member would later describe how these SERE techniques—including the notorious waterboard—were used by the CIA to torture detainees in the agency's custody. The classified full report (more than 6,700 pages) was approved by the committee in December 2012 on a bipartisan vote of 9–6. Then it took two years of battles with the Obama White House and the CIA over the content and redactions to release a redacted summary. I believe the executive branch was misusing its classification authorities to delay or prevent the release of the report, and I called its actions "totally unacceptable." Finally, on December 9, 2014, the full classified report was submitted to the Senate and a redacted executive summary was made public.

The committee report strongly condemned the CIA and its interrogation program, concluding *inter alia* that the CIA's coercive interrogation tactics were not effective and were "brutal and far worse than the CIA represented"; that the CIA impeded oversight and repeatedly misled the Congress, the White House, and the CIA Inspector General; that the CIA failed to hold personnel accountable for wrongdoing; and that the torture program damaged U.S. standing in the world.

One deeply troubling fact revealed by the investigation pertained to the CIA's destruction of the videotapes of the interrogations. I had proposed legislation in 2005 to establish a commission to look into detainee treatment, and passage of my amendment looked possible. The committee's investigation uncovered an internal email around that time from CIA acting general counsel John Rizzo, who was apparently concerned that such a commission would uncover the videos. "I think I need to be the skunk at the party again and see if the director is willing to let us try one more time to get the right people downtown on board with the notion of our destroying the tapes," Rizzo wrote. A senior CIA attorney familiar with the tapes responded that "the sooner we resolve this the better." My amendment was defeated on November 8, 2005, and the next day the CIA destroyed the interrogation videotapes.

It was a long, drawn-out battle to get the facts necessary to conduct this oversight effort and issue the SSCI report. And the tactics used by the CIA to control the committee's access to information and prevent the release of the report were things we had not seen before. Without authorization, the CIA searched the content and emails on the Senate's computers and even threatened criminal prosecution of the committee's investigative staff. But the committee in the end mostly prevailed with help from a dedicated staff led by Daniel Jones. Dan and his colleagues worked under considerable pressure for more than seven years to complete the report. I told the *Guardian* in 2016 that Dan and his team "always comported themselves in a professional manner, were diligent, and maintained the highest of ethical standards throughout this ordeal, despite all of the challenges they faced."

Notwithstanding all of our efforts, the outcome wasn't ideal—the full classified report has not been released, and the executive summary that was made public is heavily redacted. Still, the basic facts of the errant, misguided, illegal operations of the CIA interrogation program, shockingly developed by two psychologists and with the support of the agency's top personnel, did become public. The deep, ugly scar of the torture program has been exposed and is an undeniable part of our history. I'm hopeful that the documentation and findings in the reports by the SASC and the Senate Intelligence Committee will help ensure that the country never goes down that path again.

Over the years of detention of the prisoners at Guantanamo, a basic question emerged: How long can we hold these individuals captured in the War on Terror "battlefield"? In previous wars, prisoners of war not accused of war crimes were released when a truce was signed or the war otherwise ended. But in this case, with what entity or country can you sign a truce or peace treaty? The War on Terror has no clear end. Try as some of us might, we were not able to close Guantanamo. All the Republicans, and some Democrats, would not vote to close it. The right-wing media stoked fears of bringing accused terrorists to the United States for trial, as if they would be released on bond pending trial and wreak havoc. They ignored the reality that the Bureau of Prisons has space in their "super-max" prisons, that no one has ever escaped from such a prison, and that dozens of terrorists have been convicted in our courts and imprisoned in the United States. But due to the hype and hysteria, the Republican-dominated House wouldn't pass a bill to close Guantanamo.

However, as SASC chairman, I was able to work out a compromise by which those detainees not charged with crimes could be sent back to their home countries or other countries willing to accept them, under very strict supervision. Before my compromise, those prisoners couldn't be moved anywhere. American taxpayers were paying tens of millions a year for no benefit in terms of American security. As a result of our compromise, the population at the expensive Guantanamo prison was reduced from 245 to 41 during President Obama's tenure. Later, President Trump, who shamefully campaigned on bringing back waterboarding "and a hell of a lot worse" types of torture techniques, would sign a bill keeping Guantanamo open indefinitely.

STARBASE and Honors

Of all the ways I was able to utilize the defense authorization bill as chairman of the Senate Armed Services Committee, one of my favorites was my initiative to use defense dollars to connect children to the study of science and math at military bases. It is called the STARBASE program, and it stands for Science and Technology Academies Reinforcing Basic Aviation Space Exploration. It began when a wonderful Michigan teacher named Barbara Koscak used her own funds to open a summer camp for at-risk kids at Selfridge Air National Guard base in Macomb County. Brigadier General David Arendts, the wing commander, soon became her founding partner, and with a grant from the Kellogg Foundation, STARBASE began a storied life. In 1992, I was able to get $2 million authorized and appropriated for the program.

Over the next three decades the program grew to provide 25 hours of STEM, one day a week over five weeks, at STARBASE academies across the country. So far over a million kids, most of them in the fourth through eighth grade, have attended 70 STARBASE academies in 35 states, interacting with military personnel to learn about rockets and simulators and numerous other technologies with compelling hands-on experiences. The before-and-after test scores for these kids are truly eye-popping, powerful proof of the interest of young minds in science and technology when there is an opportunity to see it used in a real-world setting.

From getting it started through various points along the way, I fought many battles for STARBASE, including early ones with the DOD bureaucracy. It is firmly established now after becoming a permanent DOD program in 2000. The DOD has taken its successes to heart and holds it out as an example of how kids can be inspired to learn math and science while having a positive experience with our military. An acorn of an idea planted by one visionary teacher grew into a forest of learning. It became one of the most rewarding victories for me, not only because of the life-changing impact it has had on so many children and their teachers but because it embodies a deeper understanding of the relationship between strong math and science education and our national security. I am truly moved when Barbara Koscak refers to me as the "father of STARBASE."

Near the end of my term, and despite my opposition to many of Reagan's priorities for defense spending, the Ronald Reagan Presidential Forum decided in 2013 to bestow on me its Peace Through Strength Award. The honor is given to someone who "has applied with constant purpose a strategy to strengthen our armed forces, support our military men and women serving around the world, reinforce our nation's defense systems, and safeguard the lives and interests of the American people."

At the award ceremony I spoke about my general outlook on the military: "I think President Reagan would want us to remember that strength is important not for its own sake, but as a means to an end—a means to peace. . . . Strength means upholding our nation's most cherished values. . . . Upholding our values also means our respect for democratic government and human rights cannot be just slogans. They must guide us. This isn't just idealism. It's hard-headed reality. Look back in history and see how, at times, we've acted out of short-term expediency inconsistent with those values, and the damaging genies that were released from bottles, sometimes decades later, as a result."

It was a memorable day at the Reagan Library. I surely tried to live up to the accolade in my remaining days in the Senate.

8

Foreign Policy and America's Role in the World

My responsibilities on the Senate Armed Services Committee involved me in many of our country's military and economic challenges around the world. It gave me insight into the complexities of international diplomacy and the opportunity to play a modest role in trying to keep the peace. The backdrop for me to our relations with the rest of the world has always been that gratitude my parents instilled in me for living in America and appreciation for the struggles so many faced to get here.

The Middle East

I visited Jerusalem in late 1978, shortly after I'd been elected to the Senate but before I was sworn in. I was part of a delegation of Americans flown to Israel on a presidential plane to attend the funeral of former prime minister Golda Meir. Raised in Brooklyn, New York, Meir was a personal hero of Barbara's and mine. When I thought about her I remembered my own mother, Bess, who had been active in Hadassah.

The American delegation to Golda's funeral was led by President Carter's mother, Lillian Carter. It included several members of Congress, top administration officials, and Henry Kissinger, who, in his inimitable fashion, regaled us on the long flight about his success as Nixon's secretary of state in restoring relations with China. A number of us punctured his ego a bit during our visit. After Meir's funeral, we went to a restaurant where there was a sign out front with a picture of a female violinist who would be playing inside to entertain diners. We were in the middle of dinner and enjoying the violinist's virtuosity when Kissinger walked in with his entourage. All of a sudden, the music stopped. We saw the violinist sitting by herself, obviously upset. We invited her to our table to ask her what had happened. She said, "Mr. Kissinger asked the owner to stop the music. It was interrupting his dinner conversation." Charlie Rangel, a congressman from New York and a member of our dinner party, called the owner to our table, and we told him we didn't come to his restaurant because of the food—we came for the violin music during our dinner! Five minutes later she was playing the violin again. Kissinger never knew what hit him. We all felt a degree of satisfaction and would later reminisce about outfoxing the great strategist.

I returned to the Middle East as a senator shortly after the 1980 election, when Ronald Reagan beat Jimmy Carter and the Senate majority shifted to Republican control for the first time since 1953. I was seeking the perspectives of key leaders on how the 1978 Camp David Accords were affecting prospects for a wider peace. Leaders of neighboring Arab countries were angry that Egyptian president Anwar Sadat had broken ranks when he reached a peace agreement with Israel's prime minister, Menachem Begin, at the urging of President Carter. Those Camp David Accords were a miracle of sorts because they broke the circle of hostility surrounding Israel since its inception in 1948. Most of Israel's neighbors don't even recognize her right to exist, but the agreement between Egypt and Israel did. King Hussein of Jordan felt betrayed by Sadat, who had volunteered Jordan as the nation best suited to manage the development of a Palestinian government. And other Arab leaders, like Saddam Hussein of Iraq, became even more aggressive in their dealings regarding Israel. Egypt was suspended from the Arab League not just for forging peace with Israel but for recognizing her as a sovereign nation. At the dispute's core was the right of the State of Israel to exist.

I shared with President Reagan and the Senate Armed Services Committee my discussions and impressions and offered what I hoped would be seen as sound advice on how to continue a peace process. We spent nine days traveling through six countries, meeting with leaders and military officials in each country, including President Sadat in Cairo and King Hussein in Amman. At the time, King Hussein was not willing to either join the Camp David process or negotiate unilaterally with Israel. He told me that Camp David was a "dead horse" and that even mentioning it created a negative reaction in the Arab world. King Hussein asserted that Sadat's "sin" was recognizing the reality of Israel and that the Camp David Accords removed real pressure on Israel to agree to an "acceptable" solution to the Palestinian problem. He firmly told me that no other Arab state would make a separate peace with Israel and that Palestinians must be central to any regional peace process.

I was deeply impressed with Anwar Sadat. In his garden at his home in Alexandria, he gave me, a freshman senator, an hour of his time. He spread out his maps to give me his strategic view of the Middle East and showed me how he was surrounded by threats and violence both in and outside his country. But he was calm and seemed completely at peace with himself. I asked him, in the face of so many threats against him for forging peace with Israel, how he could maintain such a calm demeanor. He said his religion, Islam, gave him internal peace and freedom from worry over his personal safety and his own death. I still speak of Sadat, the peacemaker, so that people who are anti-Islam can get a sense of what a courageous Muslim did so effectively, and in such a positive way, to promote peace in a very difficult region. Tragically, Sadat was assassinated less than a year later, on October 6, 1981.

The main conclusion I reached from that trip and those meetings was that active U.S. engagement, namely diplomatic and military support, is essential to peace in the Middle East, and I still believe that to be true. I put my thoughts and observations in a report to the new Congress that convened in January 1981 and in a nineteen-page letter to President-elect Reagan. I urged President

Reagan to involve himself deeply in the Middle East peace process, to enhance our security assistance programs in the region to promote stability, and to renew the U.S. commitment to defend our interests in the Persian Gulf.

Given the volatility in the region and the vital importance of the area to the national security of the United States, I also described the urgent need to revamp our military command structure. Operational responsibilities in the region were divided between our Pacific and European Commands. It was clear to me that our forces in the Middle East needed one military commander—not two. Legislation cosponsored by Senator Barry Goldwater and Representative Bill Nichols, Democrat of Alabama, accomplished this in 1986 by ensuring that one commander would be in charge of all operations in a region. I was happy to be able to play a significant role in getting that legislation drafted and passed.

Of course the report did not foresee that in June 1982, the Abu Nidal Organization, a spin-off Palestinian terrorist group, would attempt to assassinate the Israeli ambassador to the United Kingdom, Shlomo Argov, in London. Israel responded by launching devastating attacks against PLO fighters barricaded in the villages of Tyre and Sidon in southern Lebanon. After heavy pounding with Israeli tanks and troops pressing in, the PLO fighters retreated to West Beirut, endangering even more noncombatants.

In July, about six weeks after Israel began the attacks on the PLO, Democratic senator Chris Dodd of Connecticut and I took a fact-finding trip to Israel and Lebanon to consider whether to support President Reagan's proposal to send U.S. Marines to Beirut to help facilitate an orderly withdrawal of PLO guerillas. At the time, Lebanon was awash in heavily armed troops fighting each other. There were 6,000 Palestinian guerillas, a U.N. peace-keeping force of about 7,000, and 40,000 Syrian troops.

We first spent an hour with Prime Minister Begin, who told us there was no deadline on efforts to find a way to peacefully evacuate Palestinian guerillas. Israel obviously held the upper hand but also wanted to avoid needless damage borne by civilians. (Caspar Weinberger, on the other hand, had earlier placed a one-week deadline on negotiations.) Then we ventured into the war zone, driving out of Israel into Lebanon. On our way to Beirut we stopped in the villages of Sidon and Tyre that had been liberated from the PLO. In the midst of the rubble and the dust, the Lebanese people were grateful that the PLO fighters and their munitions were gone. (They had left behind 6,000 tons of Soviet ammunition, not counting tanks or trucks, that the Israeli government had hauled away.)

But as we drove to Beirut, we could hear—and feel—artillery rounds hitting targets a few miles distant. Suddenly, one landed close to us, perhaps a hundred yards away. Despite my many later trips to Iraq and Afghanistan, it was the closest I came to an exploding artillery shell. Beirut at that time was a place of active combat, and from the rooftop of the hotel where we stayed, we watched as artillery rounds were exchanged just a few miles in front of us, accompanied by constant booms from rockets, heavy artillery, and mortars.

Dodd and I held a news conference in Beirut. We both said that we understood that Israel would support any effort by U.S. Marines to ensure the safe withdrawal of the PLO. But Dodd said he was against sending in U.S. Marines because they would become "too rich a target"; I said it would be worth taking that "limited risk"—*if* it was for this one mission for a limited time, and *if* all parties involved agreed to a temporary cease-fire. That was the course eventually taken.

During our time in Beirut, we had lunch with Bashir Gemayel of the right-wing Phalange party and a leader of several of the Maronite Christian groups. (Maronites are the largest Christian population in Lebanon.) Gemayel was running for president of Lebanon while leading the fight against the 40,000 Syrian militias that occupied much of the country in Syria's constant effort to dominate Lebanon. Besides the actions of the PLO, the Syrian militia was the biggest roadblock to any peace settlement.

Later that year, in August, Gemayel won the election, and two days later a Multi-National Force (MNF) of 800 U.S. Marines, in coordination with 400 French and 800 Italian troops, entered Beirut to ensure the safe withdrawal of the PLO, which occurred a few weeks later. Gemayel visited Washington shortly after his election. By then, I had heard from U.S. State Department officials that

Lebanon had, in fact, never formally asked Syria to pull out its troops. I saw Gemayel in the Capitol and asked him if that was true. He said it was true, claiming that Syria would only refuse such a request and that would humiliate his government, further evidence of Syria's efforts to dominate Lebanon and its policies. Gemayel was assassinated by a Syrian less than a month later.

Our trip left both Dodd and me pessimistic that a peaceful solution would be found anytime soon, a pessimism enhanced by Gemayel's assassination. There was much more bloodshed to come, including massacres of hundreds by Phalangists in two Palestinian refugee camps. The Marines had left after their short mission, but President Reagan sent them back to try to quell the violence. Then, in April 1983, the U.S. embassy in Beirut was bombed, killing 63 people including 17 Americans, and in October the bombing of the U.S. Marine barracks near Beirut killed 241 American and 58 French troops. Reagan withdrew our troops from Lebanon the following February.*

The Palestinians finally agreed on a framework for peace in 1993 when Israel, under the leadership of Prime Minister Yitzhak Rabin of the Labor Party, reached the Oslo Accords with Yasser Arafat of the PLO. King Hussein of Jordan was angered that he'd not been told of the secret talks between Israel and the PLO, although, ironically, he had been meeting secretly with Israeli officials—fifty-eight meetings over thirty-one years, according to published accounts. King Hussein signed a peace treaty with Rabin in 1994, a move facilitated by President Bill Clinton, who hosted them for a special ceremony at the White House that I attended that September. The peace between Jordan and Israel has endured, despite Rabin's assassination in 1995. First Sadat, then Rabin. Making peace is a dangerous venture in the Middle East.

---

* Two days after the bombing of our Marine barracks in Lebanon, President Reagan launched an invasion of the tiny island nation of Grenada, where a military coup had toppled the government and executed the country's president, Maurice Bishop. There's no way of knowing whether this was intended to be a diversion from the Marine barracks disaster in Lebanon. The United Nations voted 108–9 to condemn the invasion as a "flagrant violation of international law."

I had met Rabin on his many visits to the U.S. Senate and found him to be strategic, strong but nuanced, and measured in his actions. I was grateful I was able to attend his funeral in Jerusalem. I was standing on the porch of the King David Hotel with a group of other Americans when we spotted King Hussein, who also was attending the funeral and was sitting alone, gazing pensively at the Mount of Olives beyond the Old Town. A few of us walked over, greeted him, and thanked him for coming. He was gracious to us. I can only imagine how he felt, looking at this magnificent vista over portions of a city that had been under his control prior to 1967. My memory flew back to 1962 when Barb and I visited a divided Jerusalem. The streets were clogged with sandbags protecting the security line and the Israeli and Arab checkpoints with Arab tanks and troops directly facing Israeli forces. But looking at the Jordanian king in that setting mainly filled me with hope—Israel and another Arab neighbor once at war could live in peace.

At times I have been critical of Israel when it allows illegal settlements that undermine a two-state solution, or when I believe it uses or condones the use of excessive force—for instance, after the 1982 Israeli invasion of Lebanon and the subsequent massacre of Palestinians by a right-wing militia at the Shatila refugee camp in Beirut while Israeli soldiers stood by. I wrote to Prime Minister Begin expressing my concern. He responded, "I declare that Israel did no wrong and our detractors are the real wrong-doers." I disagreed with him on this, but I understood his passion. Israel is an island surrounded by an ocean of threats.

In 1981 Israeli jets acted against one of the greatest threats to their country's survival when they preemptively struck and destroyed an Iraqi nuclear reactor under construction a short distance from Baghdad. The attack was widely criticized by Arab countries, by the U.N. Security Council, and by many in the United States. I spent time studying the events surrounding the attack and evaluating the conflicting claims that were being made about its necessity, legality, and morality. But for Egypt and Jordan, no Arab neighbor had been willing to recognize Israel's right to exist for thirty years. They remained in a state of war with Israel, avowedly dedicated to her destruction and elimination.

It's hard for many people to fathom the anxiety felt by a country that has such opponents on its very borders. Saddam Hussein was actively pursuing nuclear weapons. He was building a reactor capable of processing the kind of enriched uranium usable for nuclear weapons. In fact, reliable reports said the reactor had no apparent purpose but to produce nuclear weapons. Once operational, no strike against the reactor would have been possible given the damage such a strike would wreak on Iraq and its people. So for Israel, the choice was to act promptly or face an unanswerable threat later. Critics of Israel's action argued that Israel had signed an arms sales agreement with the United States vowing to restrict the use of the weapons we sold them to defensive purposes. I concluded that Israel acted within the framework of that agreement because its action was taken for "legitimate self-defense." Israel's action was both defensive and defensible.

One of the most important U.S. contributions to Israel's security and regional stability was the joint development with Israel of missile defenses. I felt strongly that the significant increases that we provided in our Armed Services Committee authorization bills over the years for the development and deployment of these systems prevented a simmering situation from exploding and were also useful in advancing our own missile defense systems. The Israelis' Arrow, Iron Dome, and David's Sling missile defense systems together with the U.S. Patriot missile have given Israel the proven capability to protect its people by destroying missiles and rockets of various ranges. The United States vigorously supported the deployment and ongoing development of the Israeli systems to the tune of $700 million in the fiscal year of 2014. These investments are well worth it. It is almost unimaginable to think of what would have happened if hundreds of missiles and rockets over the years coming at Israel had not been destroyed in flight before they hit their targets.

Russia and the Soviet Union

The only Russian I knew personally before coming to the Senate was my wonderful Swarthmore Russian teacher. But the history, tragedy, and promise of the

Russian people and their vast country that spans eleven time zones have long been a fascination of mine, and I am an admirer of its novelists and composers.

My introduction to the former Soviet Union came shortly after I took the oath of office in 1979. Senator Joe Biden invited me and a handful of other new senators to join his congressional delegation (CODEL) to Moscow so he could show us the value of meeting leaders of other countries. He was right about that, and I made it a practice, when possible, to visit leaders and locations around the world that affected American security. On this first CODEL I don't remember much of the substance that came out of our meetings, but two moments stand out for me. One involved Biden's really lively, to put it mildly, debate with the number two Russian leader, Alexei Kosygin. After Kosygin was finished spouting the party line, Biden looked at him and said, "Well, that is a bunch of propaganda. I'm from Delaware and we have a saying in Delaware: 'You can't shit a shitter!' [short for 'you can't bullshit a bullshitter']." Kosygin had no visible reaction. Later, I asked our translator how she had translated Biden's words. She said she'd translated the phrase as, "You cannot fool a comrade!" a translation that sure lost some of its bite, and accuracy!

The other involved a family of seven Pentecostal Christians we met while staying at the U.S. embassy in Moscow. They were from Siberia and had been seeking asylum in our embassy. Several family members tearfully told us about what they had endured because of their religion and of their hopes to get to Israel or another country. Soviet authorities insisted the family go back to Siberia and fill out the necessary paperwork seeking permission to leave, a visit that would have ended their hopes.

Senator Dave Boren and I were deeply touched. I have always felt sympathetic to people fleeing totalitarian regimes or suffering religious persecution. Boren and I ended up trying to help that family while they continued to live in the U.S. embassy in Moscow. We brought their case to the Senate every year on June 27, the anniversary of the day we met them. Finally, in 1982, 73 of my colleagues cosponsored legislation we introduced on behalf of this family granting them status as U.S. residents living on American soil—that is, our embassy in Moscow. This was important because our immigration laws required five years on U.S.

soil before a person could become eligible for U.S. citizenship. After four years of pressure on the Soviets, resulting, I believe, from our efforts in the Senate, the family finally was allowed to leave. They were soon joined by nine other Pentecostals who had been allowed to leave, making it sixteen in all. Two of them came to Washington to thank America for keeping their plight in the public spotlight. Boren and I attended the tearful and joyful press conference where they thanked us in person. They then went to St. Louis where they were greeted warmly by throngs of Pentecostals. The family we met in our embassy eventually immigrated to Israel, where they could practice their religion freely.

In 1991, because of my efforts with the Pentecostals, I received word that I was to be given an award named for a remarkable Russian writer who had the courage to criticize Soviet leadership and whose heroism helped weaken the grip on that leadership. Christian Solidarity International (CSI), a California-based organization that defended religious liberty, announced it was giving me their Alexander Solzhenitsyn Award for contributions to religious human rights. CSI cited my "tireless humanitarian effort on behalf of human rights, giving particular attention to the persecution of Christians and Jews, in defense of their right to worship."

When I heard about the award I wrote a letter to Solzhenitsyn, who was then living in Vermont and admiring small-town American politics, citing it as the best alternative to communism or socialism. Solzhenitsyn wrote a nice note to me in English: "Thank you for the warm sentiments expressed therein. I value your fellow-feeling."

While I admire the Russian people's heart, I am always wary of Russian political leadership. I, along with the rest of the world, was stunned when Korean Airline Flight 007 was shot down by a Soviet fighter jet on September 1, 1983. The flight, which originated in New York City, stopping in Anchorage on its way to Seoul, was shot down after it accidentally flew off course into Soviet air space, killing all 269 passengers and crew. One of those killed was a Detroit woman I admired, Judge Jessie Slaton, a pioneering African American public servant. I knew her as a kind and gentle woman and a good judge. Also killed was Representative Larry McDonald, Democrat of Georgia. At first the Soviets denied shooting down KAL 007, then admitted it but said they had believed the jet was a spy plane. This was one of the tensest moments of the Cold War. Fortunately, no military exchange resulted. On the civilian side, one significant consequence was that President Reagan ordered the newly emerging GPS technology to be made available for civilian use free of charge.

A big crack in the Soviet Union's domination of Europe began in 1980 when Lech Walesa cofounded the Solidarity trade union movement and brokered the Gdansk Agreement between striking shipyard workers and the Polish government. In an attempt to prevent the crack from widening, the following year the government declared martial law and arrested Walesa. Less than three years later, Walesa won the Nobel Peace Prize, and in 1989 he brokered another agreement that led to elections and a legislature dominated by Solidarity. In 1990, he won national election as president, a newly created post. Walesa was a courageous and heroic person at a pivotal point in world history. He wasn't a great political leader in his later years, but he was an inspiring leader when it counted.

The unsteady dominos of countries in the Soviet orbit began toppling one by one after Lech Walesa won his election. Hungary, East Germany, and Bulgaria all threw off the Soviet yoke. It was a mostly peaceful transition of power from communist governments run by apparatchiks. But in Czechoslovakia, police used force against a "velvet revolution." A student demonstration on November 17, 1989, was violently suppressed, leading to larger demonstrations. Citizen groups—not armed mobs but everyday people fed up with the lies of communism—took down the barriers at the borders with neighboring countries. Barbed wire was cut, obstacles on roads and rail lines were removed, and traffic and direct communication with the outside world suddenly became a new reality.

Barbara and I went to Berlin during the holidays that year to witness and join in the celebration of the end of Soviet domination and the opening of the border between East Germany and West Germany. The Berlin Wall, no longer an obstacle to free movement, was still standing and people were hammering out chunks of it to keep or sell as souvenirs. We purchased several pieces to bring home to give to friends and colleagues. We then boarded a train to Prague and got a room in a little hotel above Wenceslas Square, which had seen recent protests of more than a hundred thousand people demanding that the communist government step down. There were candles and flowers in various places where blood had been shed in sacrifice to that cause.

Playwright and dissident Vaclav Havel's Civic Forum party had played a major role in the historic effort to achieve a peaceful transition from the authoritarian communist government to democracy. A few days after our visit, on December 29, Havel would assume the presidency of a newly formed government. We joined the exuberant mass of people suddenly free of Soviet domination and hopeful for future lives of freedom. We thrilled to their chant, "Havel na Hrad," which means "Havel to the Castle," the historic spot where he would be installed. We went to a Hanukkah celebration in the historic Jewish neighborhood in the hall that was attached to the old synagogue. Next to the synagogue was a cemetery with aged headstones askew, as if they'd been dropped helter-skelter out of the sky. In the hall, non-Jewish musicians, singers, and poets had come to celebrate Hanukkah with the Jewish community. It was a very emotional moment, the first Hanukkah celebration in decades in Prague. Afterward, we went to the historic Charles Bridge, aglow with holiday lights, where people sang Christmas carols late into the night. We walked across the bridge toward the castle that dominated the city where Havel was to be installed. There was an amazing outpouring of people celebrating their first Christmas free of communism. Those Prague moments were some of the most exhilarating and thrilling of our lives.

After the fall of the Berlin Wall and former Eastern Bloc countries separated themselves from Soviet influence, the biggest concern was what was going to happen to the nuclear weapons located in the newly independent countries. The possibility of any of them falling into the hands of terrorists was too great a risk to trust their safekeeping to financially desperate governments. It was in the interest of the United States to ensure those weapons were stored and then dismantled safely. Irreparable damage would result if the wrong people obtained even one nuclear weapon.

In December 1991, Senators Sam Nunn of Georgia and Richard Lugar of Indiana led the effort to fund, with U.S. taxpayer dollars, the securitization and reduction of the nuclear weapons that remained in the Russian inventory. Overwhelming majorities in the Senate and House passed their legislation despite disparaging comments a few months earlier of President Bush ("the needs aren't clear") and of Secretary of Defense Richard Cheney, who called it a foolish idea. I was a strong supporter from the program's inception. I called it a chance to "bury the next Hitler and Stalin before they take root." In October 2012 Senator Lugar reported that the Nunn-Lugar program had dismantled or eliminated over 7,600 warheads, 902 ICBMs, and 498 ICBM sites.

In January 1992, I joined a Senate delegation to Russia that included Republican senators Strom Thurmond of South Carolina and Connie Mack of Florida and Democrat Jim Exon of Nebraska. Our mission was to check on the status of the nuclear facilities housing the weapons that could blow us all "to kingdom come" that the Soviets had promised to dismantle. It was essential that this be a bipartisan CODEL because we were beginning to authorize the expenditure of American taxpayer dollars. The Russians, dealing with the collapse of the Soviet government and economy, were telling us that they couldn't afford to meet their commitments to reduce their nuclear inventories, and we were there to determine whether our dollars should be invested in this enterprise.

Our itinerary included Moscow; Alma Ata, Kazakhstan; and Kiev, Ukraine. In Ukraine we verified the dismantlement of nuclear missiles and bombers. I was given a clock from a Russian backfire bomber and a piece of a missile as mementos of our visit. The Russians also allowed us to visit one of their top-secret plutonium processing plants that had over the years produced more than 15,000 nuclear weapons. A two-hour bus ride took us deep into the Ural Mountains to Chelyabinsk-65, a small one-industry town that didn't appear on any Soviet maps. The mere existence of this "atomic city" was a state secret, as was the fact that an accident in 1957 at a different plutonium plant in the area had destroyed several towns, killed hundreds of people, and spread hot, radioactive particles over an area of more than 20,000 square miles. The mystery of the Kyshtym Disaster—named after the largest nearby Russian city—was first reported by the Central Intelligence Agency in late 1977. The incident was later rated as the world's third worst nuclear disaster behind the Fukushima Daiichi plant explosions following the earthquake and tsunami in Japan in 2011 and the infamous Chernobyl plant meltdown in northern Ukraine in 1986 that killed 31.

Chelyabinsk-65 had about 90,000 residents, including scientists, engineers, security guards, and community farm workers and laborers who supported the entire operation. The city was well guarded and was surrounded by a very high barbed-wire fence. We were told that there were about ten secret atomic cities in Russia, each with about 100,000 people, whose sole industry was producing nuclear weapons for the Soviet Union. Their inhabitants enjoyed the highest level of privileges. They got the best food, the best schools, and the best leisure opportunities. But now, they were desperate. They were out of work. The so-called intelligentsia (the top level of society, the physicists and other scientists and the mathematicians) were looking for work. Not only was it critical to safeguard the nuclear material and technology to keep it from falling into the wrong hands, it was essential that the engineers and scientists who had been working to develop nuclear weapons be employed to dismantle them. Without that employment, they could sell their expertise and knowledge to dangerous people like Muammar Gaddafi, Saddam Hussein, or a well-financed terrorist group.

We were also taken through another closely guarded fence to an area that is off limits to many people even inside Chelyabinsk-65. To the best of our knowledge, foreigners had never visited this site. We changed into surgical scrubs and put on heavy, lead-lined jackets. On the tour, we had to straddle a gap in the wooden floor covering a huge shallow pool to get a glimpse of submerged canisters containing highly radioactive plutonium and uranium. When we were finished, we were ushered into a locker room and told to strip and turn over our scrubs to women holding baskets in which we placed the contaminated clothing. Then we joined our hosts in a schvitz (sauna) followed by a plunge into a tank of cold water.

We were also shown a huge, unfinished new building whose purpose—if it could be completed—was to convert weapons-grade nuclear material into commercial fuel for nuclear power plants. Construction had stopped because they had no money to finish it. It was currently open to the weather and covered in snow. Some people estimated there were about a hundred tons of weapons-grade plutonium in the world, and this plant, when finished, could process a significant amount of it into commercial fuel. That would be a contribution to peace in the world and to U.S. security.

After seven days of fact-finding, we returned to Washington where we held a news conference in which we expressed concern about President Yeltsin's shaky Russian government. Senator Exon noted that the republics that had made up the Soviet Union were "in a much worse economic condition than we in the United States were in during the [Great] Depression." I told reporters, "The United States should be seizing this opportunity to reduce the world's nuclear arsenal. We don't know how long this window of opportunity will last. We don't know how long democracy will survive." Thurmond said he was uncomfortable trusting the republics of the new "commonwealth" of former Soviet states, but he supported helping to fund the completion of the half-built plutonium conversion plant we had seen. The four of us senators who had been on the seven-day trip agreed to press for an appropriation to carry out plutonium conversion in Russia. And, in fact, we joined together to make sure the money for that purpose was in the next authorization bill. But we were all amazed at how fast the security issues had seemed to change in the world, since the Soviet Union collapse had just occurred a few years before.

Senator Thurmond came away with a "gloomy assessment" of the simmering chaos and uncertainty in Russia where, he said, "no one is in charge." Senator Mack seemed more impressed with the progress and predicted that in Russia, "there isn't going to be a return to a totalitarian regime." If only he had been right.

The economic and political effects of the Soviet Union's disintegration were also dramatically evident later in 1992 when I visited Vladivostok as part of another CODEL. We stopped there in order to assess the status of the

Russian fleet based there. Their navy appeared to be held together with baling wire. Because of the instability, the government had failed to provide money needed to operate the naval base, and centralized control from Moscow had been severely weakened. People in that seaport town were desperate for hard currency. They were selling new military uniforms for a few dollars. We bought Russian sailor hats for 25 cents each. Virtually anything short of weapons was for sale. To top it off, the local Russians in charge would not allow our plane to leave for our next stop until the U.S. Army major who was escorting us paid a "fee" of $20,000—in cash.

I was worried that in the wake of the collapse of the Soviet Union, the United States would now want to disengage from Europe and the North Atlantic Treaty Organization (NATO). For more than three decades, a large share of our budget was spent on a joint defense with our allies in Europe against the totalitarian forces in the East. That was a burden we willingly carried, and it paid off in terms of freedom and security in the world. But now, the dynamic had changed. We could surely reduce the economic burden of our assistance to European defense.

Two months after I returned from Russia, I spoke at Western Michigan University and said we could safely modify our course financially and fiscally. I also said that the United States should participate in maintaining security in Europe but with a reduced role, participating through a new security arrangement, preferably with our armed forces integrated with our allies. I thought we should press European countries, particularly Germany and France, to take on a greater role and that Eastern Europe and the Baltic nations should have a role in maintaining peace. At this stage, we did not have to be the dominant power in the world; we could become a true partner with a reduced military presence. That, I said, was the transition we needed to make.

I saw a number of hurdles to jump. First, we had to overcome the opposition of those who wanted the United States to become isolationist. Pat Buchanan was arguing, for instance, that America should "come home." I, along with most Americans, wanted a changed role to reflect the new realities of Europe, but I also wanted us to remember the lessons of history, namely that

we couldn't safely totally withdraw. I deeply believed that if we did not participate in maintaining a deterrence to aggression, we would more likely have to
face new totalitarian threats that would one day emerge. That was the lesson of
history we learned too late in the 1920s and 1930s with the rise of the Nazis. We
were caught off guard, despite warnings from Winston Churchill and others.
Americans, I believed then and now, are willing to be engaged with the world,
with its "hot spots" of unrest, repression, terrorism, and war, provided that
goals are clearly set out by thoughtful and cautious leaders, and the burdens are
shared with other countries.

To ensure that we were not caught off guard by a return of nationalistic
militants fomenting rebellion in former Warsaw Pact countries, I argued that
we should support NATO and its expansion. I also thought we could safely
bring home a significant percentage of our troops stationed in Europe, which
we did starting in the 1980s.

The second challenge we faced was mainly psychological. We needed to
realize that we should no longer be the dominating partner in European security. It was not easy to accept that new role. We'd been in command of NATO
forces, just as we had been in command of the South Korean army. Our nation
developed the psychology of always being in command, and that was no longer
needed and could be safely and appropriately changed. It was finally changed in
Europe, but the change didn't happen in South Korea, despite my prodding the
Defense Department to support it.

China

China's emergence as an economic powerhouse became a major challenge in
the latter decades of the twentieth century. In December 1992, I joined two
other Democratic senators—David Boren of Oklahoma, chairman of the Senate Intelligence Committee, and Claiborne Pell of Rhode Island, chairman of
the Senate Foreign Relations Committee—on a CODEL that spent six days
in China. On two of those six days, Pell and I visited Tibet. Pell had a strong
interest in Tibet after meeting the exiled Dalai Lama in 1980, but his requests

to visit Tibet had been denied by China. He pressed General Secretary of the Communist Party Jiang Zemin and the others to let him go, which, on short notice, they finally did, but I insisted on going with him. "Claiborne," I said, "you can't go alone." Pell was then seventy-four and had a slight disability that made it difficult for him to carry things or walk rapidly. People were worried about his ability to get around a rugged landscape. So Pell and I, a couple of staff, and a doctor flew to Lhasa, Tibet's capital, with our U.S. Consul General.

After we landed at Lhasa, which is about 12,000 feet above sea level, we headed to the base of a mountain where hundreds of steep stone steps led up to the entrance of a massive old Buddhist monastery. I was trying to keep an eye on Claiborne, who was ascending a step at a time at his normal cautious, slow pace. Me? I was the one having trouble. I had developed a headache due to the altitude while the man everybody was worried about was doing great.

The monastery was extraordinary, but between the frigid December air, watching out for Pell, and my own aching head and gasps for oxygen, I didn't take in a lot of it. The monks greeted us warmly and offered tea before we made our way back down the steps to Holiday Inn Lhasa and a banquet in our honor. With little or no heat in the hotel, we were freezing, even in our overcoats, as we sampled plates of exotic food. We were at one long table with seating for about fifteen where we watched Tibetan women performing traditional dances. The Tibetans expressed delight at seeing us and showed us banned photos of the Dalai Lama, an impressive sign of their determination to preserve their religion in the presence of Chinese minders.

From Tibet we flew to Beijing, where we had a lengthy meeting with several senior government and party officials, including Jiang Zemin, the head of the Communist Party and second most powerful man in China. A humorous moment occurred at our meeting when, after Jiang welcomed us, Boren gave an opening statement and then called upon the "distinguished chairman of the Senate Foreign Relations Committee," Claiborne Pell, to make comments. As he turned to Pell, we saw that Pell was sound asleep. Since I was sitting next to Pell, I tried giving him the elbow, but it didn't work. Boren very gracefully then turned it over to me. The Chinese leaders gave an understanding smile.

At each of our meetings in China we raised three sets of issues: trade practices, human rights, and weapons proliferation. We made the case that the new administration (Bill Clinton had just been elected but not yet sworn in) would want improved relations with China but that there needed to be progress in those three areas, especially if China wanted unconditional most-favored-nation trade status. We told the Chinese leadership that this was a good moment for them to show their interest in better relations with America.

On proliferation, I made it clear that China needed to live up to its obligations under the nuclear Non-Proliferation Treaty and the Missile Technology Control Regime. That meant that China could not help any other nation acquire nuclear weapons or nuclear technology, and it must not sell the missiles that could deliver nuclear warheads. I expressed concern at news reports of Chinese sales of such missiles to Pakistan.

Dave Boren brought up reports that several missing American servicemen from the wars in Korea and Vietnam were alive, perhaps as prisoners in China, or, if dead, that China may at least know the location of their bodies. The Chinese said some American soldiers had come to China at their own request and that two of them remained, including one who was teaching English at a Chinese university. General Secretary Jiang said he would allow U.S. investigators to come to China to visit suspected sites where American planes crashed and to question people who might have knowledge of the events.

We also stressed the importance of human rights to the American people and that we deplored the treatment of the democracy activists in Tiananmen Square in 1989 when the Chinese army fired on peaceful demonstrators protesting the one-party communist state and where at least 180 people were killed. I also brought up the prison labor camps where many political dissidents were forced to work for state-run commercial enterprises. We presented letters to Chinese leaders to make our presentations more formal, and we requested information about specific political prisoners. In response to our urgent presentations about the need for progress on human rights in China if normal trade relations between our two countries were to occur, General Secretary Jiang's response spoke volumes about Chinese policies. "We have an old saying in China," Jiang said. "Business is business." Jiang's statement reflected China's behavior in so many areas—from production of counterfeit products to theft of U.S. intellectual property. China is not only the most profit-oriented country in the world, its economic behavior is often nothing short of rapacious. My comeback to him was: "We, too, have an old saying in the United States. Business is business, except when it isn't," meaning other things count, too—like whether you use child labor or have inhumane conditions in factories and dirty air to breathe and dirty water to drink and jail people for their opinions and beliefs.

We also made the case that the huge trade surplus China had with us had to be addressed and that exports made with prison labor were completely unacceptable. We said we would seek to end the one-way street where China freely sells their products to us while restricting our access to their markets or requiring our companies to make their products in China in order to sell in China. China, we said, had been allowed to ignore that unacceptable state of affairs for too long. Back in Washington, I warned my colleagues in a memo that if China is to move toward political freedom and change its behavior in trade, human rights, and nonproliferation, "we need to keep the pressure on."

But the trade and human rights abuses have continued, and the situation has not improved despite numerous efforts by members of Congress. Sandy, for instance, took the lead in the House on attacking China's illegal production of fake or counterfeit goods, including auto parts. He led the effort in 2000 to include, in legislation approving a trade agreement with China, provisions aimed at advancing human and labor rights there. That legislation also established the Congressional-Executive Commission on China to monitor progress in human and labor rights (such as prison labor) and to encourage the development of the rule of law and democracy.

It didn't take long to see that China was unwilling to live up to the spirit or the letter of agreements aimed at advancing those goals. In 2005 Congress learned that Chinese companies, obviously with the support of their government, were flooding the global marketplace with counterfeit auto parts. That October, our joint House-Senate Auto Caucus held a briefing to highlight

Chinese pirate counterfeiting that was costing U.S. automotive suppliers an estimated $12 billion a year.

In June 2006, I brought some auto parts to a hearing, including two identical-looking boxes containing nearly identical spark plug wire sets—one made by the Ford Motor Company and the other a counterfeit knockoff produced in China. The set produced in China (although it was not marked as made in China) contained substandard gauge wires that overheated with use, creating a risk of fire in the engine compartment. Here's the laughable part: while the boxes looked identical, if you looked closely, a misprint on the fake box said, "Ford Motor Company Dearbord, Michigan," a "d" at the end of Dearborn instead of an "n." Other than that, even if you used a magnifying glass you could not tell the difference in the boxes.

I testified at the hearing about reliable estimates that counterfeits constituted 15 to 20 percent of all products made in China and that they accounted for about 8 percent of the Chinese GDP. Virtually every automotive part that has turned up in the counterfeit trade was made in China, including windshield glass, brake fluid, headlights, taillights, emissions components, structural parts, sheet-metal parts, suspension parts, tires, belts, hoses, and alternators. In 2005, the Federal Trade Commission estimated that 250,000 additional workers in the United States could be hired if all trade in counterfeit auto parts was stopped. I also pointed out that China's theft of intellectual property had become so extensive that an entire U.S.-designed car had been copied, manufactured, and sold under a different name in China.

The monetary loss is only part of the risk to our country. At the hearing, I also displayed connecting rods for a Ford automobile—the steel structural parts that connect the front end of the car to the body of the car—except they weren't produced by Ford; they were made in China of inferior steel that would wear out more quickly than authentic, American-made parts, causing the front of the car to wobble and become unstable.

Although counterfeiting is a crime, the U.S. Department of Justice was doing very little about it. I testified at the 2006 hearing that there had been only one prosecution for counterfeit auto parts, and the Justice Department said it was unaware of any pending cases. The United States Trade Representative (USTR), an office created in 1962 to monitor international trade, was a paper tiger. In April 2005, the USTR placed China on a priority watch list because of its failure to improve protections for U.S. intellectual property rights. And yet, Chinese piracy and counterfeiting continued to run rampant. The rapid growth of the Chinese economy was built to a significant extent on theft and human rights abuses, including slave and prison labor.

While the federal government was twiddling its collective thumbs on the issue, the American auto parts industry created the Coalition Against Counterfeiting and Piracy. Its Detection and Enforcement Task Force issued a report that listed four strong recommendations: first, deploy an intellectual property rights staff to foreign embassies; second, have our government share information about intellectual property violators so companies can avoid becoming victims; third, address the needs of vulnerable small and medium-sized enterprises dealing with China; and fourth, use foreign trade shows to expose the counterfeiting problem. It produced few results.

The least the Department of Justice should have done was to vigorously enforce existing anti-counterfeiting laws. Unfortunately, presidents of both parties, while aware of the cheating and even talking about it, still did little about it. The sad fact is that too many American businesspeople and consumers want the lowest price on everything no matter if those lower prices come at the expense of human rights and American jobs. That's why it's vital that our government be the aggressive enforcer of our laws that make counterfeiting a crime.

We dramatized an egregious example of counterfeiting in 2011, when I was chairman of the Senate Armed Services Committee and Senator McCain was ranking member. We began investigating counterfeit Chinese parts showing up in the supply chain of the Department of Defense. Contractors for the Pentagon were unwittingly using fake electronic parts for a variety of weapons for the military. Our investigation uncovered in just the two-year period from 2009 to 2010 about 1,800 examples of counterfeit electronic parts in the supply chain, with the total number of fake parts exceeding one million. Counterfeit electronic parts showed up in thermal weapons sights delivered to the army; mission computers for the Missile Defense Agency's Terminal High Altitude Area Defense missile; and military aircraft including helicopters and Poseidon missiles. The counterfeit electronic parts originated in large measure from parts from scrapped computers. Memory chips and circuitry from computers that had been shipped to China from the United States and elsewhere were "scrubbed" of data, stamped with the code number on the part that matched American specs, and then sold to contractors and subcontractors as new.

For its part, China refused visas to our Senate staff inspectors to travel to a city near Shanghai where we believed these counterfeit computer parts were produced. McCain and I consequently included an amendment in the 2012 National Defense Authorization Act to stop the Pentagon from paying contractors and subcontractors who are responsible for counterfeit parts entering the supply chain and to require a greater number of inspections by Customs of imported parts.

We also learned during our committee investigations that members of China's armed forces, the People's Liberation Army, had increased cyberattacks on U.S. companies in order to steal our intellectual property and manufacturing techniques. I utilized the findings of the SASC in my testimony in June 2013 before the Congressional-Executive Commission on China about Chinese hacking of our private, government, and nonprofit entities in order to steal valuable intellectual property and other proprietary information. I told the commission that American companies invest hundreds of billions of dollars every year in research and development that supports the growth of those companies and the U.S. economy. I noted that General Keith B. Alexander, then head of the National Security Agency and the U.S. Cyber Command, called cyber theft of U.S. intellectual property "the greatest transfer of wealth in history." There was no doubt that China was by far the worst offender in the heist.

The U.S. economy is built on the innovation of American entrepreneurs who are free to think for themselves, develop new products, and deliver them to the world. China's actions, on the other hand, are that of a country that uses theft as a means of economic growth while, at the same time, suppressing the freedoms that encourage new ideas and innovation. When I spoke of these matters, we had already stood by for far too long while our intellectual property and proprietary information were plundered and used to undercut the companies that had developed it.

China's bargaining power at the time was the result, in part, of our reliance on China to use its huge trade surplus with us to buy our Treasury notes. If China stopped, U.S. interest rates would go up. So we are held hostage by our failure to reduce our national debt and our huge federal budget deficits. It is dangerous to our national security as well as to our economic health to allow China to have so much leverage over us.

Efforts to end our vulnerability have been totally lacking. Rhetoric over the years has at times been strong, but the concerted and cohesive effort that is needed has fallen short. The Trump administration's threats and bluster are a continuation of the trade failures with China but just dressed up differently.

Albania, Kosovo, and Belgrade

As the Soviet Union began to collapse in the early 1990s, Senator Pell and I had a friendly bet about which one of us would be the first to get into Albania, the isolated Balkan state that had no diplomatic relations with any country except China. Albania was so closed to outsiders that Albanian Stalinist leader Enver Hoxha ordered its military to kill anyone crossing the border without authorization, even swimmers who strayed into Albanian waters. Pell beat me to Albania by a couple of years, but I finally made it in June 1993.

When communist rule in Europe collapsed, a new Albanian government in Tirana led by President Sali Ram Berisha, a cardiologist, asked the United States to supply Albania with military equipment. Berisha was modest and erudite. The Albanian Air Force was comprised of only a few rickety Chinese planes, one of which I boarded for a short flight. The Albanian Naval Force base had been blasted out from a huge cliff overhanging the Adriatic Sea, but only a few small ships could fit inside. Also, the paranoid Hoxha government had urged citizens to build two-person shelters in their backyards for protection in case of a nuclear attack. They were made of concrete, looked like large mushrooms, and were completely useless, except perhaps to store trash. I supported supplying Albania with modest military equipment, and I supported supplying Albania with modest military equipment (which we did), because I had learned a lot from the friendship of Albanians in America and the support of Albania for the United States.

I was also concerned about the many Albanians living in the Kosovo region of Serbia, as I had heard from some of their relatives who were among the thousands of ethnic Albanians living in the Detroit area. The Albanians in Kosovo far outnumbered the ethnic Serbs, and the area enjoyed a protected status from 1974 until 1989 when the extreme Serbian nationalist dictator, Slobodan Milošević, began rallying Serb resentment against Albanians. Milošević renounced the special status of Kosovo and its ethnic Albanian population, prompting Kosovo's leaders to declare Kosovo's independence from Serbia in 1990, although only Albania recognized it as a sovereign nation.

Harsh treatment of Bosnian Muslims by the Serbian government over the next several years led to armed conflict with civilians paying a heavy price. The bloodshed continued for years, including the massacre of civilians at Srebrenica in 1995 by Serbian forces, despite the presence of the United Nations. To show our support for the opposition to the Milošević dictatorship, I visited Belgrade, the capital of Serbia, in 1997 with Senator Jack Reed. We met with some of the leaders of the anti-Milošević groups who were dedicated and inspirational people. We were invited to speak at a rally of fifty thousand people, where Reed called the protests a "brave struggle for democracy." I said, "We salute those people who peacefully seek democracy and work for a democratic Serbia that is ruled by law and which is at peace with its neighbors and itself."

After witnessing the intense desire for relief from a vicious dictator, we told ourselves we'd do everything we could to advance that cause. That included urging President Clinton to take military action. He finally acted in March 1999 when NATO and the United States bombed military targets, forcing Milošević's forces to withdraw from the Kosovo region. It was the first bombing campaign by NATO undertaken without an authorizing resolution from the U.N. Security Council because of Russia's veto. Milošević was charged by the International

Criminal Tribunal with war crimes during his military campaigns in Bosnia, Croatia, and Kosovo. Milošević's trial in the Hague lasted five years but ended without a verdict when he died in jail in 2006. In 2008, the Assembly of Kosovo unanimously declared independence and within days nearly a dozen countries, including the United States, recognized Kosovo's status as a sovereign state. It was a great experience to witness the birth of a new democratic state.

North Korea

Getting into North Korea was extremely difficult. But I was able to get permission in 1994 to visit North Korea in order to see for myself whether that country's oppressive dictatorship was following international rules and an existing agreement on nuclear weapons. I was in the middle of a briefing at our embassy in Beijing preparing for a flight the next day for a scheduled meeting with Kim Il-Sung in Pyongyang when we received word that the "Eternal President" had died. Trip canceled. Four years later, in January 1998, with Kim's son, Kim Jong-Il, firmly in power as Supreme Leader, I received word that I could visit. I was by then the ranking member of the Senate Armed Services Committee. I did not meet the new leader. The major purpose of our visit to North Korea was to check out the nuclear facility at Yongbyon, about forty-five miles north of the capital. An additional goal was to visit a clinic that had been sent medical equipment and supplies from the Korean American community in Michigan. I wanted to make sure the supplies had reached them and was glad to see that they had.

David Lyles, my extraordinary staff director on the Armed Service Committee, and I were first taken on a driving tour of Pyongyang, North Korea's capital. We stopped at one site with a panorama of the city. As we stood there, a young North Korean couple walked by, the man in a suit and the woman in traditional Korean dress. Both wore obligatory lapel pins memorializing Kim Il-Sung. We engaged them with the help of our interpreter-guide and learned they had just been married. I congratulated them and told them that we were Americans visiting their country and that we hoped that the barriers between the peoples of North Korea and the United States could be overcome. They looked totally bewildered by our encounter. Anti-American feelings probably had been instilled in them since birth.

The visit to Yongbyon was otherworldly. We left the capital by car on a wide, multilane highway that was almost devoid of traffic. The road to the nuclear facility was pothole free. Peasant women with brooms swept from the road the light snow that had fallen. They hardly looked up as we drove by. The reason for building such a fine highway that few vehicles used apparently allowed the Supreme Leader to quickly travel to his nuclear facility. I don't know to this day why they were open to our visit, other than at that time we had a nuclear deal with them. An American man was monitoring the facility for the United Nations. When we walked in the room where the canned plutonium was being stored in a large pool of what looked like ordinary water, the American was shocked to see us. "Senator Levin! What are you doing here?" he said. "Me? What are you doing here?" I said. He was part of a group of U.N. observers working there to ensure that North Korea was living up to its commitments.

On the way back we stayed at a nearby mountain resort for one night. It appeared there were no other guests. When we got up in the morning, our driver lit a small fire under our vehicle to warm up the crankcase—it was that cold! In fact, I don't remember any buildings with heat, whether it was the auditorium where we watched a show on North Korean culture one night, or the nuclear facility, or even the clinic in the middle of winter where patients were disrobing for physical examinations. I had other striking impressions. There seemed to be very little activity visible anywhere. The streets of the capital at that time had little traffic—vehicle or pedestrian. It almost looked like a "Potemkin Village." The countryside was denuded of trees. They'd all been cut down for fuel out of a desperate need to stay warm during the long winters. It was a repressive and depressing place that reflected the suffocation of a people by the big lie of its leaders that its actions were benefiting the people. The power of the propaganda about beloved leaders seemed relentless to this outsider and obviously unbearable to the many North Koreans who have risked their lives to escape from behind the North Korean silk curtain.

Cuba

America is at its most influential when we engage with the world. Trade, cultural, and political exchanges between the United States and other authoritarian countries, even dictatorships, don't strengthen tyranny—they weaken it. That's why the policy of successive presidents and Congress to isolate Cuba since the 1959 revolution, as well as the ill-advised and disastrous Bay of Pigs invasion in 1961, has been counterproductive.

Congress can affect our foreign policy in many ways: it has to approve sales of arms to certain countries; it can impose sanctions; it has the power to fund foreign and military assistance; and the Senate has to ratify treaties. When it came to Cuba, Congress had a huge impact on our policy by prohibiting American citizens from traveling there and corporations from trading with Cuban entities. Unfortunately, the Cuban American community centered in Florida exerted its political muscle and influence to cut off all contact with Cuba.

In 2014 I was visited by Judith Gross, the wife of Alan Gross, an American citizen imprisoned in Cuba for, among other things, conspiracy to commit espionage. These were trumped-up charges, but our lack of diplomatic relations with Cuba was hampering efforts to free her husband. Gross was a U.S. government contractor working with the United States Agency for International Development (USAID). In 2009, Gross had innocently violated Cuban law by bringing satellite and computer equipment to the Cuban Jewish community in order to get better Internet access. He even declared the equipment when he brought it to Cuba. He wasn't trying to hide it.

Barbara and I traveled to Cuba to visit Gross in prison about five years after his arrest. His mother was gravely ill, and his daughter was dealing with breast cancer. He was worried more about his family than about himself. He clearly liked the Cuban people and even liked his jailers, but he needed to go home. A number of senators were interested in his case, including Democrats Patrick Leahy of Vermont and Dick Durbin of Illinois. After our return, I joined those senators and several House members at a meeting with President Obama to urge him to help get Gross released by reducing the sentences of some of the

Cuban Five, Cuban operatives who had been convicted of conspiring to shoot down an American plane and were in prison in the United States. Not too long after our visit with Obama, a prisoner exchange with Cuba released Gross.

When a U.S. Air Force plane carrying Gross landed at Andrews Air Force Base, many of us who supported his release were there to greet him. Upon his return home, Gross supported Obama's efforts to change our policy toward Cuba. Gross thought his experience, while highly painful, should not stop the two countries from trying to achieve more normal diplomatic relations. He is an extraordinary human being. And our policy did change to a more open relationship with Cuba during the Obama administration. President Trump promptly reversed that, part of his overwhelming effort to dismantle and reverse as many Obama policies as he could.

9

Afghanistan and Iraq

The wars in Afghanistan and Iraq stand apart from the other conflicts in which the United States has been involved since Vietnam by being the deadliest and most costly for our country. They were started for very different reasons and were waged in very different ways with uncertain outcomes and still-unfolding impacts on our national security. The one commonality between them was that unlike the U.S. military actions in Lebanon, Grenada, and the Balkans, the actions we took after 9/11 in Afghanistan and Iraq were authorized by Congress. Otherwise, the invasions of the two countries were dramatically different from each other.

We took military action in Afghanistan because we had been attacked by a terrorist group on 9/11 that had clearly used Afghanistan for training and as a safe haven. Our military action in Afghanistan had the support and participation of our NATO allies and the support of the international community, including the United Nations and Muslim countries. Iraq, on the other hand, had not attacked or threatened to attack us, and our invasion of Iraq in 2003 did not have the support or participation of NATO, the United Nations, the international community, or any Muslim countries.

Those differences were important to me and were sufficient reason for me to support our military action in Afghanistan but not in Iraq. But at the core of my opposition to invading Iraq were the lies and deceptions perpetrated by the Bush administration on the American people to justify the war.

9/11

I should begin on that calm, sunlit Tuesday morning in September 2001 when a group of deranged and deadly terrorists exploited flaws in America's airline security system to hijack four passenger jets and fly them into high-profile targets in the United States. I was driving to work when I heard on the radio that a passenger jet had flown into one of the World Trade Center towers in New York City. By the time I got to my office in the Russell Senate Office Building, a second airliner had torn into the other tower, and my staff was gathered around a television watching in stunned silence. My first reaction after the horror of watching the desperate people fleeing from the collapsing buildings was a sense of dread that the unfolding scenes of terror were the beginning of a broadside attack on the United States by an unknown but highly organized entity. At 9:45 a.m. American Flight 77 struck the Pentagon, collapsing the west side of the building and killing 125 civilian and military personnel and 64 passengers. That was followed by rumors and reports that another plane could be headed for the Capitol or the White House. My staff was concerned about where I, as chairman of the Armed Services Committee, should go and what I should do. Shortly thereafter the Capitol buildings, including the Russell Building, were officially evacuated. We were told to leave the immediate area and await word. My staff directed me to a nearby office on Capitol Hill.

To our country's great fortune, the extraordinarily brave passengers on one of the flights, United Flight 93, fought with the terrorists, forcing their hijacked jet to crash in Pennsylvania, killing everyone onboard but saving Washington from what could have been another catastrophic event. When the all-clear was given, which I remember to be a few hours later, I returned to my office. Senator John Warner called and suggested that as chairman and ranking member of the Armed Services Committee, we visit the Pentagon together. I welcomed the suggestion that we show calm support for our military and our country, despite our obvious anxiety for the victims and our people. As soon as we arrived, we met briefly with Secretary of Defense Donald Rumsfeld, who was about to hold a press conference where we joined him in a show of bipartisan unity and determination to bring to justice those responsible for these barbarous acts.

A few days later I joined many other senators in traveling to New York City to see firsthand the extent of the damage and to lend support to a shaken city and its people. We viewed the still smoldering ruins of the Twin Towers and watched courageous firefighters as they searched for bodies. The mood of the delegation was somber, with everyone determined to find out whether the terrorist acts were part of a larger plot. We wanted to track down whoever ordered or participated in these terrorist acts, investigate how they could have happened, and figure out how to prevent similar atrocities from ever happening again. On our return to Washington, Barbara, my aide David Lyles, and I went to the Pentagon to show support for the civilians and the military men and women who continued to sift through the debris.

The FBI and counterintelligence agencies knew early on that a terrorist group based in Afghanistan that few of us had heard of before—al-Qaeda—was responsible, that fifteen of the nineteen hijackers were from Saudi Arabia, and that the Taliban movement in Afghanistan was giving al-Qaeda shelter.

Three days later Congress approved a resolution authorizing the president to use force against our 9/11 attackers. The administration's proposed language for the authorization would have allowed the use of our armed forces "to deter and preempt any future acts of terror against the U.S." Senator Joe Biden, chair of the Senate Foreign Relations Committee, other senators, and I thought the language was too broad, was too open-ended, and would grant authorization of preemptive military strikes against virtually any perceived threat. So we worked successfully to narrow the language so that it gave the president the legal authority to use "necessary and appropriate" military force only against anyone or any entity that had planned, authorized, committed, or aided in the September 11 attacks or those who harbored such persons or groups. The Authorization for Use of Military Force (AUMF) passed on September 14. On October 7, the president announced that airstrikes targeting the Taliban in Afghanistan had begun and, with our Special Forces already active in the border area between Afghanistan and Pakistan, Operation Enduring Freedom was underway.

At the same time, it was also important for us to learn how our Intelligence Community (IC) had failed to know about the plot to attack America. I was a member of the Senate Select Committee on Intelligence (SSCI), which began to investigate this. We had known about the Taliban in Afghanistan, of course, but most of us knew very little about Osama bin Laden or al-Qaeda. At hearings before both the SASC and SSCI, as well as from excellent reporting by the news media, we learned more about bin Laden, the Taliban, and al-Qaeda and were told about the terrorist training camps in isolated valleys in the mountains of Afghanistan.

It soon became clear that there had been a serious gap in intelligence-sharing among several federal agencies. The CIA had tracked some of the hijackers who had been meeting in Germany before entering the United States where they took flying lessons at various small airports around the country. If the CIA had alerted the FBI that a couple of potential terrorists they had been tracking and had overheard on telephone taps were in the United States, we would have likely averted this horrific tragedy. But the FBI was told nothing, even though they had done some probing with the CIA. This was a major intelligence failure, stovepiping at its worst.

For both wars, Afghanistan and Iraq, it was the duty of the Armed Services Committee to oversee the ongoing developments and expenditure of funds by the Department of Defense—everything from contracting to mission to troop support to battle plans. We carried out these responsibilities through numerous briefings, hearings, and reports, as well as personal trips to Afghanistan and Iraq.

Afghanistan

Around Thanksgiving of 2001, Senator Warner and I were flown to Karshi-Khanabad, our military base in Uzbekistan, where we met with General Tommy Franks and some of our troops. We felt it was important not only to show support but to see what was going on, in order to understand the level of military support we would need. Franks approved a plan to fly us to a forward base near

Mazar-i-Sharif in northern Afghanistan in two helicopters, over a mountain range, in the middle of the night, without lights. Before boarding the choppers, John and I had second thoughts. How could we justify putting at risk our people, who themselves had just recently arrived in Afghanistan, and using our military assets to protect us under such challenging circumstances? We didn't think we could, so we scrubbed going to the forward base and decided to go on to Pakistan instead. We got to the U.S. embassy in Islamabad in the wee hours, and I remember how hungry we were and how John quickly headed to the kitchen and found some food for us. Down-to-earth, good-humored, caring—John was a terrific travel companion. We should all live as fully as John Warner has and with his gusto for life.

The following day we met with a group of Special Forces led by a lieutenant colonel who had just launched a nighttime raid in Afghanistan going after Mullah Omar, then the leader of the Taliban. They missed him, but a point was made to show that there was no safe place for the Taliban. We told our troops what we knew to be true—that their mission was critically important for our security and that the American people supported what they were doing and thanked them for their readiness to serve. We returned home grateful that our troops on the front lines were superbly trained and prepared to take the fight to the enemy.

During a dozen or so trips to Afghanistan that I made over the years after 9/11, I always met with our troops and, when possible, tried to have joint meals with both our and Afghan troops, particularly when we were in remote areas. A critical issue for me was the relationship between the two. The Afghans may have had separate tents and different food, but it was important that they saw us as equal partners in the fight against the enemy and vice versa. During these visits, the troops from the two countries seemed genuinely to like each other. There was a spirit of brotherhood, and morale was good; our troops saw the Afghans putting their lives on the line for their country. I would also take pictures with Michigan soldiers and get the names and addresses of parents or spouses so I could drop them a note with words of encouragement on my return to the United States.

My impression visiting Afghanistan was that the people we met and their leaders were sincere in their strong support for going after the Taliban and al-Qaeda. They supported the presence of our troops and our allies' troops to help them put the country on a more secure footing. It was of critical importance to me that we were a part of a coalition that included Muslim countries and that we had international support for rooting out Islamic terrorists. I deeply believe that, with rare exceptions, we need to have that kind of broad support if military interventions in other countries are going to succeed in leaving a country secure.

The United States did far more than fight Taliban insurgents after we removed the Taliban government in late 2001. Notably, we helped villages get a boost with small grants from an Opportunity Fund to engage in development projects. Those grants (about $50,000 maximum) bought supplies for construction, for schools and hospitals, for drilling wells, and for improving sanitation. It didn't take a lot of money to do good things. While it's true that hundreds of millions of our dollars were wasted, misdirected, or outright stolen in Afghanistan, usually by corrupt officials, this modest program to provide aid to the people in small towns and villages was one of the most effective ways to help. It also helped keep the Taliban at bay, and I never heard even an allegation of misuse of these dollars from the Opportunity Fund.

In August 2009, in one of my many trips to Afghanistan, I traveled with two committee members, Rhode Island senator Jack Reed and Delaware senator Ted Kaufman. We found hopeful signs that Afghanistan could emerge from the nightmare brought on by the Soviet Union's invasion and occupation in 1979 and the Taliban domination that followed the Soviets' departure in 1988.

To highlight just one example, we visited a school that was being built to serve two adjacent villages that had pooled their Opportunity Fund money for this purpose. They built the school with their own hands, using local materials, where possible. About half of the students were girls, something that was forbidden by the Taliban. But, they said, "The Taliban will not touch this place. It's too important to all of us and the Taliban would lose whatever support they have around here if they attack this school." That may have been too optimistic.

From my distant perspective, nothing seemed to stop the Taliban in terms of what or whom they attacked. Indeed, the Taliban might attack the school *because* girls were going there. Nonetheless, the villagers seemed unafraid and very proud of what they were doing.

We witnessed other examples of progress on the civilian side of the ledger. In Kabul, we visited the American University for Afghan students that had been reestablished in a new, more secure location. When we spoke with the students, who were evenly divided between male and female, they were extremely grateful for the opportunity to learn. They were hopeful, practical, and very supportive of their country. Being able to learn together, they said, made them more unified as Afghans across ethnic and tribal lines.

In Helmand Province my colleagues and I and a few military personnel were invited to join a meeting of the elders of a small village. As we came into the meeting, the elders were sitting on the floor. We joined them on the floor and listened to their opinions—through an interpreter, of course. Referring to the U.S. military, I asked one question: Do you want us here? The answer was very significant to me and reinforced my own view of how long we should stay in Afghanistan. "We want you to train our security forces and then leave," they said. "And someday we will invite you back as guests."

I've always felt that the Afghans are going to have to make their own country function well and make it secure. We can and should assist, but we can't produce or enforce a peace. They are going to have to figure out a path on their own. First and foremost, I have always believed they need a very strong, centralized military with far greater capability and that our primary mission in Afghanistan wasn't and isn't combat but should be to train and equip Afghan troops. It is essential to create the elements for a strong military, including an Afghan air force, special forces, and an intelligence capability. We provided some training, but I continued to insist that it wasn't sufficient, either in the number of troops trained or in the type of assistance we were providing.

When we planned and then executed the invasion of Afghanistan, my question was always: If the countryside can be freed of the Taliban, then what? How could we keep the Taliban from regrouping?

As the most senior Democrat on the Senate Armed Services Committee, I conferred with President Obama on his policy decisions with respect to Afghanistan. He was always thoughtful and thorough in his analysis and believed, as I did, that America's great military force should be used with great caution. I was also able to observe how he related, as commander in chief, to the military leaders who served under him and to the political attacks he was getting from Capitol Hill. Overall, I respected the choices he made, but there were some with which I disagreed.

Reduction of Forces

I strongly supported reducing our military presence in Afghanistan and at the same time maximizing what we could do to train the Afghan military. President Obama shared the goal of reducing our troops. But in the first month of his presidency, he directed that an additional 17,000 troops be deployed to Afghanistan, as he put it, to "win quickly" and leave. I didn't support more troops. I disagreed with the president on *Meet the Press* in October 2009 and said that we should be surging U.S. trainers and the size of the Afghan army instead of the number of our combat troops.

General Stanley McChyrstal wanted the next part of a "surge" in the fall to be larger than the president wanted, 40,000 instead of President Obama's 30,000. This was a test, in my mind, whether the president would, while listening to the advice of his military leaders, make the decision he thought was right. I thought it was not dissimilar in principle to President Kennedy's situation in the Cuban Missile Crisis in the 1960s when his military leaders wanted to bomb Cuba. Fortunately for us all, a young President Kennedy asserted his leadership in a decision that possibly saved the world from a nuclear holocaust.

President Obama was also young and perceived by a segment of the public as "too liberal." Unlike President Kennedy, he had not served in the military and, perhaps as a result, felt politically vulnerable. In a conversation with President Obama in 2009, I told him what he probably already knew—that some of his critics were eager to use any disagreement with General McChrystal on the number of troops to drive a wedge between a newly installed, "inexperienced" commander in chief and his military but that he, President Obama, should make his own decisions. President Obama responded, "It [the wedge] is not going to happen."

President Obama stuck with his 30,000 number and combined it with a decision to set a timetable to start reductions of U.S. forces in July 2011. I supported the troop reduction decision. For me, setting a date to begin reductions was the best, and perhaps the only, way to force Afghanistan to take hold of their own future.

But it was a controversial decision, and a number of my Senate colleagues strongly disagreed with it. Some Republicans, including John McCain, were pressing to make the July 2011 date "aspirational" or "condition based." I made use of several opportunities to support the president's commitment to the July 2011 troop withdrawal, and each time he assured me that, despite the pressure against the withdrawal deadline, it was a "presidential order," and not a recommendation to the military, as McCain said he wanted it to be in a phone conversation he and I had with the president.

In July 2010, when flying on Air Force One and after again reconfirming the July 2011 troop reduction date, I urged President Obama to find ways to dramatize the fact that Afghan forces were taking the lead in more and more places and, in particular, were in the lead in the fierce battles that were going on in the Arghandab Valley in Kandahar Province. I thought it was important that both points reach three audiences: the Afghans, the American public, and the Taliban, whose worst nightmare was a powerful, unified Afghan army. That's because withdrawal of U.S. troops and a stronger Afghan army would mean that the Taliban would hopefully be losing both the military battles and their propaganda argument that they are fighting to remove foreigners from Afghanistan. The president said he fully shared that view.

When I told the president in September 2010 about a speech I was giving in a few days on the need to keep the July 2011 date firm, I added that I was betting on him not wavering. He suggested it was a safe bet. Thankfully, he was right.

Another part of the effort to shift the ability and responsibility to take on the Taliban to the Afghans was the issue of the size of the future Afghan army. In late 2010 many in the administration were arguing that for budgetary reasons we could not fund the Afghan army to the planned higher level. In January 2011 I told the president that Senator Jack Reed, Senator John Tester, and I had just returned from Afghanistan and that the increase in funding needed to increase the size of the Afghan army and security forces by 78,000 (with an end strength of 350,000) was essential. When the president responded that it was "under consideration," I surprised myself when I blurted out, "Do it!!" I was pleased to hear from President Obama when I was in Afghanistan in the early days of January 2013 that the 2017 end strength goal for the Afghan army and security forces would remain at 350,000 instead of being reduced to 250,000.

Afghan Leadership

Of course, Afghan leadership, or lack thereof, was key. Over the years I had met with Afghan president Hamid Karzai a number of times and found him full of himself and contradictions. What was so maddening about President Karzai was that he didn't appreciate the U.S. contribution to Afghanistan. He really went off the deep end sometimes, even suggesting that the United States had some connection to the Taliban. And then he publicly called U.S. troops an "occupying force," although he came to power in December 2001 because we and our allies forced the Taliban out, and we continued to support him for more than ten years. He was erratic and unreliable.

But the United States did not give up on Afghanistan despite years of poor leadership. Jack Reed and I were on a previously scheduled trip to that country in 2012 when we learned President Obama would be in Kabul on May 1 to sign an Enduring Strategic Partnership agreement with President Karzai that would provide for the withdrawal of all U.S. combat troops by 2014. The capture and killing of Osama bin Laden in Pakistan in May 2011 by a SEAL team that had taken off from Afghanistan gave a boost to the president's controversial troop reduction decision. The agreement called for continuing support from the United States, including more training of Afghan troops. This was very meaningful for me, since I had been calling for withdrawal of our combat troops and continuing to help Afghans help themselves. Jack and I, with a quick detour, were able to witness the signing of the agreement.

In 2014 Ashraf Ghani, a more steady and reliable leader, became president of Afghanistan. We had lunch with Ghani at his home during Ramadan. Muslims fast during Ramadan but we noticed Ghani was not fasting because of a medical condition. His Christian wife, Rula, was fasting even though she had no religious obligation to do so. She told us she was substituting for her husband, which was a moving gesture indeed.

Ghani took some steps to address the plague of corruption in his country, but they were too few. In speaking with him and other Afghans, we emphasized that unless government corruption was vigorously and successfully attacked, public support in the United States would be lost and the Taliban would benefit.

When I last visited Afghanistan in 2014, people generally were trying to live normal lives despite the terrorist attacks. You walked down the streets of Kabul, as though it were a normal, secure city. Then a suicide bombing would occur, and it was obvious that it was a dangerous place. A few hours later, shops would reopen and people would be in the streets going about their business. There was an amazing amount of life, under the circumstances. One example of that was a group of music students from Afghanistan who were visiting the United States. We invited them to give a short performance on Capitol Hill. It was moving to realize that just a few years earlier, the Taliban had forbidden the playing of music, and now these young Afghan musicians—boys and girls together—were in the U.S. Capitol playing their hearts out. It was a sign of real hope despite the constant setbacks.

Deeply troubling to me and, far more importantly, to the families of those servicemen and women who have given their lives to bring peace and security to Afghanistan is that most Americans don't believe we accomplished anything there while most Afghans believe we did much good. Why the different perspectives? The difference is that most of the people who live there see what we've accomplished, despite the Taliban and the terror that it perpetrates. There's a lot that went wrong, surely, but our media doesn't adequately report the gains that women have made there and the schools that have reopened. Nothing like that could have happened under the Taliban. Stores by the thousands are open; health in general is much better; life expectancy is longer; universities are opening. Americans may not have any feel for the gains that have been made in Afghanistan, but I have seen them.

Iraq

There is a sharp contrast between Afghanistan and Iraq. The decision by President George W. Bush with the support of Congress in 2003 to go to war with Iraq was the most misguided strategic decision by our government that I witnessed in my thirty-six years in the Senate. My opposition to the congressional resolution authorizing the attack, which passed by a vote of 77 to 23 in the Senate on October 11, 2002, wasn't a difficult decision for me. But while I didn't suffer over how to vote, I do suffer over what has proven to be the devastating consequences of that decision to go to war.

Why was I confident about my opposition? Because I knew firsthand that key information the public was being given to justify initiating an attack was misleading. The single most important decision a country could make was, in this instance, being made based on untrue claims by the Bush administration. The CIA assessment, which was, for the most part, classified, concluded that Iraq was not involved in the 9/11 attack on us and that even assuming Iraq had weapons of mass destruction, it would not use such weapons against us unless we attacked them first. So the administration's claim that we had to attack Iraq to end their nuclear threat was particularly misleading, because in fact, the opposite was true. The CIA believed that our attack on Saddam could bring about the very "mushroom cloud" that the administration was claiming they were trying to prevent.

While President Bush was publicly vowing to bring bin Laden to justice, his administration was quietly diverting its focus and energy from that mission to laying the groundwork for an attack on Iraq. According to Richard Clarke, the former White House counterterrorism chief, President Bush repeatedly told him on September 12, 2001, to look for "any shred" of evidence that Saddam was involved in the 9/11 attacks. After exhaustive research, Clarke sent a memo to Condoleezza Rice, Bush's national security advisor, indicating that "only some anecdotal evidence linked Iraq to al-Qaeda." It stated that the case for Saddam cooperating with bin Laden was "weak," adding that bin Laden "resented the secularism of Saddam Hussein's regime."

The 9/11 Commission reported that the administration was focused on Saddam from the start, finding that on September 15, four days after the attack, at the first Camp David strategy session about responding to the attack, Deputy Defense Secretary Paul Wolfowitz "made the case for striking Iraq during 'this round' of the war on terrorism." Two days later, Wolfowitz wrote a memo to Secretary Rumsfeld arguing that if there were "even a 10 percent chance that Saddam Hussein was behind the 9/11 attacks, maximum priority should be placed on eliminating that threat." In January 2002 President Bush, in his State of the Union Address, linked Iraq, Iran, and North Korea in an "axis of evil" that threatened the world. Secretary Rumsfeld was quoted as saying at a February 1, 2002, National Security Council meeting that "what we really want to think about is going after Saddam." President Bush's Treasury secretary Paul O'Neill has written that "from the start we were building the case against Saddam. . . . It was all about finding a way to do it."

Waging a war on a country that was not involved in the 9/11 attack on us, a country with a standing army, possibly weapons of mass destruction, and an unpredictable dictator, and that was not threatening us was a dangerous and unwise strategy and a distraction from the job at hand; it could also destabilize the Middle East. One thing was clear to me: Saddam was not going to commit suicide by initiating an attack against us. He was a survivalist, desperate to cling to power.

But President Bush was intent on convincing a majority in Congress and the American people that invading Iraq and toppling Saddam was essential to our security. To do this, he and his administration conjured up a series of misleading and inaccurate statements to persuade the public of two points: that Saddam had aided and abetted the 9/11 hijackers and that he possessed weapons of mass destruction.

Misleading the Nation on Saddam and 9/11

President Bush, Vice President Cheney, and other administration officials repeatedly made statements that Saddam and al-Qaeda were allies and had an operational relationship with each other. On February 6, 2003, Wolfowitz said that "Saddam's connection with terrorists started some ten years ago and with al-Qaeda are still growing every day." President Bush said on May 1, 2003, and repeated the next day that Iraq and al-Qaeda were "allies" even though the CIA and the 9/11 Commission said that Iraq and al-Qaeda were "independent actors." According to Vice President Cheney, the "best source" of information about the Iraq/al-Qaeda relationship was an assessment in a memo by Doug Feith, undersecretary of defense for policy, that claimed that "bin Laden and Saddam had an operational relationship from the 1990s to 2003," ignoring the explicit CIA determination that there was no "operational relationship" between the two. CIA director George Tenet, in his 2007 book, *At the Center of the Storm: My Years at the CIA*, noted that "much of the material in the (Feith) memo was the kind of cherry picked, selective data that Feith, Libby [Vice President Cheney's chief of staff], and others had been enamored with for so long."

Immediately after 9/11 we asked our allies for any intelligence they had on the movements and meetings of the nineteen hijackers. A few weeks later, the intelligence service in the Czech Republic reported that a "source" thought he had seen, from some distance, someone who looked like hijacker Mohammed Atta meeting with a known Iraqi intelligence officer in Prague in April 2001. There was no other confirmation of that meeting, and the CIA always doubted the report's credibility. Czech officials themselves doubted the accuracy of the report and specifically came to Washington, D.C., to tell us so. Nonetheless, Vice President Cheney and others repeatedly cited the report as evidence that

Saddam had been involved in the 9/11 attack. Cheney appeared on *60 Minutes* on November 14, 2001, saying that "I know that [Atta] was in Prague in April of this year" meeting with the Iraqi Intelligence Service. And then on December 9, 2001, Cheney told journalist Tim Russert that "it's been pretty well confirmed that he [Atta] did go to Prague and he did meet with a senior official of the Iraqi intelligence service in Czechoslovakia last April, several months before the attack." Far from being "pretty well confirmed," the only evidence that such a meeting took place was an early unsubstantiated Czech report that the Czech themselves and the CIA dismissed. In fact there was strong evidence that no such meeting took place, including travel and other records that indicated that Atta was in the United States at the time of the purported meeting in Prague.

Vice President Cheney subsequently tried to blur the fact that he had advocated for the accuracy of the unsubstantiated report. When pressed by Gloria Borger on June 17, 2004, Cheney first denied "absolutely" that he ever said that the meeting was "pretty well confirmed," although that's verbatim what he had said. He then proceeded to a new, clearly contrived, misleading formulation by saying, "What I said was the Czech intelligence service reported after 9/11 that Atta had been in Prague on April 9th of 2001, where he allegedly met with an Iraqi intelligence official. We have never been able to confirm that nor have we been able to knock it down, we just don't know."

But the contrivance falls apart because it was also factually wrong. First of all, the Czechs never "claimed" that there was a meeting. They had said early on that there was an unconfirmed report but had later even made a special trip to the United States to tell the State Department (and me) that the report was unreliable.

Second, the CIA's official position was that it had "serious doubts" about the report's accuracy and that it was "unlikely" that the meeting took place. I later pressed President Obama's CIA director, John Brennan, very hard about this issue, and he finally wrote me on March 13, 2014, in a still partially redacted letter in which he said that prior to our attack on March 19, 2003, CIA headquarters had received a communication from the field responding to a request that the field look into a single source intelligence report indicating that Mohammed Atta met with former Iraqi intelligence officer al Ani in Prague in April 2001. In that communication, the field expressed significant concern regarding the possibility of an official public statement by the United States government indicating that such a meeting took place. The communication noted that information received after the single source report raised serious doubts about that report's accuracy. . . . The field added that to its knowledge "there is not one USG [counterterrorism] or FBI expert that has said they have evidence that Atta was indeed in Prague. In fact, the analysis has been quite the opposite."

It got worse. Despite the clarity of the CIA letter, the administration kept the pressure on the Czech government to confirm that a meeting took place. Jiri Ruzek, head of the Czech counterintelligence service, wrote in his memoir about U.S. pressure on the Czech government to confirm the Atta meeting, and he chillingly noted that "the Americans wanted us to mine certainty from unconfirmed suspicion and use it as an excuse for military action."

To counter or challenge the work of the CIA and other intelligence agencies, Secretary of Defense Donald Rumsfeld in the fall of 2001 had set up a small intelligence shop at the Pentagon under the direction of Doug Feith, undersecretary of defense for policy, which had as its mission making a case for war against Iraq. Feith, who had a lengthy history of advocating for Saddam's removal and in 1998 had signed a letter urging President Clinton to use force to oust Saddam, set about scouring intelligence reports for any connections between Iraq and al-Qaeda.

In the summer of 2002, Feith's small group prepared a classified briefing on Iraq's connection to terror, highlighting the alleged Atta-Saddam intelligence meeting in Prague. The briefing, accompanied by a PowerPoint presentation, was given to Secretary Rumsfeld, the Office of the Vice President, and the National Security Council. An altered presentation that differed significantly on at least thirty points was given to the CIA. A number of slides that were provided to Vice President Cheney were omitted from Feith's presentation to the CIA, including a slide titled "Fundamental Problems with How Intelligence Community Is Assessing Information" (since declassified at my request), which criticized the intelligence community's assessment of the relationship between Iraq and al-Qaeda. Feith later acknowledged to my Senate Armed Services Committee that he had added two slides about Atta for the presentations to Rumsfeld and Cheney's office but had not included them in the presentation to the CIA (which doubted the Atta story). Two of the missing slides remained classified. CIA director George Tenet first learned about Feith's differing slideshows when I informed him during a later hearing.

Tenet would write that "intelligence was obtained that proved beyond any doubt that the man seen meeting with the member of the Iraq intelligence service in Prague in 2001 was *not* Mohammed Atta" and that administration figures "sought to create a connection between Iraq and the 9/11 attacks that would have made WMD, the United Nations, and the international community absolutely irrelevant. The first problem is that case was never, ever true." He added: "Let me say it again: CIA found absolutely no linkage between Saddam and 9/11."

Similarly, the Department of Defense Inspector General in February 2007 delivered a report on the pre–Iraqi war activities of Feith's office and confirmed what I had alleged: that the briefing slides produced by Feith's office for the president and vice president falsely represented that there was a "known contact" between Atta and the Iraqi Intelligence Service. The Inspector General found that the intelligence about the alleged meeting "was at least contradictory, but by no means a 'known contact,'" and characterized the meeting as "highly unlikely." The Inspector General also found that Feith's office "inappropriately developed, produced, and disseminated to senior decision-makers alternative intelligence assessments on the Iraq and al-Qaeda relationship which included some conclusions that were inconsistent with the consensus of the Intelligence Community." But that supposed linkage, made in statements by President Bush and Secretary Rice, promoted by the Cheney-Rumsfeld-Feith doctored briefings, helped lead a majority of Americans to believe that Saddam was complicit in 9/11 and that this justified going to war. Had I believed Saddam had aided and abetted the 9/11 attack on us, I, too, would have voted to attack Iraq.

Misleading the Nation on WMD

In addition to their misrepresentations that Saddam was involved in bin Laden's 9/11 attack on us, the administration focused heavily on the allegation that Iraq was secretly developing weapons of mass destruction (WMD), which was prohibited by the United Nations after the First Gulf War in 1991. The United Nations and coalition forces had destroyed all of Iraq's chemical and biological weapons that could be found after the 1991 war, including laboratories where Iraqi scientists were trying to develop nuclear, biological, and chemical weapons. Inspectors from the United Nations supervised the destruction of Iraq's WMD programs and watched for any signs of any new WMD. But the inspectors were forced out of Iraq in 1998, and subsequent to that, the CIA had had no human intelligence assets in Iraq. It was unknown whether Saddam was still trying to produce such weapons, though he insinuated through various covert and overt methods that he did possess them, most likely as a deterrent to attack from his neighbors, including Iran, Syria, and Israel.

I thought it likely he had WMD, but unless there is a threat that such weapons will be used against us, possession alone is not sufficient justification for attacking another country. Russia, Pakistan, and India all have WMD, but we didn't attack Russia because of that nor do Pakistan and India attack each other because of possession of WMD.

Notwithstanding the uncertainties revolving around Saddam's WMD program, in August 2002, Vice President Cheney told a Veterans of Foreign Wars convention, "Simply stated there is no doubt that Saddam Hussein now has weapons of mass destruction. There is no doubt he is amassing them to use against our friends, against our allies, and against us." President Bush also pressed the point in a national radio address in September 2002 when he said, "The Iraqi regime possesses biological and chemical weapons, is rebuilding the facilities to make more, and, according to the British government, could launch a biological or chemical attack in as little as forty-five minutes after the order is given. This regime is seeking a nuclear bomb, and with fissile material could build one within a year." What the American people were not told, of course, was that just three weeks before Bush's radio address, in early September, CIA director George Tenet told the Senate Intelligence Committee that there was no National Intelligence Estimate on Iraq's weapons of mass destruction.

National Security Advisor Condoleezza Rice also told the *New York Times* that same September that some "aluminum tubes" had been seen in satellite surveillance photos of Iraq. Those tubes "are only suitable for nuclear weapons programs, centrifuge programs," she said. She continued with her most dramatic comment of all: "We don't want the smoking gun to be a mushroom cloud." She made that statement that the tubes were "only suitable for nuclear weapons" despite the fact that the experts at our Department of Energy said in classified assessments that the aluminum tubes were not suitable for nuclear centrifuges but were consistent with rocket construction—Iraq's explanation for having them.

On September 4, 2002, as chairman of the Senate Armed Services Committee, I attended a meeting in the White House Cabinet Room with President George Bush, Vice President Richard Cheney, National Security Advisor Condoleezza Rice, Senate Majority Leader Tom Daschle, Senate Minority Leader Trent Lott, and several Senate committee chairmen and ranking Republicans, including the senior Republican on the SASC, John Warner. The topic for discussion was whether to initiate military action against Iraq. It was our first chance to ask the president direct questions about his intentions toward Iraq.

Bush gave very passionate remarks about the threat and assured us that he would seek congressional support and approval before moving forward to attack Iraq. He then opened the meeting to discussion. That assurance seemed to take the steam out of most of the congressional members. For instance, Joe Biden told the president that "we're with you and we're going to do everything we can to support you."

The issue for me, I said to President Bush, was whether, based on the information we had, there was sufficient justification to attack Iraq. Everyone conceded that Saddam was a monstrous dictator. But that didn't answer many questions: Did he have any role in the 9/11 attack on us? Did he have weapons of mass destruction? If he did, was he threatening to use them against us in the absence of our attacking him first? If we attacked, what would be the effect on the Middle East? I stated my belief that Saddam was not suicidal but interested only in his own survival and was unlikely to attack us since that would lead to his own destruction.

President Bush responded to me in a general way but didn't specifically address the questions that needed to be answered. I also urged the president to consult with senior military leaders, a number of whom I knew had concerns about invading Iraq. I said, "Mr. President, you need to hear from many of them directly." He kind of bristled but implied that he would do it or was planning to do it. I left feeling that I had also touched on some key concerns, including the possibility of large numbers of American casualties, the impact on the Middle East, and the need for an exit strategy. After the meeting, I had a chance to briefly chat further with the president. He seemed willing to hear from senior military leaders, and he assured me he really did welcome intellectual debate. That was the best thing I heard him say, and I later shared the conversation with several of the Joint Chiefs. I told them that I directly urged the president to consult with them and that he said he would welcome varying opinions. I encouraged the Chiefs to give him theirs individually so that the president heard not just from the chairman. I told them I hoped they'd get to sit down with the president and not have their opinions filtered by the vice president or secretary of defense or their neo-con ideologically driven staffs. Senator John Warner told me my remarks at the meeting with the president were on target. I knew John also had a lot of questions, but I thought in the end he would support the president.

Interestingly, neither Vice President Cheney, who sat across from the president through the meeting, nor National Security Advisor Condoleezza Rice was called on or spoke during the meeting. Secretaries Rumsfeld and Colin Powell did not attend the meeting.

When the Democratic chairs of Senate committees sat down for lunch shortly after the meeting at the White House, Senate Majority Leader Tom

Daschle told the group that I'd raised valid issues with President Bush and that discussions with the White House should be about far more than process. Senator Daschle said he was skeptical about initiating the war. He said there had been eleven hearings before the first Gulf War Authorizing Resolution in 1991, and there should definitely be many hearings now. As always, Tom Daschle was thoughtful, considerate, and receptive to the ideas of others, which helped make him such a great leader.

Shortly thereafter, I chaired the Senate informal briefing with Secretary Rumsfeld. I asked Rumsfeld whether in the previous thirty days there was anything new about Saddam seeking a nuclear weapon. I wanted to pin that down so the administration couldn't claim that there was new information that justified war with Iraq. Rumsfeld answered that he knew of no new information or intelligence.

Barbara asked me whether I thought President Bush was motivated by Iraqi oil reserves. I told her that I thought that oil might be a partial motive but that President Bush was more likely motivated by his desire to finish the business his father had left undone, and perhaps also by the allegation that Saddam had tried to kill his father. Ironically, President George H. W. Bush's advisors, including his secretary of state, James Baker, were more cautious about going to war with Saddam than were President George W.'s advisors.

On October 7, 2002, President Bush addressed the nation from Cincinnati about the threat posed by Iraq. Senate Joint Resolution 45 to authorize military action against Iraq was up for debate a few days later. I offered an amendment proposing an alternative, titled "The Multilateral Use of Force Authorization Act of 2002." My amendment required President Bush to seek support from the U.N. Security Council before attacking Iraq, while affirming that at all times the United States had the inherent right to use military force in self-defense. I urged that a multilateral approach with a coalition of other nations was critical to reduce the potential for instability in an already volatile region. A multilateral approach—as opposed to acting essentially on our own—would increase the number of nations willing to help us if we went to war by providing bases for our troops, allowing flights over their air space, and dealing with the internal security problems afterward. I told my colleagues that we would also avoid setting a precedent of initiating a war without facing an imminent threat. If we failed at the United Nations, then under my amendment the president could call us back into session and urge us to adopt a "unilateral" resolution. I included in my amendment an expedited process to ensure a vote by preventing a filibuster. My amendment failed, 24–75. The resolution authorizing the unilateral approach of the president then passed by about the same margin.

On November 8, 2002, the U.N. Security Council adopted Resolution 1441, which set up an enhanced inspection regime requiring Iraq to provide the United Nations Monitoring, Verification and Inspection Commission (UNMOVIC) and the International Atomic Energy Agency (IAEA) "immediate, unimpeded, unconditional, and unrestricted access to any and all, including underground, areas, facilities, buildings, equipment, records, and means of transport which they wish to inspect, as well as immediate, unimpeded, unrestricted and private access to all officials and other persons whom UNMOVIC or the IAEA wish to interview." The resolution contained various milestones including a report on the status of inspections to the U.N. Security Council sixty days after the inspections began, estimated to be January 27, 2003. Over Congress's holiday break I met with Hans Blix and some of his team at the United Nations. I then urged the Bush administration to give U.N. inspectors time to do their job looking for WMD in Iraq.

On January 9, 2003, as the Senate returned to begin the 108th Congress, I spoke on the Senate floor about Iraq. I reminded senators that the U.N. inspectors were due to release a report about the status of the inspections on January 27 and that we should withhold drawing any conclusions because there were still many suspect WMD sites in Iraq that were not yet examined. I said the "updates" to be provided by UNMOVIC and the IAEA were intended as interim reports. They were not final conclusions, and more updates would come over the next several months. I said that our own Intelligence Community had just begun to share some of the large amount of information that we had relative to suspect WMD sites. I told my colleagues that Iraq was complying with U.N. Resolution 1441. Iraq was required to accept the resolution within seven days, and it had done so on November 13, the fifth day. Iraq was required to provide a full declaration of its WMD programs within thirty days, and it had provided what it said was a full declaration on December 7, the twenty-ninth day. UNMOVIC and IAEA were to start their inspections within forty-five days of the November 8 U.N. Resolution, and they began their inspections on November 25, almost three weeks earlier than required. UNMOVIC and IAEA were to provide an update on their inspections to the U.N. Security Council within sixty days after inspections commenced, and they planned to do so on January 27, 2003. There was no foot-dragging at the United Nations or by Iraq.

I went on to report additional evidence that Iraq was complying and that the United Nations was able to do its inspections. I noted that on December 19, British foreign secretary Jack Straw had commented on Iraq's declaration and apparent willingness to cooperate with U.N. inspectors, saying that "what we've got today is a further step in a very calm and deliberate process to try by every means possible to get Iraq to comply with its international obligations peacefully and therefore and thereby to resolve this crisis in a peaceful manner."

On December 31, 2002, President Bush had seemed to agree, saying he hoped the Iraq situation would be resolved peacefully. "You said we're heading to war in Iraq," President Bush responded to a reporter. "I don't know why you say that. I hope we're not headed to war in Iraq." On that same day, U.N. secretary general Kofi Annan talked about the U.N. inspectors, saying, "Obviously, they are carrying out their work and in the meantime Iraq is cooperating and they are able to do their work in an unimpeded manner, therefore I don't see an argument for a military action now."

I told my colleagues that January 27 should not be considered as some kind of deadline to decide about attacking Iraq. The inspection process was in motion and was being complied with by Iraq. And, significantly, at the time, the United States and other nations with sophisticated intelligence capabilities about possible WMD sites had only just begun to share intelligence with the arms inspectors. They were proceeding cautiously in sharing their information due to suspicions that Iraqis had, in the 1990s, infiltrated the United Nations Special Commission on Iraq.

"We need to give the inspectors time needed to complete their work," I said on the Senate floor. "In the meantime, we need to provide targeted intelligence to the inspectors to facilitate their effort, without disclosing sources and methods. That is our best chance of bringing about Iraq's voluntary disarmament or, failing that, obtaining broad international backing, including United Nations authorization for a multilateral effort to forcibly disarm Iraq." I added that "if we prejudge the outcome of inspections or if we don't furnish the arms inspectors with targeted intelligence, we will not be able to obtain the international support, as represented by a U.N. authorization for the use of force that is so highly desirable and advantageous to us."

On January 28, 2003, President Bush delivered his State of the Union speech, in which he said that the British government learned that Iraq had recently sought significant quantities of uranium ("yellowcake") from Africa. We found out later the story had been cut from an earlier address on October 6, 2002, after the CIA warned National Security Advisor Stephen Hadley that the evidence was not solid because it was based on documents delivered to the U.S. embassy in Rome that purported to represent a contract between the governments of Niger and Iraq for the delivery of yellowcake that appeared to be forgeries. Our State Department was also so "highly dubious" that our intelligence experts in fact had communicated their doubts to their British counterparts, and the IAEA concluded they were forgeries.

CIA director George Tenet confirmed later that CIA staff had reviewed the yellowcake portions of the speech and had "raised several concerns about the fragmentary nature of the intelligence with National Security Council colleagues" that had led to the deletion of the allegation from President Bush's October 6 speech. The carefully and purposefully selected words in the January 28, 2003, State of the Union created the impression that the United States believed that the British allegation was true when in fact the opposite was true. (And, we had actually informed the British that we were highly dubious about it.) The American public was being misled, and the deception was perpetrated in relation to the most important issue a president and a nation face—whether to go to war—in the most important speech the president makes each year, the State of the Union. It later was revealed that neither President Bush nor National Security Advisor Rice had read the State Department report that called the yellowcake story "highly dubious." I don't know if that makes the matter more or less disturbing.

The president's State of the Union speech also represented that Iraq had "attempted to purchase aluminum tubes suitable for nuclear weapons production" according to "our intelligence sources," although our agency, which was the most capable of making such a critical assessment, disagreed.

The disinformation campaign about Iraq worked. A Gallup Poll in early 2003 found that 52 percent of Americans supported attacking Iraq. News about the hunt for bin Laden was scarce, but the administration was whipping up new headlines about what they said were serious threats against us by Saddam Hussein.

In July 2003, Joe Wilson, the diplomat who had been sent to Niger to investigate the yellowcake story, wrote an op-ed in the *New York Times* headlined "What I Didn't Find in Africa." Wilson wrote that he was surprised that the president had raised the discredited yellowcake story in the State of the Union speech. Based on his experience with the Bush administration leading up to the Iraq War, Wilson said, he had "little choice but to conclude that some of the intelligence related to Iraq's nuclear weapons program was twisted to exaggerate the Iraqi threat." About eight days later, "two senior Administration officials" leaked to conservative columnist Robert Novak that Wilson's wife, Valerie Plame, was a CIA operative and implied that she had arranged for her husband to get the assignment to Niger, as if it were some kind of taxpayer-funded boondoggle. "Outing" a CIA operative is a serious act and is dangerous not only to the individual who is outed but also to the United States. The outing of Valerie Plame showed just how far some people in the administration would go in order to push their narrative of the "imminent" threat that Iraq posed.

On February 5, 2003, Secretary of State Colin Powell spoke before the U.N. Security Council on the dangers posed by Iraq. His presentation included satellite imagery that suggested Iraq was deceiving the world. He said, "My colleagues, every statement I make today is backed up by sources, solid sources. These are not assertions. What we're giving you are facts and conclusions based on solid intelligence." The 2004 bipartisan report by the Senate Select Committee on Intelligence concluded: "Much of the information provided or cleared by the Central Intelligence Agency (CIA) for inclusion in Secretary Powell's speech to the U.N. was overstated, misleading, or incorrect. Intrusive and effective U.N. inspections were the only way to resolve this crisis peacefully. It was important for the U.S. to support the U.N. inspectors as long as they were unimpeded in their work."

Prior to the war, the CIA had identified 550 sites in Iraq as possibly having WMD or prohibited WMD materials or equipment. Of these "suspect sites," 150 were called "top suspect sites," where the CIA believed it would be most likely to find such items. The 150 top suspect sites were divided into three categories: high, medium, and low priority with 105 of the sites being either high or medium priority. At two public hearings in January 2003, I pressed Director Tenet on the issue of how many high or medium priority suspect WMD sites as identified by us had not yet been shared with the U.N. inspectors. Tenet testified that "as I said yesterday, we have briefed all of these high value and moderate value sites to UNMOVIC and the IAEA."

He didn't say "some" or "most" of such sites; he said "all." That was false, and I confronted Tenet at both of those hearings. National Security Advisor Condoleezza Rice made the same false statement in a letter to me: "United Nations inspectors have been briefed on every high or medium priority weapons of mass destruction, missile and UAV-related site the U.S. Intelligence Community has identified." At the hearings, where I contested the administration statements, I referenced classified intelligence reports showing a significant number of high- and mid-level suspect sites that had not been shared with the United Nations. I couldn't say publicly what that specific number was because it was classified, but I could and did say that Director Tenet and National Security Advisor Rice were giving false information to the American public in their effort to support the administration's rush to war against Iraq.

In January 2004, after the war began, the CIA finally declassified the number of "high and medium priority 'top suspect' WMD sites" that had been shared with U.N. inspectors before the war. The CIA acknowledged that 21 of the 105 high and medium priority suspect sites on the agency's list were not shared with the United Nations. So, ironically, it wasn't Iraq but the United States that was hiding potential WMD sites from U.N. inspectors. The Republican-led Senate Intelligence Committee's report on prewar intelligence on Iraq confirmed my claim that George Tenet's repeated representations of having shared "all" high and medium priority suspect sites with the United Nations were false. It said, "Public pronouncements by Administration officials that the Central Intelligence Agency had shared information on all high and moderate priority suspect sites with United Nations inspectors were factually incorrect."

I could only speculate on Tenet's motive. Honest answers by him might have undermined the false sense of urgency for proceeding to war. We rely on our intelligence agencies to give us the facts, not to give us their spin on the facts. The accuracy and objectivity of intelligence should never again be gamed or slanted or misrepresented to support a particular policy as it was before the Iraq War.

Days before the invasion, the White House was acting to undermine a CIA finding that raised doubt about Iraq being a nuclear threat to us. The Senate Intelligence Committee chair, Bob Graham, and I were able to get the CIA to authorize release of testimony I had solicited from CIA deputy director John McLaughlin that Saddam would not use WMD against us unless he was attacked first and felt his back was against the wall. We sent the declassified testimony to the New York Times, whose reporter called Condoleezza Rice for comment. She instead called Director Tenet and asked him to urgently call the paper to say there was "nothing new" in the CIA statement. Tenet did as he was asked. The New York Times ran the story about McLaughlin's testimony on the front page despite Tenet's comment, but Tenet's comment took some punch out of the story. The motivation for this effort became obvious when President Bush addressed the nation just days later on March 17 saying that unless Saddam left Iraq within hours, we would attack him within days. Tenet would later acknowledge in his 2007 book that it was a mistake for him to have called the *New York Times*.

Against the War

I spoke to the Senate as to why I thought President Bush's decision to proceed to war was unwise. I said that an attack on Iraq without broad support or without the support of the United Nations would "stoke the terrorism that was our number one threat." I said that without the support of other countries in the region we would increase the risk to our troops because we would have fewer overflight rights and supply routes. It would also make it "less likely that other nations would join us in the difficult task of providing stability in reconstructing Iraq in the aftermath." His argument that Saddam had failed to comply with the U.N. Resolution calling on Iraq to disarm wasn't credible, I added, since it was our action that ended the U.N. inspections that were going well, and it was the United States who pulled the plug on a U.N. vote. The completion of the work of the U.N. weapons inspectors was of critical importance relative to whether Saddam in fact had WMD. But when the president decided to move ahead with war plans, the United Nations had to withdraw its inspectors for their safety.

I told the Senate that "if there were an imminent threat against us, we would not—and should not—hesitate to use force. But attacking in the absence of an immediate threat is a very different scenario with very different risks." I reminded my colleagues in the days leading up to the war, that the Bush administration had at various times used divisive rhetoric and a denigrating attitude toward the views of other nations whose support we said we would seek. Countries were told "you are either with us or against us." The United Nations was told that while we welcomed U.N. endorsement, we would be just fine without it. The U.N. inspectors were referred to by Bush officials as "so-called" inspectors, and even before their inspections began their efforts were characterized as useless. This kind of rhetoric alienated our friends and fueled the inflammatory propaganda of our enemies. The United States came across as bullying and domineering.

I also reminded my colleagues in those remarks that while "we will prevail militarily in Iraq on our own, we need the eyes and ears of people around the world and the intelligence capabilities of other countries if we are going to detect and ferret out, deter and destroy those who care nothing for human life or international law or accept the rules of war. Historically, America has been strongest when we found common cause with other nations in pursuit of common goals. The path to a safer world and a more secure America has rarely come from a go-it-alone approach."

The administration's claim that the country we were about to attack had aided and abetted the 9/11 attack on us was false, but it was part of a deceptive narrative the American people came to believe. By the time our invasion began on March 17, 2003, upward of 70 percent of the American people believed that Saddam had played a role in 9/11 and that Iraq represented a threat to attack us.

We were going to war, and I felt it was important for our troops to know that even those of us who opposed the war supported them. So, I concluded my remarks to the Senate as follows:

President Bush has now decided to end the diplomatic effort. Those of us who have questioned the administration's approach, including this Senator, will now be rallying behind the men and women of our armed forces to give them the full support they deserve, as it seems certain we will soon be at war.

Last October a majority of both Houses of Congress voted to authorize the President to use military force with or without the authority of the United Nations. While I disagreed with that decision and offered an alternative, the overriding fact is that this democracy functions through debate and decision. The decision to give the President wide authority was democratically arrived at.

The courageous men and women whom we send into harm's way are not just carrying out their orders with bravery and the highest form of professionalism. They are also implementing the outcome of the democratic debate which this Nation protects and honors. Those men and women should know that they have the full support and the fervent prayers of all the American people as they carry out their missions.

On March 19, 2003, Operation Iraqi Freedom began with a massive bombing campaign and an invasion by more than 100,000 troops. As of 2016 more than 4,300 U.S troops were either killed in action or died of other causes in Iraq, and more than 32,000 were wounded. The estimate of Iraqi dead by the World Health Organization was 150,000. The cost to the United States is estimated to be nearly $2 trillion, not to mention the political instability the Iraq War brought to the Middle East including the growth of terrorism and the rise of ISIS.

One of the most absurd claims about our entry into the war was made by President Bush when, solemnly addressing the nation on March 19, 2003, to announce that military operations against Iraq had begun, he said that "our nation enters the conflict reluctantly." Reluctantly? When within days after 9/11 and fully aware that the perpetrator was al-Qaeda in Afghanistan, top administration officials focused on looking for a path to attack Iraq?

Reluctantly, when for the following fifteen months the president and his advisors proceeded to ignore our own intelligence assessments and concocted evidence in a concerted effort to persuade our people that Iraq was involved in the horrific attack on us on 9/11 and was an ally of the murderers?

Reluctantly, when the president and his top advisors purposely created the false impression that Iraq was seeking nuclear weapons–grade uranium in Africa?

Reluctantly, when the president and his top advisors made speeches invoking a false fear that Iraq was an imminent threat?

Reluctantly, when the president said we must address Iraq's "weapons of mass murder" now so that we do not have to deal with "them later with our own firefighters and police and doctors in the streets of our cities"?

Reluctantly, when the specter of Iraq attacking us with WMD was concocted by using false reports about Iraq seeking aluminum tubes for nuclear weapons production?

No, there was nothing "reluctant" about the Bush administration's push for war against Iraq. It was the opposite, in fact, when President Bush's secretary of defense created a special policy office in the Pentagon to provide an alternate intelligence picture, looking at Iraq through neo-con glasses, in order to undermine the CIA's assessments and promote public support for the war.

There was nothing reluctant about the Bush administration's decision to fire their Army Chief of Staff, General Eric Shinseki, after he honestly answered my question at a hearing by saying that it would take many more troops to occupy Iraq than what the administration was planning on.

There was nothing reluctant about the administration's statements that the invasion of Iraq would be a "cakewalk" or that the war itself would cost just $80 billion plus $20 billion for the restoration of Baghdad, the estimate given on March 16, 2003, by Vice President Cheney on *Meet the Press*. The reality was quite different. Brown University estimated war costs for 2003–2010 at $1.1 trillion, and Joseph Stiglitz, recipient of the Nobel Prize in Economics, estimated the cost at $3.3 trillion.

There was nothing reluctant about Tenet and Rice representing that we had shared with the United Nations information on all the high and medium suspect Iraqi WMD sites when we hadn't.

There was nothing reluctant about the administration's cutting off U.N. inspectors from finishing their work in Iraq that had been proceeding without interference from Iraq.

No, the decision to launch an attack against Iraq wasn't made reluctantly; the march to war against Iraq was consciously and aggressively orchestrated, step by step.

Perhaps President Bush engaged in the kind of deception in which presidents before him had engaged when going to war by representing to the American public that we were responding with force only after we were attacked or were threatened with an imminent attack. Presidential deception preceded the Mexican War, the Spanish-American War, and the Vietnam War. Perhaps President Bush, unlike his vice president and top advisors, who were obviously determined to take our country to war against Iraq, engaged in self-deception.

If so, it was a deception that led the American people to believe in a war that most would later regret.

Iraqi Responsibility

After the main fighting ended, I became deeply involved in the effort to force the Iraqis to settle their internal political divisions so that the violence and instability that erupted in the aftermath could be ended. To help achieve those goals, the Iraqi government committed to pass legislation that would mandate power sharing among warring factions, to share resources fairly within the country, to make needed amendments to the Iraqi constitution, and to hold provincial elections. By July 2007 the Iraqi government had kept none of those commitments and so I, along with Jack Reed, introduced at that time a bipartisan amendment with the aim of forcing Iraqi political leaders to take responsibility for their own country so that we could begin to bring our troops home.

Our amendment required the president to begin reducing the number of U.S. forces in four months and to remove most of our forces within nine months after enactment of our amendment, leaving enough of our troops to maintain counterterrorism activities, to train the Iraqis, and to protect U.S. assets in Iraq. In my remarks to the Senate on July 17, 2007, prior to the vote to end the filibuster on our amendment, I said that month after month and year after year the president had "touted progress in Iraq and called for patience" in what I characterized as a "litany of delusion." I quoted the president's words in September 2004 when he said that "we were making steady progress in completing the mission so that . . . American troops can come home." In April 2005 President Bush said, "I believe we're really making progress in Iraq," and in October 2005 the president said that "Iraq has made incredible political progress." In November 2005 the president said Iraqis are making "inspiring progress towards building a democracy," and in June 2007 the White House said that the Iraqi security forces are "growing in number, becoming more capable and coming closer to the day when they can assume responsibility for defending their own country."

The argument for our amendment was that that day would never come unless, as I said to the Senate, we acted to "force the Iraqi political leaders to take responsibility for their own country and to keep the commitments they made to meet the political benchmarks that they set and to make the compromises that only they can make." I argued that "while our troops have done everything and more of what has been asked of them, while they have risked their all and given their all, the Iraqi political leaders remained frozen by their own history, unwilling to take the political risks that only they can take." I added that the only hope of pressuring Iraqi leaders to take some risks was for the Senate to adopt "a timetable to begin reducing American forces to a more limited support mission instead of being everybody's target." I concluded: "After more than four years, over 3,600 U.S. deaths, seven times that many wounded, and expenditures of $10 billion a month that we are borrowing from the future to finance this war in Iraq, the President's pleas for patience not only have a hollow ring, it is exactly the wrong message to the Iraqi leaders."

The opponents of the Levin-Reed amendment filibustered it, and although 52 senators supported it, including four Republicans and three Democrats (Biden, Clinton, and Obama) who would later run for president, it was defeated. (We needed 60 votes to end debate under the filibuster rules.) I believe our amendment did help to get the Bush administration to begin putting some pressure on the Iraqi government, which it finally did. When President Obama came to office in 2009, he established timetables, and combat troops departed Iraq in the middle of the second year of his presidency.

I knew that Vice President Biden was a strong voice in the administration to stick with a combat troop reduction schedule. I was confident of that based on press reports of Biden's position but also because of a conversation that I had with him in October 2010 at the White House at the end of which he loaned me a book that he highly recommended by Gordon Goldstein titled *Lessons in Disaster*. The book, which was heavily underlined by Vice President Biden, describes the tragedy of Vietnam and how President Kennedy refused to Americanize the war by sending in large numbers of combat forces. The book then describes how that policy changed after Kennedy's assassination and how

President Johnson, unlike Kennedy, followed the recommendations of advisors who were well intended but whose views reflected hubris and arrogance.

The aftermath of the Iraq war is still with us. Looking back, I saw my job at the time as, first, trying to avoid the war by pressing for the completion of U.N. inspections; second, pressing the administration in numerous ways to obtain international support for going to war should the president decide to do that; third, showing not only how the administration's justification to the public for attacking Iraq was based on flawed intelligence but how accurate intelligence can be exaggerated or distorted or ignored and the way false statements were made about that intelligence, all to support the administration's decision to initiate the war; fourth, once the war began, fully supporting our troops and providing them with the equipment and support they would need to prevail; fifth, looking for ways to shift responsibility for Iraq's recovery to the Iraqi government and the Iraqi people; and sixth, doing what I could to hold those who misled us into war to some degree of accountability for their decisions, the negative consequences of which will be felt for generations.

My parents, Bess and Saul Levin, as a young couple.

Brother Sandy, sister Hannah, and me. Detroit, 1937.

Sandy and me. Detroit, May 1945.

Hannah's wedding. Sandy, Hannah, and me, 1950.

Swarthmore College, 1954.

The motorcycle I bought, rode, and cracked up in Europe. I brought it back to the United States to be fixed. Detroit, 1955. (HS19734, Carl M. Levin Papers, Bentley Historical Library, University of Michigan)

My parents and me during a trip to Europe, 1959.

My family and me riding bikes in our Green Acres neighborhood. Detroit, 1969.

City Council days. Detroit, circa 1970.

Our daughters. *Left to right*: Erica, Kate, and Laura, 1973.

Taking on HUD. Detroit, 1975.

Marching with Father Bill Cunningham and the Focus: HOPE "Walk for Justice."
Detroit, 1976. (Photo by John Collier)

Barbara and me at our house on Capitol Hill. Washington, D.C., 1980s. (HS19588, Carl M. Levin Papers, Bentley Historical Library, University of Michigan)

UAW president Doug Fraser, President Jimmy Carter, and me at the White House after the signing of the Chrysler loan guarantee legislation, January 7, 1980. (HS19596, Carl M. Levin Papers, Bentley Historical Library, University of Michigan)

Visiting with Missy Jablonksi, the 1981 National Poster Child for the March of Dimes Birth Defects Foundation. Courtesy of the March of Dimes Birth Defects Foundation. (HS19598, Carl M. Levin Papers, Bentley Historical Library, University of Michigan)

Visiting a Cambodian refugee camp in Thailand, 1980. (HS19595, Carl M. Levin Papers, Bentley Historical Library, University of Michigan)

One-on-one with Anwar Sadat, president of Egypt, at his home in Alexandria, 1981.

Greeting Menachem Begin, prime minister of Israel. Washington, D.C., early 1980s. (HS19597, Carl M. Levin Papers, Bentley Historical Library, University of Michigan)

With Senators Alan Simpson, Bill Cohen, and Sam Nunn in Moscow, 1980s. (HS19638, Carl M. Levin Papers, Bentley Historical Library, University of Michigan)

Taking a chunk of the Berlin Wall, just after it was opened, December 1989. (HS19611, Carl M. Levin Papers, Bentley Historical Library, University of Michigan)

Greeting Russian president Boris Yeltsin at the Library of Congress reception, June 1992. (HS19636, Carl M. Levin Papers, Bentley Historical Library, University of Michigan)

Meeting Vaclav Havel, president of Czechoslovakia, on his visit to the United States with Senators George Mitchell, Ernest Hollings, and Claiborne Pell, September 1998. (HS19637, Carl M. Levin Papers, Bentley Historical Library, University of Michigan)

Presenting President Reagan with his college yearbook, which I had purchased at an auction. (He didn't have a copy.) 1980s. (HS19606, Carl M. Levin Papers, Bentley Historical Library, University of Michigan)

Enjoying a letter in my office, 1980s. (HS19654, Carl M. Levin Papers, Bentley Historical Library, University of Michigan)

Barbara and me with President Clinton aboard Air Force One, February 3, 1993.

President Clinton visiting Focus: HOPE. *Left to right*: Eleanor Josaitis, a student at the Center for Advanced Technology, Father William Cunningham, President Clinton, me, and Michigan senator Don Riegle. Detroit, March 13, 1994. (HS19641, Carl M. Levin Papers, Bentley Historical Library, University of Michigan)

The Clintons at opening day of the FDR Memorial, pointing to the statue
of Fala that I was able to get included in the memorial, May 2, 1997.

A moment with Rosa Parks, June 15, 1999. I spoke at her funeral in 2005.

Conferring with Michigan congressman John Dingell before testifying together. (HS19604, Carl M. Levin Papers, Bentley Historical Library, University of Michigan)

Talking with Senator Ted Kennedy during a Senate Armed Services Committee hearing.

Huddling with Senator John Glenn at a hearing on campaign finance reform, 1997.
(Photo by Douglas Graham/Congressional Quarterly/Getty Images)

Talking it over with Senator Joe Biden before a press conference on the Democrats'
Senate agenda, January 26, 2005. (Photo by Chris Maddaloni/Roll Call/Getty Images)

Seeing the impact of the terrorist attack on the Pentagon with Secretary of Defense Donald Rumsfeld and Senator John Warner, September 11, 2001. (Photo courtesy of Department of Defense via Getty Images)

Meeting at the White House with Senate and House foreign policy and defense leaders on going to war with Iraq. *Left to right*: President George W. Bush, Senator Joe Biden, Senator John Warner, and me, September 4, 2002. (Photo by Mark Wilson/Getty Images)

Signing ceremony with President George W. Bush on the FY 2004 National Defense Authorization Act, November 24, 2003. *Left to right*: Senator John Warner, me, Congressman Tom Davis, Senator Susan Collins, Congressman Duncan Hunter.

Senator John Warner and me on *Meet the Press*, December 3, 2006. (Photo by Alex Wong/Getty Images for *Meet the Press*)

With Senators John McCain and John Warner at a
Senate Armed Services Committee hearing.

Senator John Warner and me on an Iraq CODEL, August 2007.

Eating with the troops in Iraq, August 2007.

A commander in the Russian Airborne Brigade briefing Senator Jack Reed and me during our visit to Operation Joint Guard in Bosnia-Herzegovinia. Operation Joint Guard was a multinational peacekeeping effort in support of the Dayton Peace Accords. (National Archives)

With President Obama at the White House signing ceremony for the
FY 2010 National Defense Authorization Act, which included
the Hate Crimes Prevention Act, October 28, 2009.

With President Obama at the White House, October 28, 2009.

Going after Chinese counterfeit auto parts before the U.S.-China Economic Security Review Commission, June 7, 2006. (Photo by Jay Mallin/ *The Washington Post* via Getty Images)

Signing ceremony in the White House Rose Garden on the Credit Card Accountability, Responsibility, and Disclosure Act, May 22, 2009.

At my desk in the Russell Senate Office Building.

Signing legislation while I was both acting president pro tem of the Senate and chairman of the Senate Armed Services Committee.

Swearing in Goldman Sachs witnesses at the hearing on Wall Street abuses and the company's role in the 2008 financial crisis, April 27, 2010. (Photo by Melina Mara/*The Washington Post* via Getty Images)

With Senator John McCain at a hearing.

With Senator Tom Coburn at a press briefing releasing the staff report of the
Permanent Subcommittee on Investigations on Wall Street's
role in the 2007–8 financial crisis, April 13, 2011.

Listening to witnesses at
hearings of the Senate
Permanent Subcommittee
on Investigations.

Speaking at the grand opening of the Keweenaw National Historical
Park Calumet Visitor Center, October 27, 2011.

Celebrating with members of the Michigan congressional delegation and Michigan
governor on Paczki Day. Paczki is a jam-filled Polish donut eaten just before Lent.
Left to right: Congressman John Conyers, Senator Debbie Stabenow, Sandy, me,
Congressman John Dingell, Governor Jennifer Granholm, Congressman
Fred Upton, Congressman Dave Camp, Congressman Vern Ehlers.

With Sandy at one of dozens of State of the Union addresses where we always sat together.

Conferring with Sandy before testifying at a House of Representatives
committee hearing on auto industry legislation, November 19, 2008.

Goofing off with Sandy. (HS19642, Carl M. Levin Papers, Bentley Historical Library, University of Michigan)

Sandy, Andy, and me with Congressman John Lewis at Andy Levin's swearing in as a new member of the House of Representatives serving Sandy's former district. Washington, D.C., 2018. Photo by Abbas Alawieh.

Staff photo with Sandy and Barbara, June 2003.

Barbara and me with our grandchildren at Niagara Falls, 2014.
Left to right: Ben, Olivia, Samantha, Beatrice, Bess, Noa.

10

Protecting the
Great Lakes and
the Environment

With my love for the outdoors since childhood and long believing in the value of preserving areas of pristine wilderness, I eagerly agreed to help Henry "Scoop" Jackson, Democrat of Washington, when he asked me as a freshman senator to work with him on passing legislation to protect the Alaskan wilderness. Such legislation had failed in previous sessions of Congress despite widespread, energetic support from many people across the political spectrum. Oil, mining, and timber interests had lobbied effectively to stymie passage, and Alaska's two senators, Democrat Mike Gravel and Republican Ted Stevens, were opposed to such a bill. Now, with some new members (including me) joining the Senate for the 96th Congress, Senator Jackson saw another opportunity to finally protect millions of acres of unparalleled beauty with tumbling rivers, steep-walled fjords, ancient glaciers, forest watersheds, and even volcanic craters and Arctic sand dunes, not to mention majestic mountains, including the iconic Denali (then named Mt. McKinley) where mining interests were eager to exploit a nearby tract of land.

The words of U.S. Supreme Court Justice William O. Douglas echoed in my head: "The Arctic has a call that is compelling. The distant mountains make one want to go on and on over the next ridge and over the one beyond. The call is that of a wilderness known only to a few."

The Alaska Wilderness Bill

As chairman of the Senate Energy Committee, Jackson organized eight senators to travel to Alaska to inspect ten areas of federal lands for which he proposed to provide the maximum protection possible. Jackson asked us to learn as much as we could in a few days about the area assigned to us. I was determined to be the best "two-day expert" I could be. As I flew off with the other senators, I used the flight time to read through the briefing materials provided by Jackson's committee staff. I was assigned to visit the Arctic National Wildlife Range, now named the Arctic National Wildlife Refuge, in Alaska's isolated northeast corner. It was the last portion of the Arctic coast not already committed to mineral exploration and development. The Refuge also included critical habitat for waterfowl, migratory birds, musk oxen, wolves, grizzly bears, and other wildlife and is the location for one of North America's greatest wildlife spectacles: the annual migration of the 120,000 caribou of the Porcupine River herd that come each spring to the coastal plain to calve. Unfortunately, I flew in too late to see the migration, but I got a good sense of a unique and awe-inspiring place.

My flight path took me through Fairbanks and a little village called Bettles, home to a few dozen people, that is near the Gates of the Arctic National Park and Preserve. My assignment was to speak to some local folks, inspect as much as I could by air, and then report my observations to my colleagues. There were many Alaskans who wanted the federal government's protection, including communities of Indigenous peoples such as the Inupiat and the Aleut, who depend on wildlife and hunting for survival. Six successive administrations had refused to open the area to which I was assigned to oil exploration and development. There was no doubt in my mind that protection should be permanent and not subject to the whim of some future environmentally insensitive administration.

From what I was able to learn, I concluded that there may in fact be oil reserves within the Arctic Wildlife Refuge, although the evidence indicates that the size of those reserves is less promising than in other areas of the state. And, if the Arctic Wildlife Refuge were closed to exploration, 95 percent of the highly favorable potential oil and gas lands onshore in Alaska would still be open to exploration and production. Contrary to the wild claims some were making that oil in the Arctic Wildlife Refuge could solve our energy problems, the evidence was that, at best, oil in the Arctic Wildlife Refuge could provide only a seven-month supply to fuel America's oil consumption.

When it was my turn to speak on the Senate floor in favor of Scoop Jackson's historic legislation to preserve Alaskan wilderness, I quoted one of America's foremost wildlife ecologists, Aldo Leopold: "I am glad I shall never be young without wild country to be young in."

The legislation had widespread support, but a multitude of technical issues had to be discussed and resolved. Finally, on November 12, 1980, Congress approved the Alaska National Interest Lands Conservation Act, and President Jimmy Carter signed it on December 2, 1980, a few weeks before leaving the White House. The Act provides special protections to more than 157 million acres of land, including national parks, national wildlife refuges, national monuments, wild and scenic rivers, recreational areas, national forests, and conservation areas. It was—and still is—the single largest expansion of protected lands in history, more than double the size of the National Park System.

The Great Lakes

In the late 1980s, I spent a little over a year chairing a series of hearings in the Governmental Affairs Subcommittee on Oversight of Government Management on what the federal government was doing to protect and restore the health of the Great Lakes. Our hearings documented a record of broken promises, major lapses, and serious gaps in federal programs for the Great Lakes. We uncovered multiple failures to ensure completion of remedial action plans to clean up toxic hotspots and contaminated sediments and to reduce significant disparities in the water quality rules of the states bordering the Great Lakes, as well as a lack of management plans. Pollution-control initiatives were contained in the existing U.S.-Canada Great Lakes Water Quality Agreement and the Clean Water Act, which designated the EPA as the lead agency for implementation. Unfortunately, they didn't accomplish their goals.

We held the last of the hearings on September 6, 1989, during which we disclosed that the Great Lakes suffered hundreds of spills of oil and toxic chemicals each year with very little being done about it. We initially thought those oil spills were due to oil tankers plying the Great Lakes, but our investigation revealed that they were mostly due to leakage and spills from facilities on land, including oil storage tanks. In the three years prior to the hearings, spills in the U.S. waters of the Great Lakes nearly doubled while spills in Canadian waters dropped by half because of stronger regulatory enforcement. At the same time, we found that inspections of facilities that threatened to pollute the Great Lakes were drastically cut by the EPA, from 3,600 per year in 1986 to just 1,000 in 1988. We learned that there were serious gaps in Great Lakes spill response and prevention capabilities. When I asked David Bales, then director of the Michigan Department of Natural Resources, whether we were ready to handle a million-gallon spill in the Great Lakes—which had happened in Alaska in 1984—he responded with a flat-out "no."

The Great Lakes Critical Programs Act legislation I introduced at the end of September 1989 with my fellow senators John Glenn of Ohio and Herb Kohl of Wisconsin as cosponsors was written to address a number of problems. It required the EPA to specify numerical limits that states must adhere to for the discharge of certain pollutants into the lakes. It also required the EPA to complete remedial action plans to remove contaminated sediment from forty-two identified toxic hotspots.

Since neither the Great Lakes states nor the federal government was prepared to prevent or contain oil spills, the bill required the U.S. Coast Guard to maintain an up-to-date, comprehensive list of Great Lakes spill-fighting equipment and the EPA to create plans to establish regional spill-response teams and to base at least one team in the Great Lakes region. The EPA was also required to identify high-risk spill areas and facilities and to direct federal spill research programs to consider Great Lakes concerns. The bill also increased funding authorization from $15.9 million to $25 million and ensured that the U.S.-Canadian Great Lakes Water Quality Agreement, signed in 1972, would be implemented as domestic law in the United States. The Sierra Club called my bill "the most comprehensive Great Lakes protection legislation" in a decade.

My goal was for the federal government to treat the Great Lakes as the unique, precious, irreplaceable gems that they are, so we can hand them down to future generations in much better condition than they are today. Containing 95 percent of this country's surface freshwater and serving the needs of more than 26 million Americans, the Great Lakes are essential to life as we know it.

President H. W. Bush signed the Great Lakes Critical Programs Act on November 16, 1990, under Lady Bird Johnson's willow oak tree on the south lawn of the White House. As he was signing it, the fountain pen broke in his hand, spilling ink on his fingers. The president grabbed a piece of scrap paper, pinched it to blot the ink, and set it aside. Using another pen, he signed the bill. As we left the platform, being the collector of autographs that I am, I picked up the ink-stained scrap paper containing his fingerprints. Later on, I had the bill and that fingerprint scrap framed together as a memento. Metaphorically, I mused, my fingerprints were all over the Act itself.*

In addition to working to protect the Great Lakes, I was determined to also protect the wild, pristine areas we are so fortunate to have in Michigan. The first

---

* Other Great Lakes projects in which I was involved were:

In 1983, I engaged in two days of intensive behind-the-scenes negotiations up until the final moments of the 97th Congress with about a dozen other Senators to win their approval for my amendments to a major nuclear energy bill. My amendments decreased the possibility that Michigan would be the site of a nuclear waste disposal facility.

I was a member—and often cochair—of the Senate Great Lakes Task Force (GLTF), a bipartisan subcommittee of the Northeast-Midwest Congressional Coalition comprised of members from all states bordering the Great Lakes and St. Lawrence Seaway. The GLTF worked together to improve water quality in the Great Lakes through legislation involving maritime shipping, farming, and industrial effluent and to protect against invasive species.

In 2000, I cowrote with Senator Frank Murkowski, Republican of Alaska, the National Historic Lighthouse Preservation Act that was passed by Congress to allow the transfer of historic lighthouses from the U.S. Coast Guard to state or local governments and nonprofit groups for preservation.

I sponsored legislation in 2001 to permanently ban oil and gas drilling in the Great Lakes.

Senator Debbie Stabenow, my fellow Democrat from Michigan, and I secured passage of the Great Lakes Legacy Act in 2002, which authorized funding for cleanup of contaminated sediment in the Great Lakes.

Republican senator Mike DeWine of Ohio and I sponsored the Great Lakes Fish and Wildlife Restoration Act that was passed by Congress in 2006.

I cosponsored a bill with Debbie Stabenow that provided tax equity to U.S. flagged ships operating on the Great Lakes, eliminating a provision that had put U.S. carriers at a disadvantage relative to foreign-flagged ships.

In 2007 we secured several measures to help the Great Lakes with passage of the Water Resources Development Act, including language directing the Administration to expedite projects to promote Great Lakes navigation and authorizing the Army Corps of Engineers to build a dispersal barrier in the Chicago Ship and Sanitary Canal to prevent Asian Carp infesting the Mississippi River system from entering the Great Lakes. Some $6 million was appropriated by Congress to build the barrier in 2009.

We passed the Great Lakes Compact in 2008 that established in federal law a general ban on new water diversions from the Great Lakes.

With Ohio Republican senator George Voinovich, I introduced legislation to triple the funding for new technologies to clean up the Great Lakes in 2009 and helped win Congress's approval of spending $475 million on Great Lakes restoration.

of many bills I introduced that were enacted into law was the Michigan Wilderness Act of 1987, which designated ten areas in Michigan as part of the National Wilderness Preservation System, including the stunningly beautiful Nordhouse Dunes that hug the eastern shore of Lake Michigan on the edge of the Manistee National Forest. Michigan has some of the most impressive dunes in the world, and this bill, signed by President Reagan, recognized that. It was the culmination of work with a wide range of allies over several years. In 2008 my Michigan colleague in the Senate, Debbie Stabenow, and I added a significant part of the spectacular Pictured Rocks National Lakeshore to our wilderness protection laws.

We had to follow a more difficult path when we sought wilderness protection for the Sleeping Bear Dunes National Lakeshore in northwest Michigan. The Dunes, a true wonder of the world left behind when glaciers retreated at the end of the last Ice Age, had been preserved as a national park in 1970, thanks to the late Philip Hart, the great Michigan senator known as the "conscience of the Senate." Local environmental activists and I had been advocating for wilderness designation for the Dunes, which provides an important additional protection against human impact, but there was strong opposition from some local homeowners who had property in the park.

The park designation at its inception was controversial because it involved transferring ownership of private land to public use. Some of the homeowners were able to continue living in their homes within the Sleeping Bear Dunes National Park, but there was no right to transfer ownership to anyone but the federal government. I remember meeting with the long-time occupants of a home within the park who wanted me to sponsor a bill that would allow them to transfer ownership to their children. I felt a pang of sympathy for the family, but I couldn't do it, ethically and morally, because others had given up their homes. I sat in their living room, drank the tea they kindly offered, and heard their plea to let them keep their house in paradise, but I told them I just couldn't do it. These lands should be available to belong to all Americans, now and those yet to be born.

As luck would have it, Republican congressman Dan Benishek, whose "swing" district in Michigan included the Dunes, announced he was in favor of a Sleeping Bear wilderness designation. I welcomed his support in the Republican House, which was crucial. But I suspect that was probably part of a Republican leadership strategy to blunt the criticism that he was an anti-environmentalist. This strategy was confirmed in 2018 when another Michigan Republican congressman, Dave Trott, candidly told the *Detroit News* that the Republican Party caucus leaders would identify a popular piece of legislation that he should support in order to use it as an "accomplishment" when running for reelection. "Don't worry about legislating, we'll give you a nice bill to pass, so you can talk about it in your commercials, but we don't need your help on policy or legislative matters," Trott said he was told. "That's not what I went there to do," he said. While I differed with Trott on a lot of issues, I agreed with him on that last statement—that's not what legislators are sent to Washington to do. I generally avoided trying to challenge the motive of other members of Congress, but Trott's candor made it difficult to avoid doing so in this case.

The Sleeping Bear Wilderness bill I sponsored in the Senate and Benishek sponsored in the House, which was the only wilderness bill passed in the 113th Congress (2013–2015), provided wilderness protection to almost half of the Sleeping Bear Dunes National Lakeshore. President Obama signed the bill, and now thirty-five miles of lakeshore are protected from motorized vehicles, including dune buggies and snowmobiles. Helping Benishek survive politically may have been the Republican motive, but it was an important environmental win for my state.

The Keweenaw National Historical Park

I got involved in protecting not just our wilderness areas during my Senate years but our historical heritage as well. The Keweenaw Peninsula is one such example. The Keweenaw or "Copper Country," as we call it, is a fifty-mile-long "finger" of land in Michigan's Upper Peninsula (U.P.) projecting into Lake Superior and is the northernmost inhabited spot in Michigan. One writer said that the Keweenaw "has, for my money, the most spectacular scenery and most intriguing history of any place in the state." It deserves recounting a bit of its background.

Keweenaw's history is the history of copper in America because of its extraordinary vein of copper that is deemed to be 97 percent pure. Massive, productive copper mines sprang up in Keweenaw in the late nineteenth and early twentieth centuries. It is estimated that 13 billion pounds of copper were extracted from mines in the Upper Peninsula.

Some 7,000 years ago, Indigenous people began to mine copper from shallow pits in the Keweenaw using stone to smash the rocks and fire to melt the copper in order to make tools, pottery, weapons, and decorations. Some artifacts from this pre-historic era have been found as far away as present-day Alabama, proving that commercial trade among Indigenous tribes had developed centuries before Europeans "discovered" America.

European settlers first noticed the peninsula's rich copper deposits in the 1700s, but most copper in the United States still had to be imported, primarily from Cornwall, England. In 1840, Michigan geologist Douglass Houghton, who later became mayor of Detroit, published a paper on the geology of the Upper Peninsula highlighting the potential for successful mining. The federal government that year opened a mineral land agency office in the town of Copper Harbor on the tip of the peninsula, and soon large mining companies were staking claims and digging shafts. These deposits of so-called native copper in the Keweenaw are unlike those found in most other copper-mining districts in the world because the copper ore here contains very little copper oxides or copper sulfides that require heavy processing. However, operations to process copper, such as milling, smelting, and leaching—activities that resulted in large amounts of toxic waste that was dumped into nearby bodies of water—were still necessary.

There were fortunes to be made in the Keweenaw, mostly by Easterners, and good-paying jobs for miners. Between 1845 and 1870 the Cliff Mine near Eagle Harbor made a profit of more than $2.5 million for its owners—a spectacular amount in those times. The copper mines of the U.P. played an outsized role during the Civil War because they provided most of the copper used to make canteens, uniform buttons, copper sheathing for wooden war-ships, and bronze cannons for the Union Army and Navy. Keweenaw copper also was used to make telegraph (and later telephone) lines so Union Army generals could communicate. By 1869, the mines of Michigan were supplying 95 percent of the nation's copper.

In Red Jacket—later renamed Calumet—the town fathers (not a mining company) built the opulent Calumet Opera House, which hosted well-known plays and acts from around the world, including "the man of a thousand faces" actor Lon Chaney Sr., conductor and composer John Philip Sousa, and renowned French stage actress Sarah Bernhardt.

By 1910, the Keweenaw's population had swelled to more than 100,000, the majority of whom were immigrants of about 30 different nationali-ties, principally Finns and Cornish. Pasties, which originated in Cornwall, England, are hearty pastries that were filled with meat and rutabaga and kept warm in their containers to provide lunch for miners carrying them down to cold mines. They are the U.P.'s most famous food to this day and are mailed to faraway places. There were six newspapers in the Keweenaw in its heyday, four of which were in a foreign language, 22 churches, and 74 saloons. The area was a prime example of "corporate paternalism," where the corporations brought in food, groceries, clothing, and other items and sold them to their workers in company stores.

That worked for a while, but in July 1913 about 9,000 miners walked out in a strike against unsafe working conditions and low wages. The strike turned violent, and several people were killed, including two strikers shot by sheriff's deputies and three strike-breakers gunned down in their homes by striking miners. The most tragic incident of all occurred that Christmas Eve when the Women's Auxiliary of the Western Federation of Miners threw a holiday party for striking workers and their families at the Italian Hall in Calumet. At around 4:40 p.m., just after the children received gifts from "Santa" donated by local business owners and unionists from around the country, someone came into the hall and shouted "Fire! Fire!" There was no fire, but people rushed for the exit, a narrow staircase leading down a flight to an outer door that opened only inward. Seventy-three people, including 59 children, were crushed to death in the panicked stampede for the exit. It was one of the worst labor-related disasters in modern history. The identity of the man who falsely called "Fire!" was never determined.

The strike of 1913–1914 prompted a congressional investigation and had broad implications for American labor history. Despite an outpouring of sympathy and support for the striking miners, the owners won the labor dispute and allowed strikers to return to work only if they turned in their union cards. Some of the strikers did see an increase in pay, and the companies instituted an eight-hour workday in order to appease miners who were beginning to look for new ways to make a living.

The Great Depression of the 1930s stopped most of the copper mining in the Keweenaw. Mining picked up again with World War II and then slowed down until all mining operations on the peninsula ceased in 1968. Over the decades following the boom years, the population declined sharply as miners and shop owners left for other opportunities. Many of the Keweenaw Peninsula's cities and villages began to resemble ghost towns, which is how they looked when I first campaigned there in 1978. Still, the citizens who remained in the Keweenaw loved living there despite winter snowfalls that often topped thirty feet. Their biggest worry was about economic hardship—tourism and the timber industry would never produce the high wages and profits that copper mining had. But the booming copper mining years made Keweenaw a valuable piece of history, with numerous old buildings that reflected the importance of those earlier times, and I thought the Keweenaw deserved protection and designation as a national historic park.

The idea for a national park in the Keweenaw started with a letter to the editor of the *Daily Mining Gazette* from someone who lamented that Calumet (the largest town on the peninsula), which had dwindled to 1,000 residents, resembled a "ghost town." He suggested that perhaps creating a national park would help reinvigorate the area's economy and attractiveness as a tourist destination. The newspaper ran an editorial suggesting that it was "maybe an idea worth pursuing."

Bob Davis, the Republican congressman representing the U.P. and the northern Lower Peninsula, began advocating for national park status for the Keweenaw. I soon joined in the effort, and in 1988 I introduced a bill in the Senate to create the Keweenaw National Historic Park. We were competing with a group of people from Butte, Montana, who were also trying to get national park status for their mining history, particularly the massive Anaconda Copper Mine. We had our work cut out for us.

We knew that creating a national park in the Keweenaw would draw visitors from other states and the "trolls" of the Lower Peninsula. (Yes, that's what "Yoopers"—residents of the U.P.—call folks who live below the Mackinac Bridge. That makes me a "troll.") The economics of towns along the way, like Sault Ste. Marie, Marquette, and Houghton, would also benefit from the increased traffic of tourists heading to the Keweenaw.

Against the odds, in 1992, with the extraordinary outpouring of support from Reverend Bob Langseth and a host of local enthusiasts from "Copper Country" and with Davis's partnership in the House, our bill designating a national historic park was passed by Congress and signed by President George H. W. Bush. It included towns, various mining facilities, and some areas with forests, lakes, and streams. The 1,870-acre park also includes two state wildlife parks and land surrounding two abandoned mining complexes, the Calumet and the Quincy. The Quincy has a remarkable exhibit of the "world's largest steam hoist," a gargantuan machine using a spool to run deep in and out of the mine shaft to haul miners and mining cars containing copper ore. At 9,260 feet, the Quincy shaft is said to be the deepest shaft of any mine in the western hemisphere. The building protecting the hoist is also remarkable. Made of poured concrete, it has arched windows with decorative tile imported from Italy and Spain. It is the most artistic mine entrance that I have ever seen. The bill also recognized twenty-one "Heritage Sites" on federal, state, and private land, including churches, museums, refurbished union halls, and an opera house. Appropriations for the Keweenaw National Historic Park were never large, but over time I was able to insert language in a bill that changed the ratio of local matching funds to access federal dollars for the park from one-to-one to one-to-four. As you can tell from this narrative, I'm very proud of this accomplishment.

We also began the cleanup of the harmful residue of the copper mining industry, including the 200 million tons of "stamp sand" dumped into Houghton County's Torch Lake (not to be confused with Torch Lake in lower Michigan). The EPA published its Remedial Action Plan for Torch Lake in 1987, and we were able to get it designated as a Superfund site. Work didn't begin until 1998 when we were able to get $15.2 million dedicated to the project (with $1.5 million in state funds) appropriated in the EPA budget. In 2007, the EPA reported that fish in Torch Lake had ceased showing signs of tumors and deformities while still cautioning against eating fish taken from the lake. Torch Lake was taken off the list of Superfund sites in 2014 when the EPA said the project came in $2 million *under* budget. Torch Lake will never be as pristine as it once was, but the much cleaner lake serves as a hopeful sign of progress to address the environmental sins of our past.

Thunder Bay

Preserving Michigan's maritime past was another effort into which I threw myself. One of the most dramatic chapters in our history played out in the aptly named Thunder Bay, a large area of Lake Huron east of the city of Alpena in the Lower Peninsula where more than 100 shipwrecks have occurred over the last 150 years.

A significant part of the history of the Great Lakes rests on the bottom of Thunder Bay. The shipwrecks in this area dramatically tell stories of loss, stories of heroism and folly, stories of the irreplaceable role the lakes have played, culturally and economically. But these shipwrecks were attracting increasing numbers of divers who had been removing pieces of our history, like ship bells, for souvenirs. With prodding from me in the Senate, Congressman Bob Davis in the House, and the State of Michigan, the National Oceanic and Atmospheric Agency (NOAA) created the Thunder Bay National Marine Sanctuary in 2000, some 448 square miles of Lake Huron known as "shipwreck alley" because of the dangerous weather patterns of northwestern Lake Huron that produced the disastrous demise of so many ships. We subsequently were able to get the needed federal funding for a visitors center and to expand the sanctuary by tenfold to 4,300 square miles, protecting dozens of additional shipwrecks. Today, that Great Lakes Maritime Heritage Center in Alpena welcomes 60,000 visitors a year to the Thunder Bay sanctuary with its historically significant shipwrecks, including a wooden sidewheel steamer that sank in 1844 and a 470-foot German-built freighter carrying coiled steel, which sank in 1966. It's a fabulous place to visit. There are great educational opportunities for children. In 2014, 600 students from as far away as Hong Kong and Egypt came to the center to compete in an international underwater robotics competition.

The Thunder Bay National Marine Sanctuary is unique among all the NOAA marine sanctuaries for two reasons: first, it's the only national marine sanctuary in freshwater (which preserves shipwrecks far better than saltwater); second, it was created not to protect reefs but to protect the shipwrecks. Every time I visit the sanctuary I am exhilarated by how it stimulates our imaginations and by the positive economic impact it has on the Alpena area.

Working with John Dingell

I was privileged to work on a number of environmental projects with John Dingell, who, other than Sandy, was my closest ally in the House of Representatives. John, who cared deeply about the environment, served his district for fifty-nine years in the House, making him the longest-serving member of Congress. I followed John's initiatives with bills in the Senate to protect the Great Lakes and the Detroit River. One of my fondest memories of John was when we dropped whitefish fingerlings into the environmentally restored Detroit River, restocking a fish that had been decimated by decades of pollution.

We also worked together to protect the wildlife along the Detroit River and western Lake Erie, important waterways damaged by pollution from industry lining the shores. Our efforts paid off in 2001 when President George W. Bush signed our bill, the Detroit River International Wildlife Refuge Establishment Act, which protects the wildlife found in coastal wetlands, islands, and waterfront lands along forty-eight miles of the Detroit River and western Lake Erie shoreline, including the Humbug Marsh, which has been called an "internationally significant" wetland. Since passage of the act, many wildlife species, including some endangered ones, have come back. Bald eagles, osprey, and peregrine falcons are now abundant along the Detroit River, and populations of whitefish, sturgeon, salmon, perch, and walleye have rebounded.

John and I also worked hard to create a new addition to the National Park System in Monroe County just north of the Ohio state line, the River Raisin National Battlefield Park. The park commemorates an important battle in the life of our nation, the massacre or capture of nearly a thousand Americans by British Canadian troops and their Native American allies over six days in January 1813. The captured American troops were forced to march in the cold back to Detroit; those who couldn't keep up were killed. It was considered the worst American defeat in the War of 1812, and General William Henry Harrison, who later became president, called the battle a "national calamity." But the loss prompted a rallying cry for American troops, "Remember the Raisin," that helped reverse the tide of the war and carry the fight to the British.

A fluke of politics helped me get the bill establishing that park passed in the Senate. Most of the American officers lost in the battle were from Kentucky, and many counties in Kentucky commemorate their sacrifice by being named after them. A former Detroit Tigers pitcher, Jim Bunning, Republican of Kentucky, was in the Senate at the time, and although he and most Republicans were opposed to adding to the federal inventory of parks, I was able to persuade him to make an exception and support my bill because of the Kentucky connection. Coincidence and good luck played an important role in the success of this legislation, as they had so many times throughout my career.

The River Raisin battlefield had been listed on the National Registry of Historic Places in 1982, and the State of Michigan and Monroe County opened a visitor center there in 1990. But making it a national park, as we did in 2010, has significantly raised the public's awareness of this critically important battle in a mostly forgotten war (although it was actually a second war for our independence).

Protecting Animals

And then there's my love for animals, which led me to several other legislative efforts over the years, including prohibiting commercial dog fights, improving regulation of large "puppy mills" (those that sell fifty or more puppies a year), limiting the use of chimpanzees in scientific research, and improving the treatment of horses destined for slaughterhouses. A particularly rewarding outcome came after years of effort to end the killing of northern fur seal pups in the remote Pribilof Islands off the Alaskan coast in the Bering Sea. In the 1970s, most Americans were sickened and outraged by the brutal clubbing to death of seal pups for their fur in Canada and Norway. But I learned that the U.S. government was actually paying Aleuts in the remote Pribilof Islands, part of the state of Alaska, some $5 million annually to kill 25,000 seals a year. It turned out that the United States was obligated to kill thousands of seals under the historic 1911 Northern Pacific Fur Seal Convention, a treaty signed by the United States, Japan, Russia, and Canada. The convention prohibited killing of seals in the ocean but had a provision to protect the fishing industry by requiring the United States to kill 25,000 seals on the Pribilof Islands annually and to split the harvest between Japan and Canada, using some of the proceeds to hire a company in South Carolina to process the fur under a federal government contract. The vast majority of the furs were destined for Europe. There also was a market in Asia for seal penises, believed by some to be an aphrodisiac. U.S. taxpayers were subsidizing vanity markets in Europe and Asia by paying for the brutal clubbing to death of thousands of seal pups.

When the 1911 Convention came up for renewal in 1980, I, along with Senator Susan Collins of Maine and others, called for the Senate to reject ratification. We attempted, unsuccessfully, to amend the treaty during consideration by the Senate Foreign Relations Committee. But with the support of several animal protection groups, including the Humane Society, the Fund for Animals, and Friends of Wildlife, we fought on the Senate floor during the final debate to reduce the slaughter. We convinced Alaska's Republican senators, Ted Stevens and Frank Murkowski, to accept our amendment that would at least take a step forward by authorizing development of a plan to end the seal slaughter and that would find ways to create new job opportunities for Aleuts living on the islands.

Despite the Reagan administration's desire to extend the treaty in 1985, the Senate rejected it and the commercial slaughter of seals on American soil ended, except that Aleuts and other native tribes still are allowed to hunt a much smaller number of seals for subsistence. Taxpayers no longer have to support the slaughter of seals. The Humane Society of the United States in 2009 honored Senator Collins and me for our long and successful battle.

The North Country Scenic Trail

One of the joys of my job as a senator was the opportunity my travels across Michigan gave me to enjoy Michigan's abundant forms of recreation. That included hiking along the North Country National Scenic Trail, established as part of the National Park Service in 1980 by an act of Congress that I was pleased to support. The trail was designed to run about 4,600 miles through seven states, making it longer than the well-known Appalachian Trail and Pacific Crest Trail. Senators and House members from those states worked over the years to designate portions of existing state and local trails and portions of federal lands as part of the North Country National Scenic Trail.

By 2008 about 2,600 miles of the trail had been improved. The 1980 law, while allowing donations of easements over private lands, unfortunately prohibited the federal government from paying for land or easement rights even from willing sellers. In January 2009 I introduced legislation that was signed into law by President Obama allowing the National Park Service to do so.

Volunteers keep the dream of a completed trail very much alive with the support of the nonprofit North Country Trail Association, whose office is in

Lowell, Michigan. In a typical year a thousand volunteers in seven states help add additional miles of trail and maintain the trail by clearing trees and brush and building boardwalks and bridges over streams. As of this writing, the North Country Trail is more than half finished. It won't be completed in my lifetime or maybe even the lifetime of my children, but its creation and the ongoing support for its completion, like other parts of our National Park System, reflect the vision of our people to preserve for future generations the joy our land offers to us all.

11

Earmarks and Private Bills

Detroiters have historically viewed Woodward Avenue, the major north-south thoroughfare, as the dividing line between the city's east and west sides. The two halves are part of Detroit's lore and are manifested in many ways, one of those being a 200-foot gap in the riverfront near the foot of Woodward Avenue caused by an underground stream coursing just below downtown's network of utility and sewerage tunnels before surfacing and emptying into the Detroit River.

The Bates Street Outfall, as it is called, was one of the obstacles to achievement of a decades-old dream that many of us Detroiters had and which I shared since my City Council days: an uninterrupted promenade along the Detroit River, where the public could stroll or bike the six miles from Belle Isle, a 982-acre island park east of downtown, to the Ambassador Bridge, the gateway from Detroit's downtown to Windsor, Canada, and take in the dramatic view of the freighters and pleasure boats plying the river and of Windsor across the way. While a 2002 study of the outfall conducted by the United States Army Corps of Engineers found it was in desperate need of repair, work on it was complicated because it meant disrupting the entrance and exit to the Detroit-Windsor Tunnel, used by millions of vehicles a year.

A much greater impediment to the promenade's construction was that the six-mile stretch of river had long been blocked to public access by dozens of small factories, storage facilities, the vacant Ford Auditorium, 80-foot-high cement silos, and dozens of vacant buildings, all eyesores. Since the promenade would cost far more than the city could ever raise on its own, Detroit would need hundreds of millions of corporate, foundation, private, state, and federal dollars to make it happen.

The nonprofit Detroit Riverfront Conservancy (DRFC) was formed in 2003 and was given the task of coordinating the project with the City of Detroit, the Detroit-Wayne County Port Authority, the Detroit-Windsor Tunnel, the General Motors Corporation (which in 1996 bought the riverfront Renaissance Center), and a host of federal and state agencies. The formation of the DRFC galvanized an outpouring of financial support from foundations, corporations, and private donors. In 2005 I was able to secure a Senate "earmark" of $29 million for the DRFC, including $3 million for covering over the Bates Street Outfall. That same year, the cement silos began to be dismantled and land began to be purchased. What became clear was that the vision was more than a fanciful dream. "Getting our riverfront back" was a powerful reality-changing motivator. The spectacular Riverwalk, which is what we now call the promenade, is well over half completed. Millions of people visit it each year, many benefiting from it on a regular basis. It is one of many activities helping Detroit with its truly extraordinary revival.

Earmarks

Earmarks, such as that $29 million, are appropriated funds for state and local projects specifically identified by Congress in legislation or legislative history (committee reports or statements of a bill's managers). Some oppose earmarks in principle, castigating them as "pork" or wasteful spending; others oppose earmarks unless the project is in their own district or state. Of course not all earmarks are appropriate or justified, but I think in general they are a legitimate part of the legislative process for a number of reasons that are ignored by opponents and that appear to be unknown by the public that is skeptical of them. For one thing, earmarks are carved out of a larger pot of appropriated funds assigned to a federal agency for allocation, say for cleanup projects identified as environmentally essential by the EPA. As a result, they do not increase the annual deficit. Second, members of Congress who are doing their job are surely more likely to know the needs and priorities of their state or district better than an employee in a national or regional office of a federal agency. Earmarks also serve an important purpose in helping to bring together members of different political persuasions to achieve compromise on major legislation; they help overcome differences of geography and philosophy. When the use of earmarks was ended by the party caucuses in 2011,* it ended incentives that can be critical to getting legislation passed and that helped senators like me obtain valuable support for highly useful, productive projects in their states. The ending of earmarks has also been a contributing factor to the intense divisiveness that has marked Congress in recent years because the ability of members to earmark funds provided some of the grease that allowed the wheels of the legislative branch of government to move.

It's not as though getting earmarks for your state or district is an automatic political feather in your cap. Obtaining earmarks can be challenging politically because a member of Congress can't support all the earmarks he or she is asked to sponsor. You have to say "no" to most requests of your constituents. There were dozens of requests for earmarks from all corners of Michigan every year, and my staff would read and study all of them, which helped me decide which were the most meritorious.

Although the defense authorization bill was not an appropriation measure—that is, it established programs as opposed to funding programs— it was used routinely by members for defense-related earmarks. That's because since the Senate Armed Services Committee (SASC) worked closely with the Defense Appropriations Subcommittee, including an earmark in the defense authorization bill significantly increased the chance of getting it funded.

---

* Neither the Senate nor the House has passed a rule banning earmarks. It should also be noted that in 2007 the Senate passed a rule making the earmark process much more transparent and requiring that information be posted on a website in advance of a vote. (See Senate Rule XIV.)

Also, because the defense authorization bill is the only bill that is authorized each year and addresses our nation's military needs, it is considered a "must-pass" bill and therefore highly attractive for earmarks. As chairman of the SASC I had significant power over the many earmark requests, and I had to judge the relative merit of each project: Is it important to the defense of our nation? Does it have a broad impact? Will the inclusion of the earmark help us pass the bill? I said "no" to many more requests than I agreed to include, but to the extent I was able to accommodate a meritorious project of the other members, it made it easier to pass the bill for which I was responsible.

One of the better-known opponents of earmarks was a Democrat, Senator William Proxmire of Wisconsin, who served from 1957 to 1989. He was an aggressive critic of wasteful government spending, especially at the Pentagon. Proxmire took a scatter-gun approach, often labeling any expenditure wasteful without understanding the underlying issue, especially when it came to scientific studies. Proxmire created the well-known "Golden Fleece" award to highlight projects he thought were unworthy. Many of his award winners seemed ludicrous on their face—such as the National Science Foundation grant to study why people fall in love or why prisoners want to get out of jail. But most of the projects had legitimate scientific, environmental, or economic reasons behind them. Proxmire would often seem to look at just the title of a study or project and decide that it should be mocked as a waste of taxpayer money.

Focus: HOPE

One project I strongly supported for years with earmarks was Focus: HOPE, started in Detroit by a Roman Catholic priest and an iron-willed suburban mother of five. Its goal was to bring hope to the city in 1968 when it was trying to recover from the 1967 riots. Father Bill Cunningham and Eleanor Josaitis held rallies and ran petition drives advocating for racial peace and justice and began a food distribution program with the U.S. Department of Agriculture to distribute government food commodities such as peanut butter, cheese, and dried milk. When I served on the Detroit City Council in the 1970s, the

Council approved their work, and Sandy and I admired how the charismatic Father Cunningham and Eleanor created a volunteer-based system that provided food to thousands of impoverished seniors and families with children. For people who lacked transportation to Focus: HOPE food distribution centers, Father Cunningham inspired hundreds of volunteers to use their own cars to get the food to the people who needed it.

Some become heroes by winning a big game or facing an enemy on the battlefield. The foes that Eleanor and Father Cunningham fought against were tougher and as old as humanity: bigotry, poverty, and despair. They knew that solutions are found in opportunities for education, the dignity of a decent-paying job, and an environment where everyone is accepted as equal. They had an unusual story of idealistic pragmatism in the heart of a deprived neighborhood in northwest Detroit, and they were passionate about their goals. Their story appealed to many policymakers and legislators. Their success became known as the "Miracle on Oakman Boulevard." Together, they built Focus: HOPE into an agile nonprofit powerhouse that looked for innovative ways to help people climb out of poverty.

For instance, with so many factories closing, Father Cunningham thought of a way to use empty shop floors to create something called "Industry Mall," where private machine tooling companies could share space and help support Focus: HOPE's Machinist Training Institute, or MTI. The students of MTI could be trained by retired machinists and have an opportunity to get paid apprenticeships with the for-profit companies. This program filled a large gap, namely the shortage of machinists, which was the result of many factors. The Big Three auto companies had stopped training machinists years before—primarily because after being trained, the skilled tradesmen were "poached" by other companies. Machinists in their fifties and sixties were also retiring in large numbers. As a result, much of the Motor City's specialized machining work was sent to other countries because there simply weren't enough skilled machinists around to do it. Father Cunningham looked at this dilemma as an opportunity and started from scratch by convincing Ex-Cell-O, a major manufacturer, to donate a factory down the street from Focus: HOPE and his church.

Father Cunningham and Eleanor also recruited a diverse faculty of skilled tradesmen, many of them retirees from the Tank-Automotive and Armaments Command (TACOM) center in Warren, Michigan. But they needed machining tools like lathes, drill presses, and shavers, and Focus: HOPE couldn't afford to buy them new. That's where I first came in to help. When Focus: HOPE brought the situation to my attention, I was still in my first term as a member of SASC. But after some inquiries I came upon a solution. Few were aware that the Department of Defense owned thousands of tool-and-die-making machines packed in grease for decades. They were tucked away in several climate-controlled storage facilities, including Appalachian caves, in the event of another large-scale conflict when the machines could be pulled out of storage and put to use making the war materiel the nation's defense forces needed.

I didn't see why those machines couldn't be put to use right now, so I helped Father Cunningham and Eleanor gain access to the appropriate decision makers at the Pentagon. Their convincing argument was that just having the machines at the ready was not enough to protect the nation. Our national security, they said, depended on the skilled machinists who could operate those machines. With a little nudging from me, the Pentagon agreed to loan the machining equipment to Focus: HOPE on a long-term basis.

Father Cunningham and Eleanor soon realized, however, that many of the dozens of minorities and women who applied for machinist training lacked the basic eighth-grade level of mathematics needed to operate the machinery, even if they had graduated from high school. Their solution was to create "Fast Track," a remedial education program that increased math ability for MTI candidates. Focus: HOPE also required that its student machinists be as dedicated to their futures as Focus: HOPE was. Discipline was key, and students were required to take drug tests and to be at work on time every morning.

I obtained earmarks for several Focus: HOPE projects, but none was bigger than Focus: HOPE's boldest visionary idea, the Center for Advanced Technologies (CAT). This unique combination of a high-tech, computerized training and manufacturing center created a partnership of seven engineering colleges, including Wayne State University, the University of Detroit, the University of Michigan, and Lehigh University in Bethlehem, Pennsylvania, to develop a curriculum for students to earn associate's, bachelor's, and even master's degrees in engineering with hands-on computerized manufacturing experience. Father Cunningham and Eleanor were ahead of many policymakers in realizing that post–Cold War America needed an agile defense-industrial base with "dual-use technology" that can shift quickly from producing consumer goods to war materiel. Their concept also spoke to the desire of many policymakers like me to expand opportunities to all citizens, particularly minorities and women, to compete for the high-skilled, high-paying jobs of the future. They were confident that CAT would help revitalize Detroit, discourage crime by offering young people positive role models from their own communities, and help overcome the nation's racial divide.

Again, the challenge was obtaining the machinery. We had to sell this idea to Congress, the Pentagon, the Departments of Education, Labor, and Commerce, and the White House, not to mention private, corporate, and foundation funders and state and local governments. This was a daunting task, but Focus: HOPE's mission and commitment inspired people, and its track record of success and can-do attitude earned the strong, unanimous endorsement of the Michigan congressional delegation for funding CAT. In August 1989, after two years of effort, top officials of the Departments of Defense, Commerce, Education, and Labor signed an unprecedented Memorandum of Understanding (MOU) to fund establishment of demonstration programs for advanced skills technologies for manufacturing. The MOU stated that high-technology manufacturing systems can be implemented if the skills exist to use them at peak efficiency. The one program that best fit the country's need was Focus: HOPE's CAT. Its trainees would learn to install, operate, maintain, diagnose, and repair advanced manufacturing equipment for maximum efficiency and become adept at integrating product and process improvements both as individuals and as participants on concurrent engineering teams. The MOU called Focus: HOPE "one of the nation's most capable non-profit organizations" and said its location in the Detroit–Ann Arbor area placed it at an important nexus of American manufacturing activity and technology innovation. The MOU allowed the Defense Department to spend an initial $15 million on development and purchase of the high-tech machinery needed for the project.

Focus: HOPE's Michigan delegation was strategically well placed, with me as a member, and later chairman, of the Senate Armed Services Committee and another Detroit Democrat, Dennis Hertel, serving on the House Armed Services Committee (HASC). Detroit Democrat John Conyers wasn't on HASC, but he had a good working relationship with California Democrat Ron Dellums, who served for a time as chair of the committee. Also, the legendary John Dingell of Michigan was very involved. Chuck Cutolo, my legislative director, was relentless and dogged in his support of Focus: HOPE and in the pursuit of the creation of CAT. Father Cunningham and Eleanor's ability to express their mission to the benefit of our entire country, not just their hope to serve Detroit's underserved citizens, was at the heart of the effort.

They didn't have and didn't need any paid lobbyists. No one on Capitol Hill wanted to say "no" to the two of them. Some indeed called Father Cunningham the "industrial priest" because Focus: HOPE made parts for the Big Three carmakers and dozens of suppliers. Focus: HOPE produced radiator hoses and remanufactured transmissions. For a while, the nonprofit organization actually made a profit from the transmission deal, money that went back into other Focus: HOPE programs.

One of the most unique projects of Focus: HOPE was their development of the Mobile Parts Hospital, a portable manufacturing unit that was taken to war zones to electronically repair, design, or duplicate parts that were not readily available there. Senators and representatives could see the great advantage of Focus: HOPE's technological agility and engineering skill to our nation's "defense industrial base" and the value it brought to our ability as a nation to shift to a war footing quickly.

Some of my most vivid memories as a senator are the times we brought dignitaries—generals, cabinet officers like Colin Powell, Vice President Bush, and later President Clinton—to Focus: HOPE. We told them they would thank us for getting them to visit. And sure enough, they left uplifted, some with tears in their eyes.

President Clinton's visit took place while he was in Detroit for a G7 conference in March 1994. He arrived the day before the G7, took the tour of Focus: HOPE, and addressed a large crowd gathered in the CAT. "I guess I have spent as much time in manufacturing facilities of various sorts as any person who ever occupied the presidency," he said. But, "I have never been in a place as advanced, as upbeat, and hopeful as this place.... This is a place that says 'when' ... 'when you work, when you learn, you can do, you can have a future.' So, I want you to know that you have inspired me, and I will talk about you all across this country. I remember I used to say when I was running for President, because of the little town that I was born in, that I still believed in a place called Hope. And now I can say I also believe in a place called Focus: HOPE."

Other Earmarks for Michigan

Another unique opportunity to push potential earmarks for Michigan came in 2009 when the Senate was considering President Obama's economic stimulus package, meant to jolt the country out of our economic collapse. The $410 billion legislation ultimately agreed to by Congress included billions in earmarks, and every senator and every representative—whether they voted for the stimulus package or not—fought to get a fair share to benefit their constituents. My erstwhile colleague, Senator Debbie Stabenow, and I helped win approval for earmarks totaling $150 million benefiting Michigan with sponsorships by our bipartisan delegation in the House, including some Republicans who requested earmarks but then, after they became part of the stimulus package, voted against the package itself. Much of what we requested involved protecting the Great Lakes watershed. Thanks to the earmarks, our state got funding for important projects like $500,000 for a water treatment plant in Mason, $30 million to dredge the St. Mary's River, $17 million to begin the long process of replacing a lock at the Soo, $2.1 million for Great Lakes fishery and ecosystem restoration, $500,000 for the Roseville police department to update its emergency operations center, and many more.

One earmark that was a focus of mine was the $3.8 million for the Old Tiger Stadium Conservancy. It was part of the nonprofit organization's $27 million plan to preserve the site of the historic stadium at the corner of Michigan and Trumbull near downtown Detroit. The old stadium had deteriorated over the years and was demolished in 2009, with everything gone but the historic field and its center-field flagpole.

There were many historic moments that took place at Tiger Stadium. "The Iron Man" Lou Gehrig, ailing from amyotrophic lateral sclerosis, a neuromuscular disease that would later be known as Lou Gehrig's disease, led off a game against the Tigers with a hit, then took himself out of the lineup without taking the field. It was the thirty-six-year-old's last major league game and the end of an incredible 2,130 consecutive games streak. In 1921, Babe Ruth hit what many say was the longest home run in major league history, more than 575 feet over the right-field stands. In 1934, Ruth hit his 700th round-tripper over the right-field roof in Detroit, a shot estimated at 500 feet that landed on the other side of Trumbull Avenue.

Like so many other lifetime Detroiters, I have an emotional connection to this historic spot, where baseball's greatests had played in America's "pastime." I wanted the historic field of the old ballpark preserved to inspire future generations of kids and to boost development in a struggling area of the city. The plan put forward by the Old Tiger Stadium Conservancy included a baseball field for kids with the same dimensions as the original field of the old ballpark, dugouts, seating for 5,000 in new stands, and dressing rooms for the players. The plan also included economic redevelopment projects in the adjacent, historic neighborhood known as Corktown.

My good friend Senator Tom Coburn staged a last-minute vote to eliminate eleven earmarks from the 2009 stimulus package, including mine for the Old Tiger Stadium Conservancy that he listed as number two on his "hit list." The project "looked a little stinky to me" was all he would say about why he objected. Fortunately, his hit list effort was defeated by a 61–34 vote. In 2018, the Detroit Police Department's Police Athletic League (PAL), a nonprofit devoted to the youth of Detroit, finished redeveloping the field and built a new headquarters where the left-field stands once stood. New townhouses have been built where the right-field stands once were. It is a joyous experience on summer evenings to go out and watch kids in summer leagues play. And, the Tiger Stadium development has given an additional boost to a renovated commercial area in the bustling Corktown neighborhood.

In 2010 a taxpayer watchdog group listed an energy-efficient street lighting program for Detroit sponsored by Debbie Stabenow and me as among the top "pork" earmarks that year, and, frankly, I am proud of that. None of these vital projects could even remotely be defined as "pork." The vast majority of the earmarks for Michigan that year were infrastructure maintenance projects we should have been doing all along.

I was disappointed when the ban on earmarks took effect. The public's perception of earmarks as something "wrong with Washington" misses the point that most earmarks are just as legitimate as most agency-designated projects and have the added benefit of helping make divided government work. As I feared, the effective ban on earmarks has contributed to legislative gridlock and made legislative compromise on important issues like infrastructure investment more difficult.

Private Bills

Another type of "targeted" legislation with which I was involved were private bills, legislation that affects a single person or group, most of which pertain to immigration cases. Once a private bill on an immigration matter is introduced in the Senate, the practical effect is to suspend deportation proceedings until a hearing is held. A private bill in the Senate doesn't necessarily lead to a hearing or a vote, but the immediate point is to stop a deportation until there is an opportunity to show the Senate or the Department of Homeland Security why the person or persons should be allowed to stay in the United States.

Most senators do not, as a general practice, file private bills. But I found it important and necessary to be able to address compelling individual situations, and private bills were often the only way to do that. I was willing to file private bills and viewed it as one of my responsibilities. I limited myself to introducing ten or so private bills each Congress. Many dozens of requests came to my office and I had to set a limit because I wanted to be sure that each case I accepted was thoroughly vetted by my staff.

Under the leadership of two exceptional state staffers, Cassandra Woods and Cathy Somers, our office developed a one-page guideline that included thirteen factors to consider to help make decisions on which immigration cases merited a private bill. These included whether deportation would have a permanent, significant impact on an individual's family; whether the individual has lived in the United States for a significant period of time and has set down roots in the community; and, of course, whether the individual has honorably served in the U.S. military. The actual passage of a private bill is exceedingly rare. A check with the Library of Congress by the *Detroit Free Press* in 2012 showed that only one private bill (mine) was passed by both houses that term and that only two such private bills (not mine) passed in the previous congressional term.

The bill referred to in that *Free Press* story involved a remarkable Nigerian man, Sopuruchi Chukwueke, whom I met thanks to the intercession of American nuns working in Africa. Chukwueke, who goes by his middle name, Victor, met the Rev. Mother Mary Paul Offiah of the Daughters of Mary Mother of Mercy, a Catholic order of nuns, in 2001 in Nigeria. Victor had been ostracized because of severe neurofibromatosis, a genetic disorder that causes tumors in the nervous system resulting in skin, skeletal, and facial deformities. The nineteenth-century Englishman Joseph Merrick suffered the same affliction and was known as "the elephant man" because of his disfigurement. Several books, a play, and a Hollywood movie were based on Merrick's life.

Nigeria has severely limited medical facilities with little capability to offer effective treatment for Victor's condition. He was isolated and stayed home most of the time because he was subjected to verbal abuse and ridicule. "I wouldn't go outside. I felt so ashamed," he told a reporter. "Everywhere I went, people were making jokes. All the kids would just stare at me. I couldn't face it." He could not attend a regular school.

But Victor's life took a turn for the better at age fifteen when Mother Mary Paul and the nuns who were sheltering him found a plastic surgeon in Southfield, Michigan, willing to help Victor for free. After the first surgery, he said later, he looked in the mirror and thought "it was like a new person was looking at me." It would take a series of nine major surgeries over twelve years to reshape Victor's face, even breaking his jaw to make it more symmetrical, and replace tumors with skin grafts. He did lose a right eye and has a large facial scar.

While he recovered, Victor lived in the nuns' convent in Oak Park, Michigan, studied for and passed his GED, then began taking classes at Oakland Community College. He transferred to Wayne State University, his education paid for through a benefactor known to the nuns. He made the dean's list every semester, and he graduated in 2011 with two chemistry degrees.

Wayne State raised money for a plane ticket to bring his mother to Michigan for his graduation ceremony. I helped clear the way by getting a special visa for his mother, who stayed in the United States for eleven days, taking in a Detroit Tigers ballgame and a visit to the Henry Ford Museum.

That wasn't the end of the matter, though. Victor was accepted by the University of Toledo College of Medicine, but he had overstayed his visa and was facing deportation. The private bill I introduced for him was passed by my colleagues in the Senate because Victor's was such a compelling story. His odds in the House were against him, but never underestimate nuns on a mission. They contacted religious sisters all over the country who contacted their members of Congress, including Nancy Pelosi, who weighed in on it. Approximately a year later the bill became law, and Victor was allowed to stay in the United States and go to medical school.

Another compelling immigration case I worked on involved a family man and restaurant owner from Turkey, Ibrahim Parlak. Parlak came to the United States in 1992, openly declaring that he had ties to the Kurdistan Workers Party, known by the initials PKK, and was fleeing persecution by the Turkish government. He was granted asylum here, married, and opened a popular restaurant in Harbert, Michigan. Then, in 1997, the U.S. State Department retroactively declared the PKK a "terrorist organization," and immigration officials moved to deport him over the strong objections of people in the local community who came to love and admire Parlak.

The restaurant is in Republican congressman Fred Upton's district. Upton called Parlak a "model immigrant" and introduced several private bills on his behalf every session for a decade. Unlike private bills filed in the Senate, a private bill introduced by a member of the House does not suspend a deportation because it is not referred to a committee for a possible hearing. The bills that I sponsored each Congress suspended Parlak's deportation until I retired in 2015. The delays created by those repeated suspensions worked their magic, and the court matter was settled when the Department of Homeland Security finally agreed to end their effort to deport Parlak.

It is unfortunate that most members are reluctant to sponsor private bills because private bills can remedy some of the worst injustices and delay deportation until other factors or new circumstances intervene. Doing so, however, does take staff time and requires a willingness to say "no" to many meritorious requests. But it is well worth the effort.

12

The Filibuster

When I arrived in Washington I had two conflicting preconceptions of the unique Senate practice called the filibuster. On the one hand, I had seen the movie *Mr. Smith Goes to Washington* and gained the romantic view that one senator fighting for some great cause could bring the Senate to a halt for a significant period of time and affect public opinion with the content of his remarks. On the other hand, I also thought of the filibuster as an instrument to thwart progress, particularly civil rights legislation that had been filibustered to death by southern senators until President Lyndon Johnson, who many believe had been the most effective majority leader in Senate history, strong-armed a breakthrough.

Once in the Senate, however, I found the reality to be far different than either of those images. Primarily, I learned that there were very few real filibusters where senators opposed to a pending matter would actually go to the Senate floor and take turns talking for hours or days in an effort to effectively defeat the measure. In fact, I don't think there were more than a handful of those "real" filibusters during my thirty-six years in the Senate. What were commonplace, however, indeed more and more common until they became routine, were so-called gentleman filibusters where a senator could prevent a matter from coming to the floor of the Senate for consideration by withholding consent to proceed, thus placing a "hold" on a matter. A "hold" is a request by a senator that a matter not be considered by the Senate with the implicit understanding that if the matter were to be brought up, the senator with the hold would filibuster it.

Until the 2000s the "hold" could be made informally by transmitting it orally to that senator's party leader. Over time, a letter was required, but the letter would frequently be kept confidential by the party leader. A few years later, some reformers in the Senate were able to change that practice, requiring that holds be made public. That reform didn't accomplish much, though, because most of the time senators put holds on a bill so opponents could know who opposes it and enter into negotiations for modifications or to inform the public and the media that there is opposition and why.

In addition, a hold is effective only if the Majority Leader, the person who determines the Senate schedule, wants it to be effective or, at a minimum, allows it to be effective. All the Majority Leader ever had to do to end a hold was to file a motion to proceed to the matter and force the person placing the hold to actually filibuster. But because the Majority Leader rarely did that, a mere "hold" on a matter generally succeeded in blocking consideration of that matter for a substantial length of time.

I believed that the threats to mount a filibuster were frequently hollow and had to be tested. They were hollow because "real" filibusters would require senators giving up weekends and recesses and being in session twenty-four hours, seven days a week, with resulting inconveniences to themselves, their families, and their obligations back in their states. The Senate is, if anything, a test of wills. Republican threats to filibuster President Obama's judicial opponents should have met with our determined response to "make them filibuster." I repeatedly urged the Democratic Caucus to force the Republicans to actually do what they threatened to do, that is, force them to filibuster, but to no avail, because most Democrats were unwilling to risk the same inconveniences and disruptions of a filibuster as the Republicans would face if they followed through on the threats. As a result, the Republican tactic of threatening to filibuster President Obama's nominations of judges, which should have been countered with the resolute strength allowed by the Senate rules, was allowed to thwart votes on a large number of Obama judges, leading to the use of the so-called nuclear option, the parliamentary move that violated our rules and now allows a simple majority to end debate on judges instead of a 60-vote supermajority.

The "Nuclear Option"

The dramatic moment when the "nuclear option" was used occurred in November 2013 when one of President Obama's Court of Appeals nominees was called up for Senate consideration. Majority Leader Harry Reid's frustration with the Republican tactic of putting holds on Obama's nominations boiled over. Reid moved to end the debate on the nominee. The presiding officer, Senator Patrick Leahy, the acting president pro tem, on the advice of the Senate parliamentarian, correctly ruled that it would take 60 votes to do so, as provided in the Senate's written rules. But then in an unprecedented move, Reid challenged that ruling, knowing that if he could get a simple majority to vote with him on the challenge, he could overturn the ruling of the presiding officer and allow a bare majority to end debate and proceed to the nomination, thus overriding the 60-vote requirement. Reid's challenge was upheld by the majority and thus a new precedent was created and now stands until it is overturned. Vice President Biden, who as president of the Senate often presided on critical votes, told me that he decided not to preside during this debate because he believed the nuclear option was a mistake.

It was a historic moment for the Senate. Despite concerns from a number of other Democrats, all but three supported Reid's challenge. I was one of the three for a couple of reasons. First, as I said before, I did not believe those filibustering would sacrifice the regularity of their personal lives for the confirmation of a federal judge, and second, because I feared for what it would lead to down the road. And it wasn't long before President Trump was able to get two Supreme Court justices confirmed by a Republican Senate with less than 60 votes when Majority Leader Mitch McConnell expanded the nuclear option to cover Supreme Court nominees. Would the Republicans have initiated use of the nuclear option if Democrats had not used it first? Perhaps, but we'll never know.

The Senate is unique in the democratic world. It has at times been called the "world's greatest deliberative body," and from time to time it has lived up to that appellation. Too often it does not. The reason that it has the ability to be a truly deliberative body is that, unlike the House of Representatives, its rules provide significant rights to minority party members. Central to those minority rights is the right to speak and to offer amendments until 60 senators vote to end debate. The "nuclear option" did more than partially destroy a Senate rule. It has significantly weakened the Senate as an institution and has contributed to hyperpartisanship, divisiveness, and the lessening of civility. And it could get worse. If the majority chooses, it could apply the nuclear option precedent to legislation where there would be no minority right to debate or offer amendments. The Senate, as a result, has moved in the direction of a body where the majority rules and the rules themselves can be changed by that majority at any time.

Hopefully someday the "nuclear option" precedent will be overturned. Doing so would not only help ensure the Senate's ability to be the great deliberative body it was intended to be but also increase the likelihood of compromise to resolve the great issues of the day. The 60-vote rule is a great engine of compromise. The requirement that 60 votes are needed to get serious legislation passed forces a majority of less than 60 to reach out to the minority in order to get the necessary votes. During a period of our history when political divisions seem so much deeper than usual and partisanship seems so raw and so rife, the filibuster's ability to force the majority party to reach across the aisle is particularly necessary, as my Legislative Director Rich Arenberg so persuasively argued, and should be recognized as an important value in a democratic society as diverse as ours.

Using the Filibuster for Michigan

In addition to the way they can bring senators together, filibusters and rules governing filibusters have been used to stop regressive legislation and to promote progressive legislation. One example of that value of the filibuster in which I was involved occurred during the recession of 1982. That recession hit Michigan particularly hard, with stories of people selling their blood to put food on the table. The Senate was considering a highway bill that was largely an anti-recession jobs bill. I wanted to amend it to provide unemployment benefits beyond the basic twenty-six weeks and the extended thirteen weeks provided in current law. Senator Arlen Specter, Republican from Pennsylvania, joined me in offering an amendment that on its face seemed unlikely to pass since the Democrats were in the minority and, only a year earlier, most Republicans had voted to tighten the rules on unemployment benefits as part of President Reagan's spending cut program. We looked for a way to present the amendment to avoid asking Republican senators to vote the opposite way they had voted only a year earlier.

We needed to force the Finance Committee chairman, Bob Dole, who was managing the bill, to negotiate with us. We did that by using the rules of the filibuster on the highway bill. Republican Leader Howard Baker recognized that if he cut off debate on the bill it would have the effect of preventing non-germane amendments (like ours) from being offered. So he moved to invoke "cloture" (cut off debate), which requires 60 votes and which is how the Senate defeats filibusters. Fortunately, along with strong Democratic support for our position, Senator Jesse Helms, Republican from North Carolina, and several other Republican senators voted against cloture because they didn't like the highway bill's price tag. We thus won the cloture vote, and at that point, Senator Dole had to work with us. We got most of our amendment adopted, with Michigan being among the states eligible for the most additional benefits.

Shortly after the vote, Senator Dan Inouye walked up to my desk on the Senate floor, leaned over, and said, "Congratulations, Carl. You are the first person to stop the Reagan juggernaut."

The next day, my legislative director, Chuck Cutolo, who helped design our strategy, took a call in our office. It was from a Michigan constituent. "Tell Senator Levin, thank you for saving my house." What he didn't know was that he had the filibuster rules to thank as well.

Reforming the Filibuster

That does not mean, however, that the rules governing the filibuster did not need reform. In late 2012 eight of us (four Democrats and four Republicans) got together to propose filibuster reform to the Senate leadership. Our goal was to address some of the abuses that occurred from allowing unlimited debate at all stages of a bill's consideration by the Senate. For instance, even those like myself, who see real advantages to requiring 60 votes to pass a bill where there is a determined opposition of 40 or more senators, believe the filibuster rule needed to be reformed to prevent filibusters from being used to stop a bill from even coming to the Senate floor for debate, or, once passed, to prevent it from going to conference with the House.

I convened meetings, without staff, on a number of mornings in my Senate "hideaway" (an extra, small, personal office) in the Capitol. We produced a recommendation for those reforms in a private letter dated December 18, 2012, to Majority Leader Harry Reid and Minority Leader Mitch McConnell. On January 24, 2013, at the beginning of the 113th Congress, Reid, on behalf of McConnell, Senator McCain, and myself (representing all eight of us), offered a resolution amending the Senate permanent rules to limit debate and prevent a filibuster on the motion to proceed to the consideration of a bill, on proceeding to a conference with the House, and on the appointment of conferees. The change was adopted unanimously. My colleagues who worked so well together were Lamar Alexander, John Barrasso, Ben Cardin, Jon Kyl, John McCain, Mark Pryor, and Chuck Schumer. We worked without publicity or need for recognition. That is often the key to success in a politically sensitive climate. A bipartisan effort to achieve a common goal succeeded again, and several impediments to a functioning Senate were removed.

The Case of Terri Schiavo

Part of the Senate's appeal to its members, with its rules permitting liberal debate and amendments, is that it gives individual senators an opportunity to have a significant impact. I've been involved in a number of situations where because of Senate rules, I, as a single senator, was able to make a significant difference. Two occasions come to mind where that happened. One was particularly dramatic. It involved the heart-rending case of Theresa (Terri) Schiavo. Ms. Schiavo suffered a heart attack in 1990 that resulted in severe brain damage caused by a lack of oxygen. A tube providing nutrition was inserted at that time in order to keep her alive. Her comatose condition continued for over a decade at which point Ms. Schiavo's husband, deciding that his wife would want the tube removed, pressed for its removal, but Ms. Schiavo's parents opposed it. Two Florida courts ordered that it be removed, holding that the testimony of Ms. Schiavo's husband as to her wishes should be given primary consideration over her parents' wishes. In response, the Florida legislature passed a law authorizing Florida's governor to reinsert the tube, but the Florida Supreme Court ruled that the law was unconstitutional. Ms. Schiavo's parents then came to Congress for help.

The House of Representatives passed a bill giving standing to Ms. Schiavo's parents to argue in federal court that one or more of her federal constitutional rights would be violated if the tube were removed. When the bill came to the Senate floor, a number of us objected to its passage because we did not believe there was a federal right involved. Those of us who opposed the House-passed bill succeeded in getting several amendments adopted before it was approved by the Senate. The key amendment (referred to as Section 5), which I offered, explicitly gave the federal court discretion as to whether or not to require that the tube continue to be inserted pending the resolution of the parents' federal case. This was to counter the House bill that made it mandatory that the tube remain in place during the pendency of the federal lawsuit, which could last for years.

The Senate recessed on Friday, March 18, 2005, for the weekend, not having resolved the differences between the House and the Senate bills. The tube was then removed for the third time pursuant to the existing Florida court order. Republican Majority Leader Bill Frist, hoping to get a bill passed that Saturday by unanimous consent, proposed that Section 5 of the Senate bill be stricken and that the issue of whether a court could "stay" removal of the tube pending the resolution of the federal case be left unaddressed in the final legislation. I objected because I was afraid that striking Section 5 could be read by a court to mean that Congress intended that the court would not have discretion. I worked on a colloquy with Majority Leader Frist in which he and I agreed that if Section 5 were struck from the bill that "the absence of any stay provision in the new bill simply means that Congress relies on current law . . . and that under current law a judge may decide whether or not a stay is appropriate." Having agreed to that statement in our colloquy, we both added our own statements of what we thought the court would do. Majority Leader Frist said that he assumed that the federal court would exercise its discretion and grant a stay, and I said that I did not share Frist's assumption. With that addition, the Senate bill passed by unanimous consent, and the House passed the Senate bill just after midnight on March 20, 2005.

Adding dramatic impact to his support for keeping Ms. Schiavo on a feeding tube pending a court decision, President Bush flew through the night from Texas to Washington to sign the bill. Two days later the 11th Circuit Court of Appeals denied the petition by Ms. Schiavo's parents to prevent the removal of the tube pending the Court's decision and noted the "enlightening exchange in the legislative history concerning the Senate bill that was enacted," referring to the colloquy between Majority Leader Frist and myself.

This matter is also an example of how quickly Congress can act when it wants to do so. At the time of the Senate vote, only a few senators were in Washington. Yet, working through staff and the Majority Leader, the bill was passed by the Senate.

Habeus Corpus for Guantanamo Bay Detainees

I participated in another notable colloquy on a defense authorization bill that same year with Senator Lindsey Graham of South Carolina. One of the issues in the bill was the right of aliens who are detained at Guantanamo Bay, Cuba, to have access to the federal courts, including the right to pursue habeas corpus (a hearing on the lawfulness of one's detention), which the Supreme Court had previously upheld by a bare majority.

Several pending cases were challenging the validity of the military commissions. Senator Graham introduced an amendment to the defense authorization bill that addressed the issue. His amendment provided a process for a status review of detainees being held and an appeal of that status review to a combatant status review (CSR) tribunal with a subsequent appeal to a federal court. The appeal to federal court was limited to a review of the CSR's decision in lieu of the right to seek habeas corpus. Significantly, it applied the new process retroactively, meaning it would apply to any case then currently pending before a court, including the *Hamdan* case in the Supreme Court.

While I agreed with the major thrust of the Graham amendment, my principal objection was Congress interfering with a pending Supreme Court case. I found stripping the Supreme Court of jurisdiction in a pending case highly objectionable under the separation of powers provisions in the Constitution. But the Graham amendment passed on November 10, 2005, by a vote of 49 to 42.

Shortly thereafter Senator Graham came to me and said he wanted to work out a modification of his amendment to gain the support of some of those who had voted against it. I can't think of another time when the winner of a vote on an amendment sought a compromise after winning, but I was certainly more than amenable to improving the Graham amendment. We agreed, among other changes, to strike the language in the previously adopted Graham amendment that applied the new procedures retroactively to pending cases.

During Senate consideration of the modified amendment now called the Graham-Levin amendment, I emphasized the fact that the modified amendment did not apply the new procedures to pending cases and did not affect the jurisdiction of the Supreme Court to hear the *Hamdan* case. I said that I strongly opposed the first version of the Graham amendment because "it would have stripped all the courts, including the Supreme Court, of jurisdiction over pending cases. . . . This (modified) amendment will not strip the courts of jurisdiction over those cases. For instance the Supreme Court's jurisdiction in

Hamdan is not affected." Later in the debate I also pointed out that the Graham-Levin amendment "would not apply the habeas prohibition in paragraph one to pending cases."

I reiterated the point shortly before the vote on Graham-Levin on November 15, 2005. I told the Senate that the original "Graham amendment, which the Senate approved last Thursday, includes a prohibition on federal courts having jurisdiction to hear habeas petitions. . . . The habeas prohibition in the Graham amendment applied retroactively to all pending cases—this would have the effect of stripping the federal courts, including the Supreme Court, of jurisdiction over all pending cases, including the *Hamdan* case . . . Under the Graham-Levin amendment, the habeas prohibition would take effect on the date of enactment of the legislation. Thus, this prohibition would apply only to new habeas cases filed after the date of the enactment." The Graham-Levin amendment was then adopted by a vote of 84 to 14.

Despite the clarity of the Senate debate and the Senate vote, the Department of Justice argued to the Supreme Court that the new prohibition on detainee habeas actions applied to future actions that were pending in any federal court including the *Hamdan* case in the Supreme Court.

The *Hamdan* case was decided by the Supreme Court on June 29, 2006. Justice John Paul Stevens, writing for the majority, rejected the government's argument that the new prohibition on habeas applied to pending cases for a number of reasons, including the statements that I had made on the Senate floor preceding passage of the act. Justice Stevens reviewed the legislative history, noting that the original Graham amendment applied the habeas corpus prohibition to pending cases and that the prohibition was then modified so that it would apply only to new cases filed after the date of enactment. Then Justice Stevens noted that it was the new language that "became the text" of the finally adopted amendment and that "all statements made during the debate itself support Senator Levin's understanding that the final text of the [Detainee Treatment Act] would not render [the new procedures] applicable to pending cases." The Supreme Court then ruled in favor of Hamdan, stating that the military commission system violated both the Code of Military Justice and the Geneva Conventions.

Correspondence with Justice Scalia

I was present at the *Hamdan* oral argument at the Supreme Court as well as when the Court delivered its opinion. It was very gratifying to learn that my efforts to protect the constitutional independence of the legislative and judicial branches of our government had succeeded. But I also experienced a rare insight into Justice Antonin Scalia, one of the most influential Supreme Court justices in my time in the Senate.

His comments in his dissenting opinion and when orally delivering that opinion were shockingly uninformed. He demeaned and diminished the relevance of oral debate on the Senate floor. He wrote that it is a "fantasy that Senate floor speeches are attended (like the Philippics of Demosthenes) by throngs of eager listeners, instead of being delivered (like Demosthenes practice sessions on the beach) alone into a vast emptiness. Whether the floor statements are spoken where no Senator hears, or written where no Senator reads, they represent at most the views of a single senator."

Justice Scalia continued, with reference to my statements on the Senate floor, that "the statements were made when members of Congress were fully aware that our continuing jurisdiction over this very case was at issue" and that the floor statements were "undoubtedly opportunistic and crafted solely for use in the briefs in this very litigation." He suggested that senators who participated in the debate were simply reading prepared statements that staff members had placed in front of them.

I was offended by his comments and couldn't let his ignorance of the way the Senate operates go unaddressed. So I wrote to him. I told him that his statements were "inaccurate and frankly, offensive." I wrote that I had "worked openly to modify the (first Graham) amendment after it passed." I told him that I stated that one of the three changes in the modified amendment "would allow the federal courts to retain jurisdiction over pending cases" and that "I did so to ensure that the Senate would act with a clear understanding that the changes we were considering were intended in part to undo what we had previously done." I added that "what I totally fail to understand is how you can describe the action of explaining to colleagues what we were proposing, and why they should support it, as 'opportunistic.'" I closed my letter to Justice Scalia with the following paragraph: "As to your statement from the bench about the role of congressional staff, I assure you that we rely upon our staff to assist us in much the same manner that you rely upon your law clerks—no more and no less. Your statement demeans the Senate in a way that I hope no Senator would demean your Court and its justices."

I didn't assume that I would hear back from Justice Scalia, but a few weeks later he responded, including a lengthy discussion on the word "opportunistic." He assured me that he did not use the word in a pejorative sense but as a single "action that seizes a present opportunity." He wrote that "there is surely nothing dishonorable about seizing the moment to assure, as you most effectively did, a Supreme Court opinion favoring your interpretation of pending legislation." What he missed completely was that it was not my "interpretation" of the legislation—the modified amendment was clear; it was my highlighting what the modified amendment did, so everyone was aware of the change from the previous language.

Justice Scalia then took on the issue of the relatively few members of the Senate who are on the floor during debates. He wrote, "Regrettably, the Congressional Record does not show how many of your colleagues were on the floor to hear your explanation, but it is rare indeed that more than a few are present before the vote." He totally ignored the well-known fact that debate on the Senate floor on critical issues is heard and seen in every senator's and every committee office and usually by more than one Senate staffer assigned to follow the debate to ensure that they report to their senators if comments on the floor require a response.

Finally, as to his prior comments on our reliance on staff to draft statements, Justice Scalia wrote, "Not only is the court's use of the floor debates openly selective but the fragments of senatorial speech that it relies on were (quite clearly) deliberately prepared by the staff of a tiny handful of senators to be cited in the briefs in this very litigation." Of course senators rely on staff to draft statements just as judges rely on clerks to draft orders and briefs, and, just as judges stand behind their opinions, senators stand behind their statements. The exchange with Justice Scalia was unusual, and I appreciated his writing, but his thinking in these matters was disappointing indeed.

The Line-Item Veto

Congress's sensitivity to the importance of the separation of powers concept was demonstrated in *Hamdan*, when we avoided interfering in a pending Supreme Court case. I got involved in another significant separation of powers issue when the Senate was debating, and the Supreme Court would later be deciding, whether providing a line-item veto for the president was constitutional. On March 27, 1996, the Senate approved a bill that would give the president authority to strike from an appropriation bill that he was signing those items he did not approve. Presidents had been arguing for a line-item veto power for decades, but it represented a massive shift in power from the legislative to the executive branch. Under the leadership of Democratic Leader Robert Byrd, a number of us Democrats and a few Republicans joined together in a struggle to defeat what we considered clearly to be a violation of the Constitution.

Article I of the Constitution is part of a brilliant system of checks and balances and gives the power of the purse exclusively to the Congress. I put great emphasis in my part of the Senate debate on the words of James Madison in Federalist No. 58, in which he said that the power of the purse was granted to Congress because it represents the "most complete and effectual weapon with which any Constitution can arm the immediate representatives of the people for obtaining a redress of every grievance and for carrying into effect every just and salutary measure." I argued that Congress, consistent with Article I, cannot give the power to the president to cancel provisions of a spending bill that he is signing and that we should not even try to do so. I pointed out that even though the supporters of the line-item veto argue that it would help reduce the deficit, during the Reagan-Bush years the presidents' budgets more often had greater deficits than the budgets that were adopted by the Congress.

I also cited studies by nonpartisan groups demonstrating that line-item veto provisions in state constitutions were more often used by governors for partisan political purposes, that is, governors were threatening to veto funding projects of members of their legislatures unless members would commit to vote for policies or projects that the governors favored. And even if the chief executive did not use the power for partisan or political purposes, I reminded the Senate of the Supreme Court's decision to stop President Truman's attempt to take control of the nation's steel mills where Justice Frankfurter wrote that "the accretion of dangerous power does not come in a day. It does, however slowly, come from the generative force of unchecked disregard of the restrictions that fence in even the most disinterested assertion of authority." President Nixon tried to steal the purse that the Constitution gives to Congress when he impounded EPA appropriations. The Supreme Court stopped that theft in 1975, but in its willingness to give the president a line-item veto power, Congress was now volunteering to hand over the purse, and part of its constitutional duties, to the president.

The new line-item veto authority given to the president was to take effect on January 1, 1997. Our bipartisan group of six, led by Senator Byrd, filed a lawsuit one day later challenging the constitutionality of the Line Item Veto Act. Six months later the Supreme Court ruled that we did not have standing to challenge the act. That did not end the matter, since a lawsuit had been filed by several plaintiffs who clearly did have standing. The six of us joined in support of their effort with an amicus brief. On June 25, 1998, the Supreme Court, by a vote of 6 to 3, held the Line Item Veto Act to be unconstitutional. The wisdom of the Founding Fathers remained as fresh and powerful as when they wrote the Constitution over two hundred years ago. The Supreme Court, by preserving a vital congressional power, saved us from ourselves and from our own weakness and reluctance to make tough budget decisions.

Senate Seniority

On an earlier occasion I had worked with my fellow freshman senator, Alan Simpson, a Republican from Wyoming, to change the seniority ranking of new senators, a system we thought was unfair. Seniority can matter in the Senate in a host of ways, from preference for committee assignments to office space to the location of seats in the Senate chamber. Both the Republican and Democratic caucuses had for a long time assigned the seniority ranking of new senators in the following order: highest priority was given to a senator who had previously served; second priority was given to former vice presidents; third was former members of the House of Representatives; the next highest priority was given to former cabinet members; the next to former governors; and the lowest priority to senators according to the population of their state. The unfairness arose because both caucuses made an exception to those rankings: if a new senator could get sworn in a few days before other new senators were sworn in, he or she would have higher seniority. The absurd result was that a new senator from the smallest state who had never held political office before could get higher seniority than a former governor, senator, or congressman.

Senator Simpson and I had a friendly bet as to who could get his caucus to change the procedure first. He won by a week, but both of us were able to get the rules changed so that the unfairness and quirky arbitrariness that could have a major impact on a senator's power down the road was finally ended. Senator Simpson and I and our families became very close friends over the years, and it started with that friendly bet at the beginning of our time together in the Senate.

The episode was yet another example of the importance of both the details of Senate procedures and the role of personal relationships.

13

Ethics and Impeachment

When I first ran for the Senate, ethics issues were very much in the news as the country dealt with the fallout from Watergate. That was the year Congress adopted the Ethics in Government Act, which included key provisions to create an independent counsel system to handle allegations of misconduct by high-level federal officials. Under that law, an independent counsel was to be selected not by the attorney general, who is an appointee of the president, but by a three-member panel of federal judges in order to ensure an impartial investigation and resolution of wrongdoing by top government officials. It was an important chapter in the never-ending effort to achieve an ethical government, which is so central to maintaining public support for democratic government.

For many years the Independent Counsel Law did an excellent job, including the work of Independent Counsel Lawrence Walsh, who prosecuted high-level Reagan officials for violating our laws that prohibited the sale of weapons to Iran and support for the Contras in Nicaragua and who had lied and withheld information from Congress about those activities. The Independent Counsel Law expired in 1987 and needed to be reauthorized for another five years. Republican senator Bill Cohen of Maine and I, from our positions as chairman and ranking member of the subcommittee with jurisdiction, twice led the way in the Senate for that reauthorization, once in 1987 and again in 1995. As I said during the 1987 floor debate, the Independent Counsel Law is a "invaluable achievement" that "enjoys the public's trust" and has eliminated the "uncertainty, unpredictability and skepticism that characterized investigation of high government officials prior to its enactment." The law withstood a challenge in the Supreme Court that, in 1988, upheld the act's constitutionality. But it was grossly misused by the last Independent Counsel, Kenneth Starr, in the case involving President Bill Clinton, and was allowed to die as a result.

But before we get to that sad story, there were a number of achievements in the area of ethics in the 1980s and 1990s that had a more lasting impact. In 1995 Bill Cohen and I led the successful effort in the Senate to pass a ban on gifts from special interests and lobbyists to members of Congress, in particular free travel and stays at resorts, expensive meals, and tickets to sporting events. We also prohibited the acceptance of honoraria for making speeches, most of which came from those same sources. I had always refused to accept honoraria for speeches, and nothing seemed to please audiences more when a person introducing me at a speech made reference to that fact. My stance on the subject was considerably less popular at home, because Barbara and I were struggling a bit financially, trying to put our three children through high school and college.

In other ethical advances in the 1980s and 1990s, the Senate removed several federal judges from office following their impeachment by the House of Representatives, and the Senate's own Ethics Committee recommended punishment and removal of two of our members, which led to their resignation. In a much more visible action, a special committee of the Senate recommended censure of five of our members in the "Keating Five" case, in which several senators were accused of interfering, on behalf of a contributor, with an investigation of a financial institution as part of the savings and loan crisis at that time. And, there was the investigation and resignation of Attorney General Ed Meese in which I was heavily involved, as discussed in chapter 4.

Lobbying Disclosure

In late 1995 Bill Cohen and I again led the Senate in a decades-long battle: how to bring transparency to paid lobbying. The law at the time required lobbyists to disclose their activities, but it was full of loopholes that rendered it nearly useless. Efforts to plug the loopholes had been proposed as far back as President Truman in the late 1940s. A reform bill passed the Senate in the 1960s but was never even debated in the House. In 1976 both houses passed reform legislation, but the differences in the bills could not be reconciled in a conference between the two houses.

Bill and I worked on our proposal for five years, and our efforts took some interesting twists and turns. For instance, the organization Common Cause, a watchdog group that advocates government reform, strongly supported our bill in 1992 but withdrew its support in 1993 when we separated out the provisions regulating gifts and put them in a stand-alone bill in order to make passage more likely. I said at the time that the new position of Common Cause was an illustration of an old adage: "Give them an inch, and they'll demand a mile." The Senate passed our lobbying bill, nonetheless, in May 1993 by a vote of 95 to 2. The House version did not pass until the following March when it was approved by a vote of 315 to 110. But because of differences between the House and the Senate versions, the bill went to conference. The compromise version that came out of conference in September 1994 was agreed to by the House by a vote of 306 to 112, but the travails of getting this version of the bill enacted were not over because of a filibuster in the Senate that prevented a vote on the compromise. Lobbyists had waged a major effort to defeat the bill, and they gathered outside the Senate floor for the vote to end the filibuster. When it was announced that the vote had in fact failed, their voices cheering the result could be heard from inside the chamber.

We were disgusted, but we didn't give up, and in July 1995 the Levin-Cohen bill passed the Senate after we assured the senators that it did not cover so-called grassroots lobbying (non-professional lobbying); that it contained simple, understandable ways for individuals and organizations to register; and that it avoided needless, duplicative paperwork requirements for nonprofit organizations. On November 29, 1995, it passed the House unanimously without any amendments, and the Lobbying Disclosure Act of 1995 became law. It had taken years of effort and decades of toothless laws on the books to force lobbyists to disclose whom they were representing, whom they were lobbying, on what issues they were seeking to influence Congress or the executive branch, and how much they were being paid to do so. But our efforts and patience had been rewarded.

It was well worth the effort because it closed so many of the loopholes that had bred disrespect for the previous law. For instance, some of the most effective and highly paid lobbyists are lawyers, and yet lawyer/lobbyists were exempt from disclosure until our law was passed. The previous law also was interpreted so that only direct lobbying of members of Congress was covered, ignoring lobbying of their staffs, despite the fact that most lobbying is with staffs, not members. And the previous law completely excluded the executive branch. We closed that loophole, too.

The sunshine and public scrutiny that are so essential for democracy to flourish were greatly enhanced by that act, and this was dramatized when the number of lobbyists who registered multiplied just one year after the passage of the 1995 act.

When signing the bill, President Clinton used words that I believe ring true with most Americans: "Ordinary Americans understand that organized interests too often can hold too much sway in the halls of power. They know that in Washington an influence industry too often operates in secret and gets special privileges not available to most Americans. Lobbyists in the back room secretly rewriting laws and looking for loopholes do not have a place in our democracy. . . . [This] bill is tough. It will help to restore the trust of the American people in their government." When signing the bill, President Clinton mentioned that he and I had talked about lobbying reform in the first conversation we had had after he was elected president, and he graciously noted that the legislation was "in a very real sense . . . a monument to the years and years of effort that Carl Levin has made."

Campaign Finance Reform

The 1996 presidential campaign brought to the fore the myriad problems with our campaign finance laws—dialing for dollars, paying for access, uncontrolled spending through what was called "soft money," and issue ads. The 1996 election had it all, and the Senate decided to take it on. The Governmental Affairs Committee, on which I served, was the chosen body to investigate campaign finance irregularities. Fred Thompson, Republican from Tennessee, was the chairman, and a dear friend, John Glenn, was the ranking Democrat. We were given money and staff to expose the underbelly of our campaign finance system.

At the beginning of the investigation we Democrats were optimistic that this would be conducted on a bipartisan basis—looking into improprieties by both Republicans and Democrats. But Chairman Thompson had a different view. At the committee's first meeting, Senator Glenn was presented with a laundry list of subpoenas to be issued just to Democrats and their supporters. There was no bipartisan collaboration. The partisanship by Chairman Thompson during that investigation was unexpected and unfortunate. Thompson misjudged the decent intentions of John Glenn, who was all-in on digging for the facts and exposing the abuses by both parties.

We realized we would have to fight for a balanced investigation, and that's what we did under Glenn's leadership. Through 32 days of hearings, 1.5 million pages of documents, 427 subpoenas, and 200 depositions we tried to get the story told of the improper and possibly illegal activities by both Republicans and Democrats and their supporters. In the end we had to publish our own 5,000-page minority report. But contained in the majority and the minority reports were enough accounts of end runs around the limited campaign finance laws on the books that the investigation helped substantiate the urgent need for reform, with the reformers coalescing around the legislation proposed by Senators McCain and Wisconsin Democrat Russ Feingold, the Bipartisan Campaign Reform Act (BCRA), referred to as the McCain-Feingold bill.

I had always had as one of my goals as a senator to strengthen campaign finance laws, and I did everything I could to support McCain and Feingold in their bipartisan effort. As McCain said in September 1998, "The scandal in Washington is not Monica Lewinsky. It is the debasement of our entire political process because campaign financing has run amok."

In July 1999, I objected to and blocked a request by Senate leadership to schedule just a short period of time for debate on the McCain-Feingold bill. Opponents had said they were going to filibuster the bill. The objective of the short time limit by the leadership was to quickly get to a vote on ending the filibuster, knowing that there were not 60 votes at the time to defeat it so they could move on to other business. No other senator objected to the proposal, but I wanted to force those filibustering to actually filibuster, foreshadowing my objection, fifteen years later, to the use of a "nuclear option." I accordingly said to the Senate:

> I am well aware of the opponents' desire to filibuster the McCain-Feingold bill, a bill which is supported by a majority of the members of the Senate. The opponents have every right to do that, and I respect that right. But supporters of campaign finance reform have every right not to back down in the face of a filibuster.

A few months later, we got 52 votes to end the debate on the McCain-Feingold bill, short of the 60 votes needed, and McCain-Feingold lay dormant until 2001.

Debate opened on McCain-Feingold in March 2001. I said to the Senate that the "soft money loophole has eaten the law" and that "practically speaking there are no limits . . . the truth is the public is offended and disgusted by this spectacle and well they should be and we should be too. . . . In order to get these large contributions, access to us is openly and blatantly sold. We sell lunch with a Committee Chairman of your choice for 100,000 bucks. We sell pictures with the President, access to insider meetings and strategy sessions, participation in a Congressional advisory group or a trade mission. The open solicitation of campaign contributions in exchange for access to people with power to affect the life or livelihood of the person being solicited creates the appearance of impropriety and a misuse of power."

I closed my argument to the Senate that day by saying that "permitting the appearance of corruption undermines the very foundation of our democracy—the trust of the people in the system."

We didn't get McCain-Feingold passed that year, but a year later, after fifteen years of struggle, we got the job done.

In 2003, the Supreme Court, in a 5–4 decision in *McConnell v. the FEC*, upheld the key provisions of McCain-Feingold: controlling soft money and regulating issue ads, arguing that too much money in elections can result in corruption. But when the makeup of the Court changed, the loopholes again took over. In the *Citizens United* case in 2010, the Court, in another 5–4 decision, reversed a hundred years of limits on "independent" expenditures and electioneering communications, enabling corporations, unions, and organizations to make unlimited expenditures on behalf of a campaign, so long as the expenditures are not "coordinated" with the campaign. The decision has had an enormous impact on our elections with the arrival of super PACS and spending by organizations that are not required to disclose the names of their donors.

The theory relied on by the Court was that such expenditures were different from direct contributions to those campaigns, demonstrating how distant the Court can be from the real world. The fiction the Court relied on has already shown to be just that, given the fact that those groups follow the lead of the campaigns they are supporting in the messages and the communications they fund.

The floodgates have been reopened, and unlimited money again washes over political campaigns. The issue now is how to restore limits and public trust. A constitutional amendment won't pass Congress for a number of reasons, including Republican opposition. While some Democratic candidates and officeholders benefit from the status quo, the larger number of beneficiaries are Republicans. I'm afraid it will take a change in the makeup of the Supreme Court to change course.

In the meantime, while campaigns with more funding have significant advantages, they don't always win. Candidates who oppose the current rotten system can refuse to take the offensive contributions and can run against the rot and what it buys. One way or another, only a sustained and creative effort will succeed in achieving the clear desire of our people to remove this perversion of our democracy.

The Clinton Impeachment and the Independent Counsel Law

But it was the Clinton impeachment that became the most contentious ethical controversy of the 1990s. It began with the appointment of Kenneth Starr as independent counsel in August 1994 to take over the ongoing Whitewater investigation then being conducted by Special Counsel Robert Fiske. Fiske had been appointed by Attorney General Janet Reno as a special counsel to ensure independence of the Whitewater investigation, since the Independent Counsel Law was not in effect for a short period of time between authorizations.

After Fiske's appointment, Bill Cohen and I had led our second successful effort in the Senate to reauthorize the Independent Counsel Law for an additional five years. President Clinton had consulted with me about the need for such a law and its fair application, and I had assured him of both, obviously not knowing what misuse of the law was in the offing. President Clinton signed the reauthorization bill on June 30, 1994. Lo and behold, to the shock of those of us who understood the vital need for independence under the Independent Counsel Law, the three-judge panel (Special Court) responsible for appointing independent counsels in early August appointed Kenneth Starr to take over the Whitewater investigation on the flimsiest of excuses. The Special Court was led by the very conservative Judge David Sentelle, whose mentor and advocate for his nomination to the bench was Senator Jesse Helms. It made the decision without warning and rejected the advice of Attorney General Janet Reno to retain Fiske.

The pretext the court used was the appearance of a conflict of interest because Fiske had been appointed by Reno. And while avoidance of a conflict of interest was the principal argument for the Independent Counsel Law, the phoniness of the Special Court's justification was obvious. The court replaced Fiske, who was a highly respected Republican and recognized as doing a good job, with Ken Starr, who was involved in the Paula Jones sexual harassment suit against Clinton and had recently appeared on television claiming that President Clinton did not have constitutional immunity from that lawsuit. Starr was also cochair of a highly partisan Republican congressional campaign in Virginia. So Starr had more than an appearance of a conflict; he had a real conflict. In an additional twist, Republican senator Lauch Faircloth, who had led the efforts to have Fiske removed as independent counsel, had personally met with Judge Sentelle in mid-July, just weeks before Fiske was "fired" and Starr was appointed. It sure smacked of political influence.

On August 12, 1994, in my capacity as chairman of the Senate subcommittee with jurisdiction over the Independent Counsel Law, I wrote to Judge Sentelle about my concerns about the appointment of Starr. I pointed out that in the fifteen years the Independent Counsel Law had been in effect, there had never been an issue about the independence of the independent counsel because of the care the Special Court had taken to appoint people who were not involved in partisan activity. I outlined Starr's recent partisan political activities and pointed out that the court claimed it had decided not to continue with Fiske in the position because the law "contemplates an apparent as well as an actual independence on the part of the Counsel" and that the "same standard should apply to Mr. Starr." I then urged the court to "ask Mr. Starr to provide a complete accounting of his recent political activities" and then to "issue a supplementary opinion stating whether those activities impair the appearance of independence that is so critical to the proper functioning of the independent counsel law." I concluded that the "selection of counsels who are independent in fact and appearance is the foundation of the law's success and essential to public acceptance of prosecution decisions." I sent copies of my letter to Judge John Butzner and Judge Joseph Sneed, the other two judges on the Special Court that had appointed Starr, as well as to Attorney General Janet Reno and to Starr himself. It would later turn out that Judge Butzner, the only Democrat among the three judges, had strongly opposed the appointment of Starr. His weak excuse for staying silent and not opposing Starr's appointment was that, as he reminded Judge Sentelle years later, a "dissent on this question would have been perceived as politicizing the court." Indeed, in his archived copy of my letter objecting to Starr's appointment and asking the three judges to reconsider, Judge Butzner underlined my reference to Starr's support of Paula Jones's legal position and wrote next to the underlined words, "Mr. Starr did not mention this at our interview." One can only wonder why he didn't inquire about it after he received my letter.

Six days after receiving my letter the Sentelle court entered an order with a per curiam opinion denying my "motion." (How's that for thoughtful consideration.) The opinion started by saying that I was seeking "to have the court require of the independent counsel an accounting not contemplated in the statute" and that I was seeking to put the court in a "supervisory role." That was a transparent and disturbing dodge, since I was seeking the court's reconsideration of its appointment after reviewing the evidence of Starr's conflict of interest, not its supervision of Starr.

The outrage at Starr's appointment was widespread. Lawrence Walsh, who had proven himself as an extraordinarily professional and truly independent counsel in the Iran-Contra investigation, wrote a very strong letter to the *New York Times* on the subject on August 10, 1994. He first acknowledged Starr as an "able lawyer" but went on to state that Judge Sentelle and his colleagues had replaced "an undisputedly independent investigator and prosecutor (Fiske) with an undisguised partisan (Starr)." Walsh added that "Mr. Starr has had no experience as a prosecutor" and that to "permit such an appointee to take over Mr. Fiske's work undermines the independent counsel process."

The travesty of Starr's appointment would manifest itself in numerous ways during his four-year investigation of President Clinton. While Starr had been appointed to carry on the investigation of the Whitewater matter, Fiske had basically completed that investigation by the time Starr was appointed. That didn't stop Starr, however, from continuing the Whitewater investigation for another three years, during which time he sought the opportunity to expand his hell-bent investigation into President Clinton in May 1997 when the Supreme Court ruled that Paula Jones could continue her civil case against the president. The Court denied Clinton's claim of presidential immunity in that case, since the alleged wrong (sexual harassment) had taken place before he assumed office.

One question in the *Jones* case was whether there was a pattern or practice of sexual harassment by Clinton that would help substantiate Jones's allegation. On January 12, 1998, Linda Tripp brought a tape of her "friend" Monica Lewinsky talking about her relationship with President Clinton to the Starr office, and on January 15, Starr sought an expansion of his jurisdiction to include investigation of the Lewinsky matter. Attorney General Reno approved the request, a faulty but enormously consequential decision by Reno, since Starr's political background and his extension of the Whitewater investigation way beyond what was appropriate, demonstrated his bias.

On January 17, Clinton was deposed in the *Jones* case on whether he had had "sexual relations" with Lewinsky. He swore he had not. For a statement to constitute criminal perjury, the person making the statement must know it is false at the time when it is made. Both President Clinton and Ms. Lewinsky, who had also sworn in her affidavit that she and the president had not had "sexual relations," maintained that they believed the term "sexual relations" meant that there was sexual intercourse, which had not happened. Clinton made a similar claim before the grand jury.

Starr alleged the president's denial was perjury. He added allegations of obstruction of justice and wrote a 453-page report to the House of Representatives. The report identified eleven grounds for impeachment.

A panel of five highly regarded former Democratic and Republican federal prosecutors, who appeared before the House Judiciary Committee on impeachment, testified that this case against the president would not have been pursued by a responsible federal prosecutor. Thomas Sullivan, who served for four years as U.S. Attorney for the Northern District of Illinois, and whom Chairman Hyde described as having "extraordinarily high" qualifications, said:

In conversations with many current and former federal prosecutors in whose judgment I have great faith, virtually all concur that if the president were not involved, if an ordinary citizen were the subject of the inquiry, no serious consideration would be given to a criminal prosecution arising from alleged misconduct in discovery in the Jones civil case having to do with an alleged cover-up of a private sexual affair with another woman or the follow-on testimony before the grand jury. . . . I believe the president should be treated in the criminal justice system in the same way as any other United States citizen. If that were the case here, it is my view that the alleged obstruction of justice and perjury would not be prosecuted by a responsible United States Attorney.

The articles of impeachment that were sent to the Senate were based entirely on the Starr Report. In fact, Supreme Court Justice Brett Kavanaugh, who was then on Starr's staff, acknowledged that Congress "publicly released the report without even reviewing it beforehand." The House had essentially delegated its constitutional responsibility to be the "sole" determiner on impeachment to an outside prosecutor, a known opponent of the president.

The contrast to the Watergate investigation and the impeachment of President Nixon was stark. In the Watergate investigation, the Senate had convened a select committee in February 1973 to investigate the Watergate break-in and other campaign irregularities in the 1972 election. That committee took testimony for a year. In February 1974, the House voted to direct the House Judiciary Committee to conduct an inquiry into impeachment, in keeping with the Constitution's requirement that the House of Representatives has the sole responsibility to impeach. The committee conducted its own investigation and hearings, including subpoenaing the White House tapes and calling numerous fact witnesses. The committee also obtained the report of the grand jury meeting under the authority of Leon Jaworski, the Watergate prosecutor. In deciding to allow the grand jury report to be forwarded to the House Judiciary Committee, Judge John Sirica found that the report "draws no accusatory conclusions . . . contains no recommendations, advice or statements that infringe on the prerogatives of other branches of government . . . [and] renders no moral or social judgments. The Report is a simple and straightforward compilation of information gathered by the Grand Jury, and no more."

But the Starr Report sent to the House of Representatives violated almost every standard followed by Judge Sirica. It drew a host of "accusatory conclusions" that the president perjured himself and obstructed justice in specified ways and tampered with a potential witness. It also contained a large volume of needlessly salacious detail and omitted or dismissed important exculpatory evidence. It was overall a shameful performance by Starr and the House, and in the end it cost the nation what once was a very important process, the Independent Counsel Law, because most members of Congress recognized the extent to which Starr had overreached his position and brought the country to the brink of crisis. Others didn't support the Independent Counsel Law on principle.

Although I was appalled by Starr's investigation and report, I told my colleagues during Clinton's Senate trial that the president's conduct was reprehensible. While I didn't believe his conduct in his private, consensual sexual relationship should have become public business, when it did so, Clinton had the duty to tell the truth.

During the trial itself, I had pointed out the fundamental weakness of the impeachment resolution: that its allegations were highly exaggerated and based on inference and speculation that were directly contradicted by credible sworn testimony. I cited a host of examples in my remarks to the Senate. For one, the House manager had said that "as evidenced by the testimony of Lewinsky, [the president] encouraged her to lie." In fact, Lewinsky repeatedly and under oath said that the president never encouraged her to lie. The House managers also said that when the president gave Lewinsky a carving of a bear that he had obtained in Vancouver "the only logical inference is that the gifts, including the bear symbolizing strength, were a tacit reminder to Ms. Lewinsky that they would deny the relationship even in the face of a federal subpoena." I asked the Senate how something could be "the only logical inference" when it was directly contrary to the direct, uncontroverted, sworn testimony that the gift was purchased by President Clinton on a trip that occurred long before Lewinsky's name appeared on any witness list, and even more importantly, when asked if that was the purpose of the gift, Lewinsky stated under oath, "no." The House managers didn't claim that the sworn testimony that contradicted their inferences was false or perjured. They simply ignored it and said that their inferences and speculation provided "clear" evidence. "The House managers," I said, "would have us overlook the forest of direct testimony while getting lost in the trees of their multiple inferences."

I also laid out a series of factual misstatements that the House managers made during their presentation. For instance, they claimed that Lewinsky's affidavit in the *Jones* case was obtained by promising Lewinsky to find her a job. But Vernon Jordan, a friend of the president, had been asked by President Clinton to look for a job for Lewinsky at least a month before Lewinsky was named as a potential witness in the *Jones* case. I pointed out that the House managers also represented to the Senate that the first activity to help Lewinsky occurred on December 11 and that "nothing (relative to the job search assistance for Lewinsky) happened in November 1997," while in fact our ambassador to the United Nations, at the request of the deputy chief of staff at the White House, indisputably had offered Lewinsky a job at the United Nations on November 3.

No factual and legal analysis of the House managers' overly zealous and factually erroneous presentation was as effective as Senator Dale Bumpers's closing argument against conviction. After going through some of the legal weaknesses, inaccuracies, and speculation, Bumpers urged the Senate to go beyond the legalisms. He talked about the hundreds of divorce cases he had tried and that in most of the cases where perjury was claimed, it had to do with extramarital affairs. He talked about the difference between perjury about marital infidelity in a divorce case and perjury involving the purchase of a murder weapon in a murder case and that our sense of justice would be standing on its head if somebody were charged with the former but punished as if it were the latter. He talked about the purpose of the framers of the Constitution in writing the impeachment provision and that they were determined to address corruption in the political process, offenses that were against the state, or a breach of public trust. Addressing the perjury allegation against Clinton directly, he said that "perjury concealing or deceiving an unfaithful relationship does not even come close to being an impeachable offense," an argument that more than any other carried the day and led to President Clinton's acquittal on February 12, 1999. That same day Senator Dianne Feinstein introduced a resolution of censure for President Clinton. It was a strong condemnation of President Clinton's actions. Twenty-eight Democrats, including myself, and nine Republicans cosponsored it, but it was referred to committee and never brought to the Senate floor.

There had been a number of unexpected twists during the Senate trial. One of them came late in the process, in a desperate effort by the House managers to save their sinking ship. Without notice to the Senate, Starr went to federal court to get an order to require that Lewinsky meet with the House managers for, as he put it, a "briefing." I believe he did it in hopes that Lewinsky would change her testimony. Many of us strongly objected because he had no business interjecting himself in the middle of the Senate's proceedings. Even some Republicans were offended by this precipitous ex parte intervention. Prior to the beginning of the trial the Senate leadership had appointed six senators (of which I was one), three from each party, to attempt to agree on procedures. We succeeded on a bipartisan basis but did not resolve the issue of whether to call witnesses. The House had not called witnesses because, they said, the evidence in the record was so extensive. In other words, they relied solely on Starr's investigation. Also, the House managers, prior to the trial, had not indicated the need to call witnesses. The Starr tactic was characterized by one observer as a "Hail Mary pass," and it surely was that. But with the court order in hand, the House interviewed Lewinsky. Nothing new was elicited, only a reiteration of her previous sworn testimony that President Clinton had never asked her to lie and that she had not been offered a job in exchange for making an affidavit in the *Jones* case. Subsequently, the Senate voted to take depositions from three individuals, including Monica Lewinsky, and taped segments of Lewinsky's deposition, which did not vary from her previous testimony, were presented to the Senate during the trial.

President Clinton's acquittal did not end the matter because it did not preclude criminal prosecution for the same conduct for which he was impeached. A new independent counsel was appointed to succeed Starr. The new independent counsel, Robert Ray, and President Clinton's lawyers worked during 1999 and 2000 to resolve any potential criminal liability. One day before the end of his presidency, on January 19, 2001, President Clinton agreed to a five-year suspension of his license to practice law in Arkansas. In a letter to the independent counsel, Clinton's lawyer, David Kendall, quoted what President Clinton had said to the Starr grand jury—that he "wanted to be legal without being particularly helpful" in his deposition in the *Jones* case. Kendall said that "when it comes to stating now what the President's intention was then in the deposition, all he can in conscience do is say what he told the earlier grand jury: he tried to avoid testifying falsely."

On the same day, a statement from the White House quoted the president as saying, "I tried to walk a line between acting lawfully and testifying falsely, but I now recognize that I did not fully accomplish this goal and that certain of my responses to questions about Miss Lewinsky were false." He did not admit that he had committed perjury, which would have required not that he recognize "now" that certain of his responses to questions were false but that he recognized "then," that is, when he made the statements, that his responses were false. The independent counsel, Ray, may or may not have caught, or even have wanted to acknowledge, the nuance in President Clinton's statement, when, in Ray's final statement, he blurred that distinction by simply stating that President Clinton "has acknowledged that some of his answers were false." He then declined to criminally prosecute President Clinton, which brought the saga to an end. President Clinton was found in civil contempt of court in the *Jones* case for "giving false, misleading and evasive answers that were designed to obstruct the judicial process."

One little-known effort of mine has haunted me, not because it failed, which it did, but because it could have avoided the House's impeachment. President

Gerald Ford had written an editorial in the *New York Times* that October after Starr concluded his investigation in which he had suggested that President Clinton appear in the well of the House of Representatives, not at the rostrum, and that he receive a "harshly worded rebuke as rendered by members of both parties." He said that Clinton would also need to "accept full responsibility for his actions, as well as for his subsequent efforts to delay or impede the investigation of them. No spinning, no semantics, no evasiveness." In December 1998 I wrote President Ford requesting that he consider making a "personal plea to the House members urging them not to impeach the president because of the damage that it would do to the nation and to the presidency." Referring to his pardon of President Nixon, I added, "Once before you protected the presidency and the nation from shame and decline, for which you earned a lasting place in our history." On December 12, President Ford called me and thanked me for my letter, which he said he very much appreciated. He said he had a long talk with his wife, Betty, who he said had more "common sense than anybody." He and I then had a number of calls to clarify what would be needed for him to become involved and recommend that the House censure Clinton instead of impeaching him. He said it would require an acknowledgment by President Clinton that he had committed perjury.

I made a number of suggestions to President Ford about modifying his position as stated in his editorial. He said he would consider my suggestions seriously and would do his "very best." The negotiations broke down between Ford and Chuck Ruff, Clinton's attorney, as there were many factors upon which they could not agree, including the wording of the rebuke, the nature of President Clinton's response, and the location where Clinton would be standing when he received the rebuke and gave what would need to be a limited response. President Ford was always very gracious, and I think he genuinely wished that he could have been helpful to avoid what would soon thereafter take place.

I often wondered if there would have been a difference in the tone of the nation's public debate, which was becoming more and more partisan, if a way had been found for President Clinton to receive censure while standing in the well of the House of Representatives and accept responsibility with less legalistic hairsplitting. When that didn't happen, President Clinton was able to avoid the humiliation that would have accompanied it. Perhaps if President Clinton had agreed to close the wound in that way, the continual harassment of the Clintons by the right wing over the decades might have been seen by even more people for the partisan attacks they were. Not likely, just perhaps.

14

The Permanent Subcommittee on Investigations

The capstone on my career in terms of congressional investigations came when I took over as chair of the Permanent Subcommittee on Investigations, commonly referred to as PSI, in early 2001. PSI is the premier subcommittee in the Senate for investigations, part of the Committee on Homeland Security and Governmental Affairs. PSI has no legislative jurisdiction; instead it has "the responsibility of studying and investigating the efficiency and economy of operations relating to all branches of the government . . . [including] the compliance or noncompliance with rules, regulations and laws, investigating all aspects of crime and lawlessness within the United States which have an impact upon or affect the national health, welfare and safety."

Unlike most committees and subcommittees in Congress, PSI rules allow subcommittee chairs to issue subpoenas on his or her own authority, not requiring a majority vote of the committee. That is a significant power, because it means one individual, the chair of PSI, can force a person to testify or produce documents (retaining, of course, their Fifth Amendment right against self-incrimination) and that testimony can be in a public hearing. Subpoena power carries a heavy responsibility because it can be life-altering for the person subpoenaed.

It also means that as chair you have the power to get the most critical information about an issue that may be buried in corporate files or an individual's bank account. It is the most important tool there is to getting to the bottom of an issue.

PSI has a noteworthy past. It came into being after then-senator Harry Truman, as chairman of a special investigations committee, dug into incidents of war profiteering, waste, and fraud by defense industries during World War II. Truman, who loved to drive, covered thousands of miles visiting various war production sites around the country to see firsthand what was being done. He held hundreds of hearings, issued numerous reports (all of which were unanimous), and ended up saving the war effort millions of dollars.

The success and importance of his committee's work led the Senate to establish a "permanent" subcommittee (PSI) with almost unlimited jurisdiction to investigate wrongdoing by the government or by the private sector when government action might be indicated. The result was an impressive collection of hearings over the years, from the McClellan hearings in the 1960s that exposed organized crime to the Jackson-Percy inquiries in the 1970s into energy shortages and drug trafficking to the Nunn-Roth investigations in the 1980s into money laundering and investment fraud. PSI history also includes the stain of the McCarthy hearings in the 1950s. In his investigation of alleged communists, Senator Joseph McCarthy abused the PSI chairman's subpoena authority, hauling in government officials and individuals whether they were a legitimate target of inquiry or not and bullying them in both closed and public hearings. Nobody could stop him—until he was finally censured by the full Senate.

Like the other chairs who followed the discredited McCarthy, I sought bipartisan support for the subpoenas I issued and was careful in choosing our investigative targets. At the same time, I welcomed the opportunities chairing PSI afforded me to delve into complex and unexposed issues that I thought needed to be addressed for the health of our nation. I had the good fortune to work with Republican counterparts who were committed to fact-finding and open to collaboration: Senators John McCain, Tom Coburn, Norm Coleman, and Susan Collins. Even when partisan acrimony was otherwise bringing legislative progress to a standstill, we were able to make progress on our investigations because our staffs worked together as a team. Led by my exceptional PSI staff director, Elise Bean, the staffs would draft joint document requests and subpoenas, interview witnesses together, write reports with input from both sides, and prepare joint hearing memos and press releases for committee members. It was not always possible to reach agreement on every part of a report, and there were times we had differences on recommendations for reforms, but we were clear that we wanted the facts, wherever that search might lead and regardless of whose toes we stepped on.

The more we operated in this way, the more my staff valued working with their Republican counterparts. They realized that when they investigated with only fellow Democrats, they were too often operating in an echo chamber. They missed certain facts and issues key to fashioning the type of bipartisan appeal that can facilitate meaningful reform. When they worked with staff who held different views than their own, they would uncover more facts, dig more deeply into issues, challenge unspoken assumptions, and interpret what happened with a more sophisticated understanding. In fact, it was the crucible in which each side challenged the other—in respectful, constructive ways—that produced investigative findings that were more thorough, thoughtful, and accurate than they otherwise would have been. And because both sides supported the investigations, they were also more credible to other members of Congress, experts, media, and the public.

Some of our inquiries addressed inequities in the tax system—situations where wealthy individuals and highly profitable corporations make use of egregious tax loopholes or use accounting or legal firms peddling tax-dodging strategies that cost the government and American taxpayers billions of dollars. Other investigations examined the financial abuse of consumers, including schemes by credit card companies to charge hidden and excessive fees and interest. Still others looked at the offensive practices of some of our country's leading Wall Street firms and banks and credit-rating agencies that fueled the financial crisis of 2008 and caused millions of Americans to lose their homes and depleted their net worth. The work I did at PSI consumed an enormous amount of my time in my last fifteen years in the Senate, but it was time well spent.

The 2008 Financial Crisis

The most extensive and dramatic investigation I chaired at PSI looked into the key causes of the financial crisis of 2008. Over the course of two years, we collected and reviewed over 50 million pages of documents, conducted 150 interviews, held four in-depth hearings within the span of a single month, and produced a 750-page report, the longest report during my tenure. It was the only congressional inquiry into the 2008–2009 financial crisis that was bipartisan from beginning to end and reached bipartisan findings of fact and recommendations. My partner throughout the process was Senator Tom Coburn.

The investigation was set up as a four-part inquiry. The final part, which culminated in the most contentious and widely covered hearing of the four we held, occurred when we brought the leadership of Goldman Sachs before PSI. At the time of that hearing, in April 2010, Goldman was one of the few financial institutions that had profited from the financial crisis. They earned billions of dollars from betting against the mortgage market they helped to create and many of the mortgage-backed securities they had designed, packaged, and sold through misleading representations. When confronted by our efforts to hold them accountable, Goldman tried a number of heavy-handed tactics to undermine or discredit PSI's work, including leaking a misleading set of documents the weekend before the hearing. But that was a failed effort to throw us off balance.

The Goldman hearing followed three prior hearings on the subject. The first of those focused on Washington Mutual (WaMu), the sixth largest U.S. bank that became the largest bank failure in U.S. history. WaMu had been one of the biggest issuers of mortgage loans in the country and had increased its profits by shifting from low-risk to high-risk mortgages. It enticed consumers into buying its higher-risk mortgages by offering low initial "teaser" interest rates that would later explode; and it enticed its staff to sell more high-risk mortgages by offering them higher compensation when they did so. WaMu even allowed borrowers to state their income levels on their mortgage applications without double-checking their ability to pay, all in an effort to boost mortgage production. Those so-called stated loans were later called "liar" loans. But WaMu wasn't worried about borrowers exaggerating their income or defaulting on their debts because as soon as the ink was dry on the mortgages, WaMu sold them to investment banks like Goldman Sachs. Goldman didn't care either, since they promptly issued securities whose value was linked to the revenues that presumably would come in from the mortgages being repaid and sold those securities to their unsuspecting customers.

But in between the creation and the securitization of those high-risk mortgages, two additional culprits contributed to the looming financial disaster that would be triggered by the faulty mortgages issued by banks like WaMu and securitized by investment banks like Goldman. The first was the federal regulatory agency, the Office of Thrift Supervision (OTS), that was supposed to oversee thrifts like WaMu and ensure they operated in a safe and sound way. But OTS repeatedly looked the other way despite mounting evidence of WaMu's defective loans, treating WaMu as though it were a valued client to be placated instead of a financial institution to be regulated.

The second culprit was the credit-rating companies, which were supposed to provide objective credit ratings for the mortgage-backed securities that firms like Goldman were designing and selling. The key problem was that the banks seeking ratings for their financial products were also the ones paying the credit-rating agencies for those ratings. The equivalent would be baseball umpires paid by the pitchers whose pitches had to be rated as balls or strikes. Our investigation exposed internal emails from the two largest U.S. credit-rating agencies, Moody's and Standard and Poor's, showing how, in their greed for business and profit, they pressured their analysts to issue higher safety ratings than the securities really deserved.

With all the shady mortgages, toxic mortgage-related securities, and false credit ratings used by Wall Street to sell financial products to investors around the world, it's no surprise that the poisoned mortgage market finally collapsed. The resulting financial earthquake cost our economy over $20 trillion in losses, produced a historic number of home foreclosures, reduced the value of most American homes, bankrupted businesses, cost untold numbers of jobs, and lost billions in pension fund savings for retirees. It also led to the collapse or near collapse of major Wall Street banks, forcing American taxpayers to pay billions of dollars in bailouts to stave off even worse consequences.

The PSI hearings detailing the underhanded conduct of Washington Mutual, OTS, and the credit-rating agencies unfolded over a three-week period in April 2010, building media and public interest in our bipartisan investigation. By the time we were ready to turn to Goldman Sachs, media attention was at a peak. There were more cameras, reporters, activists, bank lobbyists, and members of the public at the Goldman hearing than at any other PSI hearing I chaired. I was glad to see it, because the evidence against Goldman was overwhelming.

Goldman created securities that it peddled aggressively to its customers knowing that the securities were based on bad mortgages. Goldman took in huge fees from those sales and then shamelessly made billions more by secretly betting against the value of its own products. Goldman's negative bets would pay off only if the securities sold to its customers plummeted in value—setting up a blatant conflict of interest between Goldman and its customers, who were spending their money with the expectation that the securities sold to them were a solid investment.

Goldman's defense was a tissue of lies. The biggest lie was that Goldman claimed not to have made money betting against—"shorting"—the mortgage market and the mortgage-related securities they sold. But the bank's own documents showed that it made huge profits from engaging in what one of its own executives called the "big short," betting billions that the value of their mortgage-related holdings would fall. In one email, a Goldman executive, reacting to news that the credit-ratings agencies had downgraded some of the securities sold by Goldman to its clients, told a colleague that because Goldman had already bet against those securities, "we will make some serious money."

Actions taken by Goldman to profit off the crashing mortgage market—even at the expense of its clients—were ruthless.

The second big lie told by Goldman was that when it was selling mortgage-related securities it was simply engaging in "market-making." To be a market-maker means that a firm is willing to either buy or sell securities to meet its customers' desires rather than chase its own profit-making, but in this case Goldman was aggressively selling its own products. Goldman's own internal emails characterized its financial products as "crap," "junk," and a "shitty deal" at the same time Goldman was conducting a massive selling campaign, pushing them to buyers around the world.

At the hearing, with the expectation of obtaining some show of remorse from the Goldman witnesses for selling "junk" and "crap" to their own clients, and in my amazement at their refusal to do so, I repeated the words from their own emails over and over again. Before I did, I leaned over and asked my colleague Susan Collins whether I should use the company's own foul language. She said, "Hey, it's their words." Finally, Goldman's chief financial officer, David Viniar, got flustered and responded to my full-court press about selling what Goldman knew to be "a shitty deal" to a client by blurting out: "I think that is very unfortunate to have in an email." His response produced something between a gasp and angry snorts in the press corps seated behind him. Viniar seemed less bothered about stiffing a client than about being asked to explain evidence of the company's cold disregard for its clients.

Our four-part investigation contributed to significant policy reforms that were enacted in the Dodd-Frank Wall Street Reform and Consumer Protection Act of 2010. That law, which passed a few months after PSI's fourth hearing, stopped banks from issuing "liar loans" that they knew couldn't be repaid. A provision authored by Senator Jeff Merkley from Oregon and me prohibited banks from betting against their own clients. Another part of our provision known as the Volcker Rule—named after respected banker Paul Volcker, who zeroed in on banks' conflicts of interest with clients—barred banks from engaging in so-called proprietary trading, meaning securities transactions in which the banks put their own profits before those of their customers. The law also set up the Consumer Financial Protection Bureau (CFPB), which, as its name indicates, was established to protect American families against predatory financial practices. The law also abolished OTS, the agency that had become subservient to the financial institutions it was charged with overseeing.

That's a short list of Dodd-Frank's many accomplishments, and at the time I was proud to see Congress rise to the challenge of addressing many—though not all—of the abuses that produced the financial crisis. Unfortunately, however, the story didn't stop on that high note. Bank lobbyists and even regulators began stripping away the Dodd-Frank safeguards. Worse yet, Congress has stood by as the Trump administration has weakened the Volcker Rule and the CFPB and allowed increased levels of financial risk in our markets, making it more likely that there will be another financial crisis. Another series of bipartisan congressional oversight hearings is needed to expose the mounting dangers in the U.S. financial system and push for renewing and even strengthening the Dodd-Frank safeguards.

It was also deeply disappointing that in the aftermath of our financial crisis investigation, with all the evidence detailing the greed and client betrayals that led to the crisis, too many wrongdoers walked away not only without punishment but in some cases having profited from the mayhem they helped create.

Congressional oversight authority doesn't include the ability to throw someone in jail or impose monetary fines for misconduct. Oversight committees like PSI can't determine whether criminal conduct has occurred. That function belongs to the executive branch—in particular, the Justice Department and federal regulators. In hopes that they would act, after concluding an investigation, PSI frequently made a referral to the Justice Department, a regulatory agency like the Securities and Exchange Commission, or an agency watchdog like an agency's Inspector General. But referring a matter doesn't require the executive branch to take action to hold anyone accountable, and in too many cases little or nothing happened.

When the federal government imposes a large fine against a corporation, it is invariably part of a settlement that the written agreement state that the corporation is making no admission of wrongdoing. In the Goldman case, for example, the executive branch failed to initiate any criminal prosecutions of the firm or its executives. There were some fines, but for companies like Goldman, those were simply a cost of doing business. What is also unacceptably common is for the federal government to enter into non-prosecution or deferred prosecution agreements with corporations in the face of evidence of actual crimes. Some settlement agreements are even entered into with corporations that have repeatedly settled cases with credible evidence of wrongdoing.

But individual accountability is equally important—maybe more so—because without it the wrongdoers can simply carry on with their lives and keep most of their wrongful gains as if nothing happened. The failure to prosecute responsible individuals in those corporations that did so much economic damage to so many people and the country is a tragedy. If the excuse is that the laws are too weak to prosecute, then the laws need to be changed. Individual accountability in corporate America is essential to keep the greed in check. The government must hold large corporations and the top people in them accountable for their wrongdoing to restore public confidence in law enforcement and our financial system and to ensure that our laws are being equally enforced against the powerful.

Money Laundering

While the investigation into the 2008–2009 financial crisis received the most press, dozens of earlier investigations were also of major significance. In 1999, when I became the ranking Democrat, I initiated a series of investigations into money laundering. Money laundering occurs when people take what is essentially "dirty" money, that is, money obtained illegally, and try to use seemingly reputable banks, securities firms, or other entities as conduits to "cleanse" it by using the funds, for example, to buy houses, airplanes, paintings, or investments.

PSI's chair at this time was Susan Collins, and she was more than willing to have me lead the investigation with my staff director at the time, Linda Gustitus, who assigned it to Elise Bean (later to follow Linda as PSI staff director) and our chief investigator, Bob Roach. Our main target was Raul Salinas, brother of the president of Mexico, and the private bank at Citigroup that facilitated his money laundering. A private bank is a bank inside a bank that provides special, highly personal services for wealthy customers. Other subjects of our investigation were Omar Bongo, dictator of Gabon; Asif Zardari, husband of former prime minister Benazir Bhutto of Pakistan; and the three sons of General Sani Abacha, the recently deceased dictator of Nigeria. The investigation involved half a million pages of documents and a hundred interviews.

The hearings revealed that Citibank, through its private banking system, moved over a hundred million dollars of apparently ill-gotten gains out of Mexico on Salinas's behalf and into anonymous offshore shell corporations to hide the money. Citibank's private bank's sordid activities included the use of phony names and numbers to aid and abet corrupt leaders and their families, with one banker saying he had to keep a cheat sheet under his desk mat to remember who owned which account. As a result of our hearings, Citibank promised reforms, and the Federal Reserve and other bank regulators promised greater enforcement of existing money-laundering laws and regulations. I introduced a bipartisan bill called the Money Laundering Abatement Act at the end of 1999, but it was referred to Texas Republican Phil Gramm's Banking Committee, and our bill went nowhere.

The second part of our money-laundering investigation followed a scandal in which Russian banks moved seven billion dollars of suspicious money into their correspondent banking accounts at the Bank of New York. Correspondent banking allows one bank to open an account at another bank, enabling it and its clients to conduct business at banks worldwide. It means the bank has no need to open a branch; it just opens an account at another bank. Before our hearings there was little screening of the source of the money that went into those correspondent accounts. The lackadaisical treatment was based on an assumption that a bank was a bank and could be trusted, instead of considering that some banks might be a center of corruption.

Our PSI report looked at ten offshore banks using correspondent accounts at U.S. banks to move millions in dirty money. Some of those offshore banks had even used other offshore banks to open U.S. accounts. In order to clean up the rampant money laundering, we introduced another bipartisan bill in August 2001. Because the world changed on 9/11 and money laundering was used by some of the 9/11 attackers and would likely be used by future terrorists, the banking world became ripe for reform, and our bill became law.

Riggs Bank in Washington, D.C. (an iconic institution you can see on an old ten-dollar bill), which sat just a block from both the Treasury and the White House, was the subject of our next money-laundering investigation. We launched that investigation in 2003 after a news article claimed Equatorial Guinea, a small country in western Africa, had secret accounts at Riggs Bank with hundreds of millions of dollars in their oil revenues. It turned out that U.S. companies drilling oil in Equatorial Guinea had, in fact, paid their royalty fees, not to a bank in the home country but to an Equatorial Guinea account at Riggs Bank. At the time, Riggs specialized in opening accounts for embassies, embassy employees, foreign leaders, and their families. Over time, Equatorial Guinea had become the bank's largest single customer with government and private deposits totaling as much as $700 million.

The PSI investigation discovered that Riggs had opened accounts not only for the Equatorial Guinea government but also for its embassy, senior officials, and family members. The most dramatic findings involved Teodoro Obiang Nguema Mbasogo, president of Equatorial Guinea. PSI learned that while the bank had never opened an account in his name, it had formed an offshore shell corporation under his control called Otong, opened an account in the name of Otong, and accepted multiple cash deposits to the Otong account totaling $11.5 million. On two occasions, the banker assigned to the Equatorial Guinea accounts brought in suitcases of cash wrapped in plastic. The resulting $3 million cash deposits into the Otong accounts were made with no questions asked. Bank records showed that millions more were deposited into accounts opened for the president's wife and her brother and for corporations controlled by the president's eldest son.

That wasn't all. Riggs had also opened a set of secret accounts for Augusto Pinochet, former president of Chile and then a senator-for-life in the Chilean legislature. We eventually documented more than twenty-eight Riggs accounts opened in the name of Pinochet, two shell companies formed by Riggs for him, and Chilean military officers fronting for their former commander. By following the money transfers, we found another hundred or so Pinochet-related accounts at other banks, including Citigroup and the U.S. branch of Banco de Chile.

The bank records were full of suspicious transactions. One of the most telling was a series of transactions that sent nearly $2 million to Pinochet in Chile, using thirty-eight cashier's checks made out to Riggs Bank and never mentioning Pinochet's name but drawn on funds he'd secretly stashed in the United States. He cashed the checks in his home country while denying he had any U.S. bank accounts. We also found that he used two false passports containing altered photos and versions of his name to disguise his connection with some of the accounts.

Our report determined that Riggs Bank had acted "with little or no attention to the bank's anti–money laundering obligations, turned a blind eye to evidence suggesting the bank was handling the proceeds of foreign corruption, and allowed numerous suspicious transactions to take place without notifying law enforcement."

As a result of the investigation, the federal banking regulator that oversaw Riggs apologized for failing to force the bank to strengthen its internal controls. The Treasury Department issued long-delayed regulations strengthening U.S. anti–money laundering rules, including one that required U.S. financial institutions to exercise enhanced due diligence when opening accounts for senior foreign political figures. On top of that, after learning that the federal bank "examiner-in-charge" at Riggs Bank had left his federal job and immediately taken a position with the bank, we were able to enact a law imposing a one-year cooling-off period before senior federal bank examiners could work for financial institutions they once supervised.

The egregious actions by a bank with a sterling reputation and the constructive policy reforms we were able to achieve made the Riggs investigation one of my favorites. Pinochet, although a brutal dictator, had been viewed as honest in Chile despite his horrible record of torture. After our hearings, he was seen by his countrymen for the corrupt crook that he was. In fact, hundreds of criminal charges were pending against him in Chile for embezzlement and human rights violations at the time of his death.

Enron

Another stunning PSI investigation involved Enron, the largest U.S. energy company and the darling of the business community until it suddenly collapsed into bankruptcy, throwing its employees, business partners, retirees, and creditors into an economic tailspin. Multiple committees in the House and Senate launched investigations to understand what had happened, including PSI.

The most complex aspect of our Enron investigation zeroed in on how U.S. banks had helped Enron "cook" its books, misleading investors, credit-rating agencies, and regulators. We learned, and then exposed, how JPMorgan Chase and Citibank had separately set up secret offshore shell companies and manufactured paperwork showing fake energy trades between those shells and Enron, all to disguise the fact that each bank was actually loaning Enron billions of dollars that never showed up on Enron's books as debt. Instead, the transactions were recorded as trading operations that made Enron look like it was expanding its business when it was really loading up on loans. Enron used those so-called structured financial transactions to make its books look better than the facts justified and pump up the price of its stock. We exposed the scam just as the two banks were ramping up efforts to sell the same disguised debt tactic to other companies.

Our investigation also showed how another Wall Street giant at the time, Merrill Lynch, had participated in the fake purchase of assets from Enron so that Enron could pretend it had met its sales targets and its executives could get their promised bonuses. Enron later took the assets off Merrill's hands by selling them under the table to a company owned by its chief financial officer. Emails arranging the phony purchase and subsequent resale exposed the entire scheme.

The phony trading, sales, and structured financial transactions we uncovered were made possible because Enron's accountant, Arthur Andersen, had approved aggressive accounting practices that enabled Enron to disguise its debt, hide its losses, and inflate its earnings. Enron's disgraceful conduct, facilitated by major U.S. banks and a major accounting firm, was a financial mockery that PSI exposed to the world.

Multiple Enron investigations by us and other congressional committees led to major policy reforms. The most important was enactment of the bipartisan Sarbanes-Oxley Act, which made significant changes to clean up American business. It forced CEOs and their chief financial officers, for the first time, to personally certify the accuracy of their corporate financial statements. It created a new body to police the accounting firms auditing those financial statements. It also barred auditors from providing additional services to their corporate clients that could make the auditors less willing to point out problems with their clients' financial statements. And it took such practical steps as barring corporations from providing sweetheart loans to their executives. We'd found that, near the end, despite cash-flow problems, the Enron Board of Directors had approved a loan to its CEO, Ken Lay, for more than $7 million and then allowed him to repay the loan with Enron stock instead of cash, even though the stock price had begun to crash.

In addition to policy reforms, a number of Enron executives were indicted for misconduct. Ken Lay had a heart attack and died after a jury convicted him of fraud and conspiracy; Jeff Skilling, a key insider, was sentenced to more than a decade behind bars. Enron's chief financial officer, Andy Fastow, also went to jail as did a Merrill Lynch executive who had lied to PSI about his company's role in fake asset purchases from Enron.

PSI's ability to uncover and document Enron's financial outrages, followed by landmark legislation and multiple prosecutions, made the Enron investigation one for the memory books.

KPMG and Tax Dodging

Another memorable investigation was one that exposed how KPMG, one of the Big Four accounting firms in the United States, had engaged in aggressive mass marketing of tax shelters. In other words, KPMG, a $4 billion behemoth, was using its resources to convince American taxpayers to dodge their civic obligation to pay taxes by selling them tax scams designed by the firm.

KPMG, like the other Big Four accounting firms, was a private company with no public reporting requirements, so it took a big effort to get under the hood and find out what was going on. In particular, the PSI staff dug into how KPMG was manufacturing and peddling so-called tax products for lucrative fees. We learned that the accounting firm had set up an internal "Tax Innovation Center" and got its tax partners to contribute ideas for new ways to avoid taxes. Then its tax and audit partners promoted the tax products to their customer companies, urging their partners to "sell—sell—sell!!!" KPMG even set up a "cold call" center to contact small businesses and tell them how their competitors weren't paying any taxes and they shouldn't either if they wanted to keep up.

The IRS and Justice Department got wind of the firm's below-the-radar activities and began investigating. While KPMG was able to hold off both agencies for years, internal KPMG whistleblowers—fed up with the growing tax shelter business within the firm—gave PSI extensive documents about the tax products being sold and the clients buying them. Our hearing made it all public.

As a result, KPMG undertook a major cleanup, firing most of the tax leadership. The Justice Department indicted many of those same executives, in an effort to hold them accountable for their tax misdeeds, but the case ended on a technicality. A few other participants were convicted and sent to jail. KPMG itself paid a $456 million fine. And for years after, KPMG clients sued the firm for selling them tax products that violated the law and subjected them to tax bills and penalties from the IRS. As for PSI, the staffers who led the investigation got an award from the IRS for helping it collect billions in unpaid taxes.

After the KPMG inquiry, I asked the PSI staff to take a deep dive into the offshore tax-avoidance world. I wanted them to investigate a large number of signs that offshore tax evasion was being facilitated not just by accounting firms but also by legal, financial, and tax professionals.

The result was a series of case studies that could have been the subject of a television drama. One involved two Texas brothers, Sam and Charles Wyly, who'd made it big in business and then created a complex network of fifty-eight offshore trusts and companies to hide their wealth and cheat on their taxes. The brothers began by sending $190 million in stock options to their offshore trusts and corporations and then instructed the offshore trustees nominally in charge of those entities on how to exercise the options and invest or spend the proceeds. PSI traced how the Wyly brothers, over a thirteen-year period, used hundreds of millions of dollars from stock options for investments in real estate and to buy jewelry and art for their families, all without paying any tax on the gains.

Once exposed, policy reforms followed, in particular stronger tax safeguards when U.S. taxpayers transfer assets offshore. In addition, in 2010, the Securities and Exchange Commission charged the Wylys with securities fraud for claiming their offshore entities were independent when they were really under the brothers' control. The jury found them guilty, and the judge imposed a $300 million fine. In response, the Wylys, despite their immense wealth, filed for bankruptcy. But the IRS used the bankruptcy case to calculate the taxes and penalties owed by the Wylys for failing to declare millions of dollars in income hidden offshore for more than thirteen years. The bankruptcy judge ended up approving a second judgment against the Wylys for $1.1 billion, one of the largest tax judgments ever brought against individual tax cheats. American taxpayers had gotten a measure of justice.

A second case study identified another brazen offshore tax scam. It involved two shell companies formed in the Isle of Man, a tiny island off the coast of the United Kingdom. We were never able to learn who owned the companies; the Isle of Man formation agents claimed their laws prevented them from telling us. But we did learn that each company had been established with initial capital of around $5, and then professed to assemble a joint stock portfolio worth $9 billion. It was all smoke and mirrors, of course, but a U.S. securities firm, Quellos, set up a spaghetti bowl of offshore entities around the Isle of Man shell companies and generated paperwork depicting a complex set of phony transactions. The end product, according to Quellos, was that certain paper stock losses incurred by the shell companies' stock portfolio could be used by wealthy U.S. taxpayers to offset their income and thereby avoid paying otherwise hefty U.S. tax bills.

In 2006, PSI tracked down the wealthy taxpayers who paid Quellos millions of dollars to use the Isle of Man tax shelters to reduce or eliminate their tax bills. One was Woody Johnson, whose family owned the famous Johnson & Johnson company, who'd sold some of his company stock for a $140 million profit so he could buy the Jets football team. Another was Haim Saban, a wealthy businessman who'd sold his interest in a Fox Family television channel to Disney for a profit of about $1.5 billion. Both men had been told by their tax advisors that they could use the stock losses from the Isle of Man shell companies to avoid paying anything in tax to Uncle Sam. When confronted with the facts, Mr. Saban forthrightly testified that he had relied on legal advice and that the last thing that he as an immigrant desired was to shortchange the country that had been so good to him. He said he would pay the IRS in full, and he did. Our hearing disclosed to the world the role of securities, tax, and legal professionals in facilitating tax schemes.

The Quellos CEO and top tax attorney each got four years in prison for tax fraud. Mr. Saban tracked down his tax advisor after learning the advisor had accepted a $36 million kickback to recommend the Quellos tax scam. The tax advisor got thirty-two months in jail and had to repay millions to Saban.

As for policy reforms, I worked with my Republican partner on the offshore investigation, Senator Norm Coleman from Minnesota, and our then-colleague Senator Barack Obama to introduce two pieces of legislation to clamp down on the rampant offshore tax dodging. The Stop Tax Haven Abuse Act offered a menu of practical measures to curb offshore tax abuse. Our second bill went after U.S. shell companies with hidden owners by requiring states, when they form new corporations, to get the names of the people who own or control them—the so-called beneficial owners. Both bills were part of a worldwide effort to combat offshore abuses as well as anonymous companies being used in a wide variety of crimes, including money laundering, terrorism, corruption, narcotics, human trafficking, and tax evasion. Neither bill passed that year, but various colleagues and I introduced them year after year, refusing to give up on such important reforms.

Hidden Ownership of Corporations and Offshore Accounts

Parts of the first bill subsequently became law, but the effort to get the identity of hidden owners of corporations was stymied for over two decades despite broad support within the law enforcement community. At my request, the GAO reported on the issue. In their powerful 2000 report they described how one corporation formation agent had created hundreds of Delaware corporations for unknown parties in Russia and Eastern Europe and how those shell corporations had opened hundreds of bank accounts at Citibank and the Bank of San Francisco and had moved over $1 billion through those accounts over a period of years.

After 9/11 the real-world impact of money laundering was exposed because it was the source of financial support for the hijackers. The Patriot Act imposed a modest requirement on banks to know their foreign customers. PSI became involved, and an April 2006 GAO report we had requested described how two million corporations with hidden owners were formed in the United States in a typical year. That same year the Financial Action Task Force (FATF), the leading international anti–money laundering organization, issued a report strongly criticizing the United States for failing to require disclosure of the beneficial owners of corporations, even though the secretary of the treasury had said the previous year that our failure to do so represented a "substantial vulnerability in the U.S. anti–money laundering/counterterrorist financing" effort.

In November 2006 we held a groundbreaking hearing in PSI to lay the foundation for legislation. We had the unified support of law enforcement, and the IRS testified that the lack of ownership transparency may "rival the secrecy afforded in the most attractive tax havens." But the secretaries of state were opposed. State governments make a lot of money from their incorporation activities, and over the next year we did our best to try to work out a compromise with them. But it was to no avail. In May 2008 I introduced, with my PSI colleagues Norm Coleman and Barack Obama, a bill to require disclosure of the beneficial owners of corporations. At the time of introduction, I spoke of websites that solicit people to use their services to set up corporations with hidden ownership, saying things like "DELAWARE—An Offshore Tax Haven for Non U.S. Residents" and "no IRS information sharing." But Delaware and other states, profiting from an activity that makes our nation less secure and robs our treasury, were able to thwart our legislation.

It was not the end of our efforts, however. Momentum picked up again when President Obama's Treasury Department in 2016 issued regulations requiring banks to identify the beneficial owners of legal entities opening accounts with them. U.S. banks then became supporters, and the Chamber of Commerce, which had previously opposed the effort, went silent. The American Bar Association still opposed it, probably because many lawyers open shell corporations for their clients. But the House of Representatives passed a bipartisan beneficial ownership bill in 2019, and in 2020 eight senators, four Democrats and four Republicans, introduced a similar bill. So, as I write this memoir, there is hope we will join most European countries and end the hypocrisy of attacking other countries for being tax havens while ignoring our own corporate secrecy practices.

PSI conducted multiple investigations and hearings exposing offshore abuses. In one, PSI went after offshore banks that helped U.S. clients cheat on their U.S. taxes. The 2008 hearing showed how the largest bank in Switzerland, UBS, had set up 52,000 secret Swiss accounts for U.S. clients without declaring $20 billion in assets to the IRS. A second hearing in 2014 showed that Switzerland's second largest bank, Credit Suisse, had engaged in the same misconduct, setting up 22,000 Swiss accounts for U.S. clients with about $12 billion in assets, again without telling the IRS. We presented evidence that both banks had been sending their bankers to the United States, often on tourist visas, so they could attend yachting and art events with wealthy Americans and offer to open secret accounts for them in Switzerland.

At a key hearing, UBS sent one of its top Swiss executives to testify. To our surprise, with the cameras rolling, he admitted the bank's wrongdoing and apologized for it. UBS ended up paying a $780 million fine, turned over the names of about 4,500 U.S. clients to the Justice Department, and promised to stop opening accounts for U.S. persons without informing the IRS. Credit Suisse, which had secretly continued to service its U.S. clients after promising to close their Swiss accounts, paid a fine of $2.6 billion. The Swiss banks' surrender then led to a host of other countries promising to no longer allow their financial institutions to open secret accounts to help clients evade taxes. Tax treaties were revised worldwide to cement those promises.

On top of that, tens of thousands of U.S. taxpayers contacted the IRS to admit they had offshore bank accounts with assets on which they hadn't paid taxes. Some were afraid that the offshore banks would turn over their names. The IRS set up a series of voluntary offshore disclosure programs with reduced penalties that eventually led to 100,000 U.S. taxpayers paying back taxes, interest, and penalties totaling more than $10 billion. At the same time, the IRS and Justice Department began taking legal action against banks, lawyers, accountants, and tax professionals who'd helped those taxpayers hide their assets offshore, as well as going after U.S. taxpayers who hadn't turned themselves in, providing a measure of accountability.

A truly significant consequence of our investigation was a wave of worldwide actions to force disclosure to tax authorities of large bank accounts previously hidden from them. The United States led the way in 2010 with the enactment of the Foreign Account Tax Compliance Act (FATCA), which requires foreign financial institutions to disclose to the IRS large bank accounts opened for U.S. clients or pay a 30 percent excise tax on income produced by their ownership of U.S. treasuries, stocks, and bonds. The hard-hitting solution to that particular offshore problem was designed by Charles Rangel of New York in the House and Max Baucus of Montana in the Senate. I relished the earthquake it produced in the banking world. Large foreign banks bellowed when they learned of the bill, but the U.S. banking industry quietly supported it because U.S. banks were sick and tired of their wealthiest clients stashing assets in hidden accounts outside of the United States. Other countries followed the U.S. lead, setting up a FATCA-style system with common reporting standards that is now used by tax authorities in more than a hundred countries to exchange information about large bank accounts. Together, FATCA and the common reporting standards have made it much harder for tax cheats to use offshore accounts to hide their wealth.

We didn't stop there. Other investigations exposed corrupt foreign officials using tactics to infiltrate U.S. banks, bringing their dirty money into the U.S. financial system and using it to buy U.S. real estate, cars, and personal jets. Another exposed how HSBC Bank had allowed its foreign affiliates to transfer billions of dollars to its U.S. branch without screening the money for suspect funds. In still another, we went after the Justice Department itself for its lax efforts to shut down suspect banks. Each of the investigations targeted powerful people or institutions that, probably, only Congress was willing to take on, and we were able to do it on a bipartisan basis.

Credit Card Companies

Another set of powerful actors investigated by PSI involved corporations engaged in abusive conduct that occurred not in the offshore world but right here at home—the unfair practices of U.S. credit card companies. When I got to the Senate, the very first bill I introduced was legislation to prohibit discrimination by credit card companies against people based on the zip code in which they lived. That practice had disadvantaged poor people and minorities not just in Michigan but across the country. While my bill was never enacted, it did contribute to a movement that forced the credit card companies to discontinue that particular discriminatory practice. It showed me that progress is possible.

Years later, the credit card companies were at it again. Complaints included credit card companies imposing unilateral and retroactive interest rate hikes on people who'd never been late with a payment, charging interest on credit card debt that had already been repaid, imposing multiple late fees for a single late payment, and more. To illustrate the abuses, we scheduled a hearing featuring Ohioan Wesley Wannamacher, who, to pay for his wedding, had taken out a new credit card with Chase and went $200 over the $3,000 credit limit. Over the next six years, he tried to pay off his credit card debt. But by the time we talked with him, his $3,200 debt had ballooned to $10,700, due to $4,900 in interest charges from a 29 percent "penalty" interest rate, $1,500 in multiple over-the-limit fees despite his having exceeded the limit only once, and $1,100 in 47 late fees even though he was making his monthly payments on time. The result was that, despite his having shelled out $6,300—nearly twice what he originally owed—Chase claimed he still owed it another $4,400.

Those outrageous charges were the focus of our hearing. Wannamacher was our lead-off witness. The hearing ended with a panel of the CEOs from the three largest credit card companies, including Chase. In response, five days before the hearing, Chase informed Wannamacher that it had forgiven his debt. Two days before the hearing, Chase announced publicly that, for all Chase credit cards, it would no longer impose endless over-the-limit fees but would impose only three over-the-limit fees per violation. That policy change meant that, although the hearing hadn't even happened yet, 100 million Chase credit card holders had already won a better deal, all because we forced Chase to answer for its actions. At the hearing itself, all three credit card CEOs announced additional reforms in an effort to look more reasonable than their callous treatment of families had shown them to be, in an obvious attempt to forestall legislation to stop the abuses.

It didn't work. I introduced a bill with Senator Claire McCaskill of Missouri, a member of PSI, to curb the worst of the unfair credit card practices we'd uncovered. Senator Chris Dodd of Connecticut, then senior Democrat on the Senate Banking Committee and a champion of credit card reform, folded most of our proposed changes into a new Dodd-Levin bill that was referred to his committee. The 2008 election gave Democrats control of both houses of Congress for the first time in decades, and due in part to the visibility our hearings had brought to the issue, credit card reform was on everyone's list for early action.

A strong credit card reform bill flew through the House. Democrats could have adopted it unchanged in the Senate, but Chairman Dodd decided to negotiate with his senior Republican, Senator Richard Shelby of Alabama, to produce a bipartisan bill. The final product was not as strong as the House bill but miles ahead of the status quo, and it promptly passed both houses. I attended the presidential signing ceremony in the Rose Garden, standing behind President Obama when he signed the bill into law. Later studies calculated that, over a five-year period from 2011 to 2014, our credit card bill saved consumers about $16 billion. Not bad.

Derivatives

Another set of problems in our financial system that we tackled involved derivatives, complex financial instruments that "derive" their value from another asset. I knew that most members of Congress didn't have the time or interest to take on such a complicated subject, a MEGO, or My Eyes Glaze Over issue, as my staff called it. Their very complexity was designed to make it difficult for anyone to uncover, understand, or stop the abuses. But my staff's and my experience with Enron and the financial crisis had taught us the dangers of derivatives and gave us confidence that we could understand the details and spot the abuses. The huge amount of money involved, the power of the financial institutions, and the potentially serious consequences for U.S. markets also motivated us to dig into the issue. Never underestimate the value of a capable, determined, and hardworking staff.

One of our most important derivatives investigations took place in 2013 and involved JPMorgan Chase and the so-called London whale trades. As I had said during an earlier hearing on the financial crisis: "When Wall Street plays with fire, American families get burned." This PSI investigation caught JPMorgan playing with fire, but luckily caught it early enough that the only one burned was the bank itself.

The investigation focused on so-called credit derivatives, financial instruments used to bet on creditworthiness, such as whether a particular company will declare bankruptcy or a particular bond will default before a specified date. Only a handful of major financial institutions traded in the credit derivatives markets and made those kinds of bets. It was the financial press that first spotted a worrying set of transactions: massive credit derivative trades by a mystery trader they dubbed the "London Whale." Eventually the press discovered that the trader worked for the London office of JPMorgan and that the bank was losing big money in the market.

JPMorgan's smooth, shrewd CEO, Jamie Dimon, claimed early on that the press stories about how the huge trades were roiling the credit markets were a "complete tempest in a teapot." But the whale trades indeed turned out to be a tempest, and well worth the scrutiny. Our investigation uncovered a hidden, multibillion-dollar JPMorgan credit derivatives portfolio riddled with risk, trades that broke the bank's risk limits, derivatives that were deliberately overvalued to hide losses, and a series of bank misrepresentations that left regulators and the public in the dark about bank losses that eventually topped $6 billion.

When Dimon was interviewed by PSI staff about the whale trades, he claimed he "didn't recall" seeing the "alerts" warning that the bank's risk limits were being breached by them, even though the bank's own documents showed that he had not only been informed but personally approved risk limit increases to allow the big trades to continue. Dimon also made inaccurate statements to the media, claiming that the trades were being made for "hedging purposes," when they weren't, and that the regulators had been "fully aware" of the trades, when they hadn't been. Those false statements were made on the same day that JPMorgan's credit derivatives portfolio recorded its largest daily loss to date from the trades, a drop of $415 million.

A few days later, the bank's chief financial officer also made inaccurate statements about the whale trades during a conference call with investors, analysts, and the media, adding that the bank was "very comfortable" with its investments. But at the very time he made that statement, the bank had in its possession significant negative information about the credit derivatives portfolio including that it contained billions of dollars of assets that were rapidly losing value, that losses had been escalating for three straight months, and that it would be difficult to sell the loser assets. It took over a month for the bank to finally disclose that negative information to the public.

At the PSI hearing, Senator McCain and I laid out the stark facts about the bank's high-risk trading and deceptive conduct. The evidence was so overwhelming that regulators initiated a reevaluation of the whole fiasco. At the end of that review, the bank was required to pay $920 million in fines to U.S. and U.K. regulators for unsafe practices and misleading financial reporting, and another $100 million to the Commodity Futures Trading Commission (CFTC) for manipulating credit derivative prices. A senior JPMorgan executive later paid another $1.1 million to U.K. authorities for hiding the whale trades, but, again, shockingly, there were no successful criminal prosecutions against anyone here or abroad.

Plenty of statements of remorse and acceptance of fault for the whale trades were made by Jamie Dimon, who later called it a stupid and embarrassing situation, claimed he would take "personal responsibility for what happened," and offered the usual profuse apologies. But true accountability was dodged. The only penalty for Dimon was that his pay was cut in half for one year, but he still took home over $11 million. When asked about it, he shrugged that "the Board sets my salary," ignoring the obvious suggestion that he might have chosen on his own to return more of his millions.

The London whale trades took place less than five years after the financial crisis, proving that vigorous congressional oversight was still critical to go after wrongdoing and cover-ups driven by greed.

The next year we took on another derivatives issue—one that combined a derivatives investment with a tax dodge. The target of the investigation was the use of so-called basket options, a sham derivative used by sophisticated hedge funds partnering with major banks to magically convert millions of short-term stock profits into long-term capital gains eligible for a lower tax rate reserved for investments held for at least a year. The basket option sham was also being used to subvert important bank lending limits that protect American taxpayers from having to bail out banks financially destabilized by client stock losses after the bank financed the stock purchases.

RenTec

The largest basket option user we uncovered was a wealthy U.S. hedge fund called Renaissance Technologies, or RenTec, which we estimated used the scam to avoid paying $6 billion in income taxes. The scheme was based on a number of fictions. First was that each basket option used a trading account that was set up by the bank partnering with RenTec, either Barclays or Deutsche Bank, and, according to the bank, was owned and controlled by the bank. In fact, records uncovered by PSI showed that RenTec had made all of the account's trading decisions using a specialized computerized system that executed more than 100,000 trades per day or about 30 million trades per year. If RenTec had made the same trades directly, it would have had to pay taxes on billions of dollars in short-term gains. Instead, RenTec claimed that the trades had been made by its partner bank, which was a complete fiction.

A second fiction was that RenTec and the bank claimed that the profits did not come from short-term trades because the profits accumulated in the trading account and were paid out only after one year had passed, qualifying the profits, they claimed, for the reduced tax rate available to long-term capital gains. The kicker was that RenTec and the bank claimed the profits were paid to an allegedly independent shell company that held a one-year "option" on the trading profits. What they didn't disclose, but PSI discovered, was that the shell company was secretly controlled by RenTec, which was actually reaping all of the trading gains. The shell company's independence was another fiction. And, of course, the biggest fiction was the characterization of this derivative scheme as an "option" since RenTec's profits were already safely located in a bank account. Like any other bank account, no option was needed in any meaningful sense other than to decide when to take the money out after the one-year "cover" passed.

Giving a lower tax rate to long-term capital gains is based on the idea that long-term investments create jobs and grow the economy. But the RenTec basket option account had no long-term investments. Their claim that these were long-term investments is not even close to being true. Most of the investments were bought and then sold in seconds or minutes or hours through the use of high-frequency trading. High-frequency trading is used by some traders that use algorithms to intercept and beat out, all in a tiny fraction of a second, legitimate buy and sell orders of real investments. These high-speed traders pay to locate their computers extremely close to the computers for the stock exchange. They pay to get more information faster than anyone else. Some use secret order types. Some submit false demand with a buy and sell and then withdraw it, all in a microsecond. Tens of thousands of these trades a day, although only producing pennies, or even fractions of a penny a share, can produce millions of dollars a year in profit for a high-frequency trader. These high-frequency traders comprise about half of all trading in the billions of shares traded each day. These abominable practices should have been stopped long ago by our regulators. In the end, they are all just a private tax on real investors.

But that isn't the only problem in our modern markets. Investors also have a problem with their brokers' conflicts of interest. There's a legal requirement that brokers get their customers the "best execution" in stock transactions. That usually means the best price. Unfortunately, many brokers get paid to send their customers' orders to certain exchanges or high-frequency traders. So while your broker is supposed to be looking out for you, they're getting paid by the other side. You're right to wonder if your broker is routing your orders to get you the best price (as legally required) or to maximize its profits. When I held a hearing looking into this practice, called "payment for order flow," one retail broker executive confessed that his firm always gives their customer orders to whoever pays them the most. It's supposed to give orders to whoever has the best price. Since then, some brokers have even begun to advertise that they'll help you trade for free. It isn't free. They've just stopped charging explicit commissions and are now relying on these hidden fees.

What do these two examples have in common? Some on Wall Street bring a laser focus and concocted arguments to make a buck at the expense of legitimate investors and the rest of our economy.

The shenanigans that occurred here, if allowed to blur the line between short- and long-term gains, undermine the justification for a tax distinction between the two. Proponents of lower rates for long-term capital gains should have been part of the chorus demanding heavy penalties and reforms for basket option types of abuse. But the banking and hedge fund communities by and large remained silent when this sham became public and, by that silence, effectively condoned those abusive practices. As Senator McCain put it at the hearing, it is simply wrong for there to be one set of rules used by some of the big guys, while the rest of America complies with another set of rules.

The IRS began reviewing the basket option tax dodge even before PSI began its investigation. After our hearing, the IRS issued a multibillion-dollar tax assessment against RenTec, which the company has been fighting ever since. At the end of 2019, RenTec had still not paid its tax bill and was negotiating with the Trump administration to get out of it. As is all too typical for the IRS in recent years, it has yet to hold accountable a wealthy and powerful company, even one responsible for one of the most greed-driven schemes that PSI uncovered.

Of course, RenTec was far from alone in its tax scheming. An earlier PSI investigation, in 2008, exposed another complex tax dodge involving derivatives, hedge funds, banks, and billions of dollars in U.S. stock dividends. That tax dodge arose from the fact that the U.S. government imposes a 30 percent tax on any non-U.S. party who gets a U.S. stock dividend. In many cases, it is the only tax that non-U.S. parties pay on their U.S. investments. It is effective, because the IRS requires U.S. companies to withhold the 30 percent from any dividend payment made to a non-U.S. party and instead send the 30 percent to Uncle Sam.

Needless to say, many offshore hedge funds and other foreign investors don't want to pay that 30 percent tax. PSI uncovered a common set of schemes being used to dodge the U.S. dividend tax. We found that some U.S. financial institutions were willing to help their non-U.S. clients cheat on their U.S. taxes. They did this by making a taxable dividend payment to the offshore hedge fund look instead like a non-taxable payment to the bank, using a complex financial transaction called an equity swap or through a sham stock loan. The typical end result: after paying a 3 percent "fee" to the bank for helping it dodge the

30 percent dividend tax, the hedge fund got to keep 97 percent of the dividend amount tax-free, instead of getting only 70 percent.

The PSI investigation uncovered emails and other documents that not only exposed the scam but also showed how some offshore hedge funds were pushing U.S. banks to partner with them and at times even playing one bank against another to lower the fee charged for facilitating the tax dodge. While PSI was unable to calculate the total amount of taxes involved, the evidence suggested that, over a ten-year period, billions of dollars in taxes on U.S. stock dividends had gone unpaid.

As a direct result of the investigation, in 2010, I was able to get Congress to enact a law that put an end to the dividend tax abuse. While that stamped out dividend tax abuse in the United States, a similar tax scam later erupted in Europe, particularly in Germany, which has worked for years to stop what they call the "cum-ex" tax scandal.

Corporate Offshore Tax-Dodging Schemes

Over the years PSI uncovered a host of other corporate tax-dodging schemes as well, leading to a series of hearings on the offshore tax schemes of four iconic American companies: Apple, Microsoft, Hewlett-Packard, and Caterpillar. The American people who watched our hearings or read about the companies' complex tax maneuvering and deceptions had to be disgusted. Tax avoidance by our most profitable corporations was and is pervasive, yet these multinational corporations reap the benefit from U.S. research tax credits, take advantage of American research talent, use our infrastructure, and make use of U.S. patent protections. Yet they pay little or nothing in taxes. The Center for Public Integrity reported that in 2018, 60 corporations, including giants like Amazon, Netflix, Eli Lilly, Chevron, and Deere, paid no taxes on profits of $79 billion. And while they could have paid over $16 billion in taxes, the Center calculated that they actually got rebates of over $4 billion. Government data show that in 2018 corporations paid just 6 percent of the U.S. tax burden, while another 85 percent was shouldered by individuals paying income and payroll taxes.

President Kennedy was able, in 1963, to persuade Congress to close tax loopholes that were enabling U.S. multinational corporations to dodge paying U.S. taxes by shifting money abroad. But in the decades that followed, new tax loopholes were created by Congress or the IRS, either inadvertently or deliberately, and have once again enabled our multinationals to avoid paying their fair share. The goal of these investigations was to find out exactly how U.S. multinationals were using those loopholes and to expose their actions to the public.

Our first hearing focused on Microsoft. It showed how Microsoft had transferred the economic rights to its corporate jewels—its patented products—to subsidiaries in tax havens that provided the corporation with secret sweetheart tax deals. Microsoft then directed its sales income to its tax haven subsidiaries, paying little or no U.S. tax. The same hearing showed how Hewlett-Packard used a fake, short-term loan scheme to bring into the United States billions of dollars in offshore profits to run its U.S. operations without paying any tax on the profits brought home. Together, the facts detailed billions of dollars in unpaid taxes. The IRS reportedly went after both companies, but as of early 2020 there has been no announced outcome of its efforts—in part because federal law unreasonably prohibits the IRS from announcing any settlement with taxpayers, even for publicly held corporations.

Our second hearing was the most famous of the three. It disclosed how Apple had been stiffing Uncle Sam for years out of billions in taxes. Our investigation detailed how over a four-year period Apple had shifted $74 billion in revenues from non-U.S. countries to three Irish subsidiaries that were little more than shell operations managed from the United States, while paying less than 2 percent in taxes to the Irish government under a secret arrangement. The hearing detailed how one of those Irish subs had failed to file a tax return in any jurisdiction for at least five years—what I called at the hearing the "holy grail" of tax avoidance. At one point in the hearing, when I was attacked for investigating Apple's tax practices by Senator Rand Paul of Kentucky, Senator McCain—my partner in the investigation—provided an eloquent and moving defense of our investigative efforts. His support was a great example of PSI's bipartisan ethic and Senator McCain's political courage.

Our third and final hearing in the series examined a Swiss tax dodge that Caterpillar had paid a major U.S. accounting firm $55 million to design. The facts in this case showed how offshore tax dodging by U.S. multinationals had extended far beyond U.S. high-tech firms. After our hearing, the IRS assessed Caterpillar more than $2 billion in back taxes, interest, and penalties. But Caterpillar is still fighting the assessments and leaning on the Trump administration to settle the case for much less. That type of high-priced legal pressure just increases public cynicism and anger about the failure of America's highly profitable corporations to meet their tax obligations.

The good news is that the Apple hearing in particular triggered a worldwide conversation about how multinational corporations were refusing to pay taxes virtually everywhere they did business. In response, the Organisation for Economic Cooperation and Development (OECD) launched an effort by its thirty-six member countries, including the United States, to fight back. One early accomplishment was that all OECD members agreed to require their largest multinationals to file annual reports detailing, on a country-by-country basis, where they do business, make money, and pay taxes. That type of information had never been available on a comprehensive, annual basis, but beginning in 2018, the United States as well as its OECD partners like the United Kingdom, Germany, Japan, and Australia have begun collecting and exchanging that information among their tax authorities, making corporate tax dodging more difficult. Discussions are now underway to make the information public, which would do even more to stop the abusive practices.

In the meantime, other efforts to publish country-by-country corporate information are also underway, including a new voluntary tax transparency standard issued by the Global Reporting Initiative. The Financial Accounting Standards Board (FASB) has also begun a project to strengthen tax reporting by U.S. corporations. On top of that, a second OECD effort, launched in 2019, is calling for new taxes on digital corporations and a minimum level of corporate tax worldwide. I like to think that our hearings contributed to all of these efforts to compel multinational corporations to pay taxes to the countries where they do business.

The battle continues to make U.S. corporations pay taxes on their profits, the success of which is essential to restore public confidence in the tax system, curb our exploding deficits, and address public needs. President Trump's 2017 tax bill did nothing to restore a balance. In fact, it made things worse by drastically lowering corporate tax rates and imposing a still lower tax rate on corporate income produced outside of the United States, an ill-conceived tax differential that will encourage more companies to move operations out of the United States and encourage more offshore abuses. The tax fight is one of the most important of our generation, and I'm proud that PSI did its part to expose the facts and inform the debate.

Executive Pay

One more issue that occupied me for decades was the huge growth in the use of executive stock options that are a major contributor to the skyrocketing pay of U.S. corporate executives. Executive pay is a significant factor in the wealth and income gaps that plague our country today.

The financier J. P. Morgan, one of America's wealthiest corporate executives, once said that executive pay should not exceed 20 times the pay of the company's average worker. But in the United States, by 1990, executive pay was 100 times the pay of average workers. By 2004, that ratio had increased to 300 times. By 2007, it was 400 times. Today it is even worse.

Another complex issue, stock options are a form of compensation in which a corporation gives its executives the right to buy company stock at a fixed price for a fixed period of time, usually ten years. The idea is to create an incentive for executives to increase the company's value so the stock price will rise. But stock prices typically increase over time anyway, which means that most executives just have to stay alive to benefit. Worse, some executives, like those at Enron, began manipulating company financial statements in order to quickly boost the stock price and profit from their stock options. Some companies even began backdating stock option grants to enable their executives to benefit from past stock price increases.

Those abuses were maddening enough from executives who are already among the wealthiest of Americans, but what got PSI involved were the U.S. accounting and tax rules that put another thumb on executive pay scales. I held my first hearing on "Runaway Executive Pay" in 1991, as chair of the Subcommittee on Oversight of Government Management. I asked the Securities and Exchange Commission (SEC) to testify about an accounting rule then in effect from the Financial Accounting Standards Board (FASB), which issues "generally accepted accounting" principles for U.S. corporations. That rule, which FASB was trying to change in the face of massive corporate opposition, allowed corporations to issue stock options to their executives without recording any compensation expense at all on their books. Since it was clear that stock options had value, FASB wanted to mandate that the value be recorded in the corporate financial statements. I used the hearing to pressure the SEC to support FASB's reform effort and also led an effort within the Senate to end the accounting absurdity. It took time and a lot of courage, but finally, in 1995, FASB made the change, requiring corporations, at the time they granted stock options to an employee, to show on their books the stock options' fair market value.

But that wasn't the end of the story. While FASB had fixed the accounting rule, the corresponding federal tax rule wasn't changed to match. Instead, the tax code continued to allow companies to deduct the value of their stock option compensation on their income tax return as of the date their options were exercised, instead of deducting the value on the books when the stock options were granted. Since that exercise date was virtually always years after the grant date—sometimes ten years later—the value of the stock had typically jumped dramatically by then. That meant the corporation could claim a tax deduction that was dramatically larger than the expense recorded for the stock option on the grant date.

The tax code does not allow any other type of compensation to get a tax deduction that exceeds the actual compensation expense on the corporate books; it's a tax bonanza that executives can use to convince their boards to award them millions of dollars in stock option pay in order to get that outsized tax deduction for the corporation.

At one point, I asked PSI to investigate the tax consequences of that stock option tax anomaly. The investigation gathered data from nine corporations. The data showed that the corporations took tax deductions for stock option compensation totaling $1.2 billion, even though, under FASB's accounting rule, the expense on the corporate books for the very same stock options would have amounted to only $217 million. In other words, those corporations took tax deductions six times larger than the corporate expense. No other compensation expense generates that kind of tax windfall, and the direct beneficiary is none other than some of the most profitable corporations and the wealthiest among us.

PSI held a hearing on its findings. The IRS Commissioner testified that, at our request, the IRS had analyzed the difference between the cost to a corporation on its books and the tax deduction allowed for that same stock option compensation and did so for stock options issued by 3,000 companies. It found in the year 2004 alone, those companies had deducted $43 billion more from their taxes than the expenses shown on their books. The companies were using stock options to dodge paying their taxes.

After the hearing, I continued for years to request IRS data on the stock option book-tax gap. We once calculated that, over the five-year period from 2004 to 2009, the total amount of excess stock option tax deductions taken per year by U.S. corporations varied from a low of $12 billion to a high of $61 billion. That's a lot of forgone tax dollars from profitable corporations—tax dollars that could have supported education costs, infrastructure repairs, pollution cleanups, deficit reduction, and other public needs.

Over the years, I also collected examples of profitable corporations that used stock options to reduce or even eliminate their taxes. They include companies like Facebook, which claimed the largest known corporate stock option tax deduction when it went public in 2012, estimated at $16 billion. This deduction could be carried back two years or forward for up to twenty years; Facebook used it to get refunds from the two prior years and saved the rest to reduce its taxes in later years. Enron used stock option deductions, among other tactics, to avoid paying taxes in four of its last five years.

Twitter claimed a $154 million tax deduction for a stock option compensation expense that its books showed cost just $7 million. Netflix used an $80 million stock option deduction to avoid paying any taxes on $159 million in 2013 profits. Amazon used stock options and other tax deductions to avoid paying any taxes at all in 2018, despite being one of the most profitable corporations in the world.

I attempted to fix the problem by introducing legislation that would require the corporate stock option tax deduction to match, and not exceed, the book expense. Senator John McCain joined me in the effort, and we introduced the bill repeatedly over the years, but it has yet to become law. Today, others champion the cause. In 2019, the nonprofit Institute on Taxation and Economic Policy identified stock option tax breaks totaling nearly $11 billion, most of which went to just twenty-five corporations, and urged reform. The report stated:

> Giving massive tax deductions to a small number of corporations for handing out stock options to their executives—enabling even extremely profitable corporations to avoid paying taxes—undermines tax fairness, increases public distrust of the tax system, and deprives the U.S. Treasury of needed funds. To eliminate the double standards controlling how stock option expenses are reported by corporations to investors versus the IRS, Congress should enact a proposal modeled after the bills introduced in previous Congresses by former Senators Carl Levin and John McCain.

Corporate tax-avoiding activities and the wealth and income gaps that continue to bedevil our country have justifiably added to public anger. In this case, exposing the problem through congressional oversight was not sufficient to cure it. In my final speech to the Senate I spoke of the challenges that lie before it. One of the greatest ones, I said, "is the need to meet the fundamental economic challenge of this era: the growing gap in our society between a fortunate few and the vast majority of Americans whose fortunes have stagnated or fallen. . . . This isn't just about economic data. It is about our Nation's heart and soul. This growing gulf between a fortunate few and a struggling many is a threat to the dream that has animated this Nation since its founding, the dream that hard work leads to a better life for us and for our children. . . . And as I have said here many times, it should pay for needed investments by closing egregious tax loopholes that serve no economic purpose, but enrich some of the wealthiest among us and our most profitable corporations."

In the time since I spoke those words it's gotten worse. In 2017, three Americans had as much wealth as the bottom half of our population, or 160 million people. In 2018, a Census Bureau study found that income inequality was at the highest level ever recorded.

Throughout our complicated, high-pressure hearings, PSI maintained its bipartisanship. We did it by committing to shared fact-finding, report-writing, and hearing design. We also built PSI's bipartisan partnerships in other ways, including laying out our staff offices to make it easy for majority and minority staffs to meet in person, ending the week with bipartisan social hours on a Friday afternoon, and hosting a bipartisan lunch or late afternoon beer after a hearing's conclusion. We even arranged to take group photographs for each investigation to memorialize the work we did together. Fostering relationships on the staff level made a significant contribution to the bipartisan spirit of PSI.

Also helpful to bipartisanship was the PSI rule recognizing the minority's right to initiate investigations on topics it chooses. I was happy to recognize that right, supporting Norm Coleman's investigation into tens of thousands of government contractors who were getting paid with taxpayer dollars while owing billions of dollars in unpaid taxes; Tom Coburn's minority investigation into Social Security disability corruption; and John McCain's investigation into malicious software hidden in Internet advertising. Supporting that work not only enabled my Republican partners to exercise their own investigative muscles but expanded PSI's reach into more issues.

The investigations I led on PSI produced some of the most satisfying work I did during my thirty-six years in the Senate. The Constitution charges Congress with a range of important duties, including enacting legislation, allocating taxpayer funds, declaring war, approving nominations, and serving as a check on any executive or judicial branch abuses. To meet those responsibilities, Congress needs to gather facts so it can make informed decisions. Using its investigative powers is the key, and I am grateful I had the opportunity for so many years to fully use those powers to push for a more perfect union.

15

Bipartisanship

The PSI investigations into finance and tax abuse demonstrate the power of bipartisan, fact-based oversight to identify and correct abuses and foster positive public policy outcomes. Bipartisanship also strengthens and improves the likelihood of success for legislative efforts, and I was fortunate to have my share of those successes.

Buprenorphine

Years before the opioid epidemic arose in the United States, Republican senator Orrin Hatch of Utah and I worked together to legalize and advance the use of a substance called buprenorphine (BUP). This effort started in the early 1990s when I read about BUP as an effective treatment for heroin abuse in France. As of 1998, 50,000 addicts in France had received BUP treatment, with an 80 percent decline in heroin overdose deaths and a 50 percent decline in crime by heroin users.

At the time, methadone was the only available treatment for addiction in the United States, but it is addictive, has street value, and has to be taken daily in a controlled clinic. BUP's advantages over methadone are significant: it is not addictive, it does not have street value, and it can be prescribed by qualified physicians in their offices. When combined with a substance called naloxone, BUP prevents withdrawal symptoms that are so debilitating that they deter many people from trying to free themselves from addiction. Because it does not get the BUP user "high," it does not need to be as tightly controlled as methadone. Physicians can prescribe a week's supply in their offices, avoiding the daily, stigmatizing visit to a centralized drug treatment clinic.

Our joint effort began in May 1997 when Bob Kerry, Democratic senator from Nebraska, and I organized a forum to discuss research progress in developing BUP to block the craving of illegal addictive substances. We invited Senator Hatch, who had key committee assignments on drug issues, to attend. At the time we held the forum, the cost to society of illegal drug use was estimated to be about $70 billion a year; by 2007 it was estimated by the Department of Justice to be $193 billion; today it is much higher, with some estimates as much as half a trillion dollars. At the forum we heard witnesses from the National Institute on Drug Abuse (NIDA) discuss the barriers discouraging pharmaceutical companies from developing drugs to combat addiction. A significant barrier, we were told, was that BUP was not authorized for use in the United States. Rumor had it, shocking if true, that people involved in the manufacture and provision of methadone opposed its authorization because they didn't want the competition.

Senator Hatch and I were both moved by what we heard at the forum and agreed to work together on legislation to authorize BUP. Senator Hatch's staff and my wonderful staffer Jackie Parker made a strong team. In January 1999 we introduced the Drug Addiction Treatment Act and together fought off the opposition to the legislation, which was hard to identify. In order to get our bill passed we had to adopt a number of limitations to access BUP, including restricting to twenty the number of patients that a practitioner or a group practice could treat. The bill also had a sunset provision, that is, a limited period of authorization, that would take effect unless the secretary of health and human services and the attorney general made certain determinations. The bill also required that the participating physicians not only have a regular physician's license but also obtain a separate registration from the attorney general certifying that the physician had training and experience to treat heroin addiction and the capacity to refer patients to counseling and ancillary services. One of the strongest arguments in favor of our bill was that BUP could be administered in a doctor's office—not only avoiding the stigmatization of the methadone clinic but also addressing the very real problem that rural areas and small towns don't have methadone clinics.

By October of that year the Senate and House committees of jurisdiction had approved our bill, and the *Detroit Free Press* noted that it "seems like the kind of legislation that should be passed" particularly "in Washington's nasty partisan climate." (Yes, nasty partisanship was blocking some important legislation even then.) The *Free Press* added that it "seems like the country has nothing to lose and plenty to gain by making buprenorphine available. It sure sounds more cost-effective than throwing druggies in prison or spending billions on sporadically successful attempts to keep heroin out of the country. If everything else has been so successful to date, why is heroin usage going up?" Congress agreed, and the following year the Drug Addiction Treatment Act was signed into law. In October 2002, the FDA officially approved the use of buprenorphine/naloxone. The final bill authorized doctors to treat up to thirty patients and, following another forum we held in 2006, we were able to get the authorized limit increased to one hundred.

But it wasn't enough. Opioid addiction in the United States is a crisis, and the importance of ready access to buprenorphine has only grown. By 2015, two million Americans had a substance abuse disorder involving prescription pain relievers, and almost 600,000 had such a disorder involving heroin. There are many reasons why this scourge has continued and indeed intensified. There is not nearly enough money appropriated to Medicaid for medication-assisted treatment (MAT), and the medical profession has not stepped up to encourage more doctors to treat addiction, resulting in a severe shortage. And the limit of one hundred patients per physician for those willing to treat addiction was an arbitrary restriction. By contrast, we don't restrict the number of patients a doctor can treat for any other medical condition.

Despite these ongoing barriers, the battles that Senator Hatch and I and others fought on BUP were some of the most important battles that I waged during my thirty-six years in the Senate because they have made a difference for millions of people. That fact became clear and personalized when Senator Hatch and I held our final forum on BUP in June 2014. We heard from federal agency heads and medical professionals about the extraordinary results of buprenorphine and heard personal stories from witnesses like Dr. John Kitzmiller of Lake Orion, Michigan, who described how buprenorphine saved his own life after he became addicted to opioids and how, now that he is a full-time addiction doctor, he has seen it save the lives of many of his patients. But we also heard at that forum about additional impediments to the expanded access to buprenorphine, such as the refusal of insurance companies to cover addiction treatment for more than a year and how the cost of treatment is prohibitive for a large number of people without insurance or Medicaid coverage. And the stigma that too many physicians think exists for treating addicts will end, as I said at the final hearing on the subject, only when the medical profession and the medical schools take hold of this issue and recognize that their oath is violated when opioid addiction is ignored.

Organ and Tissue Donation

Organ and tissue donation was another cause I championed that succeeded because of bipartisan support. After my father passed away in 1960, the family learned that he had donated his corneas to help blind people see again. I was deeply moved by my father's action and how it would carry his humanitarian spirit beyond his death. As a member of the Senate Armed Services Committee, I urged the Department of Defense in 1986 to require that all persons eligible for the DOD's medical care be asked about their willingness to have their vital organs taken at death for transplantation, regardless of whether a person died in a military or civilian facility. The DOD adopted the policy in 1987, and each of the services subsequently adopted regulations to implement it. The Veterans Administration and other federal agencies then took similar action. In November 1987 the Office of Personnel Management issued a memorandum to all federal agencies encouraging their employees to become potential organ and tissue donors. In 1998 I introduced a bill to increase the amount of leave time to thirty days for a federal employee who is recovering from an organ donation. With the support of Democratic senator Daniel Akaka from Hawaii, three other Democrats, and two Republicans, the bill passed the Senate in a slightly revised form in 1999.

In February 2007 I introduced a bill that would lead to more organ donations. As the capability of surgeons to transplant organs increased over the years so, too, did the demand, and, consequently, there came to be a severe shortage of available organs. The law governing the distribution of human organs had understandably placed certain restrictions on organ donations to ensure fairness in that lifesaving distribution decision. For instance, there was a prohibition on the transfer of a human organ for payment, what was referred to as "valuable consideration." That language was construed by some to mean that a so-called paired donation was not permitted. A paired donation occurs when a transplant candidate has someone who wants to donate a kidney to them, but tests reveal that the kidney would not be a good biological match. A paired donation gives that transplant candidate the option of having another living donor who is a good match swap with the initial donor so each recipient receives a compatible transplant. Typically the donors are living family members who volunteer an organ to help another family member. My bill provided that "paired" donations would be an exception to the prohibition of "consideration" for the transfer of the organ. The bill passed the Senate that same month; the House passed it after some technical differences were worked out; and President Bush signed the bill on December 21, 2007. When I heard the president had signed it, I thought about my father's gift of his corneas and how it helped motivate me to be part of a national movement to promote organ donation. But despite all the progress that has been made, tens of thousands of people still die while awaiting a lifesaving organ to be donated by a generous soul. Continual dramatic improvements in transplant technology will help more people follow their humane instincts.

Adoption Registry

Early in my Senate career I became interested in adoption which, like organ donation, touches deep human emotions and, as I soon found out, is a completely bipartisan issue. The particular aspect of adoption that moved me to act was the effort of some birth parents and the children they gave up for adoption to find each other. A thirty-two-year-old woman from Michigan who had been adopted wrote to me in 1980 that she had been searching for her birth parents for seven years. She wrote of a young man she knew who had also been searching for his biological parents, and when he finally found them, had learned that both he and his birth mother had been falsely told by the adoption agency that the other would not "want to know and would suffer from knowledge or contact." She went on to say that "we cannot but question why this myth is being perpetuated in the face of direct refutation . . . and of sociological studies of hundreds of involved parties."

I thought it unbelievable that there could be opposition to the establishment of a system where both a birth parent and the adopted child could, later in life, provide identifying information so that a mutually sought reunion could take place. My constituent's letter went on to eloquently make the case. She wrote, "Had I surrendered a child for adoption, I know I would always secretly wonder what had happened to her, if she were alive, if she were well, if she had found a good home. I would wonder what she looked like, what sort of person she had become. I would wonder if she wondered about me. . . . The overwhelming majority of women who give up children for adoption are disturbed by these questions all their lives. Many are even haunted by guilt. . . . They can never put their thoughts to rest. If only I could speak to the woman who gave me life I could tell her how happy I am: I could tell her about the wonderful people who adopted me and the joy she brought into their lives. And for my part I could see her, discover the secret of my origin, know the country from which my ancestors came, the story that is my history. . . . For seven years I have been searching. Under our present laws, the search is difficult, frustrating and time-consuming. It is often expensive as well."

I understood, of course, why if one of the two parties did not want to be found that they should not be found or surprised. But I just could not understand why a reunion should not be facilitated if both parties wanted to find each other. I thought the argument was so compelling that there would be no opposition to the creation of a voluntary mutual adoption registry, but I was wrong. In August 1980 when I offered my approach for the first time, I did it in the form of an amendment to a pending appropriation bill. I learned a good lesson when, because of my inadequate preparation and the opposition of a single senator who mischaracterized my amendment, it picked up only 27 votes.

Defeated but not discouraged, I introduced legislation the following year, and for several Congresses thereafter, to provide for a registry that would make a match between the birth parent and the adopted child, again providing both put the same identifying information into the registry. There would be no search unless both parties on their own registered.

I introduced a strong bipartisan bill with 34 cosponsors, including Bob Dole, the Republican leader, in January 1988 at the beginning of a new Congress. Two months later I received a letter from Michael Reagan, President Reagan's adopted son. He wrote, "You should also know that my adoptive father, Ronald Reagan, supported my desire for a reunion with my birth mother. When my father helped me, it was the greatest gift he ever gave me." His letter continued that his father believed "wholeheartedly" in my bill and that he supported my efforts to make it a reality. He added that he "would have used such a registry myself . . . and that my birth mother would have also." I was grateful for Michael's letter, and I believed it would help the adoption registry become a reality.

A few days after I received the letter, Michael came to my house. He had been able to find his half brother. In a meeting that he said changed his life, he learned for the first time that his mother had not only known who he was but had kept a scrapbook of clippings about him. Michael told Barb and me, with tears in his eyes, that because he was adopted as a child, he was called a "bastard" in school, and he always believed his birth mother had given him up for adoption because she did not love him. He said he now knew from the scrapbook that his mother had always loved him. He also learned from his half brother that their mother desperately wanted to meet him but that she didn't want to impose upon him. But by the time he learned about her existence, it was too late. His birth mother had passed away in 1985.

Sadly my bill never became law because of just one or two outspoken opponents. One of those was William Pierce, who represented a number of private adoption agencies that put on a full-court press against my bill. For instance, he caught up with Bob Dole while Bob was campaigning for president in 1988 and harangued him with the false claim that our bill would open up birth records and surprise birth mothers who didn't want to be found. So Bob, under pressure on the campaign trail, withdrew his cosponsorship in June of that year. But that did not stop its forward momentum. In October, just weeks before the election, a bill with a modification offered by Senator Dole, which I readily accepted, passed the Senate on a voice vote. One hurdle overcome. But because the bill still had to pass the House and the session was running out, the bill died before the House could consider it.

I reintroduced the bill in 1989 and 1994, and it again passed the Senate, this time with the strong support of Senator John McCain, who was offended by Pierce's false representations. Senator Larry Craig, a Republican from Idaho and my chief cosponsor, was a huge help, and we had the continuing public support of Michael Reagan. But the bill failed to survive the House-Senate conference because of strong opposition by Representative Thomas Bliley, Republican of Virginia, who was the chairman of the House Commerce Committee that had jurisdiction over the bill. Bliley, who was an honorary member of Pierce's group, held the chairmanship of the committee until 2001 and was able to prevent passage by the House until then. By that time a number of privately organized computerized reunion registries were forming, lessening the necessity for a government registry.

What's the takeaway? Despite the overwhelming support in the adoption community, one organization falsely repeating a lie—that my bill would open records of adoption against the wishes of one of the parties—caused the bill to fail. The lobbying effort of that one organization with the support of one key House committee chairman who was a member of that organization was able to prevent the passage of a humane, commonsense bill that had the strong support of the adoption community, religious organizations, and pro-choice groups. While we did not achieve the enactment of a law that we worked so hard to pass, the story is illuminating about the power of a few people in key positions in Congress and the power of one lobbyist who was willing to distort facts to scare legislators.

Other Efforts for Children

I was able to achieve a better outcome on a less dramatic adoption issue aimed at providing financial assistance to families that accepted hard-to-place children into their foster care homes. A bill before the Senate was focused on providing assistance for special-needs children who were far less likely to be accepted into foster care because of various factors, such as having a severe handicap. But the bill contained a "means test," requiring a showing of financial need on the part of the foster parents, which made no sense because the government actually saved money when a child moved from an institution financially supported by the government to a private foster care home. My bipartisan amendment eliminated the means test but was strongly opposed by the Finance Committee and its chairman, the powerful Russell Long of Louisiana. We prevailed anyway because of our bipartisan cosponsorship, with a strong vote of 60–25. I experienced firsthand that it was possible, with bipartisan support and a solid argument, to take on and prevail over a senior, and likable, committee chairman. By 1984, Health and Human Services reported that almost 12,000 children had been moved from foster care to adoptive homes under the assistance program that we had authorized in 1979.

Another heartwarming, bipartisan outcome was obtained by passage of the bill I introduced with Republican senator Jeremiah Denton of Alabama in October 1981. Tens of thousands of children fathered by American military personnel were born to women in Korea, Vietnam, Laos, and other Asian countries during their wartime service, with perhaps 25,000 children being born in Vietnam alone. These children, referred to as Amerasians, had been abandoned, were often humiliated, and were outcasts in the societies into which they were born. Our bill provided a higher preference for obtaining visas and seeking permanent residence in the United States when these children obtained U.S. sponsors.

In my remarks to the Senate I quoted from a letter that I received from a couple in Grand Rapids, Michigan, who had adopted several Amerasian children. After describing the harsh conditions in which these children found themselves through no fault of their own, the letter went on to say that we should not be "too quick to blame the Asian mother's society for their insensitivity to the Amerasians without also looking at ourselves and our own responsibility to our children born in other countries." Less than a year later, in October 1982, the bill became law. President Reagan signed the bill in a moving ceremony at the White House. Our country's values were reflected in that bill and at the White House that day.

The FDR Memorial

One of my truly memorable bipartisan experiences in the Senate involved my membership on the Roosevelt Memorial Commission. A memorial to President Franklin Roosevelt had been proposed shortly after his death in 1945, and the commission was established by law in 1955. There were many delays in funding the memorial, however, in part because of opposition in the House, including from a key Democratic chairman whose argument was that President Roosevelt did not want a memorial. That was in fact true; Roosevelt had expressly told Supreme Court Justice Frankfurter that he did not want a monument other than a small block of granite with a simple inscription near the Archives building. When I testified, as a member of the commission, in support of funding for the memorial, I said that a grateful nation and an appreciative citizenry decided to build monuments and memorials to our great presidents regardless of their personal preferences about being so honored. In my testimony I argued that "the leader of a free people could never make a request for a monument in their own honor, especially if he was worthy, as Roosevelt surely was, of such a memorial." Our key members of the Senate Appropriations Committee needed no convincing. Senator Hatfield, Republican of Oregon, and Senator Inouye, Democrat of Hawaii, were staunch advocates. Their support was intensive but still had to overcome budget concerns. Indeed, one of the efforts I was involved in was to help persuade the commission after a long time of frustrated hopes that the only way we would get the monument built was to appoint Senators Inouye and Hatfield as cochairs of the commission, despite the tradition of having one commission cochair be from the House and one from the Senate. Senators Inouye and Hatfield were perfect for the job because they would not only get the appropriation passed in the Senate, they would insist upon the Senate position in a conference with House appropriators. That strategy worked, and the necessary appropriation finally came through.

Eleanor Roosevelt is the only First Lady to be depicted in a presidential memorial in Washington, which was part of the original plan for the memorial and appropriate, given her impact on the country and the world. But my unique contribution to the memorial had to do with Fala, President Roosevelt's Scottish Terrier. I proposed that Fala be depicted in the memorial. During Roosevelt's presidency, Fala had captured the imagination of the American people. He was always with Roosevelt and was even pictured at Roosevelt's feet at a historic meeting with Churchill. I had always remembered from when I was a kid what happened when the Republicans attacked Roosevelt for spending taxpayer dollars to retrieve Fala when he was left behind at a stop in Alaska. Roosevelt's humor was in fine form when he said that while he and First Lady Eleanor didn't mind the attacks, "Fala does resent them. You know, Fala is Scotch . . . his Scotch soul was furious. He has not been the same dog since." Roosevelt added that he was "accustomed to hearing malicious falsehoods about himself, but I think I have a right to resent, to object, to libelous statements about my dog." Fala is buried along with the president and Mrs. Roosevelt in Hyde Park, New York.

When I proposed that Fala be represented in the Roosevelt Memorial, the Park Service was skeptical, but the commission unanimously approved the late addition anyway. The sculptor of the monument heartily agreed and did a beautiful job of representing Fala, who sits at the president's feet. Barbara and I took great pleasure in visiting the memorial on summer evenings and watching children and, indeed, adults taking pictures posing with Fala and petting his nose, which became shiny from all of the touching. And I still enjoy looking at a picture on my wall of President and Mrs. Clinton at the opening of the memorial on May 2, 1997, that depicts President Clinton pointing to Fala with a broad smile of recognition on his face.

The Hart-Dole-Inouye Federal Center

Three senators who represented the value of bipartisanship despite having different political outlooks were Democrat Phil Hart of Michigan, Republican Bob Dole of Kansas, and Democrat Danny Inouye of Hawaii, the latter two with whom I worked closely on many Senate matters. Hart died two years before I was elected to the Senate, but he was a role model for me, and so revered in the Senate for his integrity and decency that the newest and largest Senate office building carries his name.

Before their lengthy careers in public service, these three future senators became close friends during World War II when they were convalescing at the same time in Percy Jones Army Hospital in Battle Creek, Michigan, once the largest military recovery facility in the country, with over 11,000 patients. Each was paying a heavy personal price for their valor and patriotism. Phil Hart had been wounded during the Normandy landings on D-Day. Bob Dole was wounded leading his squad of the 10th Mountain Division in the Italian Alps. His wounds were so severe that he arrived at Percy Jones in a plaster body cast and was on a recovery program there for three years. Danny Inouye, whose family was being held in an internment camp, almost lost his life leading his all–Japanese American platoon of the 442nd Combat Team, which became the most decorated unit in the European theater. Danny's extraordinary courage earned him the Medal of Honor. It cited the way he was somehow able to move through a hail of bullets from three German machine guns, hurling grenades, and destroying gun emplacements, until one enemy grenade exploded and shattered his right arm.

While at Percy Jones, these three wounded soldiers talked about their future plans and all decided on public service, including running for elected office. Danny talked with me often about his stay at Percy Jones and how the people of Battle Creek took the patients into their hearts, taking them to the theater or other recreation. He talked about how they taught him to dance with one arm and how Michigan became the first place in America he called home. He spoke of how Phil Hart, the least wounded of the three, would help him and Bob Dole through long nights, bringing water and cigarettes to their nearby beds and emptying their bed pans.

In 1954 the building where the three friends were hospitalized was converted to a federal building housing a number of agencies. In 2003 I embarked on an effort to rename the building the Hart-Dole-Inouye Federal Center, and the Senate readily agreed. Phil Hart's family was at the renaming ceremony as were Senators Dole and Inouye. They recounted their time together at Percy Jones and the way public service brought them together again in the U.S. Senate, where they became leaders. At that ceremony, I said that "in combat, these men learned a valuable lesson that shaped their work in the Senate. In the foxhole there are no Democrats and Republicans, liberals or conservatives. There are only Americans. Having fought to defeat those who would steal our nation's freedom, each of them in their Senate careers sought to ensure that all Americans would continue to realize the promise of justice and liberty, a promise in our Constitution."

The courage displayed in war by these three men must have made the political risks they took as Senate leaders seem to them mighty pale by comparison.

I am convinced that the way out of the partisanship and ineffectiveness of Congress today is to have the members of both houses work on whatever issues they can find of common interest and knit together the personal relationships that build the trust so necessary to tackle the challenging and possibly life-altering issues of our time. It's a proven approach, I know, because I experienced it with many of my colleagues.

16

The Role of an Elected Official and American Values

The Role of an Elected Official

Every person elected to public office brings a host of unique factors to the job: their origin, experiences, family background, ethnicity, religious beliefs, and financial status, as well as the characteristics and dynamics of the places from which they come. But they also have the common, overarching goal to be an effective representative of their constituents. In my case that meant being pragmatic and not ideologically rigid. It also meant being willing to compromise to get things done. I've always said if you don't come to elected office willing to compromise, you don't come wanting to govern.

Being an effective representative, I've concluded, doesn't necessarily mean voting in the way the majority of one's constituents think best. I describe my approach as that of a fiduciary, that is, a person to whom a power is entrusted to act on behalf of another. I saw my responsibility as first needing to seriously study, without arrogance or certainty, an issue with all its complexities, being open to and respecting different views on the subject at hand. Then, when the time came to take a position on a matter, I viewed it as my responsibility to do what I believed was in the best interests of my constituents in the long run, even if my position might have been unpopular at the moment. I was not a populist or a poll taker. Of course, I hoped my position might reflect the currently popular view, but I felt that doing the popular thing when not believing it to be the best approach for my constituency was really working for myself or my reelection instead of working for the people.

What I came to understand is that what people want most is to trust their representatives, and the best way for an elected representative to earn that trust is to listen and learn and then express their own authentic view and not blow with the winds of public opinion. In fact, if elected leaders publicly support positions in which they don't believe, the public can't be confident that behind the scenes, where many of the decisions are made and deals are cut, they won't be acting differently from their public stance.

Sandy and I regularly debated with our campaign pollsters over their desire to poll mainly to determine where people stood on various issues and whether we were on their side, versus our desire to poll to determine whether our constituents trusted us and found us to be fair and ethical. How often we heard from people who said that they disagreed with many of our beliefs, but they voted for us anyway because they trusted us. That was always music to our ears.

It's also true that when you ask people about the appropriate role of an elected representative it usually evokes an ambivalent response. I often met with students during my career and would ask them the following three questions: Do you want your senator to reflect the popular will? (Most students said, "Yes.") Do you want your senator to vote for what he believes in his conscience to be in the best interests of his constituents, whether or not that position is popular? (Most students said, "Yes.") Do you see those two answers as being inconsistent? (Most students laughed and said, "Yes!")

The closest I came to facing a Senate vote that I knew as I cast it could determine my future was when I voted in 1981 against the Reagan tax cut. Reagan's proposed tax cut was extremely popular, but I thought it was a mistake because it disproportionately favored upper-income folks and would have a severe impact on spending for government services, such as loans for college students and funds for economic development. I also spoke against it because it provided tax reductions for the very profitable oil companies. And I pointed out that it would add three-quarters of a trillion dollars to the deficit, which I characterized at the time as a "staggering sum."

As I was one of the relatively few who voted against it, I did so knowing that I would be attacked in television ads in my upcoming 1984 reelection campaign as being a "big-taxer." Sure enough, President Reagan, who was on the verge of winning an overwhelming reelection vote, made a television pitch for my opponent from the Oval Office, telling people that a vote for me in the Senate race would amount to a vote against him as president. I knew I had to find a formula that was authentic and would express what I believed but would also respect a popular feeling. We decided to directly address the tax issue in my major television ad. I could not honestly come out in favor of a different kind of a tax cut, and I had already refused to sign a no-new-taxes pledge. So, in the ad I looked squarely into the camera and said what I truly believed, that for the majority of the people, "the last thing we ought to do is raise your taxes." It was authentic because the people I was addressing were for the most part the people (the working and middle class) for whom I did not want to raise taxes. Showing some sensitivity to popular opinion, while trying not to pander to it, helped take the edge off the repeated attack against me that I was "pro-tax." As expected, I needed all the help I could get, since it was an extremely close victory on election night.

Another vote that was controversial enough to be a possible "election decider" was my vote against a resolution authorizing the war in Iraq in the middle of my 2002 reelection campaign. Again, I was one of only a small number who voted against very popular legislation. As I described earlier when writing about Iraq, I voiced a number of objections to the decision of President George W. Bush and offered an alternative resolution. Those who opposed President Bush's decision to go to war supported my alternative, but even many of those who favored the Bush resolution saw my alternative as a reasonable one. While having an alternative to an unpopular vote was not what motivated me to offer my resolution, it surely helped me survive my campaign opponent's predictable attacks on my opposition to the Iraq War.

But taking an unpopular position at times does have risks that cannot be mitigated by offering or supporting alternatives, and doing so on a highly visible and emotional issue has at times led to electoral defeat. When I talk to people thinking about running for office, I emphasize the importance of having something else they would be happy doing if they lost an election because they went against public opinion. In my case I felt I could be happy as a teacher or a lawyer if a vote cost me reelection.

A couple of examples stand out for me as "profile in courage" votes. Senator Henry Bellmon, a Republican from Oklahoma, cast a key vote in support of the Panama Canal Treaty, knowing full well that it would likely cost him his reelection in 1980, which it did, because of the unpopularity of that treaty in his home state. History would prove the wisdom of his vote, and it also showed the respect the people of Oklahoma had for his courage and independence when, years later, they elected him governor.

Representative Marjorie Margolies-Mezvinsky, a Democrat from Pennsylvania, is another such example. It is always tempting for a politician to tout short-term benefits because they are more readily understood and have greater immediacy and popular support. So, it took courage and entailed serious political risk when President Clinton and congressional Democrats took the long view in 1993 with the passage of the Clinton budget and tax bill—a bill that included a gas tax increase as well as a tax increase for upper-income people to help balance the budget. We did that without one Republican vote and no votes to spare. Representative Margolies-Mezvinsky's vote was the last one needed in order for the bill to pass. It was a moment of high drama. She voted "aye" knowing she would be attacked as a big-taxer. It cost her and a number of other Democrats their reelection. Representative Margolies-Mezvinsky's constituents didn't reward her, but history did. And the country benefited because the economy rebounded strongly in the 1990s, unemployment rates went down significantly, inflation stayed low, and the first budget surpluses in forty years were produced. Speaker Newt Gingrich and his supporters who became the majority in 1995 tried, during the remaining Clinton years, to return to the pattern of tax cuts for the wealthy, asserting that the revenue loss would be made up for by dubious supply-side economic theory. But President Clinton's vetoes and other forms of opposition thwarted those efforts and preserved our hard-won victory.

The Republican pattern came back to life with a roar, however, and could not be thwarted when President George W. Bush was elected in 2000 along with a Republican Congress. President Bush's father, George H. W. Bush, had labeled supply-side economics as "voodoo economics" in 1980 during his campaign for the Republican nomination against Ronald Reagan. In 2001, when George W. Bush relied on discredited supply-side theories in his budget, I labeled them "déjà voodoo" economics.

President George W. Bush and the Republican majority in the Congress were handed the gift of a budget surplus that they had not created and indeed had opposed, and they promptly took the short-term and highly political approach to a question it seemed we would never be in a position to ask: "How do we use budget surpluses?" President Bush's father was willing to take political risks to benefit the country, such as dropping his "read my lips—no new taxes" pledge in order to avoid larger deficits, an action that hurt his reelection chances. In that respect, he was like his Republican predecessor, President Gerald Ford, who took a political risk to benefit the country when he pardoned President Nixon. Conversely, President George W. Bush used the surplus he inherited to his own political advantage. He told the public that because those surpluses were "their money" he was going to give them back to the public in the form of tax cuts. Of course it was "their money"—in a democracy that's a given. But instead of tax cuts and adopting the old supply-side economic theory, that money could have been used to reduce the huge and growing national debt or to improve education, the health care system, the nation's infrastructure, or Social Security—all programs that also belonged to the public.

The Republican Congress passed President Bush's tax cuts, and unsurprisingly, they were heavily tilted to the advantage of the wealthiest among us, with the richest 5 percent getting over half the tax cut and 80 percent of the tax savings going to the upper 20 percent. In his State of the Union Address in January 2002 President Bush said that the deficit in his proposed budget "will be small and short-term." He was wrong. It was no surprise when the promises of supply-side economics were again proven false. The tax cuts helped move us further and faster toward a dangerously growing national debt that will burden our children and grandchildren. But it was not the future that the Bush administration and its Republican Congress were protecting. It was their short-term political interest that they had advanced.

They were so enamored by their tax-cut rhetoric that President Bush and his supporters would not even raise taxes to pay for the Iraq War. And, of course, bearing the burden of paying back the trillions borrowed to wage that war will fall on the shoulders of the generation that supplied most of the troops that fought in it. The short-term view that is so antithetical to great leadership is made worse when it is combined with the hypocrisy that so many former "budget hawks" have revealed when justifying the recent massive additions to our national debt. It is part of the reason that the public is so discouraged with government.

That wasn't the case with one of the most memorable examples in my career of leaders acting in the long-term interests of the country. It happened when the leaders of both political parties agreed to "hold hands and jump off the bridge together" to take painful but necessary action for the common good. Democratic senator Daniel Moynihan and Republican senator Robert Dole jointly proposed a method to protect Social Security when it was truly in danger in the early 1980s by proposing that the sacrifice required be spread to all of the component parts of the Social Security system. Seniors would have to take a three-month delay in their COLAs; current contributors would see an increase in their required payments to Social Security, resulting from a tiny increase in the tax rate and raising the cap on the amount of their income that would be subject to Social Security tax; and older workers would see a slight but gradual delay in their retirement age. The financial impact was spread fairly so that the Social Security system could be saved. What a breath of fresh air such leadership is and how respected it is by the public. In my view, people seeking elected office should be willing to take such risks, acting as fiduciaries and worthy of the public trust that comes with holding such public office.

As a schoolboy I believed that Abraham Lincoln was our greatest president. My experience in government reinforced that belief, not only because Lincoln acted in the long-term interests of the country but because he combined that with a pragmatism that helped him achieve his goals.

Though he was morally opposed to slavery, Lincoln wasn't an abolitionist. Prior to becoming president, he only supported limiting the spread of slavery to new states coming into the Union. He believed abolition of slavery in the South could cause the very split in our country that eventually occurred and that he wanted above all to avoid. Yet during his campaign for the Senate two years before the war, his pragmatism was displayed in the artful way he described to voters in the North the impact of slavery on them, reminding them that the institution of slavery was taking something from them—cheating them of their right to fair representation in Congress. Because the Constitution apportioned congressional seats based on a state's population and in so doing counted slaves as three-fifths of a person, Lincoln pointedly and pragmatically argued that, as a result, the South had undue influence not just on legislation being considered by the House of Representatives but also as to who would be elected president because of the membership of the Electoral College.

His pragmatic approach to accomplishing a purpose was also demonstrated in his first major challenge as commander in chief. Lincoln had to decide whether to use force to break the Southern blockade of Fort Sumter in South Carolina. Knowing the reluctance of the North to go to war, he ordered the Union troops to withhold their fire until they were fired upon. He wanted to make it clear that if there was going to be a war, the Confederates would fire the first shot, even though the blockade was imposing great suffering on the Northern troops inside the fort. The subsequent headlines in the North— "The South Fires on Ft. Sumter"—were essential to galvanizing Northern support to engage in hostilities and spurred enlistments in the Union Army.

Lincoln's historic Emancipation Proclamation was another example of his pragmatism. It was a military order based not on the moral issue of slavery but on military circumstances and necessity: the freed slaves in the states that had seceded could take up arms and fight as a result. He did not emancipate slaves in the states that had not seceded. Abolition of slavery would come only with adoption of the Thirteenth Amendment after the war.

I came to understand more fully Lincoln's greatness over the years. He had the courage to ask the people to follow him on a painful course of action for the long-term good of the country, and he was truthful about the reasons for doing so and the sacrifices that would likely ensue. But he also understood that it is not enough to seek to lead the people toward a noble cause. It is essential that a leader be pragmatic and sensitive to what would move people to accept that cause as their own.

American Values

I began my career in public service with a belief in the positive role government can play, and the necessary role government must play, to help the American people. I had a strong sense of our nation's history and its founding principles of egalitarianism, opportunity, individualism, freedom, and fairness, and I sought to bring those values to my work on the Detroit City Council and in the Senate. These principles serve as our North Star—the light by which we set our course as a nation. We do not always follow our star, but we know where it is and what it means, and when we go off course, we work to find our way back.

Egalitarianism is the defining feature of the American character. A belief in equality fired our founding, when rebellion against an oppressive monarchy was the "shot heard round the world" that ushered in an era of democracy, and we have maintained an instinctive distaste for classism and elitism ever since. We pride ourselves on a deep belief that everyone is entitled to the same rights, a belief that is embodied in the Fourteenth Amendment's guarantee of equal protection under the law. The Frenchman Alexis de Tocqueville, writing about America in the early nineteenth century, noted with royalist amazement how lowly workmen and educated professionals greeted one another as equals. De Tocqueville did not approve of such equality and predicted it would not last. He was wrong. Belief in equality remains fundamental to who we are. We do not disapprove of wealth—provided it is the result of honest labor. But a distrust of unearned privilege and a belief that everyone is entitled to the same treatment before the law and that nobody is above the law are at the heart of what it means to be an American. We trust in courts to fairly resolve disputes just as we trust our umpires to make impartial calls in baseball.

Yet America's history is riddled with episodes in which we have failed to live up to this egalitarian instinct. The constitutional protection of slavery and early Supreme Court decisions such as *Dred Scott* and those protecting separate but equal laws; our treatment of Native Americans and Asian Americans; and legislation and court decisions that institutionalized discrimination based on race, gender, sexual orientation, and national origin are all undeniably a part of our history. They are proof that while egalitarianism is foundational to our nation, it has often been a goal rather than an accomplishment. That still remains true. More than half a century after Reverend Martin Luther King Jr.'s "I Have a Dream" speech perfectly distilled America's egalitarian ideals, African Americans continue to be disadvantaged by the legacy of slavery and Jim Crow, and often must face overt and systemic discrimination.

Affirmative action policies that I supported throughout my career to address our prior failings and to achieve equal treatment are rooted in our egalitarian principles. Ironically, those who oppose these programs have appealed to the instinctive American distrust of "special treatment," using the Constitution's equal protection clause to argue that such programs disadvantage whites. It is ironic to me that the Fourteenth Amendment, which was driven by a desire to eliminate the vestiges of slavery, has been the basis of some Supreme Court opinions striking down programs that have the very same goal.

I became deeply involved in this issue during one such challenge to affirmative action programs at the University of Michigan. Because of my work on the Armed Services Committee, I had seen up close the value of affirmative action in working toward our egalitarian ideals in the military's selection and training of officers. That's why I helped organize an amicus brief supporting the university's programs. The brief was signed by former defense secretaries, high-ranking retired military officers, and members of Congress like me who had seen the benefits to the military and the nation of a military that made progress in overcoming the legacy of discrimination. We argued that a diverse officer corps is essential to performing the military's mission and that this vital diversity was impossible if the Reserve Officer Training Corps (ROTC) programs and service academies that educated our military leaders could not consider the legacy of racial discrimination in their admissions policies. The Supreme Court decided the case in 2003 in support of affirmative action, with Justice Sandra Day O'Connor's decision citing our brief.

American history is a story of halting progress toward our egalitarian ideal. Despite all the setbacks and inconsistencies, egalitarian beliefs are real and lie in the hearts of most Americans, and I'm ever hopeful we will continue to make progress on this front.

The distrust of affirmative action programs that led to the numerous court challenges highlights another facet of the American character: a deep suspicion of government and the exercise of power by government officials. This is why the Constitution has important checks and balances to ensure that no one element of government can exercise untrammeled power, and why the Bill of Rights was written specifically to protect individual Americans from abuses of government power. That suspicion was taken to a rhetorical extreme when President Reagan said that "government is not the solution, it is the problem" in his first inaugural address, and to a real-world extreme when Tea Party leaders rode an anti-government message into office in the 2010s and attempted to dismantle a number of important federal agencies.

Our government is surely capable of abuses. I saw that even as a college student when I helped organize action against Senator Joseph McCarthy, who abused the power of his office. My first Senate election's principal theme was opposition to abuses by federal housing officials that deeply damaged my city. The need for legislative oversight to uncover and restrict government abuses was a theme of my entire Senate career. But holding government accountable is something very different than automatic opposition to government action. I reject the notion that Americans should, or do, oppose government action to make our lives better. Surely government can and, at times, must be the solution to particular problems—and the vast majority of Americans agree.

I believe the American public's real suspicion of government abuse of power has more to do with abuses by specific individuals and not the abstraction of government itself. That's why the construct of checks and balances that our nation's founders saw as critical to the preservation of our freedoms was one of the most brilliant concepts in political history. The public's innate understanding of these checks and balances is why most Americans have consistently supported congressional oversight of the executive branch and judicial oversight of both the executive and legislative branches. It's why they consistently support other important checks on abuse of power such as the Freedom of Information Act, which guarantees public access to government information and documents; the Whistleblower Protection Act, which allows government employees to come forward to report potential abuse without fear of punishment; and the presence of independent inspectors general inside our federal agencies.

This aversion to abuse of power isn't limited to government. Americans apply the same instinctive distrust of power to individuals, corporations, and other entities. And they look to government to curb those abuses through mechanisms such as antitrust laws and regulations. I worked throughout my Senate career to use the power of legislative oversight to uncover abuses such as tax-avoidance schemes by major corporations and wealthy individuals and to fight for legislation to address them.

Another strong American characteristic is that we are highly innovative. De Tocqueville noted in his travels that Americans refused to be halted by barriers between us and our goals—we found ways around, over, and through those obstacles. We have maintained this innovative capability because of our freedom to think and speak freely, and because we are still a relatively young nation, we tend to be less cynical and more optimistic. At our beginning we had a frontier to conquer, and the drive to do so helped build the character we needed to surmount the challenges we had to later overcome. That character has driven us to constantly seek out new frontiers. The blessings of immigration and the drive that brings immigrants to our shores contribute greatly to our innovation, our optimism, and our progress. We are a forward-looking country that seeks to leave divisions and animosities behind. Looking forward also means we are less bedeviled by old divisions, as other countries so often are.

Another national characteristic is that we do not believe in starting wars. And if we go to war, we want to do so for the reasons that reflect our values and not for the aggrandizement of power. In 1775, it was the provocations of the British that prompted the first shot at Lexington. It is why President Lincoln refused to authorize the first shot at Fort Sumter and why President Franklin Roosevelt waited until we were attacked before seeking a declaration of war in 1941.

Our best military leaders, who have seen firsthand the terrible toll of war on our troops and their families, are also cautious in advising the use of force, and even when force is used against us, they urge a proportionate response. Our people believe that we should be prepared to respond to an attack, or an imminent threat of an attack, but they also believe the use of lethal force should be a last resort. That is why before we take military actions, our leaders, responding to that deeply held belief, look for ways to assure the public that they are using force only after other options have been exhausted.

Our people also want to believe that when we are going to war, we are doing the right thing, and when they believe so, they are not just willing but eager to contribute to the war effort. That's why images of Rosie the Riveter and of kids collecting cans and tinfoil to help the war effort were a prominent feature during World War II.

And when we go to war, we want the good people the world over to see us as liberators, to celebrate our willingness to free oppressed peoples from the scourge of hated occupiers or despised dictators. Nothing warms American hearts more than memories of our troops' heroism in World War II in liberating Nazi death camps and marching into European capitals to cheers and adulation.

When our leaders aren't truthful about the necessity of going to war, they feed the country's intuitive suspicion of government. American political leaders are well aware of this aversion to war, the belief that force should be a last resort, and the value we place on fighting for the freedom of oppressed peoples. And it is that awareness that has prompted too many of our presidents to use pretexts to sell wars, going back to President Tyler and the Mexican-American War, to the Spanish-American War, to President Lyndon Johnson and the Gulf of Tonkin incident in the Vietnam War, and to President George W. Bush and Vice President Dick Cheney using false information to take the United States to the costly war in Iraq.

What a contrast that was to the way President Bush's father began the Gulf War in 1991. His decision did not follow a year of misleading and deceptive statements. The Gulf War followed clear acts of aggression and occupation by Iraq against neighboring Kuwait. Intervention was supported by a broad coalition that included Muslim countries and was authorized by U.N. resolution. And the objectives of the Gulf War were limited. There was no objective on our part of regime change or a plan for our troops to enter and occupy Iraq's capital. Rather our goal was to forcibly remove Saddam's troops from Kuwait, pursue them back into Iraq far enough and long enough to severely degrade their capability so Saddam could not renew his aggression, and then leave. Those circumstances and objectives were such that I came to believe that I should have supported the Gulf War and joined the other ten Democrats who did so. Instead I joined the 45 Democrats who voted "no," resulting in only 52 votes supporting the resolution.

Finally, Americans have a sense of decency. Most strive to be good people, which means we respect others, we help others, and we form organizations to do good deeds. We also try to be good neighbors, good friends, and responsible family members. Our literature, our arts, and our movies in general try to embody the goodness of people. We like to see the teacher or parent or kid who stands up to the bully, the soldier who risks her life to recover the body of a comrade, the cowboy who stands up for law and order in a small western town. These are the images with which we grow up, and they're the images that stick with us when we think about what it means to be American.

It is not an attack on America to point out the times when we have fallen short of our ideals. That recognition is a necessary defense of those ideals and an essential step to achieving them. Most presidents have respected the law and the ideals that animate it. Most Americans continue to hold freedom and liberty dear. Most of the world's peoples continue to perceive and admire these as American values. Oppressed peoples continue to endure hardship and risk to reach our shores, drawn by the promise of equality and liberty. Tears still flow when those fleeing danger and repression step on U.S. soil for the first time. May that always be true.

17

Why I Loved the Senate, Why I Left the Senate

I loved every day of the thirty-six years I spent in the U.S. Senate. The awe-inspiring setting was a constant reminder of the rare privilege it is to work there. There is no better place to satisfy the desire to engage in public service. In the Senate, you can put into motion ideas to benefit the people of your state and the nation and try to give back something in gratitude for the opportunities and freedom that have been bestowed upon you. It is a place where policy clashes are the norm but also a place where deep friendships and trust are created, relationships that help produce meaningful accomplishments.

Unlike the House and other legislative bodies in the world, the minority in the Senate, regardless of party, has significant rights that help produce compromise, the most important one being the right to filibuster, that is, debate without limit unless 60 senators vote to end the debate. The right to filibuster is accused of causing gridlock, but the reality is quite different. When a minority member announces an intent to filibuster a bill, the majority leader can get beyond the threat by forcing the minority to actually do it—to be willing to inconvenience everyone by giving up weekends and normal family life and staying in continuous session, day and night. The majority has the power, because of its numbers, to wear down the minority and win the test of wills. Many minority filibuster threats would be withdrawn as a result. The main cause of the Senate's grid-lock, however, is not the filibuster; it's that majority leaders have not wanted to proceed to consideration of bills that would require their members to cast votes that would be problematical in close elections and jeopardize their party's control of the Senate.

Eliminating the filibuster completely in the Senate would be destructive of the Senate's ability to reach legislative compromise and to restore its place as the world's greatest deliberative body. It would turn the Senate into the House of Representatives where the majority dictates the procedures and the minority has little impact on the legislative process. That is why I fought against the "nuclear option" (that is, changing a Senate rule by breaking one) the first time it was used to end the filibuster with respect to certain judges. I hope that the nuclear option precedent will be reversed by a future Senate before it is used to eliminate the filibuster for consideration of legislation. The reversal can be done easily if the leaders of both parties, knowing that the hand of history is on their shoulders, come together to restore the Senate's unique and historic role in gaining and maintaining the nation's confidence in the political process through bipartisan cooperation.

Frustration with the Senate's gridlock was not the reason I chose to leave the Senate. Quite the opposite. Yes, over the decades I did grow weary of the increasing demands to achieve higher levels of, and commit more of my time to, fundraising, and yes, there was less time for building relationships among the members, a result of which was that debates over our differences became more caustic. But the Senate had also in some ways become a bet-ter place in which to work, particularly—and thankfully—with respect to better reflecting the diversity in our people's racial and ethnic backgrounds and in our gender and religious beliefs.

It was always a privilege and a joy to work with the extraordinary staff I was blessed to have, many of whom stayed with me for a long time. They never lost their energy or enthusiasm in the search for and application of creative solutions. Over thirty-six years there were more than seven hundred individuals who worked with me. Their names are included in the staff list at the back of this book.

So why did I decide not to run for reelection? Barbara and I thought about it for many months in early 2013. My age became the major factor. If I ran again and won, I would be eighty-six at the end of a seventh term. I had seen too many colleagues who had stayed too long and observed the decline in their intellectual stamina and their health. It turned out to be somewhat prescient, because I was diagnosed with lung cancer when I was eighty-three. Little did I know at that time that Congress would soon face its greatest institutional challenge with the election of our nation's first autocrat and serious threat to our system of checks and balances.

Donald Trump's 2016 campaign did little to hide his willingness to cross normal lines of decency. Being the reality television star that he was, he continued to feed his notoriety by damaging the feelings and reputations of others. Starting with his campaign and continuing even more cravenly during his years in office, Trump's racism, his pandering to white supremacists, his Muslim bashing, and his attacks on immigrants, including stoking crowds that were chanting "send them back," have helped to unleash a wave of racism and anti-Semitism that has contributed to attacks on black churches, mosques, and synagogues. His lying is almost pathological, and he has wallowed in a seemingly bottomless pit of self-promotion. He has upended our previously understood role of the president as the moral leader of our country.

Equally damaging has been his attempted destruction of our institutions of governance upon which we rely for fairness, honesty, competent distribution of services, and security. He has fired countless people who dare to disagree with his decisions, governing by fear and intimidation. Particularly dangerous is his firing of inspectors general, the watchdogs Congress put in place in 1978 after Watergate to check executive branch excesses and abuses of power. His summary dismissal of inspectors general doing what they are supposed to do—provide unadulterated facts directly to Congress and the executive branch—violates norms that are decades old and critical to independent fact-finding. And most significant to the authority of Congress and its role under our constitution as a check on the executive, he has dismissed out of hand congressional requests and demands for information essential for Congress to do its job. This country has not seen the likes of a president with such a complete disregard for the role of Congress.

It is with a heavy heart that I have witnessed the Republican-led Senate concede its authority to President Trump. I worked with many senators who had a deep respect for the institution and the Senate's responsibility under the Constitution to check a reckless and authoritarian president but who decided to go along with Trump's abuses, almost as though they were under his spell or in a trance.

Following the conflagration of the Trump presidency, we must restore the integrity, strength, and accountability of our governing institutions. Over the years we have developed an interlocking system of checks and balances that, while not perfect, goes a long way to protecting the values and promises of our constitution. We cannot let one ill-informed, erratic president destroy what we have taken so long to construct. An independent Congress and a judiciary not beholden to party but to justice are critical components of our government. Restoring these institutions will be a primary goal once the Trump presidency is history.

18

Retirement

Retirement has worked out well. Senator Gary Peters has very ably taken my place. Sandy's son Andy was elected to Congress in Sandy's district, and the entire family could not be more proud of his commitment to issues of racial and economic justice and the environment. Barb and I settled in Detroit full time. We were able to witness firsthand the amazing economic boom taking place in our hometown. I joined Honigman, a top-notch law firm in downtown Detroit. Also, at the instigation of Linda Gustitus and Elise Bean and with the strong support of many friends, including the intrepid Eugene Driker, and Michigan's impressive secretary of state and former dean of Wayne State University Law School, Jocelyn Benson, the law school created the Levin Center in midtown Detroit. It focuses on the essential role that fact-based, bipartisan legislative oversight plays in our nation's constitutional scheme of government with its emphasis on checks and balances. The Center got a great financial boost from Bill and Madge Berman, Detroit-born Eli and Edythe Broad, my cousin Danny Levin, and Wayne Law graduate Stephen M. Ross. Through the Levin Center I was also able to do some teaching at Wayne Law School, sharing with the students my experiences and insights as a senator.

Two very special decisions involving U.S. Navy ships were made near the end of my career and after my retirement. I had come to know Secretary of the Navy Ray Mabus, a truly visionary leader, when I was the Senate Armed

Services Committee chairman. Among his many accomplishments was how he reformed and reduced the navy's use of fossil fuels. But it was on a personal note when, during my last years in the Senate, he told me he was designating the next Littoral Combat Ship as the USS *Detroit* and Barbara as the ship's sponsor. Sponsors of ships in the U.S. Navy are women who have a relationship to the ship's namesake or to its mission. What a joy it was to watch Barb smash the traditional bottle of champagne to launch the USS *Detroit* in October 2014 at the Marinette Shipyard in Wisconsin, just across the river from Menominee, Michigan. The USS *Detroit* was commissioned (put into official U.S. service) in a great ceremony on the Detroit River, directly in front of Detroit's Renaissance Center in October 2016.

Secretary Mabus took my breath away when he called me in April 2016 to tell me that he was naming the next Arleigh Burke class destroyer DDG 120 the *Carl M. Levin* and designating our daughters, Kate, Laura, and Erica, as the ship's sponsors. We had a great keel-laying ceremony in February 2019 at the Bath Iron Works in Maine with family members and friends and were greeted by the workers with a heartwarming welcome. The launching is expected to be in 2021.

So the old saying that "there is life after leaving elected office" for retired pols like me has proven more than true. As I put the finishing touches on this memoir, Barbara and I are confined to our apartment in Detroit because of the devastating coronavirus pandemic. It gives me the opportunity to think about how the themes of this memoir relate to the circumstances in which our nation finds itself, a combination of our already massive health issues heightened by the pandemic, the resulting economic losses, the large-scale protests over police violence against African Americans in response to the brutal killing of George Floyd, and the political turmoil caused by the disastrous Trump presidency.

While the election will be over by the time this memoir is published, many of the issues discussed will be relevant far into the future. One of those issues and a constant refrain in this memoir is the value of, and need to restore, a greater level of bipartisanship in the Senate in order to accomplish common goals and to end the political civil war that envelops us. We also need elected officials to be fiduciaries, that is, to be willing to take unpopular steps in the short term, with their accompanying political risks, for the long-term well-being of our nation and the world.

Bipartisanship and a fiduciary approach to governing will be necessary to address the urgent need for a health care system that is universal, available to all who need it, and sufficiently resilient to respond to unforeseen new health threats. The pandemic has made this need starkly apparent.

It will also be necessary to address unconscionable wealth and income gaps and to institute the structural reforms that the investigations by the Permanent Subcommittee on Investigations demonstrated are needed to produce a more fair and equitable economy. Some of the most important are:

> A revised tax code that closes tax loopholes such as allowing our most highly profitable corporations to shift their profits offshore to avoid paying taxes
>
> An end to the bizarre tax treatment of executive stock options that have helped produce skyrocketing executive pay and an end to the excessive use of corporate profits for stock buybacks instead of increasing wages for average workers
>
> An end to destructive Wall Street practices such as high-frequency trading that have shifted the focus from investment in a company's and our country's future to short-term profits for a group of high-frequency traders and the entities that profit from the traders' legally dubious activities

The demonstrations against police violence and racial abuse are proof of how far we have yet to go on the long and bumpy road to achieving the promise of equality, which Lincoln placed before us at the Gettysburg battlefield. But the demonstrations of June 2020 that were so diverse and widespread, so large, and, with few exceptions, nonviolent are evidence of the depth and endurance of the promise of equality and that the struggle to achieve it will continue to drive us. It makes me confident that the enduring values I wrote about earlier that inspire us will see us through our present travails and provide support for a new president of character and heart.

Retirement has reinforced an instinct my mother instilled in me—acceptance of whatever the passage of time and Mother Nature have in store for us, as we grow old. I've always been moved by the heroine, the Marschallin, in my favorite opera, Richard Strauss's *Der Rosenkavalier*. In her haunting aria near the end of the opera she accepts with grace the impact of time and the loss of her young lover to a younger woman with the poignant words: "I promised to love him in the right way (so) that I myself still love his love for another."

Our pandemic isolation and the tragic impacts of a hellish virus also remind me of what I believe "heaven" is: receiving the love of parents when growing up, the love that Barbara and I have for each other, and the joy our three daughters, Kate, Laura, and Erica, have brought us. We watched with great pride as the bonds between them became ever tighter as they grew into strong, independent women and when they fell in love, bringing into our family sons-in-law Daniel Levin and Rick Fernandes. And to top it off, they produced six extraordinary grandchildren: Noa and Ben Levin, Bess and Samantha Markel, and Beatrice and Olivia Fernandes. The six of them bring us a slice of heaven each time we think of them or see them and when we see how close they all are to each other. Heaven for us is truly our family life here on Earth.

Acknowledgments

Many people helped me take on what for me was a daunting challenge: writing a memoir. Even deciding to take the plunge took a push from many people. My wife, Barbara, led the pack. Over the years this memoir took to write, Barb provided far more than encouragement, as needed as that was. She brought a wealth of memories, suggestions, and insights. Her ability to identify errors and omissions was derived from her innate editing skill and her thoroughness in scouring all the drafts. We spent countless hours sitting together crafting phrases and debating the meaning and impact of words. The memoir couldn't have happened without her. It has truly been a joint endeavor.

Linda Gustitus was one of the people who urged me to write a memoir. She has been a full collaborator on the project and more, just as she was more than an extraordinary chief of staff for two decades of the two investigation subcommittees I chaired and then my overall chief of staff. The staffs she supervised loved her caring ways, sensitivity, and loyalty to them and to me. Linda and I forged a strong and lasting friendship. She knew my strengths and weaknesses. She was so tuned into my thinking that at hearings, when I was struggling to find the right word in a comment or question, she knew the word I was looking for and said it just loud enough for me to hear it and use it. She brought her talents to this memoir as a volunteer. She devoted countless hours, days, and weeks, reading every draft of every chapter multiple times, proposing and crafting changes, fitting and refitting pieces together. She located people who could help along the way. Linda's contributions were more than invaluable. They were essential.

Elise Bean, who took over as PSI staff director from Linda, was a great leader, pulling together Democratic and Republican staffs to work as a team in the cause of bipartisan, fact-based, in-depth oversight. Dozens of successful investigations and hearings that resulted helped produce significant policy changes and reforms. She wrote the book (literally) and has become a national and international expert and instructor on the value and techniques of legislative oversight. She drafted the chapter in this memoir that focused on my work at PSI and, as always, brought her immense competence to the task before her, producing a draft that had fewer edits and rewrites than any other chapter.

Jack Kresnak was of great assistance in recording and organizing my thoughts in response to his questions and producing the first drafts of the early chapters and some anecdotes for later chapters. He did much of the interviewing of former colleagues, staff, and friends. He researched a number of issues at the University of Michigan's Bentley Library in Ann Arbor. He was helpful in numerous other ways, and I am most appreciative of his contributions and his friendship.

Ronit Wagman provided the needed editing of the memoir's later drafts and did so with great efficiency. She was a pleasure to work with.

Our daughters, Kate, Laura, and Erica, were always there to help jog my memory and to make valuable suggestions and corrections. My brother, Sandy, is an important part of the memoir and provided invaluable help to me in my writing it, particularly with his recollections of our early years. He brought to the memoir his great savvy about policy issues and his insider mastery of the ways of Congress gained from his own thirty-six years in the House.

Both Bob Seltzer in the early years and Gordon Trowbridge in the later years played critical roles in my elections and on my Senate staff. They also were extremely talented wordsmiths. Bob recently passed on, a great loss to all of us who knew and loved him. Both Bob and Gordon were helpful to this memoir, offering bite and poetry to its writing.

Two of my best friends in the Senate, David Boren and John Warner, as well as my dear friend Eugene Driker, who were interviewed by Jack Kresnak, were more than generous with their time and words.

Many friends and former staffers also provided helpful comments, insights, history, and fact-checking, including Tara Andringa, Rich Arenberg, Jay Brandt, Joe Bryan, Tom Clark, Jim Crutchfield, Chuck Cutolo, Rick Debobes, Chris Dewitt, Ty Gellasch, John Howes, Dan Jones, Gordon Kerr, Peter Kyriacopoulos, David Lyles, Kathleen Long, Kenneth Mahoney, K. P. Pelleran, Kathryn Polgar (Wayne University Law School Library), Marda Robillard, Kate Scott (associate Senate historian), Gina Shireman, Cathy Sommers, Nick Taylor, Rick Wiener, Chuck Wilbur, and Alison Warner. I am grateful to them for their contributions to this memoir.

I also appreciate the assistance of Director Terrence McDonald and the staff at the Bentley Historical Library in Ann Arbor, which houses my papers.

Finally, I want to acknowledge the over seven hundred staff people who worked for me in the Senate—in my personal office, in my Michigan offices, on the Armed Services Committee, and on the Homeland Security and Governmental Affairs subcommittees. (See the staff list that follows the acknowledgments.) I made every effort to include them all and to spell their names correctly. I hope I was successful. I deeply appreciate their work.

For those I overlooked here or failed to adequately acknowledge in the memoir itself, I offer my apology.

I end where perhaps I should have begun, with an expression of gratitude to the people of Michigan whose support made it possible for me to begin the adventure I recounted in this memoir and who sustained me with their goodwill and understanding through the decades.

Levin Senate Staff, 1979–2015

Abel, Matt
Abernathy, Pauline
Aboulafia, Diane
Addington, Renae
Akiyama, Amy
Allard, Wendy
Allen, David
Allen, Sandra
Aloia, Angela
Alpert, Dara
Alpert, Matt
Alvarez, Raul
Anders, Jeffrey
Andersen, Jane
Anderson, Devon
Anderson, Harvey
Andringa, Tara
Anthony, Dave
Arciero, Gale
Arenberg, Rich
Arons, Donna
Arora, Samir
Ash, Betty
Ash, Mary
Averbuch, Aaron

Bagley, Lisa
Baker, James
Bald, John
Barbaza, Melanie

Barbee, Kenneth
Barczyk, Joseph
Barr, Nathaniel
Barry, Henry
Barthel, Erin
Basch, Denise
Baum, Naomi
Bean, Elise
Belanger, Penelope
Berard, David
Berger, Michael
Berglund, Amy
Bergsbaken, Steven
Berkovitz, Dan
Berry, Shirley
Bery, Priya
Biestek, Gregory
Blacklow, Willy
Blair, Doug
Blake, Susan
Blood, Becky
Bogacki, June
Bogage, Claudine
Bolyard, David
Borawski, June
Borthwick, Stewart
Bowen, Robert
Bowers, Rebecca
Braverman, Patricia
Brennan, John

Brenner, Benjamin
Brewer, Leah
Bride, Tom
Broder, Ruth
Brody, Amanda
Brown, Anne
Brown, Geoffrey
Brown, Louis
Brown, Vonzell
Bryan, Joe
Budzinski, Carrie
Bums, Kane
Bums, Sarah
Burack, Marissa
Butler, Susan

Callow, Jim
Cameron, Susan
Cames, Melinda
Campione, Meghan
Canan, Lindsay
Canan, Martha
Cangelosi, Allegra
Cantrall, Barbara
Carlyle, Megan
Carrni, Shlomo
Carroll, Dorothy
Carter, Rick
Carver, Eric
Casey, David

Cash, Evan
Castaing, Eva
Castillo, Elizabeth
Catlin, Jessica
Cavadeas, Susanne
Chambers, Hilarie
Chambliss, Wanda
Charles, Diana
Chase, Harold
Chekan, Suzanne
Cizner, Jennifer
Clark, Allen
Clark, Jonathan
Clarke, Mavis
Coaster, Carrie
Coates, Lori
Coffman, Patricia
Cohen, Ilona
Cohen, Josh
Collier, Jacqueline
Collins, David
Colman, Jeffrey
Colona, Dorian
Confer, Eunice
Conklin-Callow, Mary
Connor, Gregory
Conway, Andrew
Cook, Steven
Cooper, Mariah
Copeland, Nancy
Cork, Fletcher
Coughlan, Jim
Courville, Jacob
Cowart, Chris
Cox, Dan
Cox, Sandra
Creedon, Madelyn
Crenshaw, Alicia
Cronin, Kevin
Crosswait, Kenneth
Crouch, Marcia
Crutchfield, Jim
Cullinan, Kathleen
Cummins, Michael

Curran, James
Cutler, Todd
Cutolo, Chuck
Cutsinger, Loran

Dallafior, Michelle
Daly, Denise
Danielson, Jack
Daugherty, Brenna
Daughtery, Miah
Davidson, Isabelle
Davis, Jeffrey
Davis, Julie
Dearmin, Diana
DeBobes, Rick
Decker, John
DeKuiper, Kay
Delgado, Ida
Dennison, David
DeVergie, Frankie
Dewitt, Chris
Diaz, Rebecca
Dick, Anna
Dickinson, Peggy
Dillon, Brandon
Dilworth, Tina
Dinning, Elizabeth
Doctoroff, Andy
Doctoroff, Mark
Dollard, Penny
Domsic, Mark
Donahue, William
Doremus, Anne
Dorman, Breton
Drobnich, Darrel
Drucker, Jon
Duckworth, Jamie
Dudley, Jennifer
Durnell, Jamie
Dyke, Judy

Eagle, Mary
Eason, Alphonso
Echols, Michael

Eichenbaum, David
Elkin, David
Ellis, Margaret
Ellman, Lisa
Elowsky, Deborah
Elwood, Philip
Epstein, Jonathan
Estrada, Kathy
Ettlinger, Elysa
Everett, Tim

Fahrer, Gabriella
Farkas, Evelyn
Farmer, Suzanne
Feinberg, Daniel
Feld, Melissa
Feldman, Eric
Fianders, Garth
Fiatow, Joel
Fieldhouse, Richard
Fife, Kittredge
Figurski, Jay
Finkenstaedt, Eliza
Fitzgerald, Virginia
Fitzwater, Sara
Fix, Jennifer
Fleishman, Sandra
Fogel, Bob
Foley, Sean
Ford, Argenia
Ford, James
Forrer, Graydon
Foster, Patricia
Foster, Shonda
Foust, Mike
Fowler, George
Frankfurter, Diana
Freedo, Kristi
Fry, Mark

Gadigian, Mark
Galen, Helen
Garabyare, Hani
Garavaglia, Marco

Garcia, Linda
Garg, Nisha
Garrett, Jessie
Gazella, Kim
Gbur, Susan
Gelfond, Deena
Gellasch, Ty
Gibson, Deborah
Giles, Allie
Gillis, Lauren
Glancy, Douglas
Glandon, Kevin
Glas, Elena
Glenn, Dwanda
Goldbaum, Keith
Goldenkranz, Laura
Goldsmith, Daniel
Gonzalez, Joseph
Goodman, Keith
Gordon, Abby
Gordon, Jan
Gore, Tabatha
Goshorn, Dan
Grabiak, Nancy
Grady, Judith
Gray, Amy
Graziani, Andrew
Green, Mary
Greene, Beverly
Greene, Creighton
Groeninger, Julie
Groman, Rachel
Grounds, Kelly
Grulke, Eric
Guglielmo, Dan
Guirey, Joanne
Gundersen, Aurora
Gustitus, Linda
Guzelsu, Ozge
Gwozdz, Janice

Hall, Jennifer
Handelsman, Dylan
Hansell, David

Hansknecht, Lisa
Hanson, Kathryn
Harder, Daniel
Harlem, Justin
Harrington, Maureen
Harris, Deborah
Harris, Micah
Harrison, Marla
Hart, Cheryl
Hart, Tess
Hartzell, Joan
Harvey, Joel
Haskell, Sandra
Hathaway, Alexandra
Hathaway, Will
Hazen, Terri
Heckart, Robert
Hekhuis, Jeremy
Helms, Bonnie
Henderson, Adam
Henry, Patrick
Henseler, Tim
Heron, Matthew
Herron, Russell
Herzig, Walt
Hickner, Andrew
Higgins, Bridget
Hill, Jason
Hilsenrad, Norman
Hobrla, Lee
Hochstein, Eric
Hoege, Howard
Hoffman, Burt
Holloman, Roderick
Horste, Melissa
Houser, Richard
Houston, Jonathan
Howard, Gary
Hubbard, Paul
Hunter, Elizabeth

Ireland, Samuel

Jacobson, Mark
Jaffray, Jan

James, Nicole
Jed, Susan
Jenkins, Judy
Jhin, Phillip
Johnson, Akisha
Johnson, Andy
Johnson, Susanne
Jordan, Bessie
Joyce, Vema

Kalec, Ann
Kampner, Alissa
Kang, Raymond
Kapustij, Carolyn
Karwacki, Chris
Kasrnir, Justin
Katz, David
Keeley, John
Keller, Heidi
Kellman, Shannon
Kenney, Thornas
Kent, Andrew
Kerr, Gordon
Kerzich, Jeanne
Key, Jennifer
Khouri, Naif
Kiefer, Donna
King, David
King, Jacqueline
Kingston, Jessica
Kinzey, Carolynn
Kirb, Dia
Kirkland, Timothy
Kirschner, Ross
Kish, Carla
Kleiman, Miriam
Klender, Mark
Kliment, Nicholas
Klitzman, Steve
Klug, Edward
Knibbs, Holly
Knowles, Jennifer
Ko, Kristina
Kochen, Manfred

Koepke, Scott
Komman, Kay
Koranda, Matt
Kosarin, Greg
Koscak, Keith
Kowalsky, Joe
Kramer, Chris
Krevait, Deborah
Kuiken, Mike
Kunkle, Liz
Kuthy, James
Kyle, Mary
Kyriacopoulos, Peter

Labarre, Andy
Lafayette, Lucy-Adelle
Lakomy, Maryann
Lane, Edward
Lang, Christine
Langton, Jennifer
Lasalle, Jeanne
Laughlin, Terence
Law, Deloris
Leed, Maren
Leeling, Gary
Legg, Christopher
Lennon, Peter
Lester, Patrick
Levi, Ari
Levin, Daniel
Levin, Devera
Levin, Matthew
Levine, Bruce
Levine, Peter
Levy, Seth
Lewis, Anne
Lewis, David
Lewis, Tanga Marie
Liebling, Mark
Lievense, Andrew
Lipner, Pearl
Lloyd, Hannah
Loftus, John
London, David

Long, Kathleen
Long, Michelle
Lossing, David
Lostracco, Elizabeth
Love, Kimberly
Luftman, Eric
Luongo, Ken
Lyles, David

Macwilliams, Joann
Maddocks, Kathleen
Mande, Lynn
Manos, Melinda
Maroney, Jason
Marshall, Laura
Mathis, Derrick
Matus, Christopher
Maxwell, Gray
Mayes, Derrick
Mazur, James
Mazyck, Nancy
McCollum, Thad
McConnell, Thomas
McCord, Mike
McCree, Karen
McCreedy, David
McGee, Susan
McGinnis, Bryan
McGuire, Daniel
McIntosh, Nicole
McLaren, Sara
McLaurin, Rashanda
McNeill, Erin
McPherson, Shani
McRill, Megan
McShea, Kathy
Meier, Kaye
Meltzer, Carol
Menkes, Allison
Merrill, Jennifer
Merritt, David
Micallef, Roseann
Michalsky, Steven
Miller, Barbara

Miller, Chris
Miller, Frederick
Miller, Patrick
Milow, Loretta
Mims, Valerie
Mitchell, Jack
Mitchell, John
Moeser, Molly
Moffitt, Paul
Monahan, Bill
Montague, Autumn
Moore, Robert
Moore, Thomas
Moran, Jim
Morgan, Kathleen
Morgan, Marston
Morse, Nicole
Morter, Kevin
Morton, William
Moscow, Joshua
Moy, Russell
Muchanic, Christine
Mulinex, Joy
Mulvaney, Douglas
Munford, Gail
Muniz, Edilson
Murphy, Allison
Murray, Brian
Mussington, Shawn
Myers, Josh
Myers, Sheila

Naccari, Jennifer
Nathansen, Laurence
Neal, Tiffany
Nelson, Steve
Neubauer, Kathy
Newman, Kendra
Newton, John
Newton, Lauren
Nielsen, Larry
Noblet, Mike
Nykaza, Madeline

O'Brien, Kathleen
O'Bryan, Michael
O'Hara, Sandra
O'Leary, Bob
O'Neal, Denise
O'Rourke, Ronald
O'Sullivan, Sharon
Oviedo, Carmen
Ozer, Elizabeth

Paisley, Kelly
Palamara, Jennifer
Paritee, Karen
Parker, Armetta
Parker, Belinda
Parker, Jackie
Parker, Nora
Parker, Veda
Parks, Celeste
Parks, Leslie
Parm, Colleen
Parr, Marilyn
Partin, Lynn
Pascale, Alison
Pasha, Ali
Patrick, Julie
Peach, Monica
Pearson, Cindy
Pelleran, Kathy
Peltier-Rand, Valerie
Pernice, Llliana
Perona, Lorraine
Perry, Amy
Petrouske, Rosalie
Petty, Aaron
Petty, Ann
Phillips, Roy
Pickell, Gregory
Pitler, Randall
Plettner, Sharon
Plumley, Nan
Polanin, Jonathan
Pollard, William
Pollock, James

Powell, Elizabeth
Powell, Leslie
Prall, Willow
Principato, John
Procida, Mark

Quinn, Laura
Quirk, John

Radike, Jack
Rahi, Christine
Raiford, Anita
Rains, Leslie
Randolph, Maggie
Record, Francis
Reed, Dorothy
Register, Louise
Rehmus, Jonathan
Revsine, Paul
Rich, David
Rico, Thomas
Rief, Julie
Risley, Paul
Rives, Robert
Roach, Bob
Robere, Chris
Roberts, Bernadette
Robertson, Mary
Robillard, Marda
Rodgers, Suzanne
Rose, Allen
Rosen, Jim
Rosenberg, Aaron
Rosenberg, Michael
Rosenblum, Dan
Rosenfeld, Jim
Ross, Cynthia
Roy, Robbie
Rubin, Benjamin
Russell, Karen

Samuelson, Linda
Savage, Barbara
Sawyer, Brendan

Schmid, Michael
Schmidt, Scott
Schneider, Gabriel
Schneider, Mary
Schochet, Bobette
Schracta, Connie
Schram, Zack
Schwab, Norma
Sebold, Brian
Seltzer, Bob
Selva, Vicki
Sen, Priyadarshi
Senor, Wendy
Seraphin, Arun
Serbinoff, S A
Serkaian, Steve
Shaffer, Russ
Shandler, Phil
Shapiro, Elizabeth
Shapiro, Joshua
Sharp, Kristin
Sheehan-Dean, Aaron
Shelton, Terra
Sheridan, John
Sherwood, Virginia
Shireman, Gina
Shoffner, Gwen
Silvasi, Guy
Silver, Charles
Simmons, Kathleen
Simodejka, Jill
Simon, Michael
Simoncic, Michael
Simone, David
Sklar, Amy
Smith, Gerald
Smith, Jonathan
Smith, Joshua
Smith, Philip
Smith, Race
Smith, Travis
Smythe, Kel
Snider, Richard
Sole, Marc

Somers, Cathy
Spiller, Donna
Spisz, Amy
Splitt, Selena
Spray, April
Spryszak, Terry
Stancil, Nick
Stein, Todd
Stemstein, Alan
Steslicki, Jeremy
Stevens, Nathan
Still, Christina
Stoddard, Penny
Stoffel, Jeb
Stoffer, Ellen
Stoll, Tina
Strack, Barbara
Strager, Patricia
Strayer, John
Strong, Carmen
Stryker, Marian
Stuber, Laura
Sturtevant, Rochelle
Sullivan, Ann
Sutey, Bill
Sybenga, Katherine
Syrja, Steven
Szuplat, Terence

Tallman, Richard
Tap, Jonathon
Tasdemiroglu, Deniz
Tash, Michael
Tausner, Diane
Thomas, Bryan
Thomas, Cheryl
Thomas, Michael
Thomas, Patricia
Thomas, Vince
Thorsen, Bridget
Thusat, Juergen
Tichon, Nicole
Todak, Alison

Todaro, Vincent
Topolewski, Gina
Tormala, Rick
Towle, Raymond
Trigg, Michael
Troost, Paul
Trowbridge, Gordon
Trujillo, Mark
Tucker, Lisa
Tucker, William
Tummonds, Dana
Tunks, Kevin
Turner, Jim
Twite, Marie

Unzicker, Lorraine
Upfal, Nathan

Vanderpool, Janet
Van Dyke, Lynne
Varadian, Mark
Veatch, Phillip
Verdery, Lauren
Verona, Lisa
Vollman, Jim

Wagner, Mary Louise
Waisanen, Robert
Walker, Barry
Walker, Kellie
Wallace, Andrew
Wallace, Clinton
Wallace, Tara
Warner, Alison
Washington, Barbara
Washington, Brittney
Washington, Mary
Washington, Vanessa
Wathel, Angela
Watson, Bradley
Watson, Doris
Weaver, Greg
Weber, Bill

Weber, Eric
Weberman, Daniel
Weinberg, Alan
Weiner, Kathryn
Weingarden, Michele
Weinstein, Lisa
Weir, Kevin
Wellington, Rosemary
Wells, Breon
Wenokur, Shari
Wertheimer, Jordon
West, Nicholas
Whalen, Bill
White, Karen
White, Mervin
White, Ralph
Wicklund, Krista
Wiener, Rick
Wilbur, Chuck
Wilkie, Edith
Williams, Jennifer
Winkelman, Laurie
Winkelman, Stephen
Wiszynski, George
Wolff, Audrey
Wolff, Erica
Wood, Mary
Woodhouse, Julie
Woods, Cassandra
Woodson, Shelley
Wright, Eliza
Wright, Sue

Yaffe, Andrea
Yates, Alice
Yatooma, Chris
Yoo, Christopher
Young, John

Zimberg, Joshua
Zimmer, Marcia
Zivian, Bruce

Index

Abu Ghraib military prison, Iraq, 105, 106–7
Abu Nidal Organization, 115
accountability, 63, 64, 248, 259, 299; Iraq and, 106, 174; regulatory, 62, 66
ADA. *See* Americans for Democratic Action
adoption, 285–86
adoption registry, 282–85
adult businesses, 29–30
affirmative action, 298–99
Afghanistan, 141, 144–48, 149–52, 170; army of, 148, 149–50; leadership of, 150; Taliban and, 143–44
Agency for International Development (AID), 56
Akaka, Daniel, 281
Alaska, 175–77, 178
Alaska National Interest Lands Conservation Act (1980), 177
Albania, 135–36
Aleuts, 176, 190, 191
Alexander, Keith B., 134
Alexander, Lamar, 212
Alexander Solzhenitsyn Award, 121
al-Qaeda, 143, 144, 146, 154, 156, 157
Amazon.com, Inc., 274
American Bar Association, 258

American Revolution, 297, 301
Americans for Democratic Action (ADA), 60
American values, 297–303
Amos, Jim, 102–3
Andersen, Arthur, 252–53
animals, protections for, 190–91
Annan, Kofi, 163
anti-Semitism, 306
antitrust laws, 300
Apple Inc., 98, 268, 269, 270
Arab League, 113
Arafat, Yasser, 117
Arctic National Wildlife Refuge, Alaska, 176, 177
Arenberg, Rich, 210
Arendts, David, 110
Argov, Shlomo, 115
Army Field Manual, 106
Arnett, Judd, 38
Aspin, Les, 95
atomic cities, in Russia, 124–26
Atta, Mohammed, 154–55, 156, 157
Authorization for Use of Military Force (AUMF), 143
automobile industry, 5, 34, 80, 131–33, 197; bailout of, 75, 76–77; Japanese, 77; NAFTA and, 81–82; trade and, 74–75
"axis of evil," 153

Baker, Howard, 211
Bales, David, 178
Ball, Don, 27, 28
bank bailouts, 245
Barrasso, John, 212
baseball, 4, 202
basket options, 264, 265–68
Bay of Pigs invasion, 139
BCRA. *See* Bipartisan Campaign
Reform Act
Bean, Elise, 242, 248, 308
Begin, Menachem, 113, 115, 118
Beijing, China, 129
Beirut, Lebanon, 115–17
Belgrade, Serbia, 136
Bell Laboratories, New York City, New
York, 13
Bellmon, Henry, 293
Benishek, Dan, 181–82
Benson, Jocelyn, 308
Berisha, Sali Ram, 135
Berlin, Germany, 122
Berlin Wall, 122–23
Berman, Bill, 308
Berman, Madge, 308
"Beyond the Bean Count" report, 90
B-52 bomber, 101
Biden, Joe, 120, 143, 159, 173, 209
Bill of Rights, 299
bin Laden, Osama, 144, 150, 152,
153, 165
Bipartisan Campaign Reform Act
(BCRA), 226–28
bipartisanship, 95, 241–42, 275–76,
277–89, 305, 309–10
Birmingham, Michigan, 1
Bishop, Maurice, 117
Blanchard, Jim, 75
Bliley, Thomas, 284
Blix, Hans, 162
B-1 bomber, 101
Bongo, Omar, 249
Boren, Dave, 65, 120–21, 128, 129, 130

Borger, Gloria, 155
Bosnia, 136, 137
Brennan, John, 155
Brewer, Mark, 51
Broad, Edythe, 308
Broad, Eli, 308
Broder, Ruth, 42
Brownlee, Les, 96
Bryan, Joe, 106
Buchanan, Pat, 127
Bulgaria, 14
Bumpers, Dale, 235–36
Bunning, Jim, 189
buprenorphine (BUP), 277–80
Bush, George H. W., 81, 124, 179, 186,
200, 294; Gulf War and, 161, 302
Bush, George W., 102, 106, 188–89, 214,
281, 294–95; Iraq War and, 152–54,
157, 158–60, 161, 163, 164–65, 167,
170–72, 292, 302
busing, 32, 34, 41
Butzner, John, 230–31
Byrd, Robert, 53, 55, 56, 219

CAFE. *See* Corporate Average Fuel
Economy
Calumet, Michigan, 184, 185
Calumet Italian Hall disaster, 184–85
campaign advertising, 41, 47
campaign finance reform, 226–29
Camp David Accords, 113, 114
Canada, 30, 81, 178
Cardin, Ben, 212
Carl M. Levin (ship), 309
Carter, Jimmy, 35, 57, 77, 177; Camp
David Accords and, 113; support
for Levin, 43, 59
Carter, Lillian, 112
CAT. *See* Center for Advanced
Technologies
Caterpillar Inc., 268, 270
caucuses, 48, 50, 51, 52, 221

Center for Advanced Technologies
(CAT), 198–201
Central Intelligence Agency (CIA), 125,
164, 166–67; 9/11 and, 144, 152,
154, 155–57; torture and, 97, 105,
106, 108–9
CFPB. *See* Consumer Financial
Protection Bureau
CFTC. *See* Commodity Futures Trading
Commission
Chase Bank, 261
checks and balances, 62, 219, 299,
300
Chelyabinsk-65, Russia, 124–26
Cheney, Dick, 107, 124; Iraq War and,
154–55, 156–57, 158, 159, 160,
171, 302
Chernobyl nuclear disaster, 125
Chicago, Illinois, 2
Chile, 250–52
China, 79, 84–85, 128–35
Chinn, Franklyn, 72, 73
Christian Solidarity International
(CSI), 121
Chrysler Corporation, 75–77
Chrysler Loan Guarantee Act (1979), 77
Chukwueke, Sopuruchi Victor, 204–5
Churchill, Winston, 128, 287
CIA. *See* Central Intelligence Agency
Citibank, 249, 251, 252, 257
*Citizens United v. Federal Election
Commission*, 228
Civil War, 183–84, 296–97, 301
Clark, Tom, 27
Clarke, Richard, 153
Clean Water Act (1972), 178
Clinton, Bill, 46, 136, 200–201, 225,
231, 288, 293–94; China and, 130;
DADT and, 102; impeachment of,
229, 232–39; Middle East and, 117,
156; NAFTA and, 81
Clinton, Hillary, 51–52
cloture, 57, 211

Coalition Against Counterfeiting and
Piracy, 133
coalition building, 88
Coburn, Tom, 98, 202, 241, 243, 275
Cohen, Bill, 68–69, 70, 73, 222, 223, 229
Cohn, Avern, 1
Cohn, Roy, 7
Cold War, 89
Coleman, Norm, 241, 256, 258, 275
Collins, Susan, 190, 191, 242, 246, 248
combatant status review (CSR), 215
Commission on Presidential
Nomination Scheduling and
Timing, 50
Commodity Futures Trading
Commission (CFTC), 264
Common Cause, 224
conflicts of interest, 100, 246, 266
Congressional-Executive Commission
on China, 131, 134
congressional oversight, 36, 63, 69, 71,
246, 264, 274, 299–300, 308
conservation, 175, 177
Consumer Financial Protection Bureau
(CFPB), 247
Cooperative Research and Development
Agreement (CRADA), 79
copper, 183–84
Copper Harbor, Michigan, 183
coronavirus pandemic, 309, 310, 311
Corporate Average Fuel Economy
(CAFE), 80, 82
corporate paternalism, 184
cost-benefit analyses, 66–67
counterfeiting, 84, 131–34
counterterrorism, 153, 156, 257
CRADA. *See* Cooperative Research and
Development Agreement
Craig, Larry, 284
credit card companies, 260–62
credit-rating agencies, 244–45
Credit Suisse, 258, 259
Croatia, 137

CSI. *See* Christian Solidarity
   International
CSR. *See* combatant status review
Cuba, 139–40
Cuban Missile Crisis, 14, 148
Cunningham, Bill, 196–99
Cutolo, Chuck, 200, 211
Czech Republic / Czechoslovakia, 122,
   123, 154

DADT. *See* "Don't Ask, Don't Tell"
   policy
Daily Mining Gazette, 185
Dalai Lama, 128
Daschle, Tom, 159, 160–61
Davis, Bob, 186, 187
Dean, Howard, 49, 50
Dearborn, Michigan, 16–17
DeBobes, Rick, 96
defense appropriations bill, 106, 196–96
defense authorization bill, 94, 99, 101–2,
   103, 105; detainees and, 106, 214–15;
   earmarks and, 195–96
defense contracting, 68, 99–100, 133–34
defense spending, 68–69, 92, 99,
   100–101
Delaware, 257, 258
Dellums, Ron, 200
Democratic National Committee
   (DNC), 49, 50–51
Democratic National Convention
   (2004), 50
Denton, Jeremiah, 285
Department of Commerce, 78, 81–82
Department of Defense (DOD), 79, 85,
   89, 91–92, 94, 102, 111, 198, 280;
   Chinese counterfeit products and,
   133–34; reform of, 92, 93; spending
   by, 68–69, 99–100
Department of Defense Inspector
   General, 157
Department of Energy, 159

Department of Health and Human
   Services, 285
Department of Homeland Security
   (DHS), 203, 206
Department of Housing and Urban
   Development (HUD), 27–29, 41
Department of Justice, 73, 216, 247,
   254, 260
Department of Labor, 60
Department of Transportation, 80
derivatives, 262–64
detainee abuse, 97, 105–8
Detainee Treatment Act (2005), 106
de Tocqueville, Alexis, 297, 300
Detroit, Michigan, 2, 3, 11, 21–22,
   193–94, 308; housing and, 27–29,
   299; Jewish religious services in, 33;
   school integration in, 32–33, 34;
   zoning and, 29–30
Detroit City Council, 22–24, 38, 57;
   adult businesses and, 29–30;
   environment and, 30–31; Focus:
   HOPE and, 196–97; housing and,
   27–29, 41; Levin's first term, 24–33;
   Levin's second term, 33–37
Detroit Free Press, 26, 36, 38, 204, 279
Detroit Legal Aid Office, 18–20
Detroit News, 27, 37, 91–92, 182
Detroit People Mover, 35
Detroit Police Department, 34
Detroit Rebellion, 21–22, 26
Detroit River, 188–89, 193–94
Detroit Riverfront Conservancy
   (DRFC), 194
Detroit River International Wildlife
   Refuge Establishment Act
   (2001), 189
Dewey, Thomas, 5
DHS. *See* Department of Homeland
   Security
Dimon, Jamie, 263, 264
Dingell, Debbie, 48–51
Dingell, John, Jr., 49, 188, 200

Dingell, John, Sr., 4
discrimination, 17–18, 35, 260, 298, 299
diversity, 6, 23, 32–33, 299, 305
DNC. *See* Democratic National
    Committee
DOD. *See* Department of Defense
Dodd, Chris, 115, 116, 117, 261, 262
Dole, Bob, 211, 283, 284, 288–89, 295
"Don't Ask, Don't Tell" policy (DADT),
    102–3
Dorgan, Byron, 81
Douglas, William O., 176
Dred Scott decision, 298
DRFC. *See* Detroit Riverfront
    Conservancy
Driker, Elaine, 23
Driker, Eugene, 23, 308
Drug Addiction Treatment Act (2000),
    278–79
Duff, James H., 8
Durbin, Dick, 139
Durkin, John, 49

earmarks, 194–96, 201–3
Earth Day, 30
education, 32–33, 63, 110–11; in
    Afghanistan, 146–47
egalitarianism, 297–99
Egypt, 113, 118
Eisenhower, Dwight, 11
elected officials, role of, 290–97
Emancipation Proclamation, 296–97
endangered species, 31
Enron Corporation, 252–53
environment, 30–31, 188–89, 201
Environmental Protection Agency
    (EPA), 178, 179, 187
EPA. *See* Environmental Protection
    Agency
Equatorial Guinea, 250
Ethics in Government Act (1978), 222
executive orders, 66–67

executive pay, 271–75, 310
Exon, Jim, 124, 126

Facebook, Inc., 273
fact-finding missions, 96, 115–17,
    124–26
Faircloth, Lauch, 230
Fala (President Roosevelt's dog),
    287–88
FASB. *See* Financial Accounting
    Standards Board
Fastow, Andy, 253
FATCA. *See* Foreign Account Tax
    Compliance Act
FATF. *See* Financial Action Task Force
Faubus, Orval, 16
FDA. *See* Food and Drug
    Administration
Federal Bureau of Investigation (FBI),
    105, 144, 156
Federal Trade Commission (FTC), 57,
    65, 132
Feikens, John, 16
Feingold, Russ, 226–27
Feinstein, Dianne, 80, 107, 236
Feith, Doug, 154, 156–57
Fernandes, Beatrice, 311
Fernandes, Olivia, 311
Fernandes, Rick, 311
Fifth Amendment, 7, 8
filibuster, 207–12, 227, 304–5
Finance Committee, 55, 70, 71
Financial Accounting Standards Board
    (FASB), 270, 272, 273
Financial Action Task Force (FATF),
    257
Fiske, Robert, 229–30, 231
Focus: HOPE, 196–201
Food and Drug Administration (FDA),
    279
Ford, Gerald, 238, 294
Ford Motor Company, 76, 132

Foreign Account Tax Compliance Act
(FATCA), 259–60
foster care, 285
Fourteenth Amendment, 297, 298
Frances Perkins Department of Labor
Building, 59–60
Frankfurter, Felix, 220, 286
Franks, Tommy, 144
fraternities, 6
Freedom of Information Act, 300
free trade, 81–82, 83, 84
Frist, Bill, 213–14
Frost, Robert, 96–97
FTC. *See* Federal Trade Commission
fur seals, 190

GAO. *See* Government Accountability
Office
Gdansk Agreement, 122
Gehrig, Lou, 202
Gemayel, Bashir, 116–17
General Dynamics Corporation, 99
General Motors Company, Detroit,
Michigan, 76
General Motors Tech Center, Warren,
Michigan, 78–79
Geneva Conventions, 106, 217
Gettysburg Address, 310
Ghani, Ashraf, 151
Gillibrand, Kirsten, 104–5
Gingrich, Newt, 293
Gladstone, Hannah, 3, 15, 24, 42
Glenn, John, 179, 226
globalization, 77
Global Reporting Initiative, 270
Goldman Sachs, 243–44, 245–46,
247–48
Goldwater, Barry, 92, 93, 102,
115
Goldwater-Nichols Act (1986), 93
Gorbachev, Mikhail, 90
Gordon, Lou, 38

Government Accountability Office
(GAO), 257
Governmental Affairs Committee,
53–56, 66, 78, 99, 100, 226. *See also*
Subcommittee on Oversight of
Government Management
Graham, Bob, 167
Graham, Lindsey, 214, 215
Graham-Levin amendment, 215–16
Gramm, Phil, 249
Gravel, Mike, 175
Great Depression, 60, 185
Great Lakes, 30, 178–80, 187, 201
Great Lakes Critical Programs Act
(1990), 179–80
Great Lakes Maritime Heritage Center,
Alpena, Michigan, 188
Grenada, 92–93, 117
Gribbs, Roman, 31, 33
Griffin, Robert, 38–39, 40, 41, 42–44
Gross, Alan, 139–40
Gross, Judith, 139
Grossman, Linda, 42
Guantanamo Bay military prison, Cuba,
105, 107, 109–10, 214–17
Guardian, The, 109
Gulf War, 302
Gustitus, Linda, 68, 71, 248, 308
Guy, Ralph, Jr., 17

habeas corpus, 214–15, 216
Hadassah, 2, 112
Hadassah Research Hospital,
Jerusalem, 2
Hadley, Stephen, 164
Halpern, Barbara. *See* Levin, Barbara
Halpern, Ben, 43–44
Hamdan v. Rumsfeld, 215–17
Harrison, William Henry, 189
Hart, Phil, 181, 288–89
Hart-Dole-Inouye Federal Center,
289

Harvard Law School, Cambridge, Massachusetts, 10–11
HASC. *See* House Armed Services Committee
Hatch, Orrin, 277, 278, 280
hate crimes, 101–2
Hatfield, Mark, 287
Havel, Vaclav, 123
health care, 63
Helms, Jesse, 211, 229
Hertel, Dennis, 200
Hewlett-Packard Company, 268, 269
Highton, Jake, 37
Honduras, 2
honoraria, 223
Hood, Nicholas, 34
Houghton, Douglass, 183
House Armed Services Committee (HASC), 200
House Commerce Committee, 284
House Judiciary Committee, 232, 233
House of Representatives. *See* U.S. House of Representatives
House-Senate Automotive Caucus, 131–32
House Un-American Activities Committee, 33
housing, 16–18, 27–29, 63, 299
Housing and Urban Development. *See* Department of Housing and Urban Development
Hoxha, Enver, 135
HSBC Bank, 260
Hubbard, Orville, 16–17
HUD. *See* Department of Housing and Urban Development
Humane Society, 191
humanitarian aid workers, 95
human rights, 85, 130–31, 133, 252
humor, 43
Hussein, Saddam, 153–55, 157–58, 161, 165; Gulf War and, 302; WMD and, 119, 152, 167

Hussein bin Talal, King of Jordan, 114, 117, 118
Hyde, Henry, 232

Iacocca, Lee, 76
IAEA. *See* International Atomic Energy Agency
ICBMs. *See* intercontinental ballistic missiles
"I Have a Dream" speech, 298
Independent Counsel Law, 222–23, 229, 230, 234
India, 158
industrial policy, 77–79
innovation, 300–301
Inouye, Daniel, 211, 287, 288–89
inspectors general, 300, 306
Institute on Taxation and Economic Policy, 274
intellectual property, 84, 132, 133, 134–35
intercontinental ballistic missiles (ICBMs), 91, 124
Intermediate-Range Nuclear Forces (INF), 90
Internal Revenue Service (IRS), 71, 254, 257, 258–59, 267
International Atomic Energy Agency (IAEA), 162–63, 164, 166
International Criminal Tribunal, 136–37
International Trade Commission. *See* U.S. International Trade Commission
Iowa, 47–51
Iran, 153, 158
Iran-Contra Affair, 222, 231
Iraq, 152–61, 165–67; Gulf War and, 302; Israel and, 118–19; opposition to war with, 168–69, 292; reduction of troops in, 172, 173; responsibilities of, 172–73; U.N. inspectors and, 162–64

Iraq War, 141, 170–73; aftermath of, 174; cost of, 171, 295, 302
IRS. *See* Internal Revenue Service
ISIS, 170
Isle of Man, 255–56
isolationism, 127–28
Israel, 2, 112–14, 117, 118–19, 158; PLO and, 115, 116; recognition of, 3
Italy, 9
ITC. *See* U.S. International Trade Commission

Jackson, Henry (Scoop), 175–76, 177
Jaffe, Ira, 38
Japan, 45, 79, 80; trade and, 74, 75, 77, 82–83
Jaworski, Leon, 233
Jerusalem, 112, 118
Jiang Zemin, 129, 130–31
job loss, 81, 83, 84; NAFTA and, 82
Johnson, Lyndon B., 22, 174, 207, 302
Johnson, Woody, 256
Joint Chiefs of Staff, 100, 102, 160
Jones, Dan, 109
Jones, Paula, 230, 231, 232
Jordan, 113, 117–18
Jordan, Vernon, 235
Josaitis, Eleanor, 196–99
JPMorgan Chase, 252, 262–64

Kabul, Afghanistan, 147
KAL 007, 122
Karzai, Hamid, 150
Kaufman, Ted, 146
Kavanaugh, Brett, 233
"Keepers of the Dream" speech, 60–63
Keith, Damon, 16
Kelley, Frank J., 16, 38, 41
Kelley, Jack, 25
Kendall, David, 237
Kennedy, John F., 12, 63, 148, 173–74, 269

Kennedy, Ted, 53, 101
Kentucky, 189
Kerner Commission, 22
Kerr, Gordon, 45
Kerry, Bob, 278
Keweenaw National Historic Park, 186–87
Keweenaw Peninsula, Michigan, 182–87
Kiev, Ukraine, 124
"killer" amendments, 58–59
Kim Il-Sung, 137
Kim Jong-Il, 137
King, Martin Luther, Jr., 298
King Hussein. *See* Hussein bin Talal, King of Jordan
Kissinger, Henry, 112–13
Kohl, Herb, 179
Korean Airline Flight 007, 121–22
Koscak, Barbara, 110, 111
Kosovo, 136–37
Kosygin, Alexei, 120
KPMG International Cooperative, 253–55
Kurdistan Workers Party (PKK), 205–6
Kuwait, 302
Kyl, Jon, 212
Kyshtym Disaster, 124–25

Lake Erie, 30, 188
Lake Huron, 187–88
Lake Michigan, 181
Lake Superior, 182
Langseth, Bob, 186
law practice, 11–12, 13, 308
Lay, Ken, 253
Leahy, Patrick, 139, 209
Lebanon, 115–17
Legal Aid and Defender Association, Detroit, Michigan, 21–22
legislative oversight. *See* congressional oversight
legislative veto, 41–42, 62, 63, 64–65

Leopold, Aldo, 177
Levin, Andy, 1, 308
Levin, Barbara, 12–15, 32–33, 38, 42,
    161, 306, 308, 309, 311
Levin, Ben, 311
Levin, Bess, 2, 112
Levin, Charles, 1, 40
Levin, Daniel (son-in-law), 311
Levin, Danny (cousin), 308
Levin, Erica, 14, 309, 311
Levin, Hannah. See Gladstone, Hannah
Levin, Ida, 2
Levin, Joseph, 2
Levin, Kate. See Markel, Kate
Levin, Laura, 14, 309, 311
Levin, Mort, 24
Levin, Noa, 311
Levin, Sandy, 3, 10, 15, 40, 56, 291; in
    House of Representatives, 1, 47, 86,
    131; in Michigan Senate, 24
Levin, Saul, 1, 2–3
Levin, Ted, 1, 2, 53
Levin Center, Wayne State University
    Law School, Detroit, Michigan, 308
Levine, Peter, 72
Levinson, Bess. See Levin, Bess
Levinson, David, 1
Levinson, Gittelle, 1
Levinson, Morris, 1
Levitas, Elliott, 41
Lewinsky, Monica, 232–33, 236–37
"liar" loans, 244, 246
Libby, Scooter, 154
Lieberman, Joe, 49
Lincoln, Abraham, 296, 301, 310
line-item veto, 219–20
lobbying disclosure, 224–25
Lobbying Disclosure Act (1995), 225
lobbyists, 76–77, 223, 224, 225, 247, 285
London, Ontario, 2
Long, Russell, 70–71, 285
Lott, Trent, 159
Lousma, Jack, 44–45

Lugar, Richard, 124
Lyles, David, 137

Mabus, Ray, 308–9
Machinist Training Institute (MTI),
    197–98
Mack, Connie, 124, 126
Maine, 70
Margolies-Mezvinsky, Marjorie, 293
Marine Corps. See U.S. Marine Corps
Markel, Bess, 311
Markel, Kate, 14, 309, 311
Markel, Samantha, 311
Maronite Christian groups, 116
Martin, Edward, 8
McAuliffe, Terry, 49–50
McCain, John, 93, 106, 134, 212,
    241, 264, 267, 274, 275, 284;
    Afghanistan and, 149; campaign
    finance reform and, 226–27; DADT
    and, 102, 103; as SASC chair,
    97–99; as SASC ranking member,
    94, 133
McCain Amendment. See Detainee
    Treatment Act
McCain-Feingold bill. See Bipartisan
    Campaign Reform Act
McCarthy, Joseph, 7–8, 241, 299
McCarthy hearings, 7–8, 241
McCaskill, Claire, 261
McChyrstal, Stanley, 148
McConnell, Mitch, 209, 212
McConnell v. the FEC, 228
McDonald, Larry, 121
McLaughlin, John, 167
Meese, Ed, 72, 223
Meet the Press, 148, 171
Meir, Golda, 112
Merkley, Jeff, 246
Merrill Lynch, 252, 253
methadone, 277–78, 279
Mexican-American War, 171, 302

Mexico, 2, 81–82, 249
Michigan, 49, 71, 76, 91–92, 211;
    environmental protection
    and, 180–83; recreation in,
    191–92; SSDI program in, 69;
    unemployment in, 75
Michigan Civil Rights Commission,
    16–18, 22
Michigan Democratic Party, 49, 51, 52
Michigan Department of Natural
    Resources, 178
Michigan Senate, 24
Michigan Wilderness Act (1987), 181
Microsoft Corporation, 268, 269
military procurement. *See* defense
    contracting
military reform, 92–93
military strength, 87–89
Milliken v. Bradley, 32
Milošević, Slobodan, 136–37
mining, 175, 183–87
missile defense systems, 13, 91, 119,
    134
Missile Technology Control Regime, 130
Mogadishu, Somalia, 95–96
money laundering, 248–52, 257
Moore, Freeman, 17–18
Morgan, J. P., 271
mortgages, high-risk, 243–46, 245–46
Moscow, Russia, 120
Moynihan, Daniel, 295
MTI. *See* Machinist Training Institute
Mullen, Mike, 102, 103
Murkowski, Frank, 191
Muskie, Ed, 64

National Association for the
    Advancement of Colored People
    (NAACP), 32
National Automotive Center (NAC), 79
National Defense Authorization Act
    (2012), 134

National Institute on Drug Abuse
    (NIDA), 278
National Oceanic and Atmospheric
    Agency (NOAA), 187, 188
National Park Service, 191
National Park System, 177, 189
National Security Council, 156
NATO. *See* North Atlantic Treaty
    Organization
Nelson, Gaylord, 30
neoconservatives (neo-cons), 160, 171
Nevada, 50, 51
New Deal, 60
New Hampshire, 47–51
New York City, New York, 143
New York Times, 52, 61, 159, 165,
    167–68, 231, 238
Nicaragua, 222
Nichols, Bill, 115
Nichols, John, 33, 34
NIDA. *See* National Institute on Drug
    Abuse
Nigeria, 204, 249
9/11 attacks, 141, 142–43, 160, 169,
    250, 257
9/11 Commission, 153, 154
Nixon, Richard, 7, 28, 220;
    impeachment of, 233–34; pardon
    of, 238, 294
NOAA. *See* National Oceanic and
    Atmospheric Agency
Nobel Peace Prize, 122
Non-Proliferation Treaty. *See* Treaty on
    the Non-Proliferation of Nuclear
    Weapons
North American Free Trade Agreement
    (NAFTA), 81–82
North Atlantic Treaty Organization
    (NATO), 90, 127, 128, 136, 141
North Country National Scenic Trail,
    191–92
Northern Pacific Fur Seal Convention,
    190

North Korea, 137–38, 153
Novak, Robert, 165
nuclear disasters, 124–25
"nuclear option," 209–10, 227, 305
nuclear weapons, 13, 54, 89, 90–92,
    123–26; China and, 130; Iraq and,
    152, 161; North Korea and, 137
Nunn, Sam, 87, 93, 94, 95, 124

Obama, Barack, 106, 139–40, 182,
    191, 201; Afghanistan and,
    148–50; DADT and, 102, 103;
    financial regulation and, 258, 262;
    Guantanamo prison and, 105, 110;
    Iraq and, 173; judicial nominations
    by, 208–9; as senator, 256, 258;
    2008 campaign of, 46, 51–52
O'Connor, Sandra Day, 299
OECD. See Organisation for Economic
    Cooperation and Development
Office of Thrift Supervision (OTS), 244,
    245, 247
offshore banks, 258–60, 310
OGM. See Subcommittee on Oversight
    of Government Management
oil, 161, 175, 177, 250
oil spills, 178, 179
Old Tiger Stadium Conservancy,
    202–3
omnibus regulatory reform, 65,
    66, 67
O'Neill, Paul, 153
Operation Enduring Freedom,
    143–44
Operation Iraqi Freedom, 170
opioid addiction, 277–80
Opportunity Fund, 146
organ and tissue donation, 280–81
Organisation for Economic Cooperation
    and Development (OECD), 270
Oslo Accords, 117
OTS. See Office of Thrift Supervision

Pakistan, 130, 145, 150, 158, 249
Palestine Liberation Organization
    (PLO), 115–16
Palestinians, 114, 115, 117
Panama Canal Treaties, 57–59, 293
Parker, Jackie, 278
Parks, Rosa, 17
Parlak, Ibrahim, 205–6
partisanship, 210, 226, 279, 289
Paula Jones v. Bill Clinton, 232, 235,
    236, 237
Peace Through Strength Award, 111
Pell, Claiborne, 128–29, 135
Pelosi, Nancy, 205
Pentecostal Christians, 120–21
People's Liberation Army (China), 134
Perkins, Frances, 60
Permanent Subcommittee on
    Investigations (PSI), 7, 8, 97, 98,
    310; basket options and, 265–68;
    bipartisanship of, 241–42, 275–76,
    277; corporate ownership and,
    257–58; credit card companies and,
    260–62; derivatives and, 262–64;
    Enron and, 252–53; executive
    pay and, 271–75; history of, 241;
    KPMG and, 253–55; Levin as chair
    of, 240–41; money laundering
    and, 248–52; offshore banks and,
    258–60; tax dodging and, 268; 2008
    financial crisis and, 243–48
Peters, Gary, 308
Petraeus, David, 107
phosphates, 30–31
Pierce, William, 284
Pinochet, Augusto, 250–52
PKK. See Kurdistan Workers Party
Plame, Valerie, 165
PLO. See Palestine Liberation Organization
plutonium, 124, 125–26
Poindexter, Thomas, 19–20
pollution, 178, 183, 187
Port Huron, Michigan, 2

Powell, Colin, 160, 165–66, 200
Prague, Czech Republic, 123, 154–55, 156, 157
presidential primaries, 47–52
Pribilof Islands, 190
private bills, 203–6
Progressive Party, 4–5
Proxmire, William, 76, 196
Pryor, David, 71, 100
Pryor, Mark, 212
PSI. *See* Permanent Subcommittee on Investigations
Pulte, William, 17–18

Quellos Group, 255–56

Rabin, Yitzhak, 117–18
racism, 16–17, 22, 306
Rangel, Charlie, 113, 259
ranking members, 68, 93, 94, 95, 98
Ray, Robert, 237
Reagan, Michael, 283–84
Reagan, Ronald, 13, 66–67, 81, 103–4, 181, 283, 286, 299; budget, 100, 211, 291–92; Cold War and, 122; Middle East and, 113–15, 117; military strength and, 89–90, 111
redlining, 34–35, 57
Reed, Jack, 97, 136, 146, 150, 151, 172–73
regulatory reform, 66–67
Reid, Harry, 209, 212
Renaissance Technologies (RenTec), 265–71
Reno, Janet, 229, 230, 231, 232
Reserve Officer Training Corps (ROTC), 299
retail politics, 50
Ribicoff, Abraham, 53–54, 66
Rice, Condoleezza, 153, 157, 159, 160, 165, 166, 171
Riegle, Don, 37, 75

Riggs Bank, Washington, D.C., 250–51
River Raisin National Battlefield Park, Michigan, 189
Rizzo, John, 108
Roach, Bob, 249
Romney, George, 28
Romney, Ronna, 46
Ronald Reagan Presidential Forum, 111
Roosevelt, Eleanor, 60, 287
Roosevelt, Franklin, 4, 60, 63, 286–88, 301
Roosevelt Memorial Commission, 286–88
Ross, Stephen M., 308
ROTC. *See* Reserve Officer Training Corps
Roth, Stephen J., 32
Roth, William, 78
Ruff, Chuck, 238
Rules Committee (Democratic Party), 48
Rumsfeld, Donald, 106, 107, 153, 156, 157, 160, 161
Russert, Tim, 155
Russia, 123–28, 124–28, 136, 158, 249, 257. *See also* Soviet Union
Ruth, Babe, 202
Ruzek, Jiri, 156

Saban, Haim, 256
Sadat, Anwar, 113, 114
Salinas, Raul, 249
Sarbanes-Oxley Act, 253
SASC. *See* Senate Armed Services Committee
Saudi Arabia, 143
SBIR. *See* Small Business Innovation Research
Scalia, Antonin, 217–19
Schiavo, Terri, 212–14
Schmitt, Harrison, 65
school integration, 32–33, 34

schools, in Afghanistan, 146–47, 152
Schuette, Bill, 45
Schumer, Chuck, 212
SDI. *See* Strategic Defense Initiative
Securities and Exchange Commission
    (SEC), 247, 255, 272
Selfridge Air National Guard Base,
    Macomb County, Michigan, 110
Seltzer, Bob, 42, 61
Senate Armed Services Committee
    (SASC), 54, 57, 79–80, 87–89, 94,
    142–43, 195–96; affirmative action
    and, 298–99; Afghanistan war and,
    144; chairs of, 92–95; China and,
    128–35; Cuba and, 139–40; DADT
    and, 102; defense spending and,
    100–101; Eastern Europe and, 135–
    37; education and, 110–11; foreign
    policy and, 112; Guantanamo
    prison and, 106–7, 110; Iraq
    War and, 144, 159–61; Levin as
    chair of, 106, 110, 133; member
    relationships, 95, 97, 98–99; Middle
    East and, 112–19; North Korea
    and, 137–38; Russia / Soviet Union
    and, 119–28
Senate Banking Committee, 75, 76
Senate campaigns, 40–47; 1978 general,
    41–44; 1978 primary, 40; 1984, 44–
    45; 1990, 45; 1996, 46–47; spending
    on, 46
Senate committees, choosing of, 53–56
Senate Democratic Steering
    Committee, 55
Senate Energy Committee, 176
Senate Ethics Committee, 223
Senate Foreign Relations Committee,
    143
Senate Judiciary Committee, 53
Senate Select Committee on Intelligence
    (SSCI), 107–9, 144, 166
Senate seniority, 221
Sentelle, David, 229, 230, 231

Serbia, 136
SERE techniques. *See* "Survival, Evasion,
    Resistance, and Escape" (SERE)
    techniques
Sessions, Jeff, 103
sexual assault, in military, 104–5
sexual harassment, 230, 232
Shelby, Richard, 262
shell companies, 251, 252, 255–56, 258
Shinseki, Eric, 171
Sierra Club, 179
Simpson, Alan, 221
Sirica, John, 233–34
60 Minutes, 69, 155
60 Minutes II, 105, 107
Skilling, Jeff, 253
Slaton, Jessie, 121
slavery, 296–97, 298
Sleeping Bear Dunes National
    Lakeshore, Michigan, 181–82
Small Business Administration, 72
Small Business Committee, 54–55, 85
small businesses, 2, 54–55, 71, 85
Small Business Innovation Research
    (SBIR), 85
Sneed, Joseph, 230
Social Security, 295
Social Security Disability Insurance
    (SSDI), 69–71, 275
Solzhenitsyn, Alexander, 121
Somalia, 95–97
Somers, Cathy, 204
South Carolina, 50
South Korea, 128
Soviet Union, 89, 90, 93, 100, 119–23,
    121; Afghanistan and, 146; collapse
    of, 126, 135; former republics of,
    126. *See also* Russia
Spanish-American War, 171, 302
Specter, Arlen, 211
Srebrenica massacre, 136
SSCI. *See* Senate Select Committee on
    Intelligence

SSDI. *See* Social Security Disability Insurance

Stabenow, Debbie, 181, 201, 203

STARBASE program (Science and Technology Academies Reinforcing Basic Aviation Space Exploration), 110–11

Starr, Kenneth, 223, 229, 230–32, 236

Starr Report, 233, 234

Star Wars. *See* Strategic Defense Initiative

State of the Union Addresses, 164–65, 294–95

steel industry, 78

Stennis, John, 57, 58, 89

Stevens, John Paul, 29–30

Stevens, Paul, 216

Stevens, Ted, 175, 191

Stevenson, Adlai, 11, 63

Stevenson, Adlai, III, 76

Stockman, David, 100–101

stock options, 255, 271–74, 310

Strategic Air Command Headquarters, Omaha, Nebraska, 91

Strategic Arms Limitation Treaties, 91

Strategic Defense Initiative (SDI), 13, 91

Straw, Jack, 163

STRESS (Stop the Robberies, Enjoy Safe Streets), 33

Student Council, Swarthmore College, 6–7

Subcommittee on Oversight of Government Management (OGM), 55–56, 68–69, 99–100, 178; IRS and, 71; Ed Meese and, 72–73; SSDI and, 69–71

subpoenas, 240, 241

Sullivan, Thomas, 232–33

Sunset Act, 64

sunset provisions, 62, 63, 85

supply-side economics, 294–95

Supreme Court. *See* U.S. Supreme Court

"Survival, Evasion, Resistance, and Escape" (SERE) techniques, 107–8

Swarthmore College, Swarthmore, Pennsylvania, 6–10

synagogues, 33

Syria, 115, 116–17, 158

TACOM. *See* U.S. Army Tank-Automotive and Armaments Command

Taguba, Antonio, 105

Taliban, 143–44, 145, 146–47, 149–50

TARDEC. *See* U.S. Army Tank Automotive Research, Development and Engineering Center

tax dodging, 253–57, 258–60, 265–68, 268–71, 274, 300; corporate, 98

taxes, 3, 71, 73; cuts, 291–92, 294–95; deductions, 272–74; loopholes, 269, 275, 310

Taxpayer Bill of Rights, 71

Tea Party, 299

Tenet, George, 154, 157, 159, 164, 166, 167–68, 171

terrorism, 105, 109, 115, 146, 151; funding of, 250, 257; Iraq War as increasing risk of, 168, 170; 9/11 and, 142, 143, 144

Tester, John, 150

Thirteenth Amendment, 297

Thompson, Fred, 226

Thunder Bay National Marine Sanctuary, 187–88

Thurmond, Strom, 93–94, 124, 126

Tiananmen Square protest, 130

Tibet, 128–29

torture, 97, 105, 110, 251–52; as damaging to U.S., 108, 109; prohibition of, 106. *See also* detainee abuse

Tower, John, 87, 92

trade agreements, 81–82, 84, 86
Treaty on the Non-Proliferation of
    Nuclear Weapons, 130
Tripp, Linda, 232
Trott, Dave, 182
Truman, Harry, 2, 3, 4–5, 220, 241
Trump, Donald, 209, 306–7, 309; China
    and, 135; Cuba and, 140; finances
    and, 247, 271; Guantanamo prison
    and, 110; rise of, 82
Tsongas, Paul, 76
Turkey, 13–14, 205
Twitter, 274
Tyler, John, 302

UBS Group, 258–59
Ukraine, 124, 125
unemployment, 75, 76
unemployment benefits, 211
United Auto Workers, 76
United Nations (U.N.), 95, 117, 138,
    141, 162–64, 166, 168, 235;
    peace-keeping force, 115
United Nations Monitoring, Verification
    and Inspection Commission
    (UNMOVIC), 162–63, 166
United States Agency for International
    Development (USAID), 139
United States Trade Representative
    (USTR), 133
University of Chicago, Illinois, 5
University of Detroit School of Law,
    Detroit, Michigan, 2
University of Michigan, Ann Arbor,
    Michigan, 2, 298
UNMOVIC. See United Nations
    Monitoring, Verification and
    Inspection Commission
U.N. Resolution 1441, 162–63, 168
U.N. Security Council, 118, 136, 161,
    162–63
Upton, Fred, 206

U.S. Army, McCarthy hearings and, 7
U.S. Army Tank-Automotive and
    Armaments Command (TACOM),
    79, 198
U.S. Army Tank Automotive Research,
    Development and Engineering
    Center (TARDEC), 79
U.S.-Canada Great Lakes Water Quality
    Agreement, 178, 179
U.S. Coast Guard, 179
U.S. Constitution, 219–20, 299
U.S. Department of Justice, 132–33
U.S. House of Representatives, 59, 210,
    221, 232–36, 258, 296, 304, 305
U.S. International Trade Commission
    (ITC), 74–75
U.S. Marine Corps, 102–3, 115, 116, 117
USS Detroit, 309
U.S. Supreme Court, 29–30, 32, 65,
    214–17, 232, 298, 299; campaign
    finance and, 228; jurisdiction of,
    215; nominations to, 209–10
USTR. See United States Trade
    Representative

Veterans Administration, 280
Vietnam War, 97, 171, 302
Viniar, David, 246
Vladivostok, Russia, 126–27
Volcker, Paul, 246
Volcker Rule, 246, 247

Walesa, Lech, 122
Wallace, Henry, 4
Wallach, Robert, 72
Wall Street, 242, 244–45, 252, 262,
    266, 310
Wall Street Reform and Consumer
    Protection Act (2010), 246–47
Walsh, Lawrence, 222, 231
WaMu. See Washington Mutual

war crimes, 109, 137

Warner, John, 46–47, 87, 94, 95–97, 106, 142, 145; Iraq and, 159, 160

War of 1812, 189–90

Warsaw Pact, 89, 90, 128

Washington Mutual (WaMu), 243–44, 245

Washington Post, 73

waterboarding, 97, 108, 110

Watergate scandal, 222, 233, 306

Wayne State University, Detroit, Michigan, 198, 205

Wayne State University Law School, Detroit, Michigan, 14, 308

weapons of mass destruction (WMD), 152, 153, 154, 158–59, 160, 166, 167; U.N. inspectors and, 162–63, 168. *See also* nuclear weapons

Weaver, Greg, 90

Wedtech, 72–73

Weinberger, Caspar, 93, 100, 115–16

Weiner, Rick, 42

Whistleblower Protection Act, 300

Whitewater investigation, 229, 231–32

Wilbur, Chuck, 49

wilderness preservation, 175–77, 181

Wilson, Joe, 165

WMD. *See* weapons of mass destruction

Wolfowitz, Paul, 153, 154

Woods, Cassandra, 204

World War II, 2, 4, 128, 288–89, 301

Wyly, Charles, 255

Wyly, Sam, 255

yellowcake uranium, 164–65

Yeltsin, Boris, 126

Yongbyon, North Korea, 137, 138

Young, Coleman A., 32, 33, 34, 35, 36, 41

Young v. American Mini-Theaters, Inc., 29–30

Zardari, Asif, 249